A COMPANION TO
THE ANGLO-ZULU WAR

'[The Zulus] were guilty of what in civilised countries are talked of as amongst the noblest virtues a nation can possess – patriotism and loyalty. But if they knew no better than to hold such antiquated notions in earnest, they must reap the consequences. Under a free course of gin and missionaries they will soon become enlightened. Probably England never engaged in so unjust a war, or on such trivial grounds set her civilised force in motion to crush an independent savage power.'

Francis Francis, *War, Waves and Wandering* (London, 1881). Francis covered the war as correspondent for the London *Times.*

A COMPANION
TO THE
ANGLO-ZULU WAR

IAN KNIGHT

Pen & Sword
MILITARY

First published in Great Britain in 2008 by
Pen & Sword Military
an imprint of
Pen & Sword Books Ltd
47 Church Street
Barnsley
South Yorkshire
S70 2AS

ISBN 978-1-84415-801-0

A CIP catalogue record for this book is
available from the British Library.

Typeset in 9.5/11pt Times by
Concept, Huddersfield, West Yorkshire

Printed and bound in England by
Biddles Ltd

Pen & Sword Books Ltd incorporates the Imprints of Pen & Sword Aviation,
Pen & Sword Maritime, Pen & Sword Military, Wharncliffe Local History,
Pen & Sword Select, Pen & Sword Military Classics, Leo Cooper,
Remember When, Seaforth Publishing and Frontline Publishing.

For a complete list of Pen & Sword titles please contact
PEN & SWORD BOOKS LIMITED
47 Church Street, Barnsley, South Yorkshire, S70 2AS, England
E-mail: enquiries@pen-and-sword.co.uk
Website: www.pen-and-sword.co.uk

CONTENTS

For Carolyn, Alex and Libby

LIST OF ILLUSTRATIONS

King Cetshwayo kaMpande, photographed in captivity at Cape Castle.

Lieutenant-General Lord Chelmsford, the commander of British forces in southern Africa in 1879.

Royal Artillery guns in Zululand.

A wooden headboard made by members of the garrison of Eshowe and afterwards placed upon the British graves at Nyezane.

Zulu dead left on the battlefields at Ulundi ... and kwaGingindlovu.

Irregular troops under Redvers Buller capturing abaQulusi cattle during the attack on the ebaQulusini homestead on 1 February 1879.

Lady Florence Dixie, seated among the British officers at the Nhlazatshe meeting on 31 August 1881.

False alarm. Panics like this were common in the British camps at night during the final advance on oNdini.

Flogging was a common field punishment in Zululand for regulars and auxiliaries alike.

Major J.F. Owen and men with the two Gatling guns of 10/7 Battery RA.

A Zulu *inyanga* or herbalist, draped in the gourds and horns containing his medicines.

Limb bones shattered by the impact of Martini-Henry bullets, as sketched by British surgeons.

A white officer, probably Henry Francis Fynn Jnr, with some of his auxiliary troops, photographed after the war.

Two men of the Victoria Mounted Rifles in typical field uniforms.

The Last of the 24th, Isandula. R.T. Moynan's 1883 painting depicts one of the last British soldiers to die in the battle.

Ernest Grandier was the only white man captured alive by the Zulus during the war.

The assault on the hospital at Rorke's Drift, represented for once from the Zulu side.

British troops looting and burning the royal homestead at oNdini.

The efficiency of Zulu rifle fire at Khambula was greatly improved by the capture of British Martini-Henrys at iSandlwana.

A studio portrait of a Zulu man, his stabbing spear and his wife.

These Swazi men attached to Wood's Irregulars fought with Wood's column; unlike the Zulu, the Swazi retained a good deal of their ceremonial costume in the field.

No quarter. 'We are soldiers; we have shown you how we can fight, and I'll show you how we can die' runs the original caption to this contemporary engraving.

The novelist H. Rider Haggard examining British graves on the Ulundi battlefield in April 1913.

Travelling shows: 'the Great Farini' (centre) and some of the Zulu troupe he brought to Europe.

Zulu prisoners under guard by men of the Buffs at the Lower Thukela in the aftermath of the kwaGingindlovu campaign.

A Zulu warrior in full ceremonial regalia.

Captain F. Glennie and men of the 2nd Battalion, 24th Regiment.

Troops unloading supply wagons at 'Dunn's camp'.

The war correspondent Melton Prior's narrow escape at oNdini.

Zibhebhu kaMaphitha, *inkosi* of the Mandlakazi branch of the Zulu Royal House.

Hlubi kaMota, the Tlokoa *inkosi* who fought for the British in 1879, photographed in about 1883 alongside representatives of the old order, the Princes Ndabuko kaMpande (left) and Shingana kaMpande (right).

GLOSSARY

Afrikaans

commando: a group, usually of Afrikaner farmers, assembled for military purposes.

laager: a defensive circle of wagons.

isiZulu

ibutho (pl. *amabutho*): guild or regiment recruited according to the common age of the members.

induna (pl. *izinduna*): state official or appointed functionary, officer, etc.

ikhanda (pl. *amakhanda*): homestead maintained by the Zulu king containing a barracks for the royal *amabutho*. From 'head', meaning of royal authority.

umkhonto (pl. *imikhonto*): a spear.

inkosi (pl. *amakhosi*): hereditary ruler, chief, king.

inyanga (pl. *izinyanga*): herbalist.

umnumzana (pl. *abamnumzana*): head of the homestead, family patriarch.

impi (pl. *izimpi*): a group gathered together for military purposes, an armed force; matters pertaining to war.

umuzi (pl. *imizi*): homestead, collection of huts usually constituting a single family settlement.

isangoma (pl. *izangoma*): spirit diviner; one who is able to commune with the ancestral spirits.

CHRONOLOGY

1878

11 December: British ultimatum delivered to King Cetshwayo's representatives.

1879

6 January: British no. 4 Column (Wood) crosses the Ncome river into territory claimed by the Zulus.

11 January: The British ultimatum expires. No. 3 Column (Glyn) crosses into Zululand at Rorke's Drift.

12 January: No. 1 Column (Pearson) begins to cross into Zululand at the Lower Thukela Drift. No. 3 Column attacks *inkosi* Sihayo's kwaSogekle homestead.

17 January: Main Zulu army leaves oNdini.

18 January: Elements leave main Zulu army to reinforce men defending the coastal districts; remainder continue towards no. 3 Column. No. 1 Column begins advance on Eshowe.

20 January: No. 4 Column establishes base at Fort Thinta. No. 3 Column arrives at iSandlwana.

22 January: No. 4 Column begins extended foray against abaQulusi positions on Zungwini and Hlobane hills. Battle of Nyezane. Pearson's column repulses an attack by an impi of 6,000 men commanded by *inkosi* Godide kaNdlela. Camp at iSandlwana attacked; 1,700 men of nos 2 and 3 Columns under Pulleine and Durnford defeated by main Zulu army (20,000 men) commanded by Ntshingwayo kaMahole.

22/23 January: Elements from the Zulu reserve at iSandlwana (3,000+ men) attack British supply depot at Rorke's Drift and are driven off by garrison commanded by Lts Chard and Bromhead.

24 January: No. 4 Column receives news of iSandlwana; breaks off engagement below Hlobane hill.

27 January: No. 1 Column receives news of iSandlwana.

28 January: No. 1 Column decides to hold position at Eshowe.

31 January: No. 4 Column moves camp to Khambula hill.

11 February: Lord Chelmsford's despatch detailing the disaster at iSandlwana reaches London. The Zulus cut communications between Pearson's force at Eshowe and the Thukela.

3 March: Improvised communication opened between Thukela and Eshowe.

11 March: First reinforcements authorised by UK Government arrive in Natal.

12 March: Stranded 80th convoy commanded by Captain Moriarty overrun at Ntombe by a force commanded by Prince Mbilini waMswati.

28 March: Attack by mounted elements of no. 4 Column on Hlobane mountain defeated by abaQulusi.

29 March: Main Zulu army under *amakhosi* Ntshingwayo and Mnyamana attacks no. 4 Column's camp at Khambula but is defeated.

1 April: Prince Imperial of France arrives in Natal to join Lord Chelmsford's staff.

2 April: Lord Chelmsford's column defeats Zulu coastal forces at
                kwaGingindlovu.
3 April: Eshowe relieved.
5 April: Prince Mbilini mortally wounded in a skirmish with a British patrol near
                Luneburg.
6 April: Serious false alarm at Mfunchini mission camp during the withdrawal
                from Eshowe.
11 April: The last British reinforcements arrive in Natal.
13 April: Lord Chelmsford reorganises British forces into 1st Division (H.H.
                Crealock), 2nd Division (Newdigate) and Flying Column (Wood).
16 April: Tpr Grandier found wandering near Hlobane mountain after his capture
                by the Zulus.
20 May: British forces on central Thukela raid Zulu homesteads opposite Middle
                Drift.
21 May: British expedition to iSandlwana battlefield to retrieve wagons and bury
                some of the dead.
31 May: 2nd Division crosses into Zululand; start of the second invasion by the
                British.
1 June: Prince Imperial killed in an ambush while on patrol.
4 June: Skirmish between British cavalry and local Zulu forces at eZungeni
                mountain.
16 June: Lord Chelmsford receives news that Sir Garnet Wolseley will be sent to
                Natal as his superior.
17 June: Flying Column and 2nd Division link up for advance on oNdini.
20 June: 1st Division advances from its bases on Lower Thukela.
25 June: Members of the Magwaza, Nthuli and Cube chiefdoms raid homesteads
                on the Natal bank at Middle Drift on the Thukela in retaliation for
                British raids of 20 May.
26 June: Elements from the Flying Column and 2nd Division destroy Zulu royal
                homesteads in the emaKhosini valley.
27 June: Combined Flying Column and 2nd Division arrive on Mthonjaneni
                heights.
28 June: Sir Garnet Wolseley arrives in Durban.
30 June: Lt Scott-Douglas (21st Regt) and his orderly Cpl Cotter (17th Lancers)
                killed near kwaMagwaza mission after having lost their way delivering
                despatches.
1 July: 2nd Division and Flying Column establish camp on White Mfolozi river.
2 July: Wolseley's attempt to land by sea at Port Durnford frustrated by the
                heavy swell.
3 July: Mounted troops under Buller skirmish with Zulus under Zibhebhu
                kaMaphitha before oNdini.
4 July: Battle of Ulundi; defeat of last major assembly of the *amabutho*.
                Mounted troops from 1st Division destroy emaNgweni royal
                homestead.
6 July: Elements from 1st Division destroy kwaHlalangubo ('old oNdini') royal
                homestead.
8 July: Lord Chelmsford resigns his command.
15 July: Lord Chelmsford hands over command to Sir Garnet Wolseley.

19 July:	Wolseley begins to accept surrenders of coastal *amakhosi*.
10 August:	Wolseley arrives at oNdini and establishes camp near the ruins of the royal homestead from which to secure further Zulu surrenders.
11 August:	The two guns of N/5 Battery lost at iSandlwana are recovered.
13 August:	Beginning of extended patrolling to capture King Cetshwayo.
28 August:	King Cetshwayo captured in Ngome forest.
1 September:	Wolseley meets with important *amakhosi* at oNdini to impose his new political settlement of Zululand.
2 September:	British evacuation of Zululand begins.
4 September:	King Cetshwayo embarks at Port Durnford for exile at the Cape.
5 September:	British attack caves in the Ntombe valley occupied by local Zulus who had refused to surrender.
8 September:	Further attacks on Ntombe caves; last shots of the war.
9 September:	Wolseley arrives at Utrecht, en route from Zululand to the Transvaal.

PREFACE

In the 1940s the Revd A.W. Lee, who had begun a distinguished missionary career working at iSandlwana in the 1900s and went on to become Bishop of Zululand, made a pertinent observation about the significance of the Anglo-Zulu War as it seemed to both participants. 'From the point of view of those who have experienced two world wars,' he wrote,

> with their widespread bloodshed and devastation, the story of the Zulu War of 1879 reads like that of a series of skirmishes carried on in an unimportant country for obscure reasons. Yet to the Zulu people it was the ultimate tragedy, involving as it did loss of independence, of self-government, and of freedom to live their lives as it seemed best to them.[1]

The popular fascination with this war continues unabated. New books appear with almost monotonous regularity and old ones are reprinted, and the output is as variable as it is varied. For the reading public, much of the appeal of the war lies in its undoubted dramatic nature, the Technicolor glamour of lines of redcoats splashed across tawny African landscapes, the bold warriors nobly defending their country against a foreign invader, the themes of courage, self-sacrifice and folly, an almost Shakespearean epic of tragically flawed heroes and the fall of a kingdom. As with most stereotypes, there is an element of truth in all this, but there is also, as Bishop Lee observed, a darker one underlying them, for only in the cinema do mythic figures battle without consequences, and for the Zulu people the consequences of the British invasion of 1879 have been hard indeed. As many as 10,000 Zulu men died fighting for their country and thousands more were wounded, many of them maimed for life, the great royal homesteads maintained by the Zulu kings were destroyed, together with hundreds of ordinary Zulu homes, while the country was stripped of thousands of head of

the cattle which represented their national wealth. Having irrevocably damaged the Zulu kingdom, the British Empire then calmly walked away, abandoning the policies that had led to the war in the first place. With tragic irony Britain imposed a post-war settlement on Zululand which, over the following decades, engendered bitter divisions and led to Zulus fighting Zulus in a cycle of civil wars which caused as great a loss of life as the British invasion. The reduction of the Zulu kingdom, part of a broader process of the spread of European domination in southern Africa, paved the way for the dispossession, exploitation and political repression of the Zulu people which lasted until recent times.

This book does not present a general history of the Anglo-Zulu War, although I have given a brief one in the Introduction to serve as a context. It is intended as a reading companion to those who have an interest in the subject, and it has been conceived essentially as a series of footnotes. Hopefully it will highlight a great many aspects of the war which there is never quite space enough to explore in a narrative history, providing some element of expansion, illumination and even, now and then and with a bit of luck, some amusement. Throughout the book I have tried to highlight the personal, to move away where possible from the broad sweeps and stereotypes, and to concentrate instead on human aspects from the perspective of both sides: what did people do, eat or believe on campaign, why did they do it, and what did it mean to them? I have also deliberately included the quirky or the absurd, as it seems to me that these are fundamental human traits too, and often all the more recognisable in times of conflict. Since it also seems to me interesting how the story of the war was communicated and perceived, both at the time and since, I have looked at the portrayal of the war in the popular contemporary media – in newspapers and works of art – and in the more recent phenomenon of the cinema. Now and then it has proved impossible for me to hide my own passions or prejudices, and in a book of this nature I am not unduly apologetic. In short I hope the book will be informative, fun, and will in some small way bring alive the people who experienced this extraordinary history.

It is of course the product of more than thirty years' association with Zulu history, and it could not have been written without the kind and patient help of many people, particularly in South Africa. My greatest debt will always remain to that remarkable and genuine *fundi* on Zulu history and affairs, Sighart 'SB' Bourquin, whom I first met in 1979 and who subsequently took me on many field trips to Zululand's historic sites. These were the days before the current tourism boom, when tourist lodges near the battlefield were an undreamed-of eccentricity. Instead SB took me camping, an experience which remains infinitely vivid in my memory, and which just then touched upon the last embers of a historic world which already seems to me now to be irrevocably lost. More recently, Eric Boswell and Ricky Crathorne have taken me the length and breadth of the country and opened it to me in a way which, I think, no others could. The 'old Zulu with family stories of iSandlwana' is largely a thing of tourist myth now, sadly, though over the years my travels have introduced me to many who have provided nuggets of insight into the past. In particular I think of L.B.Z. Buthelezi, Paul Cebekhulu and Michael Zulu (both descendants of Zibhebhu kaMaphitha), Gilenja Biyela (a descendant of Mkhosana kaMvundlana, one of the Zulu heroes of iSandlwana) and Lindiswe Ngobese, a descendant of the great Mehlokazulu kaSihayo. Graeme Smythe, during his tenure as curator at Rorke's Drift Museum, was a remarkably tolerant host, as was Gillian Scott-Berning in Durban. A mention is due, too, to Pat Stubbs, the remarkable American lady who has established the wonderful iSandlwana Lodge, and who has given me some intriguing insights into local Zulu affairs and the politics and agendas of battlefield tourism today. John Laband, without doubt the greatest scholar of the nineteenth-century Zulu kingdom, has always encouraged and shared information freely, while my old friends Ian Castle and Keith Reeves have been entertaining and refreshingly sceptical travelling companions over the years. Lee Stevenson has allowed me access to his formidable researches on the veterans of Rorke's Drift, Stephen Coan has guided my thoughts on Rider Haggard's involvement with the Zulus, and Ian Woodason has been unfailingly generous with the intriguing and occasionally bizarre pieces of information about individuals which he has gleaned in pursuing their memorials. Colonel Mike McCabe RE has provided me with telling analysis of aspects of military practice then and now, which has helped overcome my innate civilian ignorance, while Major Paul Naish has given me some interesting and stimulating perspectives on it all. Thanks are also due to Dr Adrian Greaves of the Anglo-Zulu War Historical Society, to that great iSandlwana expert F.W. David Jackson, to Colonel Ian Bennet, Dr Graham Dominy, and to my fellow enthusiasts Bill Cainan, Ron Sheeley, Tim Day, Rai England, Haydn Jones and Steven Sass. Finally, most of all, my thanks are due to my wife Carolyn and my children Alex and Libby, who have to put up with it all.

It goes without saying that any opinions let slip in this book are the responsibility of none of the above, but are my own.

Ian Knight, Chichester, 2007

INTRODUCTION:
THE ANGLO-ZULU WAR

On 11 January 1879 the British Empire went to war with a friendly power. British troops crossed into the independent kingdom of Zululand – with which they had deliberately manufactured a quarrel – on three separate fronts, intent on destroying the Zulu army and overthrowing the Zulu king Cetshwayo. The officials and military officers on the ground hoped and expected that the campaign would be brought to a quick and successful conclusion, not only to avoid the consequences of a prolonged war of attrition, but because the British Government in London had not approved the war. They were to be disappointed; on 22 January the Zulu army inflicted on the British at the foot of a distinctive rocky outcrop known as iSandlwana one of the heaviest defeats they were to experience during the Victorian age. The reverse catapulted the war and southern Africa in general into the British media spotlight; in due course it would lead to a questioning of imperial policy in the region which would destroy the career of an imperial pro-consul and result in the abandonment of the policies which had provoked the invasion in the first place. In the short term, however, there was a clamouring for revenge, for any examination of the justice of the war would have to wait until Britain's military honour had been restored.

That the British and the Zulu kingdom had advanced to confrontation at all was the result of a curiously tangled historical happenstance. In 1497, during the great age of European maritime expansion, the Portuguese explorer Vasco da Gama had rounded the extreme southern tip of Africa – known as 'the Cape of Good Hope' or, more aptly, 'the Cape of Storms' – and, hugging the coast on his tentative journey north into the Indian Ocean, had spotted a distant line of green hills and crashing surf to port on Christmas Day. He named it *Terra Natalis* in honour of the birth of Christ, and ever since the area has been known to the outside world as Natal. Yet da Gama did not linger; over the years the Portuguese established only a small trading enclave further north in Mozambique and it was left to the Dutch to establish the first European toe-hold at the tip of the continent. In 1652 the Dutch East India Company established a small victualling station in the bay at the foot of the breathtaking Table Mountain to service its ships on the long haul to that most profitable theatre of European expansion, the Indies. The Dutch had little interest in Africa for its own sake but the settlement spawned a hardy colonial society composed of French and Dutch farmers whose job it was to grow vegetables for the passing ships. When, much later, political allegiances were thrown into sharp relief in Europe by the outbreak of the Revolutionary and Napoleonic Wars, the British – who were carving out their own impressive empire in India – began to regard the Netherlands' international holdings with suspicion. Britain feared that French influence over the Netherlands might lead to a hostile French takeover of the Cape

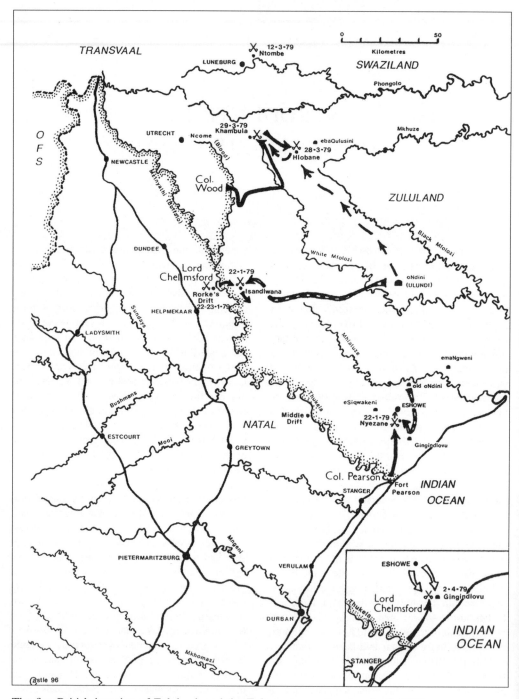

The first British invasion of Zululand, and the Zulu response, January–April 1879.

which would in turn threaten the security of Britain's Indian possessions. In 1795 Britain occupied the Cape, only to give it back – to the Dutch, of course, not the indigenous inhabitants – when peace broke out temporarily shortly after. Within a few years Britain and France were at war again, however, and in 1806 the British returned and mounted an amphibious assault, scattering Dutch forces among the sand-dunes on the beaches within sight of Table Mountain. They were to remain the dominant power at the Cape until the Union of South Africa in 1910.

The advent of British rule provided a stimulus for the expansion of settler society. Despite official disapproval – the expense of policing new territorial acquisitions was a perennial concern to colonial powers of whatever hue – this had in any case been creeping steadily across the colony's official boundaries and into Africa beyond. In the wake of the end of the Napoleonic Wars in 1815 the British themselves had been pressing forward their international economic, political and exploratory interests, and, being a maritime nation, had worked tentatively up the Indian Ocean coast. The original Dutch and French settlers – who came to think of themselves as a distinct people, 'Africanders' or, later, Afrikaners, meaning white Africans, though they were generally known as *boere* from the Dutch word for farmers – meanwhile soon came to resent British authority and looked increasingly for ways to escape it.

These movements between them brought the European world into conflict with a range of indigenous southern African societies, including the Zulus. The Zulu kingdom itself was a relatively new historical phenomenon which had emerged on the eastern seaboard, between the Khahlamba mountains (known to the first white explorers as the *Drakensberg* or Dragons' Mountains) and the ocean, early in the nineteenth century – about the time the British were first consolidating their position at the Cape. The African societies occupying this area had become stressed by a series of as-yet incompletely understood factors, and from about 1790 had been drawn into conflict with one another. The Zulus were a small group living on the south bank of the White Mfolozi river, and thus were at the geographical centre of the turmoil, but through the ambition, political acumen and military prowess of their young *inkosi* Shaka kaSenzangakhona they came to dominate many of the rest. By the 1820s they controlled the area between the Phongolo river in the north and the Thukela in the south, and exerted a patchy influence as far as the Mzimvubu beyond. The Zulu political system grafted a new administrative structure over the top of the pre-existing chiefdoms so that power was exercised by a new elite centred upon the Zulu king himself. Much of the king's power rested on his control of guilds of young men called *amabutho*. These were a part-time citizen militia and labour gang who owed their allegiance not to the regional *amakhosi* but to the king himself, and who served as an organised national army.

Ironically it was Shaka's success at state-building which drew the seeds of his nation's destruction to him. Rumours of the rise of a powerful and above all wealthy new African kingdom attracted the interest of the Cape Town merchants and in 1824 an exploratory party, led by an ex-Royal Navy lieutenant, sailed up the coast and made a hazardous entry into a lagoon known as Port Natal. Here they set up camp with the intention of trading with the Zulus. King Shaka welcomed them both for the exotic goods they brought with them and for the insights they offered into the outside world, and from this unlikely beginning all British interests in the region subsequently developed.

Over the next two decades the pace of European interest in the region accelerated. By the 1830s the Boer community living on the Eastern Cape Frontier had become disillusioned with the failure of the British administration to protect their physical safety and financial interests in the face of nagging conflicts with the local Xhosa people. From 1835 many Boers began to abandon British territory to move into the interior in the hope of establishing an administration more in keeping with their needs. Their journey – remembered today as the Great Trek, a name which imposes upon the movement a greater sense of unity than it in fact possessed – was a triumph of human endeavour in the face of terrible natural hardships, but the Boers' progress was marked by conflict with the indigenous African groups encountered along the way. In 1837 parties of Trekkers entered Natal from the interior across the Khahlamba passes. They found King Shaka dead – assassinated by his brothers in a palace coup in 1828 – but their attempts to secure land for settlement from his successor, King Dingane, led to the outbreak of a brutal war. The British settlers found it impossible to remain aloof from the fighting and allied themselves to the Boers, a decision that led to a permanent rift with the Zulu kingdom. The fighting was ultimately indecisive, but the Boers threw off whatever influence the Zulu kings enjoyed south of the Thukela river and declared the area a republic.

Their success, however, alarmed the British at the Cape who feared not only that the Boer conflicts with African societies would destabilise their own colonial possessions but that a Boer control of Port Natal would invite the influence of rival European empires into an area Britain regarded as its back yard in Africa. In 1842 British troops were marched overland from the Cape to secure Port Natal for Britain; a bizarre struggle broke out with the Boers on the very beaches of the lagoon. After a fierce tussle the British were victorious and many of the Boers retired, bitterly disappointed, back across the Khahlamba. In 1845 Natal became a British colony under the overall direction of the Governor of the Cape.

The colony grew slowly. Even though the white population was bolstered by immigration schemes which drew recruits from England with the optimistic promises of lands in the sun, the settlers remained heavily outnumbered by the African population. The political fortunes of the colony and the neighbouring Zulu kingdom were inextricably entwined, if only because many in Natal's black population were tied to Zululand by a shared history that pre-dated the arrival of the whites. Nevertheless, successive Zulu kings strove to remain on good terms with the British administration while trade in the Zulu country was for many years an economic prop of colonial Natal.

In the 1870s, however, the British adopted a more aggressive policy in southern Africa. The economic stimulus for this was the discovery of diamonds in what became Kimberley, north of the Cape, in 1868. Hitherto British imperial strategists had regarded wider involvement in southern Africa, with its complex web of mutual hostilities, as too high a price to pay for the security of the maritime highway to India. Now, however, its potential as a source of mineral wealth made it possible to imagine the economic development of the region as a whole. To bring it all under some form of British control begged the question of how the objections of the Trekker republics – who owed their existence in the first place to the rejection of British authority – and indigenous African groups might be overcome. In 1877 an experienced imperial pro-consul, Sir Henry Bartle Frere, was sent out as High Commissioner for the Cape with instructions to do just that. Even as Frere arrived in Africa the British took advantage of a financial and political malaise among the Boers to annex the Transvaal republic.

Along with the Transvaal Britain inherited a long-standing dispute between the Boers and the Zulu kingdom. Although an Anglo-Zulu accord in the 1840s had stipulated that the border between Natal and Zululand should follow the lines of the Thukela and Mzinyathi rivers, this line became blurred in the sparsely populated northern districts as the rivers meandered towards their headwaters in the mountains. Here Dingane's successor, King Mpande, had allowed republican Boers trekking away from the British to settle and found the village of Utrecht. In time Utrecht attached itself to the Transvaal and the claims of Boer and Zulu began to overlap. The dispute had spluttered on for twenty years and at times had threatened to break into violence but the Zulus – who enjoyed an undoubted military superiority – held their hand, partly for fear of offending the British in Natal.

For Frere the Transvaal boundary issue was symptomatic of the wider problems besetting southern Africa as a whole. He saw in it an undercurrent of the widespread resistance of indigenous communities to the inexorable spread of European domination, a resistance that would need to be suppressed if the Boers were to be persuaded of the advantages of renouncing their historic antagonism towards British rule. Against the vision of a British-driven unity of white southern Africa pushing forward economically into the African hinterland, the power and independence of the Zulu kingdom seemed to Frere anachronistic and assumed in his mind a degree of hostile intent that its ruler – Mpande's son Cetshwayo – did not in fact possess. To Frere, who was by nature a global imperialist, the security of southern Africa within the wider empire was also dependent on its ability to reduce internal dissent. These threads drew him inexorably to a single conclusion, that the path to successful confederation lay through a short successful war against the Zulu kingdom.

Frere had little doubt that the British would win, an assumption based largely on the apparent disparity of weapon types and military discipline. The British Army was possessed of the most sophisticated weapon types in the world, and – since they were experienced in warfare all over the world – its men knew how to use them. The Zulu army was armed with shields, spears and antiquated second-hand firearms. The one political drawback for Frere was that the British Government, which was even then tumbling into a fresh entanglement in Afghanistan, was reluctant to sanction the use of force in southern Africa. But Frere was accustomed to taking difficult decisions on his own responsibility, and he gambled that the benefits of breaking up the Zulu kingdom could be attained before the Home Government had time to object. He began deliberately trying to manipulate a confrontation. Ironically, however, a boundary commission set up to inquire into the history of the disputed territory, and whose findings Frere hoped to exploit to produce a crisis, found largely in favour of the Zulu cause. While he was considering how best to react, however, the family of an important Zulu border *inkosi*, Sihayo kaXongo, played into his hands. Two of Sihayo's wives had fled across the border into British Natal with their lovers, and in July 1878 Sihayo's sons went looking for them at the head of an armed band. They found the

women, dragged them back into Zululand, and, in accordance with Zulu law, executed them.

This was the excuse Frere needed. He instructed the senior military commander in southern Africa, Lieutenant-General Lord Chelmsford, to mass British troops on the Zulu borders. King Cetshwayo was invited to send delegates to a meeting at the Lower Thukela on 11 December 1878, ostensibly to hear the long-delayed boundary commission report. In fact they were presented with complaints about Sihayo's followers and a demand for redress which took the form of an ultimatum. This required virtually the disbandment of the *amabutho* system and the complete subjugation of Cetshwayo's authority to the British.

King Cetshwayo was given thirty days to comply. He did not; Frere had never thought that he would. On 11 January 1879 British troops invaded Zululand.

The prospect of a campaign against the Zulus had provided Lord Chelmsford with a number of strategic challenges. Because the Government in London had not approved the war, he was short of troops, and only had those British forces already in southern Africa – just eight infantry battalions and two batteries of artillery. Victorian commanders were routinely expected to achieve spectacular results with inadequate resources, and Chelmsford had bolstered his forces with mounted units raised from the settler community and with auxiliary units drawn from Natal's African population. Conscious that the Zulu army was a highly mobile one, he had resolved to invade from a number of separate points along the border with the intention of reducing the Zulu capability to mount a counter-attack. He had initially planned on five separate offensive columns, but shortage of transport wagons forced him to reduce the invading columns to three, with two in reserve. One column – no. 1, the Right Flank Column, commanded by Colonel Charles Pearson – was to cross at the Lower Drift on the Thukela, near the coast. Another, the no. 3 or Centre Column, commanded by Colonel Richard Glyn, was to cross the Mzinyathi along the central border at Rorke's Drift; Chelmsford intended this as his main thrust, and accompanied it himself. The third offensive column, no. 4, the Left Flank Column under Colonel Evelyn Wood, was to advance from Utrecht on the Transvaal border. Of the smaller defensive columns one – no. 2, under Colonel Anthony Durnford – was placed on the Middle Thukela border (between columns 1 and 3) and the other, no. 5 under Colonel Hugh Rowlands, was placed north-east of Wood's at a spot where the Transvaal, Zulu and Swazi borders met. The invading columns averaged about 3,000 men each, a mixture of regulars and auxiliaries; the total manpower at the command of King Cetshwayo was estimated at more than ten times that.

The Zulus made no initial attempt to oppose the first British moves into their territory, however. Men living in the border regions were ordered to watch the invaders, and the king assembled his *amabutho* at his royal homestead of oNdini and waited to gain a sense of the British objectives before deciding his strategy. On 12 January Chelmsford himself directed an attack by Centre Column troops on the private homestead of the border *inkosi* Sihayo, whose followers had committed the border transgression six months before. Sihayo's followers were dispersed and his homestead burned. When the news reached oNdini Cetshwayo and his councillors decided to direct their main response against the Centre Column. On 17 January some 25,000 men set out for Rorke's Drift, while smaller detachments were sent to reinforce local groups opposing the flanking columns.

The result was a wave of fighting which took place across the country over several days from 20 January. In the north, Colonel Wood had been keen to suppress the resistance of a particularly ardent local Zulu group, the abaQulusi, whose military operations were conducted from the security of a series of flat-topped mountains north-east of Wood's base. On the 20th Wood marched out and drove the Zulus off the first of these mountains, Zungwini, and for the next three days manoeuvred with a view to taking the next, Hlobane. In the south, meanwhile, a Zulu *impi* had attempted to intercept Pearson's column as it passed the kwaGingindlovu royal homestead on the 21st but mis-timed its advance.

Instead the Zulus retired behind a line of hills overlooking the Nyezane stream with the intention of ambushing Pearson on the march. In fact Pearson's scouts blundered into the Zulu vanguard, hiding in long grass, on the morning of the 22nd, and unleashed a premature Zulu attack. Pearson hurriedly deployed into a long line on the slopes above the river as the Zulus swept down from the heights, but the Zulu attack was poorly coordinated and ground to a halt under heavy British fire. The Zulus finally withdrew and Pearson, pausing only to bury his dead, resumed his march. The following day he occupied the deserted Norwegian mission station at Eshowe, where Chelmsford had instructed him to build a supply depot.

By far the most severe fighting occurred on the central front, however. Here Chelmsford had moved forward from Rorke's Drift on the 20th to establish a camp beneath a rocky outcrop known as iSandlwana. Rumours reached him that day that a large Zulu army might be approaching him, and on the 21st he ordered a sweep through the rugged hill-country on his right flank. Late that evening his patrols discovered a Zulu force in the Mangeni hills, 12 miles from iSandlwana. When news reached him in the camp at about 2.30am on the morning of the 22nd, Chelmsford decided to split his command, taking a mobile force out to confront what he thought was the main Zulu army, and leaving his baggage and tents behind under a strong guard. He also ordered up Durnford's column – which he had previously moved from the Middle Thukela to Rorke's Drift – to reinforce the camp at iSandlwana. Chelmsford reached the Mangeni at daybreak but only small parties of Zulus were visible, and he dispersed his men to pursue them.

In fact the big Zulu *impi*, some 25,000 men under the command of Ntshingwayo kaMahole and Mavumengwana kaNdlela, had already passed across Chelmsford's front, moving on the 21st into a sheltered valley 5 miles north-east of iSandlwana. According to Zulu custom, the 22nd was an inauspicious day to launch an attack and Ntshingwayo pushed out scouts to watch the camp while his men rested quietly. The scouts were clearly seen from the camp, however, and

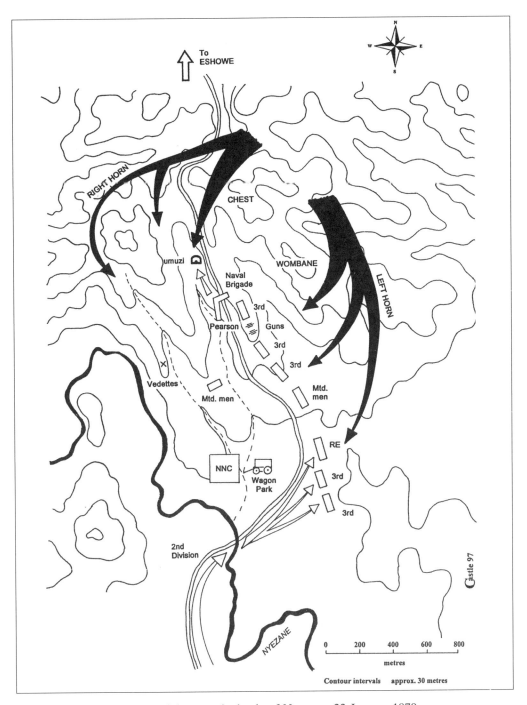

The first major engagement of the war: the battle of Nyezane, 22 January 1879.

when Durnford arrived at about 10.30am he decided, in the absence of more specific orders from Chelmsford, to investigate the Zulu presence. At about noon on the 22nd detachments from Durnford's command blundered into the concealed Zulu army, provoking a spontaneous Zulu attack.

The Zulu attack developed over a wide area and the British, initially unaware of its true extent, deployed in scattered formations to meet it. Driven in by the great encircling sweep of the Zulu advance, the British tried to hold a line in front of the camp but, in danger of being outflanked, they then retired upon the tents. The Zulus pursued them with a determined charge which destroyed a British attempt to reform, and eliminated the infantry companies piecemeal. Many of the defenders were killed fighting on the slopes beneath the peak of iSandlwana; others were driven down into the valley of the Manzimnyama stream beyond before being brought to bay and killed. Of some 1,700 men, black and white, in the camp at the start of the battle, 1,300 were killed, among them all the senior British officers. Fewer than a hundred of the survivors were Europeans. Yet the battle proved to be a costly victory, too, for over a thousand Zulus were killed, and many more were wounded, large numbers of them mortally.

The battle largely exhausted the *amabutho* who fought in it. A strong reserve, some 4,000 men, commanded by the king's brother Prince Dabulamanzi kaMpande, which had been employed in cutting the British line of retreat, crossed the Mzinyathi into Natal, however, hoping to loot the vulnerable border. Here many of them dispersed but a large body, perhaps 3,000 altogether, moved to attack the supply depot the British had established at the mission-station at Rorke's Drift. Here a garrison of some 150 men, under Lieutenants Chard and Bromhead, had been warned of the impending attack by survivors of iSandlwana, and had barricaded the post with sacks and boxes of supplies. The Zulus had probably expected to find the post unprepared and they launched a rather undisciplined attack at about 4.30pm. Throughout the late afternoon they repeatedly assaulted the post, driving the

British out of the old mission house – which they had converted into a makeshift hospital – and setting it on fire. As darkness fell, however, they were unable to make any headway against a fierce British defence of the last remaining building. Sporadic attacks continued throughout the night but shortly before dawn the Zulus withdrew.

Lord Chelmsford had spent a frustrating day at the Mangeni hills before a series of curious reports from the camp persuaded him to return to iSandlwana. He found the camp devastated and strewn with the bodies of the men he had left there. With his own men tired he had little option but to spend a night upon the dreadful field, and the following morning he marched back down the road to Rorke's Drift, where he had started his invasion less than a fortnight before. Along the way he passed the defeated Zulu troops withdrawing from the attack on the mission – neither side had the will to resume the fight.

The reverse at iSandlwana was a political and military calamity. Any hopes Frere had entertained of winning the war quickly and quietly were shattered at a stroke, and Chelmsford's invasion plan lay in tatters. Yet the fighting – which had cost the Zulus at least 3,000 dead on all fronts – had also shocked and temporarily incapacitated the *amabutho*. Although the British feared a Zulu counter-thrust into Natal, King Cetshwayo lacked both the political resolve and sufficient fresh troops to accomplish it. Chelmsford's flanking columns were left unsupported; Pearson opted to dig in at the Eshowe mission while Wood moved his camp to a more secure position on the Khambula ridge and began a low-intensity campaign directed at local Zulu loyalists.

Although Pearson reduced the strength of his column almost by half, sending his mounted men and auxiliaries back to the Thukela to preserve his supplies, his remaining 1,700 men were destined to spend nearly three months cooped up at Eshowe. King Cetshwayo was indignant that the British seemed to have settled down as if they already owned the country, but, with the experience of Rorke's Drift fresh in his mind,

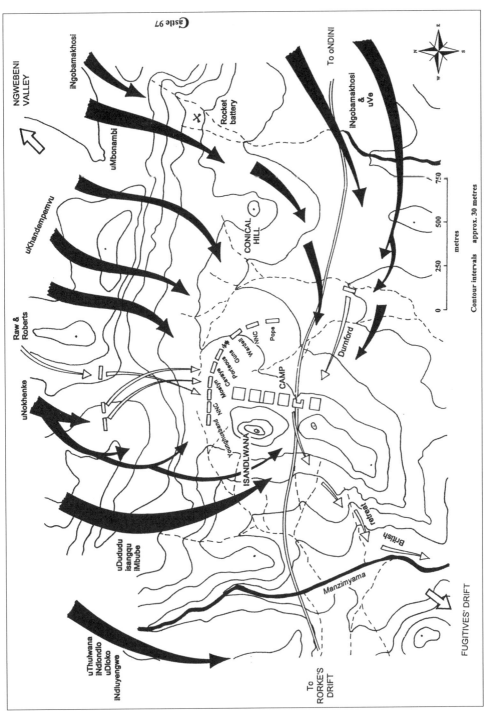

The climax of the battle of iSandlwana, 22 January 1879.

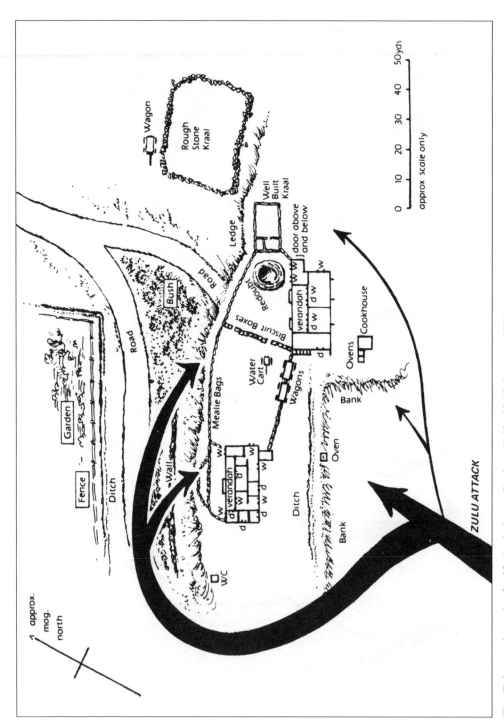

The Zulu attack on the fortified mission at Rorke's Drift, 22/23 January 1879.

he dared not order a direct attack on Pearson's fortified positions. Instead he cut Pearson's line of communication with the Thukela and placed a cordon around Eshowe. Pearson was effectively under siege.

Yet by his reluctance and his inability to take the war across the borders, King Cetshwayo allowed the military initiative, which his men had won so painfully at iSandlwana, to slip back to the British. The British Government was concerned at the news of iSandlwana and in due course would ask searching questions of Sir Bartle Frere, but it regarded it as essential that its military security be restored first. British reinforcements, denied Chelmsford at the start of the invasion, were now hurried to Natal.

Chelmsford's immediate concern, once he had sufficient fresh troops, was to relieve Pearson's command. By late March he was making definite plans to do so, and he asked his remaining commanders along the borders – particularly Wood – to make demonstrations to draw attention away from him. Wood had, in any case, been particularly concerned at the activities of the abaQulusi, working from their base on the Hlobane mountain. On 12 March a convoy of supply wagons escorted by the 80th Regiment had been attacked as it lay stranded across the flooded Ntombe river a few miles outside the exposed border settlement of Luneburg. The attack had been well timed and perfectly executed; most of the convoy's escort had been killed, and crucial supplies were lost. The attackers had been local Zulus and abaQulusi commanded by the renegade Swazi Prince, Mbilini waMswati, who had a homestead on Hlobane. Chelmsford's request persuaded Wood to make a determined attack upon Hlobane – a decision which may also have been influenced by the large numbers of abaQulusi cattle gathered for safety on the summit.

Wood's plan was to assault either end of the mountain with mounted detachments at dawn on 28 March. Although his men attained their start positions under cover of darkness well enough, the party tasked with attacking the western end of the complex, commanded by Lieutenant-Colonel John Russell, found its route up to the summit

impractical. At the far eastern end, however, the detachment commanded by Lieutenant-Colonel Redvers Buller successfully stormed the summit at daybreak and began to round up the cattle they found there. The abaQulusi rallied below the mountain, however, and moved round to cut the routes by which Buller's men had gone up. Wood himself, following behind Buller, found some of his men pinned down by determined Zulu rifle fire from among the boulders at the foot of the Hlobane cliffs. In the fire-fight which followed, two of Wood's own staff were killed and Wood himself, badly shaken, returned to his base at Khambula.

The British position on the mountain steadily deteriorated. Buller's men were retreating across the summit, under growing abaQulusi harassment, when they spotted long columns of Zulus advancing rapidly through the valleys to the south of Hlobane. This was the main Zulu army – the same *amabutho* which had triumphed earlier at iSandlwana – and its appearance at this crucial juncture was purely coincidental. King Cetshwayo had watched Chelmsford's troops mustering again on his borders and had reassembled his army. Bowing to pressure from Mbilini and the abaQulusi he had dispatched it to attack Wood's base at Khambula, and it had come over the iNyathi ridge south of Hlobane at first light, just in time to see the British attack developing in the distance. One wing of the army had hurried forward to assist the abaQulusi, dividing in two to sweep round Hlobane on either side.

The appearance of this *amabutho* was enough to cause the British position on the mountain to collapse. One detachment, forcing a way through the abaQulusi at the eastern end of the mountain, ran straight into the approaching *amabutho* and was pinned down above a line of steep cliffs and all but wiped out. Wood himself had seen the *amabutho* coming and ordered Russell to withdraw from the heights; Buller's men, exposed without support, could only scramble down as best they could. Their route took them down a steep staircase of rock, later called the 'Devil's Pass', and here the abaQulusi struck them, turning the retreat into a rout. Buller's men fled

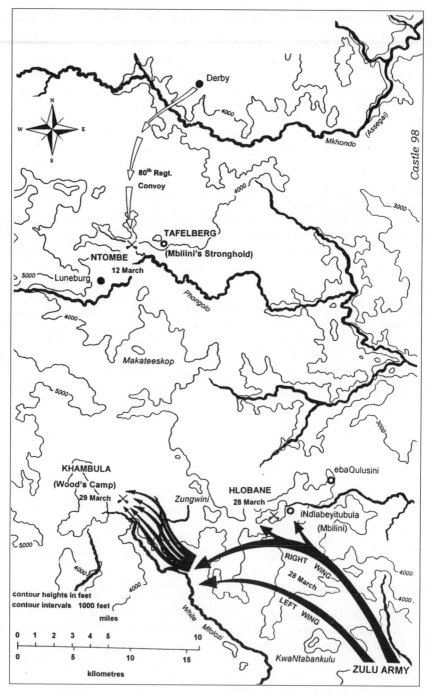

The war in northern Zululand, March 1879. This was the turning-point in British fortunes.

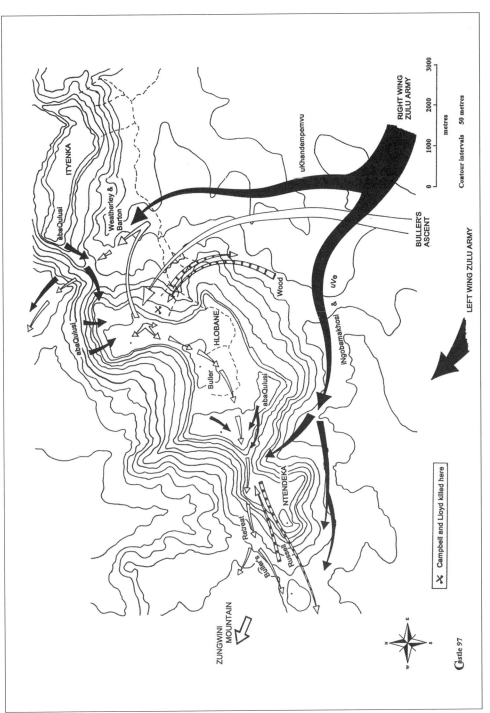

The battle of Hlobane, 29 March 1879.

down the slopes and fell back towards Khambula in disarray, leaving nearly 200 dead on the field.

That night the Zulu army bivouacked on the headwaters of the White Mfolozi while Evelyn Wood prepared his camp to be attacked. His position consisted of a chain of laagers and a redoubt cresting a rise on the open ridge-top. His men could clearly see the Zulu army approaching miles away. It was commanded by *inkosi* Ntshingwayo, the victor of iSandlwana, and accompanied by Cetshwayo's most senior councillor, *inkosi* Mnyamana kaNgqengelele Buthelezi. Mnyamana's presence was an indication of the importance the king placed on the expedition; if the Zulus won the coming battle they might halt the British build up, cause the invaders to lose faith in the invasion, and bring them to the negotiating table. If they lost they would wipe out all the advantages they had won at iSandlwana.

Yet from the first the battle went badly for the Zulus. The approaches to the British camp were difficult and the *amabutho* of the right wing were in place before the centre and left were in position. Wood saw his opportunity and seized it; he ordered his mounted men to ride out and provoke the right horn to launch an unsupported attack. His men dismounted just 50 yards from the Zulu line, fired a volley and retreated quickly on the laagers, drawing the Zulus after them. Once the mounted men were safely inside the British position the defenders opened up with a devastating fire which drove the Zulu right to ground. The Zulu left and centre then hurried up but they had lost the initiative and throughout the afternoon they frittered their attacks away piecemeal. Even so, Zulu marksmen armed with Martini-Henrys captured at iSandlwana were able to make some of the British positions untenable and Wood was forced to abandon one of his laagers. At times the Zulu attacks rushed right up to the British positions before being shot down. By late afternoon, however, the Zulus were growing tired and they began an orderly retreat. Seeing them go, Wood ordered his own mounted men – many of whom were survivors of the Hlobane debacle of the day before, and burning for revenge – to drive them from the field. Under the British pursuit order among the *amabutho*

collapsed and hundreds of Zulus, too exhausted even to defend themselves, were cut down.

The battle of Khambula would prove a turning-point of the war. The Zulu losses were at least as great as at iSandlwana, probably more, and many leading *izinduna* had been killed as they tried to encourage their men. But for Cetshwayo worse was to follow, for within days Lord Chelmsford had inflicted another defeat upon him at the other end of the country.

Lord Chelmsford had crossed the Thukela with a relief column at the end of March. The Zulus investing Eshowe had been reinforced, and on the morning of 2 April they contested Chelmsford's advance near the ruins of the royal homestead at kwaGingindlovu. Chelmsford's column was drawn up around its overnight camp, however, the wagons still laagered and protected by a trench and rampart. The Zulus were unable to penetrate the curtain of British fire, and as they began to withdraw they too were mercilessly chased from the field. The following day Chelmsford led a flying column forward to relieve Pearson at Eshowe.

These two decisive victories allowed Chelmsford the time to plan a fresh strategy. He had no need now to hold Eshowe, and instead pulled his men back closer to the border, forming Pearson's old command and the relief force into a new column, the 1st Division. In the north, Wood retained his command, now redesignated the Flying Column, while reinforcements newly arrived from home were formed into a new column, the 2nd Division. Chelmsford's plan was that the 2nd Division and Flying Column would advance together to attack Cetshwayo at oNdini while the 1st Division would suppress resistance in the coastal districts.

In fact the Zulu kingdom was now beginning to feel the effects of the repeated battle casualties and King Cetshwayo recognised that the *amabutho* had at best the capacity to mount one last effort at defence. The defence of the borders, already compromised by the British advance, was largely abandoned, and no stand was to be made in the coastal districts. Instead the army would be mustered only in defence of the royal homestead at oNdini.

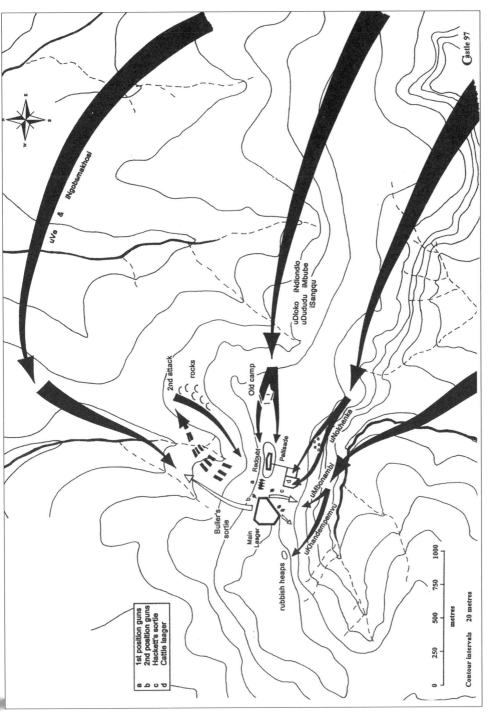

uVe & iNgobamakhosi

uDloko iNdlondlo
uDududu iMbube
iSangqu

2nd attack

rocks

Old camp

Redoubt

Palisade

Buller's sortie

Main Laager

uMbonambi

uKhandempemvu

uNokhenke

rubbish heaps

Castle 97

a 1st position guns
b 2nd position guns
c Hackett's sortie
d Cattle laager

0   250   500   750   1000
              metres
Contour intervals 20 metres

The battle of Khambula on 29 March 1879 provided the decisive British victory of the middle war.

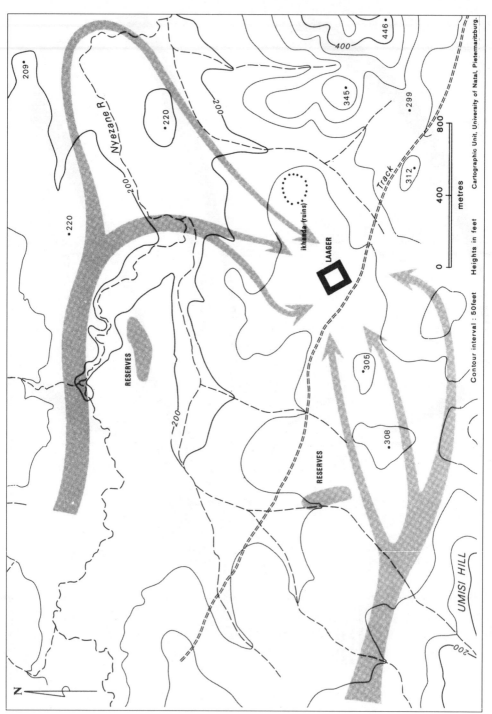

The battle of kwaGingindlovu, which broke the Zulu cordon around Eshowe, 2 April 1879.

Even so, the new invasion began badly for Chelmsford. On the very day the 2nd Division began its advance – 1 June – the exiled Prince Imperial of France, who had gone to the front as an unofficial observer, was killed when a patrol he was accompanying was attacked by a Zulu scouting party. The incident caused a sensation in the British press and, since Chelmsford himself had chosen to accompany the 2nd Division, it added to his growing list of embarrassments.

The second invasion was slow and painstaking, making up for the carelessness of January. As he pushed deep into the Zulu heartland, Chelmsford ordered his troops to destroy Zulu homesteads and crops in the hope of undermining the Zulu will to resist. The effectiveness of this policy is open to debate; it in fact encouraged many of the regional *amakhosi* to retain men at home to defend their property, and the British advance was carried out in the face of constant skirmishing.

Yet Chelmsford was under pressure in other directions, too. The British Government had finally lost faith in him, prompted not so much by his defeats as by the escalating cost of the war and by a growing friction between the military and the colonial authorities in Natal. General Sir Garnet Wolseley was sent out to the Cape with plenipotentiary powers which superseded both Frere and Chelmsford. But while Wolseley was desperate to reach the front to take command, Chelmsford was equally determined to win the battle that would restore his reputation before Wolseley arrived.

He succeeded. By the end of June the 2nd Division and Flying Column had reached the valley of the White Mfolozi. Many of the old and venerable royal homesteads in the emaKhosini valley – where the ancestors of the Zulu kings were buried – were destroyed and on 3 July Chelmsford probed across the river, scouting out ground to fight close to oNdini itself. Before dawn on the 4th he crossed the White Mfolozi with over 4,000 men, ten field guns and two Gatling machine-guns – the largest British force yet fielded for battle in southern Africa. He drew his men up in a square, the infantry in ranks four deep and the artillery carefully placed among

them, and then manoeuvred into position on the plain facing oNdini. The Zulus had been expecting them, and ironically had hoped to trap the British on that same ground. At about 9am the *amabutho* emerged from their overnight bivouacs and advanced towards Chelmsford's square on all sides. Yet they could not hope to withstand the hail of fire the British laid down, and despite some gallant individual attacks – which reached to within yards of the British lines before being cut down – they were driven back. As they began to retire Lord Chelmsford sent out the 17th Lancers who launched a smart attack into the retreating *amabutho*, turning the retreat into another rout.

The battle of Ulundi – the name by which the British called oNdini – was clearly decisive, and having ordered his men to set fire to oNdini and a cluster of royal homesteads nearby, Chelmsford withdrew that day across the Mfolozi. Within days he had resigned his command; Wolseley was welcome to what was left of the war.

There was indeed little to do beyond mopping up, and imposing a new political order. King Cetshwayo himself had not stayed to witness the slaughter of his men in the final battle, and had retired to the homestead of *inkosi* Mnyamana Buthelezi in the north. Wolseley reoccupied oNdini, and from there he pressured Zulu *amakhosi* to make their formal surrenders. He also dispatched patrols to capture the king. Cetshwayo did his best to elude them, but was finally captured by British dragoons in the remote Ngome forest. He was taken to oNdini where Wolseley informed him that he was deposed and would be sent into exile. He was taken to the coast and put aboard a steamer, destined for captivity in Cape Town.

Wolseley then disposed of Cetshwayo's kingdom. A change of administration in London – the fall of Disraeli's Conservatives and the rise of Gladstone's Liberals – had brought a further reluctance to formalise British entanglements in Zululand, and Wolseley had been instructed to impose a peace which was broadly favourable to British interests without the expense of annexation. His solution was to divide up the country among thirteen chiefdoms, distributing

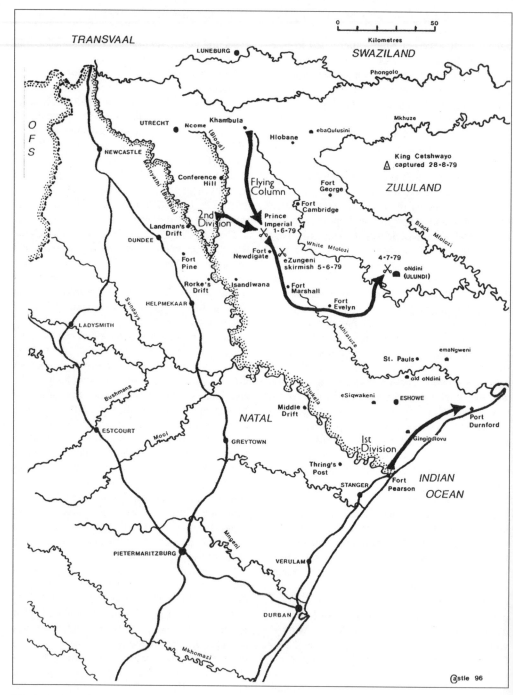

The British second invasion of Zululand, June–July 1879.

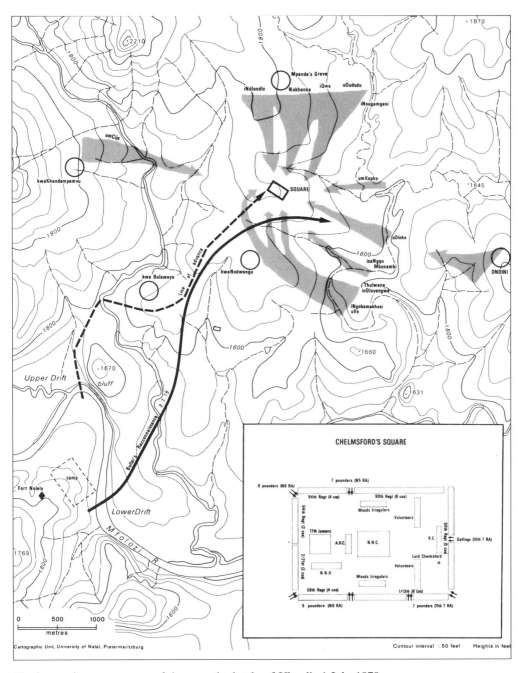

The last major engagement of the war: the battle of Ulundi, 4 July 1879.

these among groups who were known to be hostile to the Zulu Royal House and therefore in sympathy with the British. Here and there a few pockets of resistance still had to be subdued by force, but by the middle of September British troops had largely withdrawn from Zululand.

In many respects the invasion of 1879 proved to be just the first step in the systematic reduction of Zulu power and independence. Wolseley's settlement unleashed powerful tensions within the country which the Zulu kings had largely kept in check. Most ordinary Zulus remained loyal to their exiled king, and were resentful of the British-backed new order, which in turn reacted to dissension with violence. Within two years Wolseley's settlement was in danger of collapsing into civil war. By that time the image of the Zulu king among his enemies had undergone a radical transformation, and he began to be perceived in London as the means by which a lasting stability might be returned to Zululand. In 1883 Cetshwayo was allowed to return but only on condition that he did not revive the *amabutho* system, the means upon which so much royal authority depended. Since the British were also reluctant to abandon their protégés in Zululand, a large part of the country was set aside and reserved for those who were opposed to Cetshwayo's return.

The result was an almost immediate and catastrophic outbreak of civil war. Cetshwayo returned to oNdini in February 1883 and his jubilant supporters promptly attacked his former general, Zibhebhu kaMaphitha, who had become the focus in his absence of anti-royalist sentiments. Zibhebhu was a gifted commander, however, and severely defeated Cetshwayo's followers at the battle of Msebe in March. Both sides then began to arm, but Zibhebhu struck first, launching a surprise attack on Cetshwayo's rebuilt oNdini homestead on 21 July. The royalists were caught by surprise and scattered. Cetshwayo himself escaped but was wounded in the process;

dozens of his most prominent *izinduna* were killed, including Ntshingwayo, the victor of iSandlwana.

The battle of oNdini effectively destroyed the last vestiges of Cetshwayo's administration. The king himself went into hiding before surrendering to a British official at Eshowe. He lived there in exile until he died suddenly in 1884.

The king's death ushered in a new wave of misery and civil war. His successor, his teenage son Dinuzulu, recruited the help of the Transvaal Boers and defeated Zibhebhu. The prospect of Boer influence in Zululand provoked the British to intervene, however, and in May 1887 the British finally annexed Zululand. Dinuzulu refused to accept the annexation and called his supporters out in revolt, and in 1888 British redcoats were again marched into Zululand. There was to be no repeat of the large-scale bloodletting of 1879, however, for the Zulus were too weak and divided; after a series of skirmishes Dinuzulu, together with several of Cetshwayo's brothers who had supported him, gave themselves up to the British. Dinuzulu was sent into exile at St Helena.

Dinuzulu returned from St Helena in 1898. During his absence much of Zululand had been opened to white settlement and the country was firmly under colonial control. When, in 1906, a rebellion broke out among the Africans in neighbouring Natal – a reaction to decades of impoverishment and exploitation – the rebels called upon Dinuzulu to add the enormous prestige of the Zulu Royal House to their cause. He refused, and the rebels were mercilessly dispersed by colonial militia armed with machine-guns. Such was the suspicion of the Royal House in colonial circles that Dinuzulu was in any case found guilty of abetting the rebels. He was sent into exile in the Transvaal and died in 1913.

The process set in motion by Sir Bartle Frere in 1878 had reached its logical conclusion.

A COMPANION TO
THE ANGLO-ZULU WAR

Ammunition Boxes

The influence of British ammunition-box design on the course of events during the battle of iSandlwana has become part of the enduring mythology of the war.

The fundamental pattern of Army small-arms ammunition boxes had changed only slightly since the introduction of brass-cartridge breech-loading ammunition in the 1860s. It had been tweaked slightly in 1871 to accommodate the issue of a new rifle, the Martini-Henry, and the subsequent design was only amended in minor details over the next decade. The Mark V or Mark VI pattern boxes, both authorised in 1876, seem to have been the types employed in Zululand.[2] These were stout wooden (teak or mahogany) boxes with dove-tailed joints at the sides and a wooden base fixed in place by copper nails. Each was lined with tin to protect the contents from damp. Although the construction of the box was solid enough it was further held together by two copper retaining bands (copper was used because there was less risk of friction causing sparks), fastened with thirteen brass screws. Rope handles were provided at either end for carrying. Access to the contents was by means of a wedge-shaped sliding panel in the top. This was retained by a single brass screw. The lining was fitted with a wire handle at the top which could be pulled back, like a modern ring-pull, once the wooden panel had been removed. The rounds themselves were wrapped in brown paper packages of ten,

tied round with string. Each box contained 600 rounds. A full box represented a considerable weight – just under 80lb – and while one man might drag it for a short way over grass, it needed two to carry it any distance. The same design of box was used to carry both Martini-Henry rifle and carbine ammunition, and ammunition for the previous military issue firearm, the Snider, with which some auxiliaries were still equipped.[3]

The alleged difficulties in opening the boxes have become part of the mythology of the war but are not generally supported by eyewitness accounts. Self-evidently the boxes were designed to be robust in order to protect their contents from the rough handling which often accompanied a march over difficult terrain. The proper way to open them was with a screwdriver, with which battalion quartermasters were equipped. Because, however, only the central panel had to be removed to allow access, a number of other means were employed during an emergency. A heavy blow to the outer edge of the access panel caused the retaining screw to bend and the washer housing to split away from the wood. Perhaps the tools best suited to this job were the mallets which were used to drive tent-pegs into the ground; every British camp in Zululand, including that at iSandlwana, would have had these in quantity.[4] In dire circumstances the butt of a rifle could also be used, although the curve of the butt-plate meant that rather more precision was needed in striking the edge of the lid. Once the lid was open it took a few seconds to lift out the first of the tightly packed packets of rounds; after that extracting the packets became easier.

In evaluating the debate concerning the question of ammunition supply or failure at iSandlwana, it is worth noting that a number of bent retaining screws from the centre panels have been found over the years on the battlefield, indicating that a significant number of boxes were forced open in this way. During the 2000 archaeological exploration of iSandlwana a number of the tin inner-lining handles, with pieces of lining panel still attached, were discovered along the line of the British firing positions on the rise above the iNyoni dongas. A sketch of the battlefield by Lieutenant W.W. Lloyd of the 24th in September 1879 clearly shows an open ammunition box lying near British forward positions.[5] The overwhelming agreement among Zulu veterans of the battle that they continued to be fired upon until the final stages of the hand-to-hand fighting on the nek at the end of the battle (when all means of supply had inevitably broken down) is further indicative of the earlier success of British attempts at re-supply.

Given that the battalion reserve supply of ammunition for both 24th battalions (a total of some 320,000 rounds) was present in the camp at iSandlwana – carried in at least 530 boxes – together with supplies for the other units, it is interesting to note that there are no surviving references to full unopened boxes being discovered on the battlefield after the event.[6] The vast majority of those boxes present during the battle were either opened by the British during the fighting or later by the Zulus. The fact that the Zulus – most of whom would have had little previous knowledge of items of European manufacture – successfully opened the boxes they captured, either using the rounds with looted Martini-Henry rifles or extracting the powder to use with muzzle-loaders, surely confirms that the boxes could be opened with a combination of ingenuity and force.

It is also worth noting that B Company 2/24th had its company reserve of ammunition present at Rorke's Drift – and fired off most of it –

and that no mention is made of any difficulty in opening the boxes during the battle (despite the absence of a quartermaster). At the battle of Nyezane – also on 22 January – Captain Arthur Hart, the 2nd NNC's staff officer, begged a supply of ammunition from the 3rd Regiment's Quartermasters and then carried it forward to a position held by the NCOs of his regiment and distributed it before assaulting a Zulu position – all without reference to any difficulty opening the boxes. The same pattern of boxes was used in every other battle in the campaign, and there are similarly no recorded difficulties in accessing the supplies.

Ammunition Supply (British)

In his *Field Force Regulations* Lord Chelmsford specified that ammunition was 'to be constantly in possession of regiments and detached companies in the field ... at a rate of 270 rounds per man, viz. 70 in possession of each soldier, with a reserve of 200 rounds'.[7]

The ammunition carried by each soldier was distributed between two pouches worn at the front of the belt, each containing 20 rounds, and 30 rounds carried loose in a black 'expense' (i.e. available to be expended) pouch which was usually worn hanging from the belt in front of the right hip. The expense pouch was not a particularly efficient item – it came open easily and the rounds dropped out – but it was probably subject to some unofficial modifications by the men and the wastage would only have become apparent to a few individuals after very heavy expenditure.

The reserve ammunition was kept in boxes of 600 rounds which were intended to be carried on transport wagons designed to take thirty boxes apiece. Since these wagons were not available in southern Africa, locally produced mule-drawn 'Scotch carts' were used by most battalions instead. A Scotch cart could easily accommodate thirty boxes, although the weight may have proved heavy for the mules. Chelmsford's regulations specified that carts and wagons should bear a small flag for ease of identification – red for ammunition wagons, blue for the commissariat, red and the colour of the regimental facings for regimental transport, red and white for the staff and red and blue for artillery. According to the usual plan for military camps of the period, regimental transport and ammunition wagons were usually parked immediately behind the last row of tents so that they could be easily accessed when needed.

Individual battalions were responsible for distributing ammunition from the reserve to the front-line companies. Seventy rounds represented a heavy expenditure and it was extremely unusual for such a high and sustained rate of fire to be reached to expend all the rounds in the men's pouches. Although a modern marksman in ideal conditions on a firing range, with rounds laid out beside him, might hope to achieve a rate of twenty aimed rounds in a single minute, the emphasis in training manuals in the 1870s was upon a controlled rate of accurate fire. By carefully pacing the rate of fire commanders stood a greater chance of achieving their tactical objectives through a higher rate of hits. The inevitable nervousness which afflicts men in battle leads to a tendency to blaze away rapidly, producing a higher rate of fire but a low rate of hits. This, by encouraging the enemy through the apparent ineffectiveness of the fire, might produce exactly the opposite to the intended result. Rapid fire of the Martini-Henry also produced a greater volume of smoke which obscured the target – and again reduced the rate of hits. Slow, disciplined fire was therefore regarded as essential and the *Musketry Instruction Manual* of 1887 – when the Martini-Henry was still in service – recommended that in field practices:

One minute will be allowed for each of five volleys, counting from the first command 'ready' ... It should distinctly be understood that the section commander is under no obligation to fire five volleys; on the contrary, it would be wiser to fire only four volleys if he thinks the results would be better.

A slower rate of fire also allowed for more time to be spent observing targets, to redirect fire as circumstances changed, and to allow the smoke to clear between volleys. Moreover, no unit in battle fires at a consistent rate without interruption simply because events alter situations; the unit itself might cease firing to manoeuvre, and targets might move in or out of range or go to ground. In all battles long breaks between short bursts of firing are the norm. Battlefield statistics from the 1879–80 period tend to support this. At Khambula – arguably a more prolonged and sustained battle even than iSandlwana – Evelyn Wood noted that 'the line battalions were very steady, expending in four hours an average of 33 rounds per man'.[8] At kwaGingindlovu an officer of the 60th noted 'the average number of rounds fired per man was rather under seven; that of the Marines next to me was sixteen'.[9] At Ulundi the average was ten rounds per man expended in half an hour's fighting. At the battle of Charasia, in the 2nd Afghan War (6 October 1879), 'the 72nd fired 30 rounds a man, being heavily engaged for some hours',[10] while at Ahmed Khel (19 April 1880) the expenditure was only ten rounds a man. At El Teb (29 February 1884) and Tamai (13 March 1884) in the Sudan – both battles in which the enemy made extremely determined attacks – 'the troops most committed fired about 50 rounds a man'.[11] It is worth noting that the men of the 1/24th at iSandlwana were specifically complimented on their slow and steady rate of fire, while at Rorke's Drift – undoubtedly the most prolonged and sustained battle of the war – the defenders fired off the best part of a company reserve of 200,000 rounds in about ten hours. Much of the latter part of the battle was fought during the hours of darkness, of course, and there were by then long gaps between the Zulu attacks – nevertheless, it remains significant that the *average* rate of fire was rather under 15 rounds per man per hour.

All of which meant that, while company officers undoubtedly ordered fresh supplies of ammunition to be brought forward long before the men had emptied their pouches, it remained unusual for re-supply to be necessary in action, and no formal system seems to have existed. It was left to battalion officers to improvise when the situation required it. Some idea of how this worked is provided in a revealing letter by Captain Edward

Essex of the 75th Regiment, who was the Transport Officer for no. 3 Column and who survived iSandlwana. Essex was well known to the officers of the 1/24th, and had joined those companies (Mostyn and Cavaye's) which had been sent up on to the iNyoni ridge at the start of the engagement. After a period of firing which it is difficult now to estimate, Essex noticed that these two companies were

> now getting short of ammunition, so I went to the camp to bring up a fresh supply. I got such men as were not engaged, bandsmen, cooks, etc., and sent them to the line under an officer, and I followed with more ammunition in a mule cart. In loading the latter I helped the quartermaster of the 2nd Battalion 24th to place the boxes in a cart, and while doing so the poor fellow was shot dead. The enemy's fire was now increasing and I could hear the whiz of bullets all over the place.[12]

This short passage holds many insights into the tortured question of ammunition supply at iSandlwana. Essex is adamant that he dispatched first a group of men, presumably carrying boxes between them, and then a cart; how many boxes thus dispatched can only be guessed at but, given the capacity of a cart, it was unlikely to have been less than 20 and probably not more than 40. Significantly, a number of wire handles from the tin lining of the boxes were found along the British firing positions during the archaeological survey in 2000. The officer he mentions was, most probably, his junior in the transport department, Lieutenant Horace Smith-Dorrien, 94th Regiment. Since Smith-Dorrien's accounts are also crucial to the debates it is worth pausing to consider what he said:

> I will mention a story which speaks for the coolness and discipline of the regiment. I, having no particular duty to perform in camp, when I saw the whole Zulu army advancing, had collected camp stragglers, such as artillerymen in charge of spare horses, officers' servants, sick, etc., and had

taken them to the ammunition boxes, where we broke them open as fast as we could, and kept sending out the packets to the firing line ... When I had been engaged at this for some time, and the 1/24th had fallen back to where we were, with the Zulus following behind, Bloomfield, the quartermaster of the 2/24th, said to me in regard to the boxes I was breaking open, 'For Heaven's sake man, don't take that, for it belongs to our battalion.' And I replied, 'Hang it all, you don't want a requisition now, do you?'[13]

Much has been made of this account, written late in his career, and upon it is based the myth of obdurate quartermasters sticking to their orders at the expense of their duty. Yet, in a letter to his father written from Helpmekaar immediately after the battle, Smith-Dorrien offered a subtly different emphasis, merely remarking that 'I was out with the front companies of the 24th handing them spare ammunition'.[14] Quartermaster Edward Bloomfield was, of course, protecting the 2/24th's reserve ammunition – which, being drawn up behind the 2/24th camp, was nearer the firing line than the 1/24th's – a supply that Lord Chelmsford had ordered to be kept ready to dispatch to his troops (which included the 2/24th) should it be needed. His exchange with Smith-Dorrien must have taken place early in the fight – according to Essex Bloomfield was killed soon after – and it is highly likely that Bloomfield did not at that stage consider circumstances were desperate enough to warrant his overriding Chelmsford's instructions. Smith-Dorrien was, it should be noted, both very young and very junior at the time; Essex's evidence implies, however, that Bloomfield relented under Essex's greater rank and authority. It should not be thought that Smith-Dorrien contradicted his earlier account – merely that, years later, some events had come to assume a greater importance in his memory than they did at the time.

A similar incident had occurred, with one telling difference, earlier that same morning at the battle of Nyezane on the coast. At the height of the battle Captain Arthur Hart, Staff Officer to the 2nd NNC, had attempted to lead an attack by the European NCOs of his unit on a key Zulu position. He had noticed, however, that most were running low on ammunition:[15]

> I knew that our ammunition reserve was a long way off, so fearing that there might be a difficulty, I rode back myself to where Colonel Pearson was still engaged with the guns and the 'Buffs' ... and I got leave to take ammunition from the first supply, no matter to whom it might belong. I thus got a supply at once, and got some of our natives who were crouching about to carry it ...[16]

Hart, in other words, had anticipated the objection to issuing supplies to unauthorised units – the same complaint Smith-Dorrien faced just a few hours later at iSandlwana – but had taken the precaution of gaining authorisation beforehand and as a result secured what he needed.

In fact there is no evidence that a failure of supply contributed to the tactical decisions made by the officers of the 24th at iSandlwana. It is perhaps closer to the truth to suggest that a failure of firepower – of the ability of the front-line troops to halt or break up the Zulu attack owing to the extended front, the small numbers of men in the firing line and the determination of the enemy – was responsible for the decision to retire on the tents which led to the British collapse.

The situation among the auxiliary units is less clear-cut. One man of the NNC, Malindi, observed that 'our ammunition failed once but we got fresh from the camp, and remained firing until the Zulus were within 100 yards'.[17] After protracted firing from both detachments of his men, however, Durnford's command undoubtedly grew short of ammunition. Although he sent men back to gain fresh supplies they were hampered by the fact that Durnford had left iSandlwana while his baggage train was still on the road from Rorke's Drift; while his ammunition wagons had subsequently arrived in the camp, in the confusion of battle no one knew where they had been parked. Shortage of ammunition may well have been a factor which prompted Durnford

to abandon his defence of the forward donga; arguably more pressing, however, was the fact that his position had become untenable as the Zulus were outflanking it on both sides.

During the subsequent major actions of the war – Khambula, kwaGingindlovu and Ulundi – the British fought from defensive positions close to their ammunition carts. This must inevitably have eased any difficulties of re-supply, but in fact the expenditure of ammunition in each case does not seem to have warranted any undue efforts.

Artillery

Travelling through Zululand in 1882, Bertram Mitford had the opportunity to interview a number of Zulus who had fought in the war, one of whom gave him a frank opinion on the capabilities of British artillery:

> 'Ubain-bai? Haow! Didn't like them at all. First the warriors tried to dodge them, and scattered when they saw them coming, till at last on one occasion when a lot had dispersed from where the missile was expected to fall, it astonished them by dropping right in the thick of the group that had just dodged it. Arms, and legs, and heads flew in every direction' went on my informant, with an expressive gesture. 'This event caused them to lose heart more than anything, as they found that they could not get out of the way of the "bain-bai" so easily. At Sandhlwana the big guns hardly fired at all, and even then, when they did, they scarcely hit anyone.'[18]

The discrepancy between the performance of the guns in the early stages of the war and that during the key battles later, as it seemed to the Zulus on the receiving end, reflected the difference in the types of guns available to the British.

On the eve of the invasion, as in so many areas, Lord Chelmsford was woefully short of artillery. He had just two batteries of light guns to support his entire army, N Battery, 5th Brigade, and 11th Battery, 7th Brigade.[19] N/5 had been in southern Africa since 1878 and had taken part in the closing stages of the 9th Cape Frontier War while 11/7 had been based in the Natal garrison.

Both batteries were equipped with a type of gun known technically as the 7-pdr 200lb RML or 'Rifled Muzzle-Loader'. This type of weapon technology was enjoying a late popularity for it had in many respects already been superseded. Muzzle-loading weapons had of course been the mainstay of the great battles against Napoleon and even of the Crimean War twenty-five years before but the technology had existed for several years to produce functioning breech-loading weapons. In the 1860s the Royal Artillery had largely re-equipped its batteries with 9-pdr or 12-pdr breech-loading Armstrong or Whitworth guns, and some had been employed in New Zealand against the Maoris with good results. The technical problems posed by a hinged breech had not been entirely eradicated, however, while the experience of the American Civil War – where much of the fighting took place at close quarters and powerful smooth-bores were more popular than the more accurate breech-loaders – had led to the triumph of conservatism and the re-introduction in the 1870s of muzzle-loading models.

The 7-pdr was a lightweight and versatile weapon. Introduced in 1873, it was regarded as a 'mountain gun', in that either the barrel could be carried on a small, lightweight carriage drawn by mules, or the gun itself could be dismantled and the parts carried on pack-mules. The barrel was rifled – it had three grooves down the inside of the barrel which made the shell spin in flight, with a marked increase in accuracy and range over the old smooth-bore round-shot – and a range of about 3,000 yards (2,800 metres). A choice of projectile was available, ranging from common (explosive) shells to shrapnel shells (named after the inventor, Henry Shrapnel; these shells were filled with lead balls and timed by means of a fuse to explode in an air-burst above the target), and case-shot. The latter consisted of lead balls in a container which was designed to disintegrate on firing so that the contents sprayed out of the barrel like a giant shotgun; it had a limited useful range but was highly effective against personnel.

On the Eastern Cape Frontier N/5 had found that the mountain carriages of the 7-pdr were unsuitable for work over rocky terrain or on narrow tracks through the bush since the narrow wheel-base made them unstable. Instead, they were mounted on 'Kaffrarian' or 'Colonial' carriages which were a slightly modified version of the carriage supplied for the heavier 9-pdr gun. The carriages were made of iron with wooden wheels and included distinctive seats on the axle-tree for use by the gunners when on the march. The carriages were painted in battleship grey paint as a preservative. The heavier carriage was far more stable when drawn by a limber but was too heavy to be dragged by mules; instead both N/5 and 11/7 drew their guns by means of teams of six horses.[20]

When planning his strategy Chelmsford intended that the Centre Column should be his main thrust into Zululand. N/5 was therefore attached to the column in its entirety, much to the delight of its members who had served alongside the 24th Regiment on the Cape Frontier. In contrast, the 11/7 Battery was split between the two flanking columns. Two sections (four guns) were attached to Wood's column and one to Pearson's; Pearson's shortages were to some extent made good by two 7-pdr guns, two rocket tubes and a Gatling provided by the Royal Navy. Two unattached 7-pdr guns, pulled by mules and perhaps mounted on mountain carriages, and commanded by Lieutenant Frederick Nicholson RA, were also deployed with Wood's column.

It was N/5's guns that covered the crossing into Zululand at Rorke's Drift on 11 January, and they accompanied the advance to iSandlwana on the 20th. When, early on the morning of the 22nd, Chelmsford decided to split his force in response to reports that there were Zulus in the Mangeni hills, he instructed the commander of N/5, Lieutenant-Colonel Harness, to accompany him with two sections of the battery (four guns). One section – two guns – was left together with the battery's logistical supports in the camp under the command of Lieutenant Henry Curling. Because of the difficult terrain Harness's guns lagged behind Chelmsford's advance, and at one point, reacting to a report that the camp was under attack, turned back towards iSandlwana, only to be ordered to resume the march. When Chelmsford, having failed to find the main *impi* at Mangeni, decided to advance the camp to join him, Harness's second-in-command, Major Stuart Smith, was sent back to supervise packing up the battery. He arrived just as the Zulu attack developed.

The two guns formed the anchor of the British defence. There was no tactical doctrine in the 1870s which allowed guns to shell an enemy over the heads of their own men – the fuses on the shells were too unreliable and the dangers too great – so the guns were placed well forward, with the 24th extended on either side. They began shelling the Zulus as they descended off the iNyoni heights to their front; at one point a shell seems to have exploded prematurely over the head of Lieutenant Roberts' troop of mounted auxiliaries, who were retiring down the slope, killing Roberts himself. At the height of the battle one gun was moved briefly to the right to fire at the Zulu left in support of Durnford's stand in the donga.

According to one of the survivors, the civilian interpreter James Brickhill, the results were decidedly mixed:

The Artillery threw about 25 shots from different parts of the field during the battle. Four of these were very effective, each tearing up what appeared to be an acre of ground in the enemy's masses. One of the guns, however, always appeared to shoot high, whilst one shot burst half-way, nearly over the head of our foot Native Contingent.[21]

The reference to 'tearing up an acre of ground' provides a vivid impression of how effective shrapnel shells could be. Nevertheless, this account implies that the guns were too few and too light to have a more decisive effect on the battle. Their performance provoked some controversy in the military press afterwards where it was argued that the muzzle velocity of the 7-pdr was too low, and the bursting charge of the shell too light, to make it truly effective against a determined mass attack.

Certainly the Zulus do not seem to have been unduly daunted by the guns at iSandlwana. One survivor noted that, as they drew closer, they learned when the guns were about to fire from the drill of the crew who stood back before each discharge. The Zulus would then throw themselves down in the long grass calling out '*Moya!*' – 'the wind'.

During the final stages of the attack the guns switched to firing case-shot at close range. By this time the infantry had retired towards the tents and the guns were left exposed for a few moments, as Curling afterwards recalled:

At this time, out of my small detachment, one man had been killed, shot through the head, another wounded, shot through the side, and another through the wrist. Maj. Smith was also shot through the arm but was able to do his duty. Of course, no wounded man was attended to, there was no time or men to spare. When we got the order to retire, we limbered up at once but were hardly in time as the Zulus were on us at once and one man was killed (stabbed) as he was mounting the seat on the gun-carriage. Most of the gunners were on foot as there was no time to mount them on the guns.[22]

Curling later said that he assumed that the guns were being withdrawn to a new position, and this may well have been the case for a concerted stand closer to the tents was probably what Durnford and Pulleine had in mind. In the event it was too late, however, for the left of the Zulu 'chest' had pushed forward into the British camp, and Curling found that even as he rode through the camp Zulus were running up to attack his men. Most of the gunners were killed as they ran alongside the guns; finally, as they crested the nek and descended into the Manzimnyama valley, the guns themselves came to grief:

When we had gone about 400 yards, we came to a deep cut, in which the guns stuck. There was, as far as I could see, only one gunner with them at this time, but they were covered with men of different corps clinging to them. The Zulus were in them at once and the drivers pulled off their horses. I then left the guns.[23]

Both Curling and Major Smith then abandoned the guns and tried to escape; Curling managed to get away but Stuart Smith was killed during the final descent into the Mzinyathi valley.

When the first burial details visited the site on 21 May 1879, they found one of the gun limbers still stuck in the donga above the Manzimnyama valley, the dead horses lying in their traces. The other limber was found on the plain in front of the camp, having been apparently dragged away by the Zulus. Neither gun was present.

In 2000 an archaeological investigation of parts of the iSandlwana battlefield was allowed to excavate a cairn which was falling away into a donga at the head of the 'fugitives' trail'. It was found to contain the long bones of between four and six horses, as well as at least one human bone. The metal remains – studs and buckles – from leather harnesses were scattered nearby. These were, presumably, the remains of the horses and men killed when the limber became stuck in the donga.

The guns themselves were dragged by hand all the way to oNdini – as a prisoner of war, Ernest Grandier, later saw them there. There had been no time to spike them[24] and the Zulus tried to make them serviceable. They understood enough of the principles involved to attempt to detonate the charges by forcing rifle percussion-caps into the vents in place of friction tubes but this proved unsuccessful. The guns were later dragged away towards the oLandandlovu royal homestead, which lay between the White and Black Mfolozi rivers. On 11 August, during the extensive British patrolling in pursuit of King Cetshwayo, the guns were discovered lying in the empty veldt, not far from the homestead. The barrels had been removed from the carriages and left in the grass, while nearby were leather harnesses which had apparently been used to drag them, as well as shells and rockets. The barrels were mounted back on the carriages and the guns taken to Sir Garnet Wolseley's camp at oNdini. They were later returned to N/5 Battery,

rather to Harness's embarrassment. To lose a gun in action was the artillery equivalent of the infantry's disgrace at losing a Colour, and Harness was uncertain how to react at their recovery. Eventually the guns were returned to England, and there they disappear from history.

Elsewhere 11/7's guns had also seen action at Nyezane on 22 January, and they accompanied Pearson's advance to Eshowe, where they were emplaced in the British earthworks throughout the siege.

At Khambula on 29 March Wood was able to deploy six 7-pdr guns, in contrast to Pulleine's two at iSandlwana. The detached section commanded by Lieutenant Nicholson was placed in the redoubt, but the four guns of 11/7 Battery, commanded by Major E.G. Tremlett, remained in the open throughout the battle. Positioned between the redoubt at the main wagon-laager, they were able to change their face to meet each Zulu attack. Certainly Wood himself was impressed by their performance:

The men belonged to Garrison companies, but I have never known a battery so exceptionally fortunate in its Subalterns. Lieutenant Nicholson, standing on the gun platform, fought his guns with the unmoved stoical courage habitual to his nature. Major Tremlett was renowned as a fearless sportsman, and both Bigge and Slade were unsurpassable; they with their gunners stood up in the open from 1.30pm till the Zulus retreated at 5.30pm, and by utilising the ridge were enabled to find excellent targets with cover during the first attack on the southern slope and later on the northern slope, and suffered but little loss.[25]

Among those losses, however, was Lieutenant Nicholson, who was hit by a Zulu bullet as he stood on the parapet directing his guns.

The reports of the details told off to bury the dead confirm that the artillery had caused considerable execution. At one point, as the Zulu left emerged from the valley to the south of the camp and mounted a determined charge at close range, the guns had fired several rounds of case-shot. Afterwards Sergeant Edward Jervis of the 90th Regiment wrote home to his brother: 'A more horrible sight than the enemy's dead, where they felt the effects of shellfire, I never saw. Bodies lying cut in halves, heads taken off, and other features in connection with the dead made a sight more ghastly than ever I thought of.'[26]

After iSandlwana, reinforcements were hurried to Natal, including three field batteries (M/7, N/6, 8/7), a Gatling gun battery (10/7), and an ammunition train (O/6). Most of the field batteries were equipped with 7-pdrs but N/6 had the 9-pdr 8-cwt RML gun, which was in fact standard issue for field service. This had a slightly greater range than the 7-pdr – its maximum range was 3,500 yards (3,231 metres) – and a greater muzzle velocity. Because of the heavy calibre, the shells, too, had a greater bursting charge. The guns were mounted on the same carriage which had been adapted to provide the 7-pdr's 'Kaffrarian' carriage. In addition to the artillery reinforcements, the Navy also landed a number of guns with its additions to the Naval Brigades.

All of this potential firepower was, of course, distributed among Chelmsford's reorganised columns. In the event, those batteries attached to the 1st Division, on the coast, were destined to see no action but on 4 July the combined 2nd Division and Flying Column defeated the main Zulu army at the battle of Ulundi. Chelmsford's forces on that occasion included a concentration of guns unprecedented in the British Army's history in southern Africa – two of N/5 Battery's 7-pdrs, six 9-pdrs of N/6 Battery and four 7-pdrs of 11/7 Battery. In addition the two Gatling guns of 10/7 Battery were heavily involved in the action. The battle was short, for the Zulus were growing disheartened by the end of the war, and the British were in any case able to lay down an impenetrable wall of fire around the square. Although the number of rounds fired by the guns was much lower than in the protracted fighting at Khambula, at one point N/6 still had to fire case-shot to halt one particularly determined rush, and afterwards clumps of bodies were found lying within 50 yards of the guns, where they had been cut down. During the retreat, too, when the Zulus

showed signs of rallying on high ground, where the pursuing cavalry could not reach them, they were subject to well-placed shells fired at longer ranges which dispersed them.

As Mitford's informant had recognised, while the Zulus had the courage, discipline and numbers to withstand the losses necessary to take a position protected by just two 7-pdrs, as they did at iSandlwana, the fire from concentrated batteries was far more destructive, and all the more discouraging because its effects could not easily be avoided. Perhaps nothing demonstrates more clearly the essentially unequal nature of the struggle in 1879.

And why did the Zulus call field guns 'ubainbai?' Perhaps the earliest recorded explanation can be found in the writings of the Revd Allen Gardiner, the first missionary to work at Port Natal, who wrote in 1836 that

> the origin of this term is somewhat curious. Lieutenant Farewell RN, who was the first settler at Port Natal, had constructed a fort round his house, on which some carriage-guns were mounted. These guns excited much curiosity among the natives, and he was frequently questioned by them as to their use. His usual reply was 'You shall see bye and bye'; until hearing the last words so frequently repeated in reference to the guns, they naturally concluded that was the proper name.[27]

The term is still widely used in rural Zululand today.

BaSotho

Throughout the war in 1879 the British had a habit of referring to their mounted auxiliaries as 'Basutos'. This was a reflection of the favourable impression the baSotho had made on the British consciousness rather than a statement of fact; in reality only one troop of mounted auxiliaries was Sotho in origin.

These were the followers of Hlubi kaMota Molife, *inkosi* of a group of Sotho-speakers living in Natal called the Tlokoa. The Tlokoa had originally lived on the upper reaches of the

Mzinyathi river but had been driven over the Khahlamba mountains by the violence which characterised the rise of the Zulu kingdom. They had wandered the interior for a number of years, earning a fearsome reputation under their queen, MaNthathisi. After MaNthathisi's death the main section of the Tlokoa remained in the high veld under her son Sikonyela, but a section under Sikonyela's brother Mota apparently quarrelled with its neighbours and crossed the mountains into Natal. Mota had previously established a relationship with the amaHlubi people, and his son – born about 1835 – was named Hlubi to commemorate this. The Tlokoa settled in the foot-hills of the Natal Midlands with the amaHlubi as their neighbours.

In 1873, however, the Hlubi *inkosi*, Langali-belele kaMthimkhulu, fell foul of the colonial authorities and attempted to move his followers in the opposite direction, across the mountains. Natal's Secretary for Native Affairs, Theophilus Shepstone, sought support from Natal's African population to prevent the amaHlubi escape and the Tlokoa, their historic links to the Hlubi over-ridden by the need to maintain Shepstone's good-will, agreed to provide a contingent of mounted men.

Unlike most African groups south of the Limpopo, the southern Sotho had recognised early in their contacts with Europeans the value of the horse and by the 1870s sure-footed mountain ponies had become a major factor in Sotho war-fare. The Tlokoa, therefore, were ideally placed to assist the troops dispatched by Shepstone into the mountains. They were led by Hlubi himself, then a young man, and were attached to a small column commanded by (then) Major Anthony Durnford RE. Hlubi acted as Durnford's personal guide. Also present was a contingent of Christian Africans from the Edendale mission outside Pietermaritzburg. On 4 November 1873 Durn-ford's command intercepted a strong column of amaHlubi attempting to cross the Bushman's Pass into BaSotholand. In the ensuing skirmish Durnford was wounded and several of his men killed but the black auxiliaries retained their discipline and covered his retreat.

When Durnford was asked in late 1878 to draw up a plan for raising auxiliary forces he naturally turned to both the Tlokoa and Edendale men. Hlubi, by now in his forties, agreed to raise a troop of fifty men. Armed with Swinburne-Henry carbines, and dressed like most of the mounted auxiliaries in hard-wearing yellow corduroy, and with their hats wrapped round with a red band, they were attached to Durnford's no. 2 column.

The column was initially deployed at Middle Drift but was ordered to Rorke's Drift to support the advance of the Centre Column. They arrived at iSandlwana on the morning of the 22nd, and Durnford's decision to probe Zulu movements on the iNyoni heights led to an encounter with the Zulu army and precipitated the battle. His men – including Hlubi's BaSotho troop – made a determined stand in a donga in front of the camp but retired when their position was outflanked and their ammunition nearly spent. During the retreat Hlubi kept his men together, fighting their way through the Zulu right 'horn' and retreating towards the crossing at Rorke's Drift. At the crossing they halted briefly to rest their exhausted horses, then crossed by way of the Drift and reported to Lieutenant Chard at the Rorke's Drift post. At Chard's request they deployed in a screen to the south of the Shiyane hill, but after firing a few shots at the advancing Zulus they broke and rode towards Helpmekaar.

After iSandlwana the Tlokoa and Edendale men were based at Helpmekaar and patrolled the exposed border. When the auxiliary units were reorganised they were posted to Colonel Wood's column. During the battle of Khambula on 29 March they formed part of the mounted sortie which rode out to harass the Zulu right into a premature and uncoordinated attack. Rather than retreat towards the dubious safety of the British laager, however, a number of the auxiliaries preferred to trust to their horses and remain in the open. They stayed outside through-out the battle and harassed the Zulu flanks.

Despite their failings at Rorke's Drift – which even Chard was prepared to forgive them – the Tlokoa had earned a good reputation among the British. Hard-riding, resourceful and courageous, they seemed to represent the best that the auxiliary forces could offer, and their tough, wiry ponies epitomised their spirit to the extent that the British took to calling all mounted auxiliary units after them.

The Tlokoa took part in various patrols towards oNdini at the beginning of the second invasion in June 1879, and formed part of the mounted force which skirmished across the White Mfolozi on 3 July. On the following day they played a major role in the battle of Ulundi, at first harassing the Zulu attack, then riding back to take shelter in the British square before riding out again during the pursuit.

After the war Sir Garnet Wolseley, in implementing a political settlement on Zululand which best served British interests through indirect rule, offered Hlubi chieftainship of a swathe of land on the eastern bank of the Mzinyathi. His intention was to provide a sympathetic buffer beyond the Natal border and to eradicate the influence of the prominent royalists, the amaQungebeni, who lived there. Hlubi and his followers arrived in the area in October 1879 and built a homestead in the Batshe valley, not far from the ruins of *inkosi* Sihayo's old homestead. Throughout the 1880s Hlubi repaid his appointment by turning out his men several times to support British intervention in the successive crises which wracked post-war Zululand. In 1882 the traveller Bertram Mitford suggested the extent to which Hlubi associated himself with the European world:

A middle-aged man, rather stout, with an intelligent face, dressed in a velveteen jacket, tweed trousers, and flannel shirt, and with a general air of native well-to-do-ness, such is the chief Hlubi. His aspirations tend in the direction of comfort, for he lives in a substantial stone house with a verandah, and uses tables and chairs. Furthermore, he drives his own trap, an American 'spider' – albeit given to loading up the same rather inordinately: for to drive seven full-grown persons in a vehicle constructed to seat four *is* inordinate loading-up. At the time of my arrival the chief was engaged in presiding over a 'trial-at-law' . . . About fifty natives – Zulus and Basutos – were squatted around

in a circle, with the defendants, six in number, in the centre; the 'court' was held in the open air, Hlubi being the only man who affected a chair, the others sitting on the ground tailor-fashion.[28]

As this passage suggests, Hlubi's Sotho formed the governing elite of the Mzinyathi border community, a position he maintained successfully for more than a decade. With increased British intervention in Zululand following the Dinuzulu rebellion of 1888, and the subsequent annexation, Hlubi found himself increasingly marginalised, his power restricted to his immediate followers in the Batshe valley. Ironically Hlubi discovered a truth which underpinned the advance of British imperial interests across southern Africa – that it ultimately undermined the power and prestige of all traditional African leaders, whether collaborators or no.

Hlubi became ill in 1897, showing signs of mental instability which may have been the result of long-term exposure to malaria. He died in October 1902. He was succeeded by his son Isaak Lenega but in the 1940s the South African Government effectively removed what remained of Tlokoa authority in Zululand and their influence there effectively came to an end.

Their influence can still be seen among their descendants, however, in the number of cutstone round Sotho-style huts still to be found in the Nquthu and Nondweni districts.

Beards (British)

In the British Army of the Victorian era Queen's Regulations stated that men should not shave their top lip. Moustaches were equated with manliness and military panache. With the exception of infantry Pioneers, however, troops stationed in the UK were barred from growing beards. This prohibition was relaxed on active service at the discretion of the commanding officer, and a full growth of beard was almost universal in the field, partly because of the impracticalities of insisting upon a daily shave in areas where water might be scarce, and partly to exaggerate a business-like military appearance. Faced with the prospect of at least three weeks' inactivity on the boat en route to southern Africa, many men began growing beards on the ship, and officers' letters suggest the daily growth was the subject of some competition. Lieutenant Nevill Coghill, a week into the invasion of Zululand, wrote home to his sister that he had grown 'quite a present-able Van Dyke, but I shall be very glad indeed when I take it off'.[29] Indeed, throughout the war beards seem to have been equated with veteran experience and the lack of them with inexperi-ence; Evelyn Wood himself marvelled at the courage of his younger staff at the battle of Hlobane, commending it all the more because they were 'beardless boys'. Among the Royal Navy it was also considered desirable to grow beards.

At the end of the war, however, Sir Garnet Wolseley, determined to assert his own authority over the forces under his command, instructed the troops to smarten up. Helmets and cross-belts dyed buff with tea and coffee on campaign were cleaned, torn and battered clothing was repaired – and beards were shaved off.

Big Game Hunting

In the 1930s, looking back wistfully over a life rich in adventure, George Mossop – who would serve in Zululand as a teenage trooper in the Frontier Light Horse, and leave an extraordinary account of his participation in the battles of Hlobane and Khambula – recalled a brief spell spent in 1876 in the company of professional hunters in the Transvaal. There was then, he said, 'game, game everywhere, as far as the eye could see – all on the move, grazing. The game did not appear to be moving; the impression that I received was that the earth was doing so, carrying the game with it – they were in such vast numbers, moving slowly and steadily, their heads all in one direction.'

Yet that extraordinary sight – and 'no one who has not witnessed such a scene can form any idea of what it was like' – was even then in the passing. After millennia of living to their optimum population levels in the rich South African environment, only marginally affected by the limited hunting activities of black Africans, the game was already, by 1876, in the process

of being devastated by the arrival of European hunters armed with efficient firearms. Mossop himself knew it, and came to regret it:

On our old hunting-ground I do not think that a dozen head of game could be found to-day; certainly not one black wildebeest ... The old man Visajie told me he seriously began shooting when he was a lad of ten years of age. He said that in the Orange Free State the game had so diminished [by 1876] that it no longer paid to shoot there; that the game were at their last gasp, and were making their final stand in that section of the eastern Transvaal in which our camp was situated. Here they were in their hundreds of thousands, and if this was their last gasp and last stand it makes one wonder what the country looked like when they were at full strength.[30]

A similar process had already occurred in Zululand. The environment is different there, of course, and the country never supported the huge quantities of savannah animals that thrived in the open grassland of the interior; indeed, historically the human population was also always more dense. Nevertheless, Zululand boasted an ancient and rich fauna which, similarly, was already under pressure from European hunting techniques by the 1870s. The Zulus themselves were efficient hunters, but usually on a limited scale; only those hunts organised by the Zulu kings and involving the participation of hundreds – even thousands – of men made any significant impression on wild-life population levels. In the 1820s, for example, King Shaka had organised a large-scale hunt as part of the cleansing ceremonies following the death of his mother; several *amabutho* took part, driving game *en masse* towards the confluence of the Black and White Mfolozi rivers where animals were trapped in prepared pits and killed. Perhaps the greatest impact caused by the Zulus themselves was on those smaller species of animals whose pelts were desirable as part of the ceremonial regalia of the *amabutho*, in particular spotted cats such as the genet or serval. Only men of rank were entitled to wear leopardskin; if a leopard was killed by a commoner, he was required to present the pelt to his *inkosi*.

It was, however, the arrival of the whites (from 1824) which precipitated the reduction of Zulu game. Almost from the first, white settlers augmented their trading activities with commercial hunting – there was a growing international market for ivory and skins. The Zulus had only rarely hunted elephants prior to this, and had no tradition of making ivory ornaments and bangles; realising that the whites would pay handsomely for tusks they soon collaborated in the trade, however. With the expansion of settlement in Natal in the 1840s, commercial hunting in Zululand increased. White hunters were required to obtain permission from the Zulu kings, and certain areas were considered out of bounds as being royal hunting grounds; nevertheless, the activities of well-organised hunting parties caused widespread destruction among natural populations of elephants, hippos, buffalo and those antelope whose skins or horns were considered desirable. Even by the 1870s the number of white hunters operating in Zululand had begun to decline because animals were no longer as plentiful as they once were.

By the time of the Anglo-Zulu War, although small groups of animals still survived across the country, the larger concentrations had retreated to areas less accessible to man, in particular the wild country along the Black Mfolozi and the flats of Maputaland ('Thongaland') beyond the barrier of the Lebombo mountains. Furthermore, the movement of large armies of men, whether white or black, further reduced the chances of encounters with wildlife.

Nevertheless, the possibility of discovering game was greatly anticipated by the troops, the British in particular. Most of the regular officers had come from backgrounds where field sports – hunting, shooting, fishing, steeplechasing – were popular pastimes, and many of them looked forward to the opportunity to enjoy some sport at the expense of African wildlife. There was a more prosaic reason, too; game meat offered a desirable alternative to the monotony of daily rations. Ordinary soldiers were not, of course, permitted to waste ammunition in hunting but

officers were able to indulge their interests, and indeed some had brought their personal hunting weapons on campaign with them. Members of the Irregular and Volunteer corps generally enjoyed more freedom in this regard too. Captain W.E. Montague of the 94th recalled the enthusiasm which greeted one encounter:

a troop of hartebeests showed about a mile away, and a couple of sportsmen started at once in pursuit. The ground was favourable; and the column, having halted for the mid-day meal, was able to watch the whole of the chase. Presently the horsemen dismounted for a shot, and the excitement vented itself in loud cries and directions from the men.

'Keep your head down, captain darlin'!'

'Don't you see that big one with the two horns; he's a cow, he is, not a deer at all, at all.'

'Holy mother, but them's pretty creatures to shoot!'

Just then, puff went the smoke of the two rifles, and off galloped the hartebeests untouched ...

Equally typical was another incident, also related by Montague:

Far out on this sea of grass we had been watching a speck moving constantly, which might be a horse, an ox, or some wild animal. The glasses made it out to be like an ox; to imaginations fired with accounts of South African sport, it was a wild buffalo. So a sportsman was soon in the saddle, and rode off with a rifle to solve the question. His progress was eagerly watched: the leaving the pony in a hollow, which instantly galloped home – the stalk, and the final shot, when the great beast fell over heavily – were all intensely interesting. Our anticipations of sport were, however, rudely shattered when the sportsman returned with the news that he had only shot a tame ox, wandering about ownerless on the veldt ...[31]

Major Anstruther, also of the 94th, certainly took the opportunity to shoot whenever he could. 'I go out every day shooting,' he wrote in letters home,

> but there is lamentably little. On Monday I got a wild duck and on Tuesday I made a great bag, 2 wild turkeys (small ones), 2 plover and 2 brace of quail – did not miss a shot. The turkeys and wild duck were awfully good eating but I have given up shooting quail as cartridges are scarce and you can't buy them.

A month after Ulundi, he noted, 'Brook and I have been out shooting all morning and we saw hartebeest and some bush buck but I did not have a shot.'[32]

For the most part, however, the presence of so much concentrated humanity was enough to make the game scarce. According to Dr Doyle Glanville, who served with the Flying Column,

> Marching along these solitary wastes but few signs of life are visible – not even a bird, save now and then when we kill oxen, and the vultures mysteriously appear. Occasionally we come across the track of some startled hare, or perhaps a buck, when the excitement is for the moment tremendous ... [Yesterday] a buck sprang up and ran through the column. In an instant a lot of soldiers and natives went pell-mell after it, many coming to grief, and sprawling over the ant-bear holes that abound in the long grass. The numbers were too much for it, the game was duly bagged, and the happy hunters were rewarded at their dinner by a change from the usual fare ...[33]

When, after the relief of Eshowe, Lord Chelmsford personally led a foray to destroy eZulwini, the personal homestead of Prince Dabulamanzi kaMpande, the troops disturbed a small antelope on the return trip. Guy Dawnay, a gentleman adventurer who had attached himself to the NNC, was sorely tempted by the sport: 'on the way

I nearly got a good shot at a duiker not eighty yards off, bounding along; Dunn just missed it, but I couldn't fire, as it was on the ridge over which the General had disappeared.'[34]

The sort of bigger game that would engage the true sportsman's instincts of course kept well away from the progress of the armies. Lieutenant Baskerville Mynors of the 3/60th, who had come out with the reinforcements after iSandlwana and had fought at Gingindlovu, dreamed of bagging a serious trophy even as he lay in his sickbed after the battle, suffering the first pangs of the dysentery which would soon kill him: 'Two rhinoceroses have been seen near here feeding; I wish I could get a shot at them, but can't get leave to go out.'[35]

It was during the pursuit of King Cetshwayo during August 1879 that British patrols encountered the most game. The king had retired north of the Black Mfolozi river, and the troops pursuing him moved through less densely populated country – once regarded as Shaka's personal hunting ground, and in modern times incorporated into the Umfolozi Game Reserve – which was thick with bush teeming with wildlife. One night, when Captain Lord Gifford's patrol was camped near a Zulu homestead, an ox from the settlement was taken by a lion, while 'several kinds of antelope of the larger sort, waterbucks, and hartebeests appeared, and as the troopers managed to wound and ride down several, their nightly bivouac in the forest was solaced by a feast of excellent venison.'[36]

Perhaps the most poignant encounter with wildlife occurred on 4 July. Lord Chelmsford's troops had just finished manoeuvring their square within sight of the royal homestead at oNdini, and the first Zulu *amabutho* were beginning to advance towards them across the plain, when a duiker, a small grey antelope, disturbed by all the movement in the grass, broke cover and dashed off down one face of the square. In the tension of the moment the troops broke into a cheer. It was a fitting tribute to two very different aspects of a timeless Africa, both of which were in the process of being irrevocably destroyed.

Boers

Towards the end of 1878 Lord Chelmsford wrote to Evelyn Wood asking him to use his influence to try to persuade the Transvaal Boers to join the invasion of Zululand. Chelmsford remained short of men, and he hoped that the Boers of the Utrecht district – which lay squarely in the 'disputed territory' – might be persuaded, especially as many had petitioned for military protection in the tense months running up to the outbreak of war. The Transvaal was of course a British colony by that time, and Chelmsford was aware of the bitter fighting which had taken place between the Voortrekkers and the Zulus a generation before. Wood was ideally placed to secure their support, for his column began its advance from Utrecht, and Wood prided himself on the good relations he enjoyed with individual Boer farmers.

Both Chelmsford and Wood were to be disappointed. The annexation of the Transvaal was bitterly resented by the majority of Boers in the rural areas, and many had no intention of risking their lives in a war between two groups whom they both feared and distrusted. As Petrus Lefras Uys ('Piet' Jnr), a prominent farmer in the Utrecht district, explained to Wood,

> He doubted any Dutchmen coming out. He said if I could persuade Swart Dirks Uys and Andries Pretorius to join us, they would bring over many others. Piet Uys told me that the feeling of his countrymen was so intensely bitter that he doubted whether any of them would come out, but he would do his best to help, not because he loved us, but because he realised the importance of the Border question.[37]

When Wood then interviewed A.L. Pretorius – 'Rooi Adrian' – he was told bluntly that any support was conditional upon the outcome of negotiations then under way regarding the future of the colony: 'We have sworn an oath to be true to Messrs Kruger and Joubert, who went to England to see your Government, and we will not move until we hear the answer to the deputation, and we will not help you until the Transvaal is given back to us.'[38]

In the event, only Piet Uys agreed to give his support, for largely personal reasons. The representative of a great Voortrekker family, Uys had lost his father, Piet Snr, and his brother Dirk to the Zulus at the battle of eThaleni during the disastrous *Vlugkommando* of 1838. Moreover, Uys's own farms were directly threatened by the boundary dispute with the Zulu kingdom. Uys raised a commando of 45 men, many of them connected to him by family ties and patronage. Although Wood offered to pay them 5 shillings a day plus rations and fodder, many of Uys's men seem to have agreed to fight on the promise that they would get a share of any looted Zulu cattle.

Wood developed a close personal relationship with Uys and relied heavily on his advice during the early stages of the war when much of the fighting involved long-range mounted expeditions and raids, a type of warfare at which the Boers were adept. The commando was present with Buller's detachment during the attack on Hlobane on 28 March, but during the retreat down the 'Devil's Pass' Piet's eldest son 'Vaal Piet' lagged behind and his father turned to help him. A Zulu, clambering over the boulders in-between, managed to spear Piet Snr through the back. His death, and the fact that it proved impossible to remove his body from the field, demoralised his followers, most of whom abandoned the war that evening, returning to protect their families on the exposed northern frontier.

Although Uys's sons continued to serve with Wood throughout the war, Hlobane effectively ended Boer support for the British cause. Uys's body was later recovered and buried on his farm, and Wood himself instigated a memorial to his memory.

Such was the feeling against the British that other farmers were more inclined to support the Zulus. Along the Phongolo frontier – where Boer, Zulu and Swazi claims overlapped, and where the war assumed a distinct character of raid and counter-raid – there is evidence to suggest that some Boers living on remote farms offered intelligence to Zulu raiding parties in return for their property being spared.

In December 1880 the Transvaal Boers rose in arms and threw off the British domination of the Transvaal.

Border Raids

Although attention has been traditionally focused on the major campaigns during the Anglo-Zulu War a low-intensity war was none the less practised by both sides along much of Zululand's borders with both Natal and the Transvaal. Indeed, the fear of Zulu incursions largely shaped the response of the colonial administration to the conflict. In fact, however, King Cetshwayo was reluctant to authorise a major strike into British territory, and as a result the British retained the strategic initiative, and all the major battles took place on Zulu soil.

None the less both sides engaged in small-scale border strikes throughout the war. Although it is seldom considered as such, the action at Rorke's Drift falls into that category; it was not a planned offensive but rather an opportunistic raid which gave the Zulu *amabutho* who had remained in reserve at iSandlwana a chance to secure both loot and glory. The exact number of Zulus who crossed the Mzinyathi that afternoon will never be known but it was certainly in excess of 4,000; of these, some 3,000–3,500 went on to assault the position at Rorke's Drift. The rest dispersed in smaller bodies along the Mzinyathi valley, raiding deserted white farms and African homesteads. Some pressed up to the foot of the Helpmekaar escarpment while others ranged downstream towards Eland's Kraal. Numbers of abandoned homesteads were burnt, and official returns show that the raiders carried away several African women and children. Even the great *induna* Zibhebhu kaMaphitha abandoned his command responsibilities when he reached Sothondose's Drift, crossed into Natal and looted cattle on his own account – narrowly avoiding Lord Chelmsford's force at iSandlwana when he returned to Zululand that night.

In the weeks after iSandlwana, when British defences along the Mzinyathi were in disarray, minor Zulu incursions were common. These were apparently mounted by the amaQungebeni people, the followers of *inkosi* Sihayo or his

brother Gamdana, for whom the temptation offered by empty homesteads and deserted farms proved too much. On 16 February, for example, sixteen armed Zulus attempted to cross the river but turned back after they were spotted and fired upon by black Border Guards. At the end of February a large party of Zulus crossed at Robson's Drift, upstream from Rorke's Drift, but retired again when the Volunteers based at Fort Pine rode out to intercept them. In early March a small party of Zulus, dressed in great-coats looted from iSandlwana, crossed the river and attacked three African homesteads, shooting one man in the thigh and carrying away five women, twenty children and a number of cattle. Occasionally this activity persuaded the British, cooped up at Rorke's Drift, to retaliate; Commandant George Hamilton Browne of the 3rd NNC frequently led small patrols, consisting of his white NCOs, across the river to harass the Zulus. On one occasion they spotted an *inyanga* and her assistant burning medicine over a fire in the hope of driving away the invaders – Hamilton Browne and his men shot them both dead.

The incidents along the Mzinyathi remained minor affairs, however. Further north, where Zululand bordered the Transvaal, raids and counter-raids became not only endemic but far more serious. Here the village of Luneburg was at the eye of the storm. Luneburg had been founded by a German missionary community on land recognised at the time as being Zulu – King Mpande had granted the permission – but it lay close to both the Transvaal and Swazi borders and became, through the 1870s, the focus of many of the claims and counter-claims of the infamous 'boundary dispute'. Cetshwayo, both as a prince and later as king, was particularly keen that Zulu claims in the region should not be lost by default, and partly for that reason had given the exiled Swazi prince Mbilini waMswati permission to settle in the Luneburg valley nearby. The abaQulusi section, who lived further south around the Hlobane and Zungwini mountains, were also directed to watch Zulu interests in the region. When the war broke out, therefore, the British recognised that Luneburg was particularly vulnerable, and it had effectively been straddled by two British columns – Evelyn Wood's Left Flank Column further south, and Colonel Rowlands' no. 5 Column to the north-west. A garrison was also established at Luneburg itself.

Despite this, Luneburg remained firmly at risk. Prince Mbilini was to emerge as the most dashing and daring guerrilla leader of the war, and he had cultivated strong ties with other groups in the area, notably the Khubeka of *inkosi* Manyanyoba kaMagonondo, who lived in the Ntombe valley just outside Luneburg, and the abaQulusi. In October 1878 Mbilini had signalled his defiance by orchestrating a number of raids on African settlements outside Luneburg, and at the end of December 1878 all of these groups undertook the rituals necessary to prepare them for war.

Evelyn Wood had recognised the strength of his opposition and was determined to counter it. From the beginning of the war he targeted the abaQulusi, sending Redvers Buller to probe their strength around Zungwini mountain on 20 January, and on the 22nd leading a strong foray of both infantry and mounted men himself. Wood drove the abaQulusi off Zungwini in a running fight that spilled over several days but was forced to withdraw when news reached him on the 24th of the disaster at iSandlwana. For several days Wood was preoccupied with securing his own position – he retired to his camp at Fort Thinta, then moved to Khambula hill – but he was determined not to abandon the initiative and on 1 February he dispatched a mounted force under Buller to destroy ebaQulusini, the royal homestead which served as the administrative centre of the abaQulusi. The move caught the abaQulusi by surprise and Buller destroyed the homestead – which contained 250 huts – and carried away 270 cattle.

This activity did not, however, discourage Zulu resistance outside Luneburg. Early in February Mbilini and Manyanyoba assembled their followers, reinforced with numbers of abaQulusi, and on the night of the 10th they laid a major raid, directed not against the Luneburg settlers themselves but against their Christian African followers, many of whom had been left in charge of white-owned farms while the settlers had retreated to the safety of the village laager. The raiders struck before dawn, moving from farm to farm using spears rather than guns where they could, and killing 41 men, women and children. When the Luneburg garrison heard of the attack and set out to intercept them, they swiftly retired, carrying away hundreds of cattle and thousands of sheep.

The raid provoked Wood into sending Buller to attack Manyanyoba in retribution. On 15 February Buller attacked Khubeka homesteads in the Ntombe valley, burning five and killing 34 Zulus, and carrying away cattle and sheep. Manyanyoba and most of his followers retired to caves in the hillsides, however, and Buller failed to drive them out. Responding to the need to re-assert British fortunes in the north, Colonel Rowlands also launched two minor forays against hills used by the Zulus as a refuge in the Luneburg area. On 15 February his men attacked Talaku mountain – where it was said the live-stock captured on the 11th had been hidden – and on the 20th Makateeskop. Although the Zulus were driven off the strongholds they merely reoccupied them once the British had departed.

The nature of these raids intensified through-out March. On the 12th Mbilini struck a supply convoy of the 80th Regiment that was stranded on the Ntombe river, killing most of the escort. The British again responded by ravaging the Ntombe valley but Mbilini himself withdrew to join his abaQulusi allies on the Hlobane moun-tain. Wood was particularly keen to deny this refuge to the Zulus and when, on the eve of Lord Chelmsford's march to relieve Eshowe, he was asked by Chelmsford to mount a diversion in the northern sector he opted to attack Hlobane. The foray took place on 28 March but proved a disaster; the abaQulusi, assisted by Mbilini, mounted a spirited defence and the British dis-comfort was exacerbated by the arrival of a large Zulu army en route from oNdini to attack Khambula.

The repulse of that army the following day at the battle of Khambula swung the fortunes of war in the north decisively in favour of the

British. Not only was the main army defeated but the abaQulusi suffered so heavily that they abandoned their position at Hlobane. Mbilini himself – who may have been slightly wounded at Hlobane on the 28th – had already moved north. Once back in his fastnesses on the Ntombe, he and Manyanyoba led a raid against the whites in the Phongolo valley on the night of 4 April. Once again the farm owners were absent but several of their retainers were killed and their property was thoroughly looted. Late on the evening of the 4th a mounted patrol dispatched from Luneburg intercepted a small party of Africans on horseback. One man was killed – he proved to be Tshekwane, a son of Sihayo Ngobese – while another was shot through the body but managed to escape. He proved to be Prince Mbilini, and he died shortly afterwards.

The death of Mbilini, following so soon upon the British victory at Khambula, severely weakened the ability of the Zulus in the northern sector to resist, although sporadic skirmishing continued throughout the war, and indeed some of the last shots fired were against Manyanyoba's followers in the Ntombe valley.

In the meantime the same directive issued by Chelmsford to Wood, which had prompted the attack on Hlobane, had provoked other raids along the Natal/Zulu border. On 20 May the British had mounted a strong raid into Zululand across the Thukela at Middle Drift. This area – a recognised point of entry into the Zulu kingdom – had been occupied by the British from the beginning of the war. Durnford's command had originally been stationed there before he was ordered to iSandlwana, and a sizeable detachment had been left in earthwork forts high on the escarpment above the river. On 20 May the local commander, Major A.C. Twentyman, led a strong raid against Zulu settlements on the opposite bank in support of Chelmsford's advance on Eshowe. Twentyman's men – Natal Volunteers and African auxiliaries – crossed at three separate points and apparently caught the Zulus by surprise. They destroyed a number of homesteads and carried off cattle before retiring to the Natal bank. Although the raid was a success, Twentyman was somewhat deflated when, as his men

struggled back up the escarpment, a party of indignant Zulus crossed behind him and burned a number of Natal African homesteads in retribution.

The Lower Thukela also saw limited activity at this time – on 28 May the local commander, Captain G.A. Lucas, crossed with a party of auxiliaries and destroyed two homesteads on the Zulu bank.

The policy of border raiding – encouraged at the time by Lord Chelmsford – aroused the opposition of Natal's Lieutenant-Governor, Sir Henry Bulwer, however. Bulwer was worried about the long-term impact on the relationship between African groups on either side of the border, and concerned that the Zulus would, at some point, retaliate.

He was right. At daybreak on the morning of Wednesday 25 June two black Border Guards standing watch over the Shu Shu hot springs upstream from the Middle Drift were alerted by the sound of movement in the water. It was a misty morning and it was not until they were 30 yards away that the guards saw a large *impi* crossing the river. The guards fired shots at them but received such a heavy volley in return that they fled. The Zulus were in fact one part of a two-pronged raid – the other had crossed below Middle Drift – launched by members of the Magwaza and Nthuli chiefdoms, both of which had suffered during Twentyman's raid of 20 May. The Zulus, about 500 strong, swept through the valley below the escarpment, destroying African homesteads, capturing cattle, and killing about 30 men, women and children. They then retired by way of the Middle Drift, harassed by a section of local Border Guards. The raid had been so swift and well planned, however, that the Zulus were back on their side of the border before the bigger detachment of Volunteers and auxiliaries could be moved down from the heights to intercept them.

By the time the raid of 20 June took place the war was already moving against the Zulus, however. On 4 July Lord Chelmsford decisively defeated the main Zulu army at the battle of Ulundi, and the cycle of raid and counter-raid which had spluttered along the border since the beginning of the war came to an end. Nevertheless, the defiance displayed by the Magwaza and Nthuli had been noted, however, and when British troops were withdrawn from Zululand Lieutenant-Colonel Clarke was ordered to retire by way of Middle Drift to intimidate the local chiefdoms. By that stage of the war, however, the Zulus had little to gain by a show of resistance and Clarke's passage went unopposed.

The 'Boys' of iSandlwana

Late on the evening of 22 January Lord Chelmsford's command returned to the camp it had left at the foot of iSandlwana mountain before dawn that same morning. There had been some light left as they drew near the camp, enough to confirm that the rumours of the day – that the camp had been taken – were true, for Zulu stragglers could still be seen among the tents, or retiring away, carrying their wounded and loot, on to the iNyoni escarpment. There were delays, however, before Chelmsford reoccupied the camp, for his men had to be formed up in expectation of Zulu resistance, and by the time the men reached the ruins of the tents it was quite dark. And it would get darker still, for there was no moon and after an hour or two a light drizzle descended, the clouds blocking out even the starlight. It was so dark that men talking in close, hushed voices could not recognise each other's faces. Some tripped over corpses or lay down to sleep only to find later that they had been lying next to disembowelled bodies. Here and there a few officers lit lanterns, but the only fragile light otherwise was from the smouldering remains of the tents, some of which had been set alight by the Zulus hours before. And everywhere was the presence of death, of human bodies jumbled up together with the carcasses of hundreds of oxen and horses, all of them victims of a close-quarter slaughter. The British dead had mostly been repeatedly stabbed and were disembowelled, the Zulu dead were disfigured by bullet and bayonet wounds – the state of the animals can only be imagined. The slopes below iSandlwana had been transformed into the floor of an abattoir; in places the ground must have been awash with blood. A heavy, foetid smell hung in the air; far off, jackals howled. In this desperately overwrought atmosphere, a trooper of the Newcastle Mounted Rifles, Sam Jones, believed he saw a dreadful sight:

> One sight, a most gruesome one, I shall never forget. Two lads, presumably little drummer boys of the 24th Regiment, had been hung up by butcher's hooks, which had been jabbed under the chins, and then disembowelled; all the circumstances pointing to the fact that they had been subject to this inhuman treatment while still alive.[39]

This story went round Chelmsford's men like wildfire. 'Even the little drummer boys that we had in the band,' wrote one man of the 2/24th, 'they were hung up on hooks, and opened like sheep. It was a pitiful sight.'[40] The pathos of the scene is enshrined in one of the most famous images of the war, the artist Charles Fripp's painting *Last Stand of the 24th, Isandhlwana*, in which a young drummer boy, no more than 12 years old, takes centre stage in the composition.

That the Zulus would have killed boys as well as men need not be doubted. In battle the Zulus made no distinction between their enemy's soldiers and non-combatants; since the days of Shaka it had been common practice to 'sweep everything clear', to destroy the enemy in whatever way possible to bring a firm end to a conflict. Non-combatants were, in any case, regarded as guilty by association; if they supported an enemy, then they were as legitimate a target as the enemy themselves, and it is no coincidence that the Zulu boy Muziwento, when marvelling at the dead lying on the battlefield a few days afterwards, referred to as one the 'dead white men ... and the people who had served them, and fought with them'.[41] Several times in Zulu history non-combatants accompanying an army were caught up in the fighting – notably when King Shaka finally defeated the amaNdwandwe at Ndolowane hill in 1826, and when Prince Cetshwayo defeated his brother Prince Mbuyazi at 'Ndondakusuka in 1856 – and a catastrophic loss of life ensued. Nor was any shame attached to the act of killing a non-combatant in battle – indeed, James Stuart told Rider Haggard that

King Dinuzulu had earned the right to wear the *iziqu* bravery necklace (awarded only to those who were among the first to kill one of the enemy) for stabbing a boy as he emerged from a hut during fighting with the rival Mandlakazi faction.[42]

There was, moreover, a feeling of great indignation prevalent among the Zulu army which attacked the camp at iSandlwana, an anger at the presumption of the British who had come to take their country from them. Anyone found among the British forces was by definition an invader, and was considered fair game. And any little 'drummer boys' had taken the Queen's Shilling and wore her red coat – and were now taking their chances.

Yet still something does not ring quite true about that best known of iSandlwana horror stories. Lord Chelmsford deliberately instructed that his men should not be allowed to wander the camp that night; not only did he not want to demoralise them, but the possibility of a renewed Zulu attack was very real. Sentries were posted, a few officers were required to go the rounds, and some men made excuses to seek out relatives or property they had left in the camp that morning. Most, however, had no opportunity to do so, and at least one officer, Lieutenant Maxwell of the 3rd NNC, was sceptical of the gruesome descriptions he heard the next morning on the road to Rorke's Drift: 'on the way I heard some terrible stories about mutilated bodies. These were invented for the occasion, as it was impossible for those who told these yarns to distinguish anything in the night, it being exceptionally dark.'[43]

And were there 'young boys' in the ranks of the 24th Regiment? It is certainly true that 'Boy' was a rank in the British Army. In 1795 three experimental regiments had been formed to relieve parishes of the burden of feeding 'boys between the ages of 10 and 16'. This experiment seems to have been abandoned once the boys grew old enough to enlist in the regular army, but during the Napoleonic Wars infantry battalions were authorised to maintain 'a certain number of boys' as drummers or non-combatants. By 1876 the practice had largely been regulated, and battalions were allowed to maintain 1 per cent of

their strength as boys to serve as musicians and 0.5 per cent to serve as tailors and shoemakers. Boys could be recruited from the age of 14 while the age of enlistment for an adult was officially 18 (although it was not unknown for men to lie about their ages – and much else besides – on enlisting). In that regard it is interesting to note that the Elementary Education Act of 1870 provided provision for the education in Britain of children between the ages of 5 and 12; once a boy reached 13 he was expected to earn his own living. In fact, however, most Boys on the Army strength were the sons or orphans of serving soldiers and were taken on as part of the responsibilities of the Army community. They were not, for the most part, drummers; this role was open to adult soldiers and most of them were mature men. Although sometimes called upon to play the drums on parade, the main duty of the drummers by 1879 was to play the bugle-calls by which orders were transmitted on the battlefield. Of the twelve 1/24th drummers killed at iSandlwana the two youngest were each 18 and the oldest was in his late 30s.

The band of the 1/24th had been left at iSandlwana when Chelmsford marched out on the morning of the 22nd – most were employed as stretcher-bearers during the fighting, and were killed there – as were some elements of the 2/24th. Altogether there were five Boys in the camp: Thomas Harrington and Robert Richards of the 1/24th and Daniel Gordon, James Gurney and Joseph McEwen of the 2/24th. None of them was a drummer, although they may well have been in the battalion bands. Although the records are incomplete, Joseph McEwen appears to have been the youngest of these Boys at 16 – officially – on 22 January – not quite the innocent boy of popular myth.

Would the Zulus have hung them up on butchers' hooks? There is no reason to suppose so. At the height of the battle, in the adrenalin rush of the final assault, and amidst all the confusion of smoke and dust, the Zulus stabbed at anything that moved – men, boys, animals – and a few things that didn't, like mealie-sacks piled up on wagons. To have hung the 'little drummer boys' up by the chin would have required a degree of deliberation which seems highly unlikely under the circumstances, not to mention an uncharacteristic sadism. Even Captain William Penn Symons of the 24th – who was out with Lord Chelmsford that day and later wrote an important history of the Regiment – went out of his way to state categorically that 'no single case of torture was proved against them. The wild stories current at the time, and repeated in the English papers, were untrue.'[44]

Bertram Mitford's Zulu informants, who had participated in the battle, agreed: 'all were killed on the field, and at once; no white men were tortured: it is the Zulu custom to kill everyone on the spot; prisoners are never taken.'[45]

That the Boys of the 24th were killed, with the rest, at iSandlwana, cannot be doubted, although the manner of their deaths is unlikely ever to be known. Simeon Nkambule of the Edendale contingent found one whom he described as a 'drummer boy' (age unknown) guarding a supply of ammunition in the camp; the drummer refused to allow the Edendale men to plunder his charge, and refused also the chance to escape with them. He was supposedly seen later flinging his regulation-issue drummer's sword at the approaching Zulus. No other reliable fragments survive in relation to their fate.

The story that young boys had been hung up on meat-hooks nevertheless was widely and quickly circulated among surviving British troops, and it exacerbated the ruthlessness which characterised British behaviour in later battles. It was certainly well known by the time the first burial expedition to iSandlwana took place on 21 May, and may have coloured the accounts of what was found there. One man claimed to have seen the body of a boy lying near the butchers' scaffold; he may well have done. Others claimed to have seen the mutilated bodies of 'young drummer boys' elsewhere on the battlefield. But what they thought they saw, and what they really saw, is little more now than a matter for speculation.

There were, of course, almost certainly other boys in the camp, some quite possibly younger than the 24th's teenagers. It is possible that some of the civilian wagon-drivers had their sons with them, but since they were not on the Army rolls no official record of their loss exists. Many of the black *voorloopers* who walked beside the wagon-teams driving the oxen with their long whips were young lads, too.

Certainly the Zulu boy Muziwento noticed the bodies of youngsters on the field when he visited it a few days after the fight: 'We saw some boys who had died in a tree, [lying] underneath it. They were dressed in black clothes.'[46]

Who were these 'boys'? Dressed in black (or even dark blue or brown, affording Muziwento's account some leeway), they were not the 24th's drummers, certainly. It is not clear whether Muziwento thought them boys or youths; the clothing suggests they may have been members of the Natal Volunteer corps. It is not inconceivable, even, that these were the 'boys' seen by Sam Jones – himself a Volunteer – in the faint lurid light of smouldering tents on the night of the 22nd, and the tree his butchers' scaffold. Then again, perhaps Sam Jones, his mind overwhelmed by the dreadful reality of mass slaughter, merely mistook the butchers' meat-carcasses for slender human bodies.

There were lots of young men on the Zulu side, too, many more of them, and possibly hundreds of boys. The uVe *ibutho*, which formed the tip of the left 'horn', and which suffered heavily pursuing Durnford on the way to his donga, was composed entirely of young men of about 19 or 20 years, while the *izindibi*, the boys who carried mats for their elders on the march, were as young as 9 or 10. It was the practice to leave the *izindibi* behind at the last bivouac before making an assault, but the boys themselves were usually caught up in the excitement and were desperate to see something of the action. There are many family traditions of boys accompanying the attack at iSandlwana; some even apparently crossed the Mzinyathi with their fathers in the reserve *amabutho*, and watched the fighting at Rorke's Drift from the hillsides nearby. At kwaGingindlovu one mat-carrier actually reached the British entrenchments and was taken prisoner; at the battle of oNdini on 21 July 1883 one white mercenary who took part noted that two prominent Zulus were 'run down' and killed by his mat-carriers.

How many of these boys took part in the battle of iSandlwana, and how many were killed there, will never be known.

Brevet Ranks

Throughout most of the nineteenth century in the British Regular Army a brevet rank was awarded to enable selected serving officers to hold a temporary commission at one rank above their own substantive rank. They did not usually receive the pay of the brevet rank but were sometimes eligible to be appointed to a post in the higher rank, and so perhaps receive most or all of the specific allowances associated with the new rank and appointment. A brevet rank generally conferred seniority within the Army above the lower substantive rank. For example, a brevet colonel would be deemed to have seniority below any substantive colonels, but above other lieutenant-colonels. However, for the purposes of substantive promotions, where seniority in a substantive rank was a considerable influence, an officer with a brevet rank would normally remain in competition for promotion with officers of his own substantive rank. Brevets were usually awarded as a reward for distinguished service in the field, or to bring an officer up to the rank necessary for a specific field command. Though the award of brevet rank could indicate the likelihood of a substantive promotion it provided no guarantee of it. During his time on the Cape Frontier Chelmsford (then Thesiger) would appear to have appointed most already in-country imperial officers of suitable rank and experience into command appointments in the 'full' colonel rank. By doing so, he could prepare more decisively for war with officers already known to him and was not then vulnerable to having other unfamiliar commanders imposed on him by Horse Guards. In an era before the British Army had any permanently constituted brigades (a situation largely unchanged until 1906 except in India) improvised field force units were usually commanded by colonels, sometimes temporarily designated as 'brigadiers' or 'brigadier-generals', unless or until a general officer of more senior rank was appointed in their stead.

Buried Treasure

In his classic history of the war, author Donald R. Morris has an intriguing story of the panic which ensued close to the border as news spread of the Zulu victory at iSandlwana. Speaking of a convoy on the road between Greytown and Helpmekaar, he says,

> The 2nd/4th entrenched a camp near Sand Spruit, and detachments along the road hurried on. An officer escorting a supply train buried a large quantity of ammunition on a bare hillside before abandoning his wagons and hastening to the next laager; it was several weeks before he was able to return to the site and by then rains had washed away all trace of the digging. The cache was never located.[47]

It is a story calculated to intrigue those with a taste for historical mysteries – a treasure-trove of historical artefacts, abandoned in the very real confusion of war, perhaps still there to this very day.

Sadly, like most lost treasure stories – Captain Kidd's treasure, the Kruger millions – a close reading of the sources suggests it never really happened. It is true that a convoy of 22 men of the 2/4th under Colonel Bray were on the march to Helpmekaar on the 22nd escorting 28 wagons, of which 15 contained ammunition. They were approaching the Msinga magistracy when survivors streaming down the road from the direction of Helpmekaar broke the news of the battle. Bray made for the nearest defensive position – the magistracy itself – which was hastily fortified. The buildings were loopholed, rooms knocked through, and Bray's wagons drawn into laager. No attack developed, however, and after a few days Bray marched his men across the road and took up a better defensive position on a knoll beside the road. Later he marched on to Helpmekaar and the NNC built Fort Bengough on the same knoll.

Bray's actions are well documented, both in his own reports and in the accounts of border officials and magistrates, and no mention is made by any of them of burying the ammunition supply, nor is it recorded in the 4th's regimental digests. Nor does it seem necessary when Bray had apparently opted for the more secure alternative of including the wagons within a defensive perimeter. The burial of any large supply of ammunition would have represented an expense to the government large enough to bring on an attack of the vapours for any battalion quartermaster, and it is unlikely that any search for quantities buried and lost would have been easily given up – yet no official reports of recovery expeditions survive.

How then did the story come about? Like most missing treasure myths it is impossible to say, but it almost certainly owed its origins to a local memory of the confusion of those first terrible hours after iSandlwana.

Rather more reliable – perhaps – is a story published in the Natal press on the 50th anniversary of the war, that the pay-chests of the 1/24th were lost in the camp at iSandlwana. These were captured by the Zulus, so the story goes, and hidden in caves on the Hlazakazi mountain. For many years afterwards the story captured the attention of wandering adventurers, and in particular one unnamed (as they so often are, in such tales) prospector. After searching in a haphazard fashion for many years it was noted that this old prospector was suddenly able to pay his bills in the remote trading stores and hostelries of Zululand with rather more readiness than had been his habit. Where he got the money he never said; others thought he had simply stolen it.

That there was money in the camp is highly likely; private individuals and contractors no doubt had their ready cash with them, and there were perhaps some regimental funds with the colonial Volunteer units. As to the 1/24th, certainly Paymaster Francis White was killed in the battle, and he may well have had some of the battalion's petty cash with him. In 1913 officers of the then South Wales Borderers, on a visit to the battlefield, were asked whether they had lost a pay-chest there – and their opinion was that it was unlikely. Many of the Zulus, indeed – coming from an economy that was not based upon cash as the main means of exchange – might not have understood the significance of large amounts of coin, although there were no doubt some among them who did. Whether a large chest or chests might have been dragged any great distance is another matter; it is far more likely that whatever money was in the camp on the fatal day was simply distributed among those Zulus who happened to discover it. Much of it no doubt made its way back into the colonial economy through the trading stores which gradually spread across Zululand in the years after the war.

One story that does have a grounding in fact is that King Cetshwayo ordered his personal belongings to be hidden by the girls of his *isigodlo* in the weeks before the battle of Ulundi. One of his attendants, Nomguqo Dlamini, confirms that items were lowered by ropes into caves on the Hlopekhulu mountain, overlooking the White Mfolozi. The British – with stories of other looted palaces in mind (gold taken from the King of Asante's palace in West Africa in 1873, and riches appropriated in China in the 1860s) – fondly hoped to find great things at oNdini when they entered it after the Zulu defeat on 4 July. They were disappointed to find little beyond artefacts of Zulu manufacture – shields, head-rests, milk-pails, sleeping-mats – in large quantity (now ironically considered treasures) and a framed picture of Queen Victoria, presented to Cetshwayo years before. Once it became known that the king had hidden his possessions, however, some optimism returned and several officers made inquiries as to their whereabouts, but, as Charley Harford relates, the British were too late:

> Jim [his servant] came to me to say that he knew the spot where Cetewayo's crown and other paraphernalia presented to him on the occasion of his Coronation by 'Somtseu' were buried, and asked if he might go and make a search … However, it turned out that they had been removed, and squatting down, snapping his fingers to emphasise matters, he declared that it had only been done that very day, as the earth in the hole was quite fresh. I should much like to have gone with him afterwards, to have a look at the spot, but I never got the chance.[48]

Nomguqo Dlamini confirms the essence of the story; she understood that, after Cetshwayo was captured, the men charged with hiding his possessions simply went back and stole them.

Throughout the war the British recovered a great many items taken from them at iSandlwana and hidden in caves near the homes of men who took part. No doubt they missed a good deal too, although it is unlikely there were ever great riches of any sort hidden away. Stories of a search for enemy treasures are a feature of most wars, but in this case they are confused by the very different value-systems of the opposing sides. Most of what the Zulus took at iSandlwana and treasured was conditioned by its practical or novelty value; to them the riches were to be counted in efficient British weapons and items of exotic luxury manufacture, like great-coats, camp-beds, wooden boxes and trinkets. These to the British remained mundane, even when they recovered them and – in an economy which counted its wealth in cattle – the hopeful stories which circulated among the British of lost gold or diamond caches in Zululand proved to be as illusory as anything imagined by the novelist Rider Haggard.

Burying the Dead

A few weeks after the battles of iSandlwana and Rorke's Drift, Henry Harford, a young lieutenant in the 99th Regiment, temporarily attached as Staff Officer to the 3rd Natal Native Contingent, decided to ride out from the fort at Rorke's Drift to look for traces of the recent fighting and

> came across the body of a very fine speci-men of a Zulu in the skeleton stage, which I took Surgeon Reynolds out to have a look at. He too was impressed with the stature and splendid proportions, and brought away one or two bones of scientific interest, and the soles of the feet which had become detached and were just like solid pieces of horn. I also took one of the collar bones and lesser bones of one of the arms, which I intend one day to give to the Durban Museum.[49]

It is a telling incident, both because it illustrates the impact the mass killings of the major battles had on the landscape, and because it reveals much about the attitudes of Europeans at the time to human remains. In the aftermath of the fighting the battlefields were littered with dead, not merely in the areas where the concentrated killing had taken place, but for miles around where the wounded had crawled away to die. In accordance with their beliefs, the British, where they could, usually made some effort to bury the fallen – their own, of course, but also those of the Zulus – but this was usually only possible where they had remained in possession of the field after the fighting. For the Zulus the propitiation of a dead man's spirit was more important than the disposal of his body, and often only a token burial was attempted. When they were able to do so, the Zulus dragged the bodies of their own fallen into the grain-pits of deserted homesteads, or tipped them into dongas; often it was considered sufficient to place a man's shield over his corpse.

In almost all of the battles of 1879, the dis-posal of the dead after the fighting was only partial, and in some cases human remains littered the sites for decades to come, arousing the curiosity of passers-by, like Harford, and even in one case outright avarice. The immediate response to the dead was largely framed by the strategic conditions which pertained in the immediate aftermath of an engagement. After the battle of Nyezane on 22 January – the first of the war – it was the British who were left in possession of the field. While 15 British troops, black and white, had been killed, the British estimated that some 400 Zulus had died, and, given the nature of the terrain, it is likely that many more corpses lay uncounted in the long grass and bush. The British buried their dead in a mass grave close to a wagon-track, but the British commander, Colonel Pearson, considered it a strategic necessity that the column resume its advance as soon as possible, and no time was therefore spent collecting the Zulu dead for burial. Because the British aban-doned the site immediately, advancing to occupy the mission station at Eshowe, it is probable that Zulu non-combatants living locally made some attempt to seek out the bodies of friends and family and to cover them over. The vast majority of the dead were, however, left where they fell, and indeed British convoys moving along the road between the Thukela and Eshowe commented on the heavy smell of decay which hung around the site for weeks afterwards. Indeed, these same convoys also noted that many wounded Zulus still lay out on the site over the same period, and could be heard calling out for help as the soldiers passed by; most, of course, must in the end have succumbed to their injuries. Nevertheless, because the dead were scattered over a wide area at Nyezane, and because there were only a few of them relative to later battles, their remains appear to have been absorbed by the environment – broken up by scavengers and birds of prey, or in the streams and gullies which drain into the Nyezane river.

The same cannot be said for the other great battles of 22 January – iSandlwana and Rorke's Drift. ISandlwana was a hugely destructive battle; some 1,300 British and allied troops were killed, while Zulu losses numbered at least 1,000 dead, probably more. Huge numbers of animals were also killed – the total number of transport oxen attached to nos 2 and 3 columns ran to nearly 2,000; while it is impossible to know exactly how many of these were in the camp at the time of the battle, the majority were undoubtedly killed. So too were 200–300 mules and a large number of horses. The dead lay spread thinly on the approaches to the camp – where the Zulus had fallen to artillery and long-range rifle-fire – then grew thicker in a constricting circle around the British positions and into the camp. Behind the tents, and on the nek below iSandlwana mountain, where protracted fighting had raged at hand to hand, the bodies of men and animals lay so thick that members of Chelmsford's command, returning to the battlefield that night, could hardly walk over the field without stepping on them. Many more were killed in the running fight to the banks of the Manzimnyama stream and along the Mzinyathi at Sothondose's ('Fugitives') Drift. When the victorious Zulu army retired that night to its bivouac in the Ngwebeni valley, it took many of its wounded with it. Some died

along the way; others reached the bivouac but could go no further. Many wounded individuals simply crawled away, often for miles, only to die in agony alone.

Nor was the day's toll over. In the fierce and protracted fighting at Rorke's Drift 17 British soldiers were killed while 450 Zulu dead were subsequently collected from around the British barricades and many more lay further off or on the line of retreat; it is estimated that as many as 600 Zulus died altogether.

The concentrations of dead on the two sites could not easily be disposed of by the survivors. At iSandlwana, where the Zulus were left in possession of the field, some attempt was made to dispose of their own dead. A large number of bodies were dragged into the dongas which run off the foot of the iNyoni heights, while others were piled into the grain-pits of abandoned homesteads nearby. The obligation to perform this grim duty fell to friends and relatives of the fallen but so many were the dead that large numbers were not recognised, and these were simply covered over by their war-shields. The British dead were left where they fell.

At Rorke's Drift, by contrast, the British were left in command of the field. The British dead were buried on the morning of 23 January in a plot between the post and Shiyane hill (a small graveyard stands on the spot today). The Zulu dead immediately surrounding the post were dragged away for disposal. The British tried to use African auxiliaries attached to Lord Chelmsford's command for the task but many were reluctant to do so because of a fear of *umnyama*, the dark supernatural forces which were thought to linger around fresh corpses. According to Lieutenant John Maxwell of the 3rd NNC,

Orders were out for the burying of all dead, the Contingent and the 24th to provide the fatigue parties. And it was arranged that the first mentioned should dig the holes, on account of their prejudice against touching the dead, and that the 24th should place them therein. And so the dead were buried at Rorke's Drift, occupying some two or three hours: we digging large holes in various places and the 24th with the assistance of reins, placing the bodies therein.[50]

The exact location of these graves has remained something of a mystery; a large depression in the soil in front of the site of the old hospital building, which apparently dates to the period of military occupation, was tentatively identified as a possible burial site until an archaeological investigation proved it to contain no remains. Many Zulu bodies lay only a short distance away from the post but were not discovered immediately. Colonial troops sleeping that first night in the cattle-kraal awoke to discover that at least one body lay under the straw on which they had been sleeping; many more were discovered on the slopes of Shiyane hill, or were only located in the long grass and bush when the stench of decomposition revealed their whereabouts. According to Maxwell,

at various times for a period of six weeks, bodies were found in the caves and among the stones on the mountain, and two months afterwards two brother officers and myself discovered in a cave near the summit three bodies, which were quite hard and sound. These had been wounded and managed to crawl thus far to die.[51]

It is equally possible that these were men of note whose bodies had been dragged away and given the most respectful burial that circumstances would permit.

The disposal of the dead at iSandlwana remained more problematic. Although Lord Chelmsford's force had been forced to bivouac on the battlefield on the night of 22 January, they had deliberately evacuated the site of the devastated camp at first light on the morning of the 23rd, and there had been no time to attempt to bury the fallen. In the weeks afterwards the possibility of a Zulu strike into Natal seemed very real, and Lord Chelmsford could not afford to risk his scant resources by undertaking an expedition across the border simply to bury the dead. Some of the outlying bodies were none the less buried by patrols from Rorke's Drift; the remains of

Lieutenants Melvill and Coghill were first discovered on the hillside above Sothondose's Drift on 4 February. They were covered over on that occasion but later properly reinterred at the foot of a large stone a few yards away from where they fell (where they still lie today).

It was not until 14 March that any attempt by the British was made to investigate the state of the iSandlwana battlefield proper. Major Wilsone Black of the 2/24th led a small patrol to the outskirts of the battlefield where he lingered just long enough to experience the dreadful smell of decay which still hung over the site and to observe that the dead were not yet fully decomposed. He then returned, under fire from Zulus living locally, to recommend that a proper burial expedition be delayed for at least another month.

In fact there was far too great a concentration of dead things at iSandlwana for the environment to absorb so quickly. The bodies rotted, of course, although the Zulu habit of disembowelling enemy dead had encouraged in some cases a primitive form of natural mummification, with flesh and skin drying out on the bones. Where uniforms or clothes were left on the British dead this also helped to keep the remains intact. Some remains were broken up by scavenging wildlife but the quantity of carcasses was too great for local population levels of scavengers. Probably the most destructive animals were nocturnal bush-pigs, some of which still inhabit the Manzimnyama valley. There may have been a few hyenas still living in the Mzinyathi valley by 1879, although they were already scarce close to areas of European settlement. Certainly there were a few Cape Vultures – although these too were rare in areas where there was little natural game to sustain them – and kites, crows and rodents undoubtedly did their part. Equally destructive were domestic dogs, either from nearby Zulu homesteads, or – with gruesome irony – the former pets belonging to the column. Abandoned and starving, these ran wild in packs in the countryside around the battlefield – and fed on whatever they could find.

Some idea of the condition of the battlefield is suggested in an account by the Zulu boy Muzi-wento who lived nearby. Zulu men occasionally visited the site to search out remaining loot, but for the most part Zulu non-combatants avoided it for fear of the dead. Like boys the world over, Muziwento and his friends could not resist exploring it, however, despite the warnings of their parents, and his description of what they found there has an apocalyptic ring:

We went to see the dead people at Isandhlwana. We saw a single warrior dead, staring in our direction, with his war-shield in his hand. We ran away. We came back again. We saw countless things dead. Dead was the horse, dead too the mule, dead was the dog, dead was the monkey, dead were the wagons, dead were the tents, dead were the boxes, dead was everything, even to the very metals ... We saw boys who had died in a tree [lying] underneath it. They were dressed in black clothes. We saw white men dead (they had taken their boots off, all of them), and the people also who had served them, and fought with them, and some Zulus, but not many ...[52]

Although pressure mounted on Lord Chelmsford to give the British dead a proper burial, he did not feel that it was safe to do so until his troops along the border had been heavily reinforced. At the end of March – with the defeat of the Zulus at Khambula on 28 March and Gingindlovu on 2 April – the tide of war began to turn in his favour. By May he had begun to assemble a new column and a fresh invasion of Zululand was imminent. On the 15th Wilsone Black again led a patrol to the battlefield, reporting that it was now possible to walk through the long grass which covered the battlefield, and that many wagons still remained upon it. As a result, prompted at least partly by the need to recover serviceable transport wagons from the battlefield, Chelmsford finally authorised the first of a series of burial expeditions on 21 May.

The expedition was a large one to counter the possible threat of a Zulu attack. It consisted of the newly formed Cavalry Division – the 17th Lancers, 1st (King's) Dragoon Guards and Natal Volunteers – commanded by General Frederick Marshall. It started in two divisions from Rorke's Drift early in the morning, following the old line of advance by way of the Batshe valley, and burning Zulu homesteads along the way. A journalist, Archibald Forbes, left a powerful description of what they found on the battlefield:

dead men lay thick, mere bones, with toughened, discoloured skin like leather covering them, and clinging tight to them, the flesh all wasted away. Some were almost wholly dismembered, heaps of yellow clammy bones. I forbear to describe the faces, with their blackened features and beards bleached by rain and sun. Every man had been disembowelled. Some were scalped, and others were subject to yet ghastlier mutilations. The clothes had lasted better than the poor bodies they covered, and helped to keep the skeletons together ... I came across a gully with a gun-limber jammed on its edge, and the horses, their hides scored with assegai stabs, hanging in their harness down the steep face of the ravine. A little further on was the broken and battered ambulance wagon, and around lay the corpses of the soldiers, poor helpless wretches, dragged out of an intercepted vehicle, and done to death without a chance of life ...[53]

As the cavalry harnessed up the serviceable wagons, officers and volunteers wandered across the stricken field, trying to identify some of the dead lying strewn in the long grass. Durnford's body was recognised, and buried where he fell – although it was later exhumed and reinterred in Pietermaritzburg. Colonel Glyn of the 24th had asked that his regiment be allowed to bury its own dead, but since no members of it were present with the expedition most of those still wearing a redcoat were left unburied. The rest – those readily discovered in the camp area – were hastily buried in shallow scrapes in the ground, and covered over with stones. Another journalist, Melton Prior, sketched the process but his drawings were only published in a highly sanitised form, devoid of the grinning skulls which so dominate the originals.

As the war moved on it became possible to give attention to those dead remaining on the battle-field. With the start of Lord Chelmsford's new invasion in June, the Zulu largely abandoned the defence of the Mzinyathi border, and it became possible to mount regular patrols from Rorke's Drift to bury the remains of the 24th. On 20 June Black – now a lieutenant-colonel – led a party of 80 Dragoons, 140 2/24th, 360 Border Guards and 50 men of Teteleku's Horse from Rorke's Drift to iSandlwana. They were accompanied by Major Dartnell of the Natal Mounted Police and representatives of the Natal Volunteers. Large numbers of 24th dead – by now quite unrecognisable – were buried in shallow graves and stones piled over the bodies, while the Volunteers were more successful in identifying their own dead. Black returned again on the 23rd and the 26th. By the time they had finished, those bodies most recognisable as Europeans had largely been buried. The bodies of Africans – it was largely impossible to tell if they were Zulu or NNC – were left where they were, as were the skeletons of horses and oxen. It was at this time – rather than during the May expedition – that three photographs were taken by the Durban photographer James Lloyd.

The dead were, however, buried in the shallowest of graves and by September the reports of troops passing the site of bodies exposed by the rain persuaded Sir George Colley, then Chief of Staff in South Africa, to dispatch a party under Brevet Major C.J. Bromhead – Gonville's brother – to tidy the site. Bromhead and two companies of the 2/24th camped at iSandlwana on the night of 19 September and carefully searched the field. Those graves which were disintegrating were rebuilt and a number of outlying bodies, missed by the earlier details, were also interred. Bromhead instructed his men to build three large cairns on the spots where he judged the 24th's resistance to have been greatest.

Nevertheless, the haste with which the early burials had been completed meant that graves continued to wash open. In March 1880 Lieutenant M. O'Connell of the 60th Rifles was sent to iSandlwana accompanied by a detachment of the Natal Mounted Police. O'Connell found that on the slopes which drained into the dongas many graves had become disturbed. His methods in redress were nothing if not practical:

Each man was provided with a sack to carry any bones he might find, and every third or fourth man had a spade or pick to dig up the bones in those places where they had not been properly buried, and where the ground did not seem to be such as to make the recovering of old graves desirable. I extended my men in a line across the place where Lord Chelmsford's camp had been, and moved them slowly backwards and forwards. They put all the uncovered bones they could find into the sacks, and renewed the stones and earth over the graves that required it. As soon as three or four sacks of bones had been collected in this way, I caused them to be carried to [a specified spot] and there buried them in two large deep graves ...[54]

Of course, by this stage it must have been difficult to tell European bones from Zulu ones and even from some animal ones. When the archaeological team investigated some areas of the iSandlwana battlefield in 2000, they found a pit at the head of the 'Fugitives' Trail' containing large numbers of long bones, apparently from the RA gun-limber team. In among them was a human thigh bone.

In the meantime the war had, of course, moved on, adding a fresh crop of bones to the landscape. On 12 March a British convoy was overrun at the Ntombe river. On 28 March Wood's foray against Hlobane mountain was repulsed but the following day the same Zulu army which had triumphed at iSandlwana was decisively beaten by Colonel Wood's column. A few days later, at the other end of the country, Lord Chelmsford himself dispersed the Zulu forces investing Eshowe at kwaGingindlovu.

The disposal of the dead in each case reflected the patterns established in the January fighting. At Ntombe the Zulus, although victorious, abandoned the battlefield almost immediately in the face of a British foray from the nearby town of Luneburg. The British were therefore able to collect most of their dead, who were interred in a large grave on the site of the action. A few bodies were lost in the flooded Ntombe river. At Hlobane, where the Zulus were also victorious, the British dead – 15 officers, 79 white troops and at least 100 African auxiliaries – were left on the field. Some attempt was made early in the fight to recover or evacuate the bodies of officers killed in the early skirmishing, but this had to be abandoned as the fighting intensified. The British dead were therefore left scattered over a wide swathe of difficult country where they had fallen, from Ityenka Nek on the eastern slopes of Hlobane, across the top of the mountain, down the so-called Devil's Pass, and across a very scattered line of retreat to Khambula. Even after the victory at Khambula Wood made no attempt to trace and bury the dead until nagged to do so by the Irregulars. On 20 May he led a patrol around the southern and western slopes of Zungwini, where the remains of Lieutenant C.C. Williams (Wood's Irregulars) and Captain Charles Potter (Hamu's Followers) were found and buried. Not until August 1879, during pacification operations, were some of the remains of Weatherley's Border Horse discovered on Ityenka Nek at the eastern foot of Hlobane. According to Captain Montague of the 94th,

On the crest of the narrow neck we found numerous skeletons, many a good deal broken up, probably by the monkeys; on the lower plateau were a few; and at the base of the mountain they lay thickly enough, in a broad line, gradually getting thinner, till only detached bones were met, these extending for three miles from the actual mountain. All were perfect skeletons, the rags hanging here and there about them; some with the hair still attached to the scalp. Weatherley was recognised by his long fair moustache lying by his side, and the skeleton of a boy, his son, not many yards from him. We gave them what burial we could, and paid the last marks of respect to our soldiers' graves.[55]

Both horses and men had tumbled off the steep cliffs that line the northern edge of the nek, and local Zulus recall that bones could still be found at the bottom to within living memory. The body of the Boer leader Piet Uys was recovered from the Devil's Pass by his relatives, who recognised the remains of his clothing and removed him to his farm at Utrecht. Although a cairn was at some point later erected at the top of the pass – it has since been dismantled – it is unclear what became of the rest of the remains left there; many were probably never buried, and some perhaps still lie there, undetected, jammed in crevices between inaccessible rocks at the foot of the surrounding cliffs.

Certainly Evelyn Wood, who must bear most of the responsibility for the disaster, was troubled by the lack of attention accorded the dead officers. In particular, he was concerned that a personal friend of his, Lieutenant Robert Barton of the Grenadier Guards, attached to the Frontier Light Horse, who was killed in open country between Hlobane and Khambula during the rout, had not been properly buried. As a result he contrived to influence the Empress Eugenie, on her way to pay homage at the spot where her son, the Prince Imperial, had died, to divert her route via Hlobane in 1880. Wood then made inquiries regarding the death of Barton, and on the strength of this summoned an *induna* named Sitshitshili kaMnqandi, who had killed him, to search for the body:

I said, 'Do you think you can find the body?' 'Yes, certainly,' he said, 'but you must lend me a horse, for it is a day and a half.' I sent Trooper Brown VC with him next day, and, with the marvellous instinct of a savage, he rode to within 300 yards of the spot where fourteen months previously he had killed my friend, and then said, 'Now we can off-saddle for we are close to the spot,' and, casting round like a harrier, came in less than five minutes upon Barton's body, which had apparently never been disturbed by any beast or bird of prey. The clothes and boots were rotten and ant-eaten, and tumbled to pieces on being touched. Brown cut off some buttons from the breeches, and took a Squadron Pay book from the pocket filled with Barton's writing, and then buried the remains, placing over them a small wooden cross painted black, on which is cut 'Robert Barton, Killed in action 28th March 1879'.[56]

The site of this grave has since been lost.

After the action at Khambula the following day the British buried their dead on a slope below their camp. Nearly 800 Zulu bodies were collected from the area immediately around the British positions, a task which took three days; they were loaded in wagons and taken a hygienic distance from the camp where they were buried in two large mass graves. Many Zulus had been killed during the particularly ruthless pursuit, of course, and as usual wounded men crawled many miles, often only to succumb to their injuries. No attempt was made to dispose of these remains, and British observers noted the strong smell which blew from the direction of the retreat, and the numbers of birds of prey to be seen in the sky. A particularly graphic description of the effect of so much killing on the environment leaves little to the imagination:

They have nearly succeeded in burying the dead in the vicinity of the camp, but I hear there are so many bodies of the fallen Zulus lying about in the veldt at the distance of two-and-a-half miles from camp that it will take a long time to bury them all. Now and then we get a sniff of the stench wafted towards the camp whenever the breeze blows from that direction. We had a heavy shower of rain yesterday, which was very acceptable, as it washed the brains and pools of blood that were saturating the ground down the hill and ravine, making the smell a little sweeter.[57]

In 1882 Bertram Mitford noted that 'three or four dark spots of a different growth show the places of sepulture of the Zulu dead, who were buried in hundreds after the battle'.[58] The exact location of these graves is not, however, known today.

Much the same circumstances applied after the battle of Gingindlovu on 2 April. Here the British dead were buried in a small graveyard outside their entrenchment. Some hundreds of Zulu dead were collected together and buried in several mass graves; the site of these is unknown now, although they were probably dug some distance in front of each face of the British square. Because of the more extensive under-growth – long grass and bush – many bodies further away were not spotted, and the battlefield was noted for the large number of remains left unburied. Some bodies later turned up in the Nyezane river – presumably those of men killed during the pursuit – where they had a detri-mental effect on the quality of the water drawn for nearby British camps. Others still lay on the field when a Durban photographer passed by in June. Today the area is covered with sugar-cane, and farmers still plough up fragments of bone and teeth.

It was at oNdini, however, that the dead left their greatest mark on the landscape. On the morning of 4 July Lord Chelmsford had finally defeated the main Zulu army on the open grass-land in front of King Cetshwayo's principal residence. He had advanced from his camp on the White Mfolozi only that morning, and had lingered on the northern bank just long enough to win the battle and destroy the surrounding royal homesteads; by late afternoon he was back in the camp again. The British therefore had time to bury their own dead, but not those of the Zulus.

It is not known how many Zulus were killed during the battle but they numbered in the region of a thousand, and they lay in a great circle around the site of the British square. Once the British had withdrawn, non-combatants living locally emerged from hiding and tried to identify and cover over loved ones among the dead. Since the army had consisted of men living right across the country, however, the vast majority of remains went unrecognised and unburied. Their skeletons were a feature of the site for decades to come. A photograph of the field, probably taken in September 1879, shows the field, stripped bare by a grass-fire, littered with long bones and skulls; at that time Captain Arthur Hart, ordered to survey the site, noted that,

The frequency with which I have come suddenly upon human skeletons in the grass has been quite forbidding. When one is not alone, the light of one's companion's presence dispels all the gloom and horrors, just as the arrival of a lamp spoils a ghost story!

There is nothing so dead and harmless as a skeleton, yet when you contemplate them in solitude they appear to possess a life of their own, especially when there are so many together. Some look angry, some threatening, some foolish, some astonished, and those that are on their faces seem to be asleep.[59]

Bertram Mitford, on a moonlight stroll across the battlefield in 1882, found many of them still there:

I wander on; at every step, skulls, gleaming white amid the grass, grin to the moon with upturned faces and eyeless sockets. Yonder, shadowed forth in dark contrast on the moonlit plain, lie the ruins of Ulundi and Nodwengu, dim and mysterious, like mystic tracings from the wand of some grim wizard of the wilderness.[60]

In the years after the war the fate of the Zulu dead aroused little interest among the victorious British administrators or the settler community in Natal. The condition of the iSandlwana battlefield remained of considerable concern, however, not least because the annual summer rains constantly exposed the British dead in their shallow graves. In 1880 a traveller, R.W. Leyland, found the battlefield

the most unpleasant sight ... many unbleached human bones. They had been washed by heavy rains out of the shallow graves in which they had been interred ... We noticed some bodies partly exposed, portions of their skeletons visible. In one instance the leg bones, encased in leather

gaiters, protruded at the bottom of a grave, and close by were the soldier's boots, containing what remained of his feet.[61]

When an Anglican mission, St Vincent's, was first established at iSandlwana in 1880 by the Revd Charles Johnson the site had first to be cleared of the skeletons of a number of Zulu dead. Johnson, indeed, did what he could to ensure that 'the bodies of those slain in the battle ... had been reverently gathered as far as was possible and buried',[62] and when bones were washed out of the dongas at the foot of the iNyoni heights, near the mission, they were collected together and buried just outside the mission church.[63] Nevertheless, the persistent stories of damage to British graves eventually persuaded the Lieutenant-Governor of Natal to dispatch a work party under a civil servant, Alfred Boast, to tidy the battlefield properly. Boast stayed at iSandlwana from 12 February to 9 March 1883 and during that time all known graves were exhumed and the remains reinterred in graves 3 feet deep and 18 inches wide. Boast then had stones piled on top of each grave – the origins of the cairns which mark the site today. Boast's meticulous report lists a total of 298 graves, each containing the remains of between two and four individuals.

The Zulu remains on the other battlefield continued to attract the curiosity of chance passersby. Nor was Henry Harford alone in collecting them for his own purposes. Attitudes towards the collection of human remains were very different in the nineteenth century to those current in the West today. As the British Empire had expanded so there was a burgeoning curiosity about the natural world. The apparent differences between the species were the subject of considerable speculation and, at a time when it was commonplace to kill living creatures and preserve them for study in the name of science, or to mount the heads of animals as sporting trophies, few saw any inherent disrespect in collecting the human traces of other peoples. Their motives ranged from a genuine interest in science and medicine to simple morbid curiosity. Lord Grenfell, who had served on Chelmsford's staff as an ADC, and had been present at the battle of Ulundi, described how he had been tempted to take a human skull as a souvenir when passing the battlefield with Redvers Buller in 1881:

I told Buller that I had seen a Zulu Induna shot in the head by Owen's machine-guns, of which there were two at this corner. He was leading his men on and got as close as eighteen yards from the square, for I had measured it after the action. I again paced the eighteen yards and came to my old friend, a splendid skeleton, his bones perfectly white, his flesh eaten off by the white ants. I felt I could not part with him, so I put his skull into my forage bag, and brought it home with me.[64]

Grenfell was by no means alone; at one stage the Natural History Museum in London had over fifty skulls presented to it by travellers returning from the Zulu battlefields, although the entire collection was apparently destroyed during the bombing of London in the Second World War. The fate of any other such remains in British collections is obscure as most institutions are acutely sensitive to the issue of bones collected in very different times, and are reluctant to admit to any that may still exist.

Perhaps the most disturbing aspect of the treatment of the Zulu dead concerns a suggestion that, when British troops reoccupied oNdini in August 1879, they had deliberately desecrated the grave of the Zulu king Mpande kaSenzangakhona, which lay within sight of the position of Lord Chelmsford's square. According to a Natal Native Pioneer who was present, a detachment set out one day from Wolseley's camp to find the thicket which marked the site of the grave:

The soldiers first pulled up the stakes and made fires with them to cook their food. Then came two soldiers with spades, and another with a pick, together with Colonel – and Mr. –. They dug up the King's grave, and came first upon some stones and wicker-work, and then they took out his bones wrapped in his blankets. I stood near

enough (about ten or fifteen yards off, as indicated) to see that there had been four blankets of different colours wrapped around the body, one inside the other, and outside there had been a kaross made of jackal-skins; but this last was quite rotten, and three of the blankets were also much decayed, although one seemed to be sound and held together. The white men were surprised and said, 'How is it that the blankets have lasted so long (seven years)?' The black people asked our captain, 'What are you doing, digging up a man's bones?' Said he, 'We are doing it in order to catch the King; for, now that we have dug up his father, we shall soon catch him.' So they took out all his bones, a soldier belonging to the hospital handling them, and I saw the bones of the King, and the skull with the teeth, and the leg bones – they took them all, and put them into a box which had held food (biscuits), and shut it up, and put it in a mule-wagon to carry it away. We asked our captain, 'What would be done with them?' Said he, 'They will be carried across the sea to be looked at.' Then they put back the stones upon the grave, and covered it over, and we went away.[65]

The fate of these remains has never been resolved; if the bones of one of the great Zulu kings still survive in a British collection somewhere, no one has so far been willing to admit to it. Ironically, however, it is possible they were not the bones of King Mpande at all, for oral tradition suggests that at least one of his councillors was buried with him during his funeral.

There is, at least, no evidence to suggest that skulls were ever collected as trophies from fresh Zulu dead in the way that often happened during the earlier Cape Frontier Wars. Such practices usually reflect a wearing down of the perception of the enemy as human, a process which usually occurs after protracted and bitter fighting. On the Cape Frontier there are descriptions of surgeons 'boiling down' freshly severed heads to obtain medical specimens, and of volunteers collecting skulls as trophies. No evidence of any similar mutilation of Zulu dead in 1879 has emerged; the grim fact remains that there were plenty of naturally decomposed bones available on the battlefields for years to come.

There were so many, indeed, that one enterprising individual sought to turn them into a business opportunity. The Golgotha noted by Mitford at oNdini in 1882 was added to by a subsequent slaughter on the same spot, which took place shortly after his visit. In February 1883 King Cetshwayo was restored to Zululand, and built a new oNdini homestead a short distance from the ruins of the one destroyed on 4 July 1879 by Lord Chelmsford. Cetshwayo's return proved to be an unhappy one, however, for it provoked a civil war with an anti-royalist faction which had gained support during his absence. On 21 July 1883 Cetshwayo's new oNdini was attacked by forces led by his erstwhile general, Zibhebhu kaMaphitha. Cetshwayo himself barely managed to escape, his supporters were scattered, and hundreds of them – including many prominent leaders from 1879, among them Ntshingwayo kaMahole and Sihayo kaXongo – were killed. Many of them fell as they tried to flee across the site of the old 1879 battlefield.

As a result, during the mid-1880s the site was noted for the concentration of dead to be found there, and the experiences of H.P. Braadvedt, the son of a missionary living at Mahlabathini, was by no means unusual:

One day we went for a picnic to the junction of the Ntukwini and Mbilane streams close to the site of the old Ulundi royal kraal. We fished and had excellent sport, as the river was teeming with large scalies and bream. Strolling along the river bank, I was considerably startled by the sight of two almost complete skeletons behind a bush. Probably these men fell in the Ulundi battle, as at one time numerous skeletons lay scattered over the Ulundi plains.[66]

Eventually, a storekeeper living at Ulundi recognised that such a quantity of bones was not without value. He

offered to barter salt and sugar for old bones. As a rule Zulus show the greatest respect for the dead, but evidently the temptation proved too strong, because very soon long files of women and girls daily wended their way to the trader with baskets full.

Eventually a considerable heap of the remains of the gallant Zulu warriors was collected and dispatched to what in those days was called a bone manure factory in Durban.

But on the arrival of the gruesome load there was an immediate outcry against such desecration, so the bones were buried instead.[67]

Visiting the site in 1914, the novelist Rider Haggard heard much the same story. Guided around the battlefield by a local man, Simpofu, who had been present during the battle with the iNgobamakhosi, Haggard

asked Simpofu what had become of the remains of his people as we saw no skeletons lying about the veldt. He replied, 'The white men came and took them away in wagons.' Mr Gibson says also that he remembers seeing piles of bones lying at a store in this neighbourhood, so I suppose that the end of the mortal part of those Zulus was to be ground into bone dust for manure.[68]

Small wonder that even Haggard – a supporter of the British invasion when he had worked as a clerk on Theophilus Shepstone's staff in 1877 – was moved by 1914 to ponder 'what will become of the poor Zulus? Truly their case is sad and they have been ill-treated.'[69]

Zulu people still visit the many battlefields of Zululand to carry out the ceremonies necessary to honour the spirits of their fallen ancestors.

Cattle

In a speech given at a banquet thrown by the Fishmongers' Company at the beginning of October 1879 to honour him upon his return from Zululand, Evelyn Wood spoke frankly of the manner in which he waged war. 'I am aware', he said, 'it has been said that we lifted many cattle, committed much arson. I plead guilty. As regards the cattle, they are in Africa the sinews of war.'[70]

It was at least a fair admission, for Wood and his subordinate Redvers Buller had emerged as the most enthusiastic cattle raiders of a war which had seen thousands of head carried away from Zululand by the invaders. Wood recognised that cattle were essential to the Zulu way of life, and that by targeting cattle he was striking a blow not only at the logistical infrastructure which supported Zulu armies on campaign, but at the ability of Zulu society itself to resist the invasion.

For the Zulu cattle represented far more than meat, milk and hides. Indeed, although milk curds were a staple food, cattle were far too important to slaughter merely to provide meat, except on the most important social and religious occasions. In a society which lacked a cash economy, cattle were the only means of assessing wealth and status, and they performed crucial roles in social interaction. An exchange of cattle from the bride's family to the groom's, known as *ilobolo*, was central to the marriage contract, while cattle were confiscated as punishment for criminal actions or distributed as rewards. The slaughter of a beast, moreover, provided an essential bridge between the living and the spirit world during the performance of most religious rites. In practical terms cattle provided hides for cloaks and shields or to work into reims (ropes), and horns to be crafted into utensils.

The Zulu – like most other African societies – were also deeply in love with their cattle, seeing in them a point of reference to define the world around them. This stream might be likened to a tail, those hills to a herd of calves, that one to a piece of cow's intestines, while the sunrise – when cattle are first visible against the lightening sky – was labelled 'the horns of the morning'. Furthermore, the Zulu reserved some of their best poetic expressions for their cattle, and the vocabulary describing the colours and combinations of markings on a cow's hide was rich and intense. The names for these patterns evoked imagery of speckled eggs, of patterns of shadows cast by the branches of a tree, of the markings on a type of snake, or even of 'a wife crossing the river' (a dark beast with pale legs – an analogy reflecting a married woman's pale untanned legs as she hitches up her leather skirt to wade through a stream). A Zulu herdsman prided himself on his ability to recall the characteristics of an individual beast in a herd which might number hundreds.

Cattle were owned by *abamnumzana*, homestead-heads, individually, or by the state, as represented by the king. Cattle taken in war or as fines imposed by the king belonged to the nation, and were kept either at royal homesteads about the country, or were distributed among ordinary Zulus as a mark of favour. Although the recipients were expected to care for the animals, return them when required and report on natural increases or wastage, they were allowed in return to enjoy the milk the cows produced. At the coronation of King Cetshwayo in 1873 John Dunn estimated that over 100,000 head of royally owned cattle were paraded before the king to celebrate his accession.

Yet even before the invasion Zululand was suffering a significant loss of cattle resources. European-introduced diseases – particularly bovine pleuro-pneumonia ('lung-sickness') – had spread throughout the kingdom, ironically stimulated by the great review of 1873, while traders from Natal took thousands of head each year in profits. It is certainly true that cattle were regarded as a legitimate military objective in African warfare in the region; the nation's wealth owed much to Shaka's successful military conquests fifty years before. Cattle were also one of the few means of supplying a Zulu army on the march; the British had a hazy understanding, too, of the principles of royal ownership, and therefore considered 'royal herds' fair game as a means of applying pressure to the state administration. As the war progressed, the British largely abandoned this distinction, seizing whatever cattle they could and destroying ordinary homes and crops as a means of undermining the Zulu will to resist.

There were also other reasons why the British regarded cattle as a target. It was a common practice in Victorian warfare for men to receive a share of any 'prizes' captured during the fighting, the value of which was determined by appointed prize agents. In his *Standing Orders* of November 1878 Chelmsford specifically noted that

> On any cattle or other prize being taken, the officer commanding the corps or party making the same will at once report the circumstances and number or nature of the prize to the officer in charge of the operations, who will thereupon determine what troops will share, and will appoint prize agents to arrange for the disposal of the cattle, &c, and to distribute the proceeds according to the following scale, viz -
>
> Trooper or private – 1 share
> NCO – 2 shares
> Captain or subaltern – 3 shares
> Field Officer – 4 shares
> Officer in command of the operations
> – 6 shares
> Officers of the staff – shares according to their rank

Of course men serving in mounted corps stood a far greater chance of being involved in the sort of operations where cattle might be captured, and this perhaps explains why Wood and Buller were openly spoken of as 'great cattle thieves', and why Buller's Irregulars, in particular, directed many of their operations against Zulu cattle.

There is, indeed, a certain amount of evidence to suggest that Wood chose to assault Hlobane mountain on 28 March, in pursuit of Lord Chelmsford's request that he make a diversion to distract from the advance to relieve Eshowe, at least partly because it was well known as being the place where the abaQulusi sheltered their cattle when under threat. Some estimates put the number of cattle on the mountain on the day of the battle as high as 2,000 head; certainly most of Piet Uys's followers seem to have been under the impression that they were embarking on a cattle raid. Once the assault had begun, and the British had reached the summit, their first act was to round up the cattle they found there. These were then sent off the mountain under the escort of the auxiliaries of Wood's Irregulars.

Once the battle began to turn against the British, however, the Zulus made particular efforts to recapture these cattle, and Wood's Irregulars suffered many casualties as they tried to drive them away towards the British camp at Khambula. Most of the cattle were indeed retaken.

In the last stages of the war King Cetshwayo attempted to ward off the catastrophe of defeat by opening negotiations with the British. It was too late, of course; by that time Lord Chelmsford, heavily reinforced, knew that he would win the war, and needed only a decisive victory to restore the damage wrought to his reputation by iSandlwana. Chelmsford was prepared to offer terms to Cetshwayo, but only such terms as would ensure his abject humiliation. With the prospect of disaster imminent, Cetshwayo sent a herd of 100 of his personal herd of white oxen – a type known as *inyonikayipumule*, 'the bird that never rests' (an allusion to the busyness of cattle egrets resulting from the wealth of the Zulu kings) – down to the White Mfolozi drift with the intention of offering it as a token of goodwill to the British. But the herd was turned back by men of the uKhandempemvu *ibutho* guarding the drifts who were unwilling to see the king prostrate himself while they were still willing to fight.

Two days later Cetshwayo's kingdom was effectively destroyed at the battle of Ulundi.

Caves

Although the psychology of the Zulu army was essentially aggressive – conflicts were resolved by seeking out the enemy and attacking him – there was none the less an acceptance that non-combatants, possessions and cattle might have to be secured by defensive means from an enemy attack. This was accomplished through the use of *izinqaba*, natural strongholds which could be fortified to make secure places of shelter. These were carefully selected for their geographical features which made them difficult to attack; Hlobane mountain, for example, with its flat summit largely surrounded by cliffs, was an ideal stronghold. The abaQulusi had further fortified the mountain by blocking with stone walls the cattle paths which wound precariously on to the top.

One highly desirable feature affecting the choice of a stronghold was the presence of caves. Much of the geology of Zululand consists of sandstone or volcanic rock like dolerite, neither of which lend themselves to particularly large underground cave complexes. Nevertheless, a combination of erosion and natural fissures in the strata has left its mark on the landscape, creating overhangs, gaps between fallen boulders, and here and there passages which extend back into the sides of mountains. The presence of these caves was usually well known to a local community, but often hidden from outsiders; in times of stress women, children and cattle might be driven up into them, the entrances barricaded with stones and guarded by fighting men. Often items of value were simply hidden away in caves in the hope that they might escape detection by any passing enemy.

For all the popular attention given to the large-scale battles of the campaign, Zulu defensive operations around caves featured heavily in the fighting. On 12 January Lord Chelmsford attacked the followers of *inkosi* Sihayo kaXongo in the Batshe valley. Sihayo himself, his principal sons and many of his followers were absent, having gone to oNdini to attend the general muster of the king's *amabutho*, but a number of men had been left to guard crops and cattle under Sihayo's younger son, Mkhumbikazulu. The action which followed was typical of Zulu defensive tactics. Women, children and cattle were hidden among the caves formed between fallen boulders at the foot of a line of cliffs on the kwaSokhege ridge. Mkhumbikazulu's men then hid among the rocks and taunted the invaders, daring them to come up. A fierce scrimmage then took place among the boulders, as Lieutenant Henry Harford, who was present with the 3rd NNC, described:

Confronting me across the bend was a large, open-mouthed cave, apparently capable of holding a good number of men, and hanging below it were several dead Zulus, caught in the monkey-rope creepers and bits of bush. They had evidently been shot and had either fallen out, or been thrown out, by their comrades when killed ... It was an uncommonly difficult place to get at, as it meant climbing over nothing but huge rocks and in many places having to work one's way like a crab, besides which the loss of a foothold might have landed one in the valley below.... Clambering at once over a big piece of rock, I got rather a rude shock on finding a Zulu sitting in a squatting position behind another rock, almost at my elbow. His head showed above the rock, and his wide-open eyes glared at me; but I soon discovered he was dead. Scarcely had I left this apparition behind than a live Zulu ... suddenly jumped up from his hiding place and, putting the muzzle of his rifle within a couple of feet of my face, pulled the trigger. But the cap snapped, whereupon he dropped his rifle and made off over the rocks for the cave, as hard as he could go ... I went after him, emptying my revolver at him as we scrambled up. Out of my six shots only one hit him, but not mortally ... Speaking to him in Kaffir, I called upon him to surrender, explaining that I had no intention to harm him in any way ... He then squatted down in submission.[71]

This description has much in common with the skirmishing which took place at the foot of the cliffs on the southern side of Hlobane mountain early on in the assault of 28 March. Here both men of the Border Horse and Evelyn Wood's personal staff had come under close-range fire from Zulus concealed in the gaps between the huge fallen boulders. It is known that Prince Mbilini waMswati had a homestead nearby, and this spot may have been chosen as his personal refuge. Wood himself described the Zulu positions:

Umbellini, who shot Campbell, was in a hole at the end of this passage, which was about six feet wide, seventy feet long, and the walls were about eleven feet high. The footway, if such it can be termed, was composed of masses of rock with intervening spaces. The passage was open at the top to the sky, the den having been formed by a great fall of rock from the top of Hlobane, which stands about 400 feet above ...[72]

Captain Ronald Campbell, Wood's ADC, led Wood's personal escort to attack this spot but as he entered it he was hit by a bullet which took off the top of his head. Wood's orderly, Lieutenant Henry Lysons, and Private Edmund Fowler of the Mounted Infantry climbed over Campbell's body and fired into the cave, driving the Zulus further down the passage, from which they emerged to clamber up the mountain.

Oral tradition today among the abaQulusi suggests that women and children had been concealed in other caves on the mountain before the British attack.

Prince Mbilini, indeed, had a number of secure places in northern Zululand from which he launched his effective guerrilla war against the British in the northern sector. As well as a home on the flanks of Hlobane he had another high on the Tafelberg mountain, overlooking the Ntombe river. This too had caves in the cliffs above, which he used as a stronghold. Further upstream in the Ntombe valley the Khubeka people of Mbilini's close ally Manyanyoba also had a number of caves in which to protect themselves. After Mbilini and Manyanyoba's successful attack on the stranded 80th convoy at the Ntombe on 12 March, the attackers retired to these caves and were largely successful in defying British punitive assaults.

Indeed, the Ntombe caves saw the last shots of the war. Although Mbilini himself was killed in a skirmish on 5 April, both his followers and Manyanyoba's had refused to surrender to the British despite the dispersal of the royal *amabutho* at Ulundi on 4 July. On 5 September British troops under the command of Colonel Baker Russell began several days of concerted attempts to drive the Zulus out of the Ntombe strongholds. On 8 September two NCOs of the 4th Regiment were killed in skirmishing outside Mbilini's caves and in retaliation the British decided to seal up the mouths of the caves with gun-cotton, despite the fact that there were some

thirty people still sheltering inside. According to one report:

> The Engineers, under Captain Courtney, were employed blasting the rocks; but I believe their efforts were fruitless, at least as far as the outcasts were concerned. For, despite the incessant shocks from the concussion of the slabs of dynamite, which were employed on the occasion, we were totally unsuccessful in driving them from their location.[73]

The Engineers eventually succeeded in sealing the caves; none of the Zulus emerged alive. And upon this rather inglorious note the slaughter of the Anglo-Zulu War ended.

Throughout the war the Zulus concealed items of importance in caves to prevent the British from finding them. Some of these caves were later discovered, and were found to contain weapons and items looted from the British camp at oNdini. Nomguqo Dlamini, a girl in King Cetshwayo's royal household, recalled that she and others were deputed to hide the king's personal possessions as the British advance drew near:

> We carried all the king's goods and chattels to Hlophekhulu and had to ascend the mountain, which is the home of hyenas and contains deep caves, to just below the white kranzes. With the aid of a rope the king's belongings were lowered into a deep cave. We returned immediately and on the following day we carried our own possessions into hiding. On that day we consisted of a particularly large group; we were almost an army of our own. On our return we reported to the king that all was safely hidden. In reality ... when the king was captured and taken away, his possessions were retrieved by the men who had hidden them, and who enriched themselves thereby ...[74]

Later in the war, when Sir Garnet Wolseley had established a camp near the ruins of oNdini, patrols were sent out to the royal homestead of oLandandlovu, between the Black and White

Mfolozi rivers, to investigate reports that a store of powder had been discovered nearby:

> they came upon a deep cave, extending under huge ledges and overhanging rocks, below one of the rugged mountain spurs of this wild country. This cave was found to contain 500 wooden 5lb kegs, supposed to be of Portuguese importation from Delagoa Bay – in other words upwards of a ton of gunpowder. Sir Garnet decided that it should be destroyed at once; but to avoid the tremendous noise which an explosion in the cave would produce, and perhaps create alarm in the neighbourhood, the powder was removed to the summit of the hill and there destroyed.[75]

The end of the war and the British withdrawal brought no return of peace and security to the Zulu people, and indeed with the breakdown of the Wolseley settlement and the outbreak of civil war between pro- and anti-royalist factions, many Zulu women and children were again forced to resort to their natural strongholds. Some idea of just how impressive these could be comes from a description by Nomguqo Dlamini of an impressive edifice, undiscovered by the British, in northern Zululand:

> The men entered the cave first, to see that everything was in order and safe; then they called out to us, 'Come inside! All is well and it is safe!' I was one of the last to enter. I was afraid that some of the huge boulders might come tumbling down on us. By the friction of two sticks ... fire was made and all parts of the cave were lit up, enabling us to select nice dwelling places within that large cave. Penetrating the cave ... we found inside a large pool of water ... The smoke from the fires was dissipated through fissures in the rocks; they were such that no sunlight ever penetrated ... Our enemies were afraid to enter ... We kept very quiet and stayed deep inside the cave until they moved off ... Our men, who were concealed near the mouth of the cave, would have immediately stabbed any entrant to death ... The cave was very large indeed. The cattle entered it from the west, and we from the east. The cattle suffered no hardship: there was sufficient grazing and water.[76]

Even today the exact location of many of these places of refuge remains unknown to outsiders.

Cinema

The Anglo-Zulu War has long attracted the attention of film-makers around the world. Although South Africa boasted an early film industry – some of the world's first movie footage was shot during the Anglo-Boer War, and a number of short films were made about African (including Zulu) life at the beginning of the twentieth century – the first feature film inspired by the war was actually shot in the USA as early as 1914. The Edison film company produced a two-reel extravaganza directed by Mr Ridley and apparently called *Rorke's Drift*. It was filmed in Jacksonville, Florida, and apparently included 'thrilling battle scenes, hand-to-hand encounters, hairbreath escapes, and [worked] up to a magnificent climax when the reinforcements arrive after the savages have succeeded in setting fire to the soldiers' flimsy barricades'.[77] Nothing appears to have survived from this historic film by which to judge its quality, but since it had no discernible connections with either Africa or the British Army it is perhaps safe to assume that it was exciting rather than accurate.

Equally intriguing are two films shot by African Film Productions in South Africa. The first, *De Voortrekker*, shot in 1916 and directed by Harold Shaw, was a tribute to the Boers' 'Great Trek' of the 1830s. Considerable efforts were made to ensure a degree of historical accuracy and the script was written by Gustav Preller, a noted historian of the Trek, while the descendants of several Voortrekkers took part. Artefacts from the Trek were loaned for use in some scenes. The film concentrated particularly on the experiences of the Trekkers in Kwa-Zulu-Natal, and on their war with the Zulu king Dingane kaSenzangakhona. The climax featured a dramatic reconstruction of the battle of Ncome/ Blood River. Most of the film was not shot in KwaZulu-Natal, however, but nearer the film studio in Johannesburg. According to the film's publicity, the Ncome battlefield was sculpted by blasting a donga in a hillside and creating an artificial river. The film was made at a crucial time in South African history; after a century of conflict the various independent Boer republics and British colonies had been united by the union of a decade before, and Afrikaners were, in particular, searching for a new sense of identity in the wake of their defeat in the Anglo-Boer War. The battle of Ncome was already at that time beginning to achieve an iconic status as a defining moment in Boer history. The film was premiered at Krugersdorp on 16 December 1916, the anniversary of Ncome, and was rapturously received by a predominantly Afrikaner audience which included General Louis Botha.

Moved by the success of *De Voortrekker* AFP embarked on an extraordinarily ambitious project in 1918, a patriotic study of the Anglo-Zulu War called *Symbol of Sacrifice*. The film was written and directed by F. Horace Rose – then editor of the *Natal Witness* – and was proudly proclaimed to be 'the world's biggest battle picture'. Certainly the scale was striking by the standards of the time – over 1,600 British uniforms were made for the film, together with 160 tents, while specially constructed sets portrayed the interior of Windsor Castle and King Cetshwayo's oNdini complex. The film itself was a typical silent movie melodrama and featured two pairs of star-crossed lovers – one settler, the other Zulu – whose stories are interwoven with a series of historical tableaux.

The film remains remarkable in a number of respects. Its patriotic tone was deliberate for it was made during the last year of the First World War, a conflict which – coming so soon after the Anglo-Boer War – had divided white South African society. Although the Union Government had supported British involvement in the war, and former Boer commando leaders like Louis Botha and Jan Smuts had fought in the British cause, many old Boer 'bitter-enders' had sympathised with Germany. The film put on a determinedly united front, drawing British, Boer and French characters together in the common cause of fighting the Zulu. The 'Symbol of Sacrifice' of the title was of course the British flag, which apparently appeared several times as a motif, most noticeably in the iSandlwana sequence when Lieutenant Melvill dies with the 1/24th's Queen's Colour wrapped round him.

The film is also unique in its attempts to offer a comprehensive history of the war. Staged sequences include British troops crossing the Mzinyathi river into Zululand, the battles of iSandlwana and Rorke's Drift, the battle of Hlobane, the death of the Prince Imperial and, finally, the battle of Ulundi. Surviving sequences suggest that these were extraordinarily epic, the Hlobane sequence being particularly good and containing a convincing representation of the death of Piet Uys amidst the smoky confusion of the descent down the 'Devil's Pass'. The story of the Prince Imperial is used to evoke contemporary attitudes towards Britain's First World War ally France, and his death is suitably poignant. The Ulundi sequence includes a representation of the British square and the burning of the royal homestead at oNdini.

The film was remarkable, too, in its attempts to tell the story from the Zulu perspective as well as from a white one, although the Zulu hero's actions are contrasted with the villainous attitude of King Cetshwayo. No other feature film has so far offered a convincing Zulu perspective about the events of 1879, despite the rather lame attempts in *Zulu Dawn* (1979).

Symbol of Sacrifice was made at a time, of course, when the Anglo-Zulu War was still within living memory, and indeed at least one veteran of the war played a prominent part in the film. Johann Colenbrander was an adventurer of note who had fought with the Natal Volunteers at the battle of kwaGingindlovu in 1879 and had later, as an adviser to *inkosi* Zibhebhu, played a prominent role in the Zulu civil war of the 1880s. In the 1890s he had ventured to Zimbabwe with Cecil Rhodes and had been heavily involved with Rhodes' dealings – and conflicts – with the amaNdebele ('Matabele') people. Colenbrander was employed by the film to advise on the management of the African extras and agreed to take a small role as Lord Chelmsford. Tragically, it was to be his last adventure; on 10 February 1918 he was filming a scene where Chelmsford and his staff crossed the White Mfolozi river prior to the battle of Ulundi when his horse stumbled in the strong current and he was swept away and drowned – all before the lens of the camera.

Colenbrander died not in the Zulu heartland, however, but in the Klip river near Henley-on-Klip, south of Johannesburg. The entire film was shot in the then-Transvaal, partly for practical reasons, not least its proximity to the film studios, and partly because of a wariness of the unsettling effect it might have on the black population of KwaZulu-Natal who, only ten years before, had suffered heavily during the Bhambatha Rebellion.

Sadly, it was common practice in silent-movie days for producers to cannibalise the prints of previous films when making new ones, and *Symbol of Sacrifice* seems to have fallen victim to this habit. No complete print has so far been discovered, and the only surviving example has much of the action sequences – including the battle of iSandlwana – almost entirely missing. Nevertheless, surviving fragments and still photographs suggest that, allowing for the cinematic conventions of the time, it displayed a considerable degree of accuracy. Nevertheless, although the film proved hugely popular in South Africa, it did not entirely convince those in the audience who remembered something of the real events. One commented that 'Rorke's Drift shown in the picture is as like Rorke's Drift as the Durban Club is',[78] while a survivor of iSandlwana, Richard Vause, admitted to his grandson that it did not accurately reflect his experience of the real thing!

African Film Productions was still around in the 1930s and produced another historical epic, this time to celebrate the centenary of the Great Trek which was fast becoming a symbol of twentieth-century Afrikaner identity. Unlike the earlier films, this one was a talkie, which in itself posed problems in a country where there were two white languages; the result was that Joseph Albrecht's 1938 *They Built A Nation* was filmed in both English and Afrikaans versions. Realistically the black cinema-going population was in any case small, but since the film was a celebration of white South African history it did not, in any case, offer any significant sympathetic black viewpoint. The film was an episodic look at the settlement of South Africa and again featured the Voortrekkers' war against King Dingane heavily, including the slaughter of the Trek leader Piet Retief and a spectacular reconstruction of the battle of Ncome/Blood River.

It is significant that all of these films were produced within South Africa, and indeed the mainstream British and American cinema industry took little interest in South African subjects until the 1960s. Only one aspect seemed to appeal to them – the similarity of the ideology and experience of the Boer Trekkers and the white pioneers moving west in America. In 1955 a leading Hollywood action director, Henry King, made *Untamed*, essentially a straightforward Western story transposed to southern Africa. With a distinctly hazy understanding of historical chronology, it features the trials of a wagon-train which sets out in the 1850s to discover and settle new lands. Along the way it is attacked by a marauding Zulu *impi* – in much the same manner that Hollywood settlers were routinely worried by Indians – and the 'promised land' is finally wrested from the British in a shoot-out which is rendered entirely in Wild West terms. The film starred Tyrone Power and Susan Hayward – neither of whom actually filmed their sequences in South Africa – and much of it is over-blown and tedious. The battle sequences, filmed at Otto's Bluff outside Pietermaritzburg, are both accurate and exciting, however, and give a good impression of the effectiveness of a Boer laager. Interestingly, the depiction of the Zulus – the way they line the hill-tops, chant and drum their shields with their spears – foreshadows their similar treatment in Cy Endfield's 1964 *Zulu*.

The superficial similarity between the Western genre and settler history in South Africa led to the production of a number of similar films in the 1960s. Indeed, a low-budget version of Stuart Cloete's Trek novel *The Fiercest Heart* was filmed in 1961 starring American athlete Raffer Johnson and Stuart Whitman as a deserter from the British Army. The film was produced entirely in America, has little sense of an authentic African backdrop (new close-up sequences featured Zulus wearing war-paint, presumably intended to complete their identification in the audience's mind with Native Americans) and, indeed, boasts some truly bizarre British uniforms. It did, however, re-use the battle sequences from *Untamed* to provide a dramatic climax. Other films at the time which similarly merged genres were *The Hellions* (1961), in which British stalwart Richard Todd played a Transvaal policeman menaced by a gang of outlaws, including James Booth (of *Zulu* fame), and *The Jackals* (1967), with Vincent Price as a South African prospector who, with his daughters, is similarly under threat from an outlaw gang. It is interesting to note that in films of this period and type black Africans were largely marginalised or absent altogether.

Undoubtedly the most enduring and famous film about the Anglo-Zulu War has been Cy Endfield's epic recreation of Rorke's Drift, *Zulu* (filmed in 1963, and premiered in London on 22 January 1964). Based on an original article by the historian John Prebble, who went on to co-write the script, the film was very much the personal project of Welsh actor Stanley Baker. He was apparently attracted by the element of Welsh heroism inherent in the story and co-produced the film along with director Cy Endfield, an American living and working in the UK since the days of the McCarthy anti-communist witch-hunts in America. Baker himself also played Lieutenant Chard, and the cast included both established actors and newcomers, often cast, intriguingly, against type. Jack Hawkins, the firm-jawed hero of many British war-films, played the flawed missionary Otto Witt, whose entirely fictional pacifist sympathies (the real Witt supported the British invasion) crumble under the strain of the impending attack, while Michael Caine was cast as the aristocratic Lieutenant Bromhead rather than the working-class roles for which he would later make his name. The film was shot not at Rorke's Drift – which was decided early on to be both impractical, because

of the existing mission buildings, and not sufficiently cinematic – but in the amphitheatre of the Royal Natal National Park in the Khahlamba mountains, one of the most impressive landscapes in KwaZulu-Natal. The film was shot, of course, at the height of the apartheid era, and the South African authorities insisted on the strict separation of the Zulu extras and the visiting film crew, and the filming was carefully monitored throughout by the security police.

Zulu remains a marvellously rich piece of cinema-making, the story driven by conflicts within the isolated garrison and offset by a striking visual sense which draws heavily on the contrasts between the appearance of the protagonists and the surrounding landscape. Red coats and white helmets stand out vividly against the cloud-swept mountain backdrop and the blue of the sky, and dappled shields and cowtails speckle the tawny hillsides. The film benefits greatly from the fact that the white extras were loaned by the South African army, while the principal actors also had some experience of military life, if only through National Service. In many respects, while clearly revelling in the spectacle of battle, the film fits into a very 1960s context of British film-making, dealing with issues of class conflict and the questioning of Empire which were not, in fact, contemporary to the real battle. Indeed, for all its well-deserved popularity, it must be said that *Zulu* takes serious liberties with the historical record, altering the personalities of protagonists – there is no evidence of any disagreement between Chard and Bromhead during the battle, the real Hook was not an insubordinate malingerer, the real Colour Sergeant Bourne was a young man at the time of the battle, Margaretta Witt was a child, and so on – and adding far more structure to the battle than was in fact the case. The real battle took place largely at night – which would not, presumably, have made for such a satisfying cinematic experience.

The film is also responsible for some of the most enduring popular myths about the war. Baker's Welsh stamp – and in particular the inclusion of Welsh baritone Ivor Emmanuel, who rallies the garrison at the height of the battle with a stirring rendition of '*Men of Harlech*' – has created a misleading impression of the make-up of the defenders, only a few of whom were actually Welsh (the 24th Regiment was not re-designated the South Wales Borderers until 1881). And while the Zulus did indeed take the rifles from the British dead at iSandlwana, as in *Zulu*'s enigmatic opening sequence, they did not use them at Rorke's Drift for the simple reason that the Zulu reserve, which attacked the mission outpost, had not taken part in the earlier looting of the camp.

One aspect of the film which has provoked some controversy is its treatment of the Zulus. Despite the one-word title – intended to evoke a popular reaction to the name which itself harks back to the impact the news of iSandlwana made upon the wider world – and a brief appearance of the then-emerging political leader *inkosi* Mangosuthu Buthelezi, playing his forebear King Cetshwayo, the film offers no authentic Zulu perspective. Yet within its dramatic parameters, this is entirely justified, for the Zulus instead are characterised as an extension of an alien land-scape – they appear menacingly in long lines over hill-tops, or rise up silently from the long grass – which threatens to swallow up the isolated garrison. The sense that the defenders are out of place, in a situation they cannot entirely understand and over which they have no effective control, offers one of the film's most effective critiques of imperialism. As, indeed, does the final image, in which Richard Burton intones the names of the VC winners, not over shots of exultant soldiers, but over a vista of wounded men and fresh graves.

The success of *Zulu* prompted Baker and Endfield to plan a second Anglo-Zulu War film, to be about iSandlwana. Sadly this project was curtailed by Baker's premature death from cancer at the age of just 48 in June 1976, and the project was sold on, to emerge in 1979 as *Zulu Dawn* (some idea of Endfield's original concept for the film can be found in his novel of the same name). Despite a big-budget approach, however, *Zulu Dawn* failed to capture much of the power of its predecessor. Director Douglas Hickox handled the crowd scenes with rare dexterity,

and the film stars a host of well-known British character actors including Peter O'Toole, Sir John Mills, Bob Hoskins, Simon Ward, Peter Vaughan and Phil Daniels, while American investment was secured through the participation of Hollywood star Burt Lancaster as Durnford; however, the lack of a strong script and character-driven drama reduced most of them to mere cameos, and the film rarely comes alive. The locations were arguably better than in *Zulu* – the scene in which the Centre Column crosses into Zululand was actually shot at Rorke's Drift, albeit in reverse (from the Zulu to the Natal side), the 'Fugitives' Drift' sequences were shot on the true location, and there is a long-shot at one point of the real iSandlwana mountain. Since the presence of monuments on the battlefield made filming there difficult, the main battle-scenes were shot at the foot of iSiphezi mountain (where the Zulu army had actually bivouacked on the night of 20 January 1879). Much effort clearly went into the attempt to portray the wide variety of uniforms worn by the British troops with some accuracy, although many have a mass-produced synthetic fibre look and the pale blue uniforms worn by the officers of Sikhali's Horse are pure fiction. The battle scenes certainly have some spectacular appeal, but they are curiously bloodless – both because of a lack of close-up action sequences of the sort which worked so well in *Zulu*, and because of a reluctance to portray violence too graphically. Indeed, production of the film was plagued by rumours of financial problems and wrangles among investors, and some of the more bloody sequences – the killing of wounded soldiers in the field hospital and the death of minor characters – were cut before release to ensure a family certificate. Nevertheless, the film was given only limited cinema distribution, and it was many years before it was made available on DVD or video.

Unlike *Zulu*, *Zulu Dawn* made a half-hearted attempt to add a Zulu perspective to the story, but in the final cut this was largely confined to conversations between characters explaining the action, leaving *Symbol of Sacrifice* as the only 1879 film to date with a fully developed Zulu story line. Although the film adopted a 1970s ideological stance which was largely critical of British policies in Zululand, it remained conservative in its assessment of the British defeat, attributing it in part to the reluctance of Quartermaster Bloomfield – a wonderfully bravura performance from Peter Vaughan – to issue ammunition without proper procedure.

From the 1960s to the 1990s the South African film industry was largely isolated from the world cinema industry. Nevertheless, South African director David Millin made three big budget films on historical themes which received only limited international distribution. The first, *Majuba* (1968), was based on another Stuart Cloete novel, *Hill of Doves*, and concerned the British disasters in the Anglo-Boer War of 1881. As with earlier South African films, it was shot in both English and Afrikaans versions. Even by the standards of the time, Millin's style seems slow and dated and the script was uninspired, Cloete's story offering little more than a family melodrama interspersed with historic tableaux. Nevertheless, the film includes surprisingly epic reconstructions of the battles of Bronkhorstspruit, Laing's Nek and Majuba itself, weakened only by a lack of close-up shots – which makes the action seem curiously distanced – and by any credible depiction of the violence. Millin's second film, *Shangani Patrol* (1970), is perhaps his strongest, and concerns the fate of a patrol of British South African troops cut off and wiped out by the amaNdebele during the war of 1893. Although similarly sanitised – particularly at the end – and of course uncritical of BSA Company policies, it recalls *Zulu* in its sense of a small group of men facing hopeless odds. Millin's last historical epic was an Afrikaans film set during the war between the Voortrekkers and King Dingane in 1838, *Die Voortrekkers* (1973). This again featured the death of Piet Retief, and included a good reconstruction of the abortive Trekker expedition in April 1838 (the *Vlugkommando)* and the battle of eThaleni, in which the Boer leader Piet Uys (father of Piet Uys of Hlobane fame) was killed.

By the 1980s the arts in South Africa were increasingly dominated by the political tensions within the country. These framed the artistic vision of one of the most complex and controversial epics about Zulu history, William Faure's mini-series *Shaka Zulu* (1985). This told the story of Shaka's childhood, his supposed problematic relationship with his parents and his rise to power through military conquest against the background of the first contacts with white interlopers (led by Edward Fox and Robert Powell). While there is certainly much to criticise in *Shaka Zulu* from a historical point of view – it encapsulates the essentially contradictory nature of white myths about Shaka as both hero and tyrant, misrepresents the motives of the British characters, introduces a fantastical element and absurdly exaggerates some aspects of Zulu traditional costume – it remains compulsive viewing. Despite being at times over-bloated and lurid, the central performance by former football-player Henry Cele as Shaka is compelling, and the series has a remarkable grandeur, using the Zululand landscapes to striking effect. If its attempts to turn Shaka's story into a mythic epic do not always succeed, it remains a bold attempt to place the Zulus at the centre of their own history. The series was the subject of a belated sequel – *Shaka Zulu II; The Citadel* (2001) – again starring Henry Cele and with David Hasselhoff playing a disillusioned slave-trader and singer Grace Jones as Shaka's mother. Following production problems in South Africa the series was largely shot in Morocco, and publicists readily admitted it 'made no claims to historical authenticity'. It is, indeed, entirely without historical – or apparently artistic – merit, and is only interesting in its exploitation of the image of Shaka as an iconic African warrior-hero.

Much more entertaining was a low-budget South African series filmed in the wake of *Shaka Zulu*, and using many of the same sets. *John Ross* (1987) was based around the adventures of the first British ivory traders to land in Natal, and in particular of a young apprentice named Charles Rawden Maclean who ran away to sea under the name John Ross. The film follows Ross (Darryl Robertson) from his escape from the life of a Glasgow street-urchin to the epic walk from Port Natal to Delagoa Bay to secure a supply of medicines, a feat for which he is remembered by posterity. Aimed at a family audience and lacking both *Shaka Zulu*'s pretesions and its gore, it presented an essentially predictable series of adventures with wistful charm and was filmed against stunning backdrops.

It is interesting to note that the most recent representations of Zulu history have been preoccupied with the rise of the kingdom rather than its fall; the definitive film about the events of 1879 has perhaps yet to be made.

Climbing Kranskop

Above the Middle Drift on the Thukela river, standing out from the high escarpment on the Natal side, is an isolated pillar of rock known to the first Afrikaner settlers as Kranskop ('cliff head') and to the Zulus as Itshe lika Ntunjambili ('the rock with two holes', so-called from a gap below a bridge of fallen stone lying between the pillar and the face of the escarpment). This feature is so distinctive that over the years a number of folk-tales have accumulated regarding it. It used to be variously said among the local African population that a spirit lived in the hole and would sometimes emerge to carry away lazy children who lingered too long in its vicinity, or that it was once the secret hideaway of cannibals who could open the magic hole at will; on a windy day the voices of the lost souls are said to whisper in the sighing winds.

In 1879 there was considerable military activity in the Kranskop area; although the terrain is steep and rugged, the Middle Drift crossing was one of the few viable fords across the Thukela and it commanded the central Natal/Zulu border. Lord Chelmsford had originally intended to mount a strike into Zululand by this route but when a shortage of transport wagons made this idea impractical he opted instead to exploit its defensive possibilities and Colonel Durnford's no. 2 Column had originally been stationed on the escarpment within sight of the Kop. When Durnford was moved up to Rorke's Drift to reinforce the Centre Column, detachments of his column were left behind to guard a series of posts above the border and throughout the course of the war

there were a number of raids and demonstrations across the river from both sides.

For the most part, however, life in the Kranskop garrisons was one of unmitigated boredom, constrained by the need to keep a watchful eye out for Zulu movements in the valley far below. The burden of duty fell to various auxiliary units, notably detachments of Durnford's 1st Battalion, 1st NNC, together with local Border Guards and Border levies, and a few Natal Volunteers. Although the posts offered breathtaking scenic views, life there was uncomfortable for the Thukela valley was hot, dry and airless. Many of the NNC officers drank too much – nearby Greytown afforded a source of ready supply not available to the troops serving across the border in Zululand – and at least one of them shot himself.

Commanding the 1/1st NNC in the area was Commandant Alexander Montgomery, a former regular – he had been a captain in the 7th Fusiliers – who had brought his large family to Natal and had established himself among the local gentry as an estate-owner and a Justice of the Peace. Although middle-aged, Montgomery was a restless man who was clearly irritated by the constraints of the duties in which he found himself. He organised sports for his officers and spear-throwing competitions for his men in an effort to keep them amused, and on one occasion a mock-battle. These excitements were still not enough for him, however, and one day in the middle of February he decided to climb Kranskop.

The Kop itself is a great elliptical column of weathered sandstone, broken off from the point of a narrow grassy ridge on the side of the escarpment. A bridge of rock which once connected it to the ridge collapsed aeons ago into a broken arch of boulders and the domed summit of the Kop is now completely isolated, the cliffs rising up several hundred feet from the steep valley sides. It was said among local settlers that not even a baboon could reach the summit. Montgomery was a keen climber, however, and set off with two friends one morning to accomplish the task. Scrambling down the escarpment to the base of the column, they worked their way gingerly around it until they came to a fissure which was large enough to give them purchase and foot-holds. Montgomery successfully eased himself up and eventually emerged on to the summit. After surveying the extraordinary views of the Thukela valley some 2,000 feet (800 metres) below, he put a match to the grass and started to make his way down. By the time he reached the bottom safely, the whole of the summit was ablaze; it was a clear day, and a tall pillar of smoke rose up into the sky which was visible to the Zulu population for miles across the river.

At the time Montgomery's achievement was regarded as an act of psychological warfare. It encouraged his own men, while the Zulus were apparently astonished by the sight of the Kop in flames, and could not understand how the British had achieved it – many, indeed, preferred to believe that it was the result of a natural lightning strike. In today's greener world, however, it might be seen as one of ecological vandalism; the summit of the Kop is home to the rare Zulu-land cycad, and black eagles, kestrels, falcons and rock pigeons nest there.

Colours

In the 1870s every infantry battalion (excluding Rifle regiments) in the British Army carried Colours, both as a demonstration of national allegiance – a national flag by which troops could be identified on a smoky battlefield – and as an evocation of a regimental tradition. As a result, each battalion had two Colours, the national flag, known as the Queen's Colour, and a Regimental Colour which bore distinctions and honours particular to each battalion. It was still the practice to carry Colours into action, although by 1879 there was a growing sense of awareness that their practical functions belonged to an earlier age, and that they were not entirely appropriate on a modern battlefield in the age of increasingly accurate and long-range weapons. The main function of Colours in battle was to provide a fixed point of reference to the men when manoeuvring in formation, and in particu-lar to provide a focus for rallying a battalion when it was under pressure. They also served to boost morale by reminding the men in the

ranks of the traditions they were upholding. The Colours were carried by junior subalterns on parade and in action, and it fell to the Colour Sergeants – historically the most senior rank of NCO in the British Army, created originally to honour distinguished service – to protect them. By this time the practice of carrying cavalry Colours into battle had been discontinued.

Both the Queen's and the Regimental Colours were of the same size. From 1855 Colours were 6 feet wide by 5 feet 6 inches tall, but in 1858 they were altered under regulations to 4 feet by 3 feet 6 inches, and in 1868 to 3 feet 9 inches by 3 feet. Colours were presented by the monarch, either in person or by an appointed representative, and most battalions proudly carried their Colours for as long as possible before they were laid up and new ones presented; not only did they often carry Colours of an obsolete pattern, therefore, but the wear and tear of previous campaigns was borne as a badge of honour. As Kipling wryly observed, most long-standing Colours actually resembled 'the lining of a bricklayer's hat on a chewed toothpick'. In 1879 several battalions carried the post-1868 pattern of Colours but many still had the old 1858–68 pattern, and one – the 58th (Rutlandshire) – carried the even earlier 1855–58 pattern. The Colours themselves were made of silk.

The Queen's Colour was in each case the Great Union flag with the regimental numeral in the middle surmounted by a crown. In those cases where a regiment consisted of more than one battalion – i.e. the first twenty-five Line battalions – the second battalion in each case was distinguished by a scroll under the numeral embroidered with the words 'II BATT'N'. The Colour was edged on the three free sides with a fringe of crimson and gold, while the envelope of silk by which it was attached to the pole on the fourth side was also crimson. Two cords and tassels of mixed crimson and gold were attached to the head of the pike. The pike itself – also called the Colour pole – had been 9 feet 10 inches long since 1768 but was changed in 1873 to 8 feet 7 inches. The old pike was topped by a gilt spear-head, but this was changed in 1858 to a device of a crown surmounted by a lion.

All the battalions present in Zululand seem to have had the post-1873 Colour pole and crown device with the exception of the 58th, which seems still to have had the old spear-head point on its Colours.

The Regimental Colour was markedly different in each case. It was the distinctive colour of the regimental facing in each case (thus buff for the 2/3rd Regiment, 90th and 99th, blue for the 2/4th, 1/13th, 2/21st, green for the 1st and 2nd 24th and 94th, yellow for the 57th, 80th, 88th and 99th and black for the 58th). In each case the first quarter – the top corner nearest the pike – bore the Union flag, while in the centre was a red circle bearing either the regimental number (in Roman numerals) or the regimental badge, surrounded by a scroll bearing the regimental title. Above the central device was the royal crown and surrounding it was a Union wreath of roses, thistles and shamrocks. On either side of the central device, in scrolls on the facing-colour background, were regimental battle-honours which had been approved and awarded by the monarch. In some cases additional devices – which had been granted as a particular distinction in the past – were also carried. For those battalions with red, white or black facings the design of the regimental Colour was different; in 1879 only one battalion, the 58th, fell into this category, and their Colour was black with a scarlet St George's Cross, and the usual Union flag in the upper canton and regimental devices. Battle honours were often awarded some time after an event, and were sewn on to existing Colours still later, so some battalions went into battle carrying Colours that did not yet bear honours that had been awarded years before. When not on parade or in action the Colours were carried in a heavy black leather sheath, topped with brass, known as a case. Since the Colours were consecrated and blessed when they were presented to a battalion, they could also be used for 'drumhead' church services in the field.

Colours were unfurled in action in several of the battles of the Anglo-Zulu War. The 3rd (Buffs) had their Colours flying at Nyezane, and while there is no evidence that Colours were unfurled at Khambula (a defensive action in which the men were fighting from behind wagons and barricades) many of the battalions certainly carried their Colours at Ulundi.

There is nothing to suggest that either battalion of the 24th carried their Colours in action during the battle of iSandlwana. Indeed, the Regimental Colour of the 1st Battalion was with a company then still at Helpmekaar; the Queen's Colour of the 1st Battalion and both Colours of the 2nd Battalion were, however, in the camp at iSandlwana. There is a tradition that during the British collapse Colonel Pulleine ordered the adjutant of the 1/24th, Lieutenant Teignmouth Melvill, to escape with the 1/24th's Queen's Colour to prevent the disgrace of it falling into the hands of the enemy. Although this story was widely circulated after the battle, perhaps by Colonel Glyn himself, it is not mentioned by any of the survivors and cannot be substantiated. It is in fact more likely that the Colour was brought out by Melvill – either on his own initiative or under orders – to serve as a rallying point, but by then the situation had deteriorated so rapidly that this was no longer possible and instead he decided to save it. In this regard the comparison with the 2nd Afghan War battle of Maiwand (27 July 1880) is interesting. Maiwand bears a number of similarities to iSandlwana, not least in the way a British infantry battalion, in this case the 66th, attempted to make a fighting withdrawal under heavy pressure from overwhelming enemy forces. With the British in danger of collapsing completely, Colonel Galbraith of the 66th ordered the Colours to be unfurled and tried to rally his battalion. Some 200 men rallied to him but Galbraith was cut down almost immediately and the 66th was broken up into smaller parties, many of which were overwhelmed.

When Melvill rode out of the camp at iSandlwana the Colour was still in its case and carried across his saddle. The Colour would have been heavy and cumbersome and very difficult to carry on horseback, especially across such difficult country; it presumably snagged on bushes as Melvill rode, and one of the survivors, Lieutenant Horace Smith-Dorrien, reported that when he saw Melvill he thought the Colour-pole had broken because the top was dangling down; he later became convinced that the case had merely been dragged half-off since the pole was intact when recovered. Along the way – possibly on top of Mpethe hill, above the Mzinyathi valley – Melvill met Lieutenant Neville Coghill, also of the 1/24th. The two attempted to swim across the flooded river but Melvill – still carrying the Colour – was swept out of his saddle by the current and clung instead to a rock which was just breaking the surface. Coghill swam his horse across to the Natal bank but, on emerging on to dry land, looked back to see Melvill in the water. Turning, he rode back into the river to rescue Melvill, but his horse was shot by Zulus who now lined their bank. Undeterred, Coghill swam to Melvill, and together with a lieutenant of the 3rd NNC, Walter Higginson, he managed to help Melvill across to the Natal bank. In the process, however, the current finally pulled the Colour from Melvill's hands and it sank into the river. Melvill, Coghill and Higginson emerged safely on to the Natal bank – probably some of the last white men to do so – but both Melvill and Coghill were caught and killed as they struggled up the steep slopes ahead.

On 4 February Major Black of the 2/24th led a patrol from Rorke's Drift to investigate the story that Melvill had been seen with the Colour. Descending from the heights above the river towards Sothondose's ('Fugitives') Drift, the patrol found the bodies of Melvill and Coghill. Melvill's tunic was unbuttoned to see if he had the Colours wrapped around his body. As he did not, the bodies were covered over with stones and the party picked their way down to the river. The water-level had dropped since the battle, and both banks were scattered with bodies and debris. Here Lieutenant Harford (99th Regiment attached to the 3rd NNC) and Lieutenant Harber (NNC) came across

the Colour case mixed up with a heap of other things, and picking it up I said to Harber, who was closest to me, 'Look here! Here's the case! The Colours can't be far off!' We all three then had a look at it,

putting it on a conspicuous boulder, and went on. Then, as Harber was returning to his position, I noticed a straight piece of stick projecting out of the water in the middle of the river, almost in line with us, and said to him, 'Do you see that straight bit of stick sticking up in the water opposite you? It looks to me uncommonly like a Colour pole.' He waded straight in, up to his middle, and got hold of it. On lifting it out he brought up the Colour still adhering to it, and on getting out of the water handed the standard to me, and as he did so the gold-embroidered centre scroll dropped out, the silk having more-or-less rotted from the long immersion in the water.[79]

The Colour was taken back to Rorke's Drift. The sentries posted on Shiyane spotted them and a guard turned out to greet the men with the tattered Colour. Colonel Glyn himself received them – and it was an emotional moment as it was he who had received the Colours when they were presented to the battalion at the Curragh in Ireland in June 1866. The following day the Colour was escorted back to Helpmekaar and formally returned to the surviving companies of the battalion. For the last part of the journey Harford was allowed to carry the Colour – a moment of great pride to him, for it is extremely unusual for an officer of another regiment on duty to be allowed to carry the Queen's Colour.

The tattered Colour was brought home to England in October 1879. Queen Victoria expressed an interest in it, and on 28 July 1880 a Colour-party from the battalion presented it to her at Osborne House on the Isle of Wight. The Queen placed a wreath of Immortelles – dried flowers – on the Colour to commemorate the battalion's 'immortal bravery'; subsequent Colours of the battalion have borne a silver wreath around the crown on top of the pole to commemorate this, and a wreath was assumed by the regiment as a badge. The Colours were carried on parade by the battalion until 1933, when they were laid up in Brecon Cathedral. The original wreath of Immortelles was kept for many years in a silver-mounted wooden box, at first in the officers' mess and later in the cathedral. It was stolen in 1980, apparently for the silver, and later found abandoned in a ditch. Both the wreath and the box were recovered, but the original wreath was damaged beyond repair – the flowers currently on display are replacements.

The two Colours of the 2/24th lost at iSandlwana were never recovered. At the end of March 1879 a wood-cutting party from Rorke's Drift found the gilt crown finial from one of the Colours in the garden of a deserted farm-house 4 miles downstream from Rorke's Drift. It appeared to have been unscrewed by someone familiar with the construction of a Colour-pole, but how it got there remains a mystery. The pole from which it had been removed was discovered by vedettes of the 1st (King's) Dragoon Guards in a Zulu homestead about 2 miles from iSandlwana during the burial expedition of 21 May. It is not clear, either, how pole and crown became separated. No trace of the Colours themselves were found, although the homestead was put to the torch by the Dragoons before being thoroughly searched – rather to the 24th's regret.

The days of carrying Colours in action were in any case numbered. They were carried by some battalions in Afghanistan during the 2nd Afghan War – notably by the 66th at Maiwand – but in 1881 a series of events occurred which demonstrated just how out of place they were on a modern battlefield. In the aftermath of the Zulu campaign the Boers in the Transvaal attempted to overthrow the British administration there. Many of the British garrisons were invested, and when an infantry battalion – the 94th – was marched to relieve the Pretoria garrison it was shot to pieces (in the battle of Bronkhorstspruit on 20 December 1880). The 94th had previously fought at Ulundi, and was carrying its Colours on the march. When the troops surrendered to the Boers the Colours were hidden under the bed of Mrs Fox, one of the soldiers' wives who was wounded in the action, in an ambulance wagon. They were later smuggled to safety to prevent the Boers capturing them.

In order to prevent British troops hurrying up from the garrison in Natal to relieve those under pressure in the Transvaal, the Boers occupied the Laing's Nek pass through the Khahlamba mountains. On 28 January 1881 troops under the command of General Sir George Colley attempted to force the pass. Among them was the 58th, carrying the Colours it had carried in Zululand. The troopers of the 58th were ordered to march up a steep slope to assault the Boers entrenched at the top; they marched up in column, the Colours carried by Lieutenants Baillie and Peel. As they neared the summit they deployed into line to launch an assault, only to find that they were exposed to fire from Boer trenches at close range. Both Peel and Baillie were soon shot and wounded; as Peel went to help him, Baillie told him to take the Colour instead but Peel tripped in an ant-bear hole and fell. Sergeant William Bridgestock, thinking Peel dead, picked up both Colours. By this time the attack had clearly failed and Bridgestock carried the Colours down the hill under fire. A fellow officer, Lieutenant Hill, attempted to drag Baillie away, but while he was doing so Baillie was hit again and killed. Hill did rescue several other wounded men, however, and was later awarded the Victoria Cross. Sergeant Bridgestock was awarded the DCM for saving the Colours.

The devastation wrought among the Colour Party at Laing's Nek was a stinging reminder of their conspicuousness and vulnerability when in action against an enemy armed with accurate breech-loading rifles. Sir Garnet Wolseley himself commented that any commander sending his men into action with Colours under those circumstances should be tried for murder; they were subsequently banned by regulation from being carried into battle, and the 58th achieved the distinction of being the last British infantry battalion to have done so.

Disease

In the middle of June 1879 Frances, the wife of Bishop Colenso, described the state of the British forces as they seemed to her, living as she was in Natal and away from the front line. What she noticed was not the extent to which Lord Chelmsford's forward columns were closing in on the Zulu capital but rather the physical cost and spiritual malaise engendered by prolonged hard campaigning:

> Everything here is in a deplorable case. Fever is decimating the troops; at the hospitals belonging to the Coast column there are over 400 sick and and the deaths are at the rate of nearly two a day! I suppose camp life at this time of year must be very unhealthy and unspeakably wretched. Fancy sick men without mattresses and pillows, only blankets on the ground. The habits of savage life must give great advantage to the Zulus, and you may read in the colonial newspapers pitiful complaints of the unfairness of the match between the light marching equipment of the enemy, the comparative fewness of their wants, and their powers of endurance, and the complicated arrangements of the English soldiers. I fear that the spirits and courage of our army are flagging ...[80]

She paints a dismal picture which contrasts starkly with the imminent victory in the field – the battle of Ulundi was only weeks away – but one which none the less contains a great deal of truth. For the British Army on campaign during the nineteenth century disease normally incapacitated more troops than enemy action – a statistic that might well have been true of the Zulu campaign too, had iSandlwana not upset the reckoning. A total of 76 officers and 1,007 British and colonial troops were killed in action in Zululand, and a further 37 officers and 206 men wounded. The official returns indicate that 604 African auxiliaries were killed – a figure that is probably significantly under-estimated. By contrast 17 officers and 330 men died of disease during the war, and a total of 99 officers and 1,286 men were invalided from active duty owing to sickness or accidents. A staggering total of 53,851 medical treatments were recorded, and there were base hospitals at Durban, Pietermaritzburg, Ladysmith and Utrecht. The sick were cared for mostly by doctors from the Army Medical Department and support staff from the Army Hospital Corps. There were a number of civilian

doctors – both employed by the military and volunteers – and a number of civilian nurses who volunteered in England for the job.

The main causes of sickness among the British troops were poor hygiene leading to water-borne diseases such as 'enteric' – typhoid – fever. Although medical science understood the connection between cleanliness and good health, the appreciation of the means by which diseases actually spread remained hazy. Thus Surgeon Norbury of HMS *Active*, Pearson's contentious senior medical officer in invested Eshowe, pondered whether the outbreak of sickness there could be attributed to

> a soil consisting almost entirely of vegetable matter placed over a watery sub-soil [which] in so hot a climate could not be healthy ... The ground became saturated every few days and then a burning sun would cause a copious exhalation ... The result was that the malarious emanations from the ground could not escape, and these becoming mingled together with the exhalations from the bodies of men, so closely packed together, produced a poisonous atmosphere, which they sometimes inhaled for days together ...[81]

Perhaps rather closer to the mark, according to modern scientific principles, he also attributed the garrison's failing health to

> the very heavy work which was required of the men under the broiling sun, when on a reduced scale of diet; the alternations of heat and cold, the thermometer standing one day at 97°, and the next at 67°, with fogs and rain, and, lastly exposure – men at their posts frequently lying in the mud the greater part of the night, with the rain pouring on them, and without any protection beyond their overcoats. The cases of purely typhoid fever at Ekowe were undoubtedly caused by some soldiers belonging to the working party having foolishly filled their water-bottles at a small stream which flowed

directly from the cemetery, and which also drained the ground which was set aside for the burial of dead bullocks.[82]

What Eshowe suffered as a result of the enforced containment of a force of 1,700 men within the confines of a small mission complex also beset the other columns to a lesser degree, and Norbury's account admirably sums up the causes of the sickness noticed by Frances Colenso. The fundamental problem faced by a British army on campaign, particularly in a climate of extremes like that of Zululand, was that its very presence inevitably polluted its immediate environment with unfortunate results for the health of the men. All British camps in Zululand were equipped with specially dug latrine trenches, but the African auxiliaries, accustomed in their civilian lives to choosing their own bush, regarded them with suspicion and distaste and could seldom be persuaded to use them. Moreover, the camps teemed with animals – horses, oxen, mules, dogs – all of which soiled the ground freely. When an army was camped in one place for any length of time it was almost impossible to keep the sources of water – which for defensive reasons needed to be close by – free from pollution.

Moreover, as Norbury hints, the men in the ranks tended to assess water from its face value, filling their water-bottles from any source which looked clean. Both the water-bottles carried by individual soldiers and the water-carts used to transport drinking water on the march were made of wood; once a source of infection had entered them it was likely to remain in the wood even when water was emptied out and refilled.

At Eshowe, Pearson and his officers were well aware that, by containing virtually the entire garrison within the confines of the fortified post at night, they were inviting disease, and they worked hard to prevent it. During the day areas outside the fort were specified as latrines while large wooden tubs were provided for use at night. Nevertheless, the weather was poor for much of the siege, and the heavy rain, combined with the passage of men and animals, meant that the interior of the fort was a sea of mud which, during particularly heavy storms, was washed

freely about the interior. Under the circumstances it is a remarkable achievement that so few of the garrison were to die of disease before the post was relieved.

It is no coincidence that Frances Colenso noted that the scourge of sickness fell most heavily on the columns operating in the coastal district. One of the simplest ways for an army to avoid sickness was to keep moving, to abandon a campsite as soon as it became fouled and to select another. For the most part the 2nd Division and Flying Column advanced towards oNdini at a slow but steady pace. The 1st Division, in any case operating in a humid sub-tropical coastal climate, was hampered by inadequate transport facilities which limited its advance from one static supply-depot to another. A journalist visiting the camp near the old battlefield at kwaGingindlovu in mid-April was appalled by what he found there:

I found on my arrival there ninety-three serious cases on the sick list, nearly all being cases of dysentery, colic, and diarrhoea. As for the officers, a more woe-begone lot it has never been my fortune to see. Thanks to the paternal care of Major Bruce of the 91st, and some of the officers left behind on the Tugela, the officers of this admirable regiment presented a better appearance than did those of either the 57th or the Naval Brigade. Private supplies of food had been forwarded to them, and they had not been obliged for weeks to live on that abomination in the way of food, 'Chicago tinned beef'. They therefore looked better, though of course far from well. When, however, I came to the 60th Rifles, and saw them, so cadaverous were their looks, so utterly changed and wasted down from what I had left them but ten short days before, I felt quite dazed when they surrounded me. The colonel was sick and unable to move; the senior captain was doubled up, and a whole row of fine young fellows were lying for shelter from the burning sun under wagons, eking out their shade with an old tarpaulin – shaking with low fever, and exhausted by continuous dysentery – nine hundred men in the ranks, and only three officers fit to take charge of them, though others were manfully struggling against their sickness and holding the field.[83]

It was perhaps fortunate for Lord Chelmsford that, following their recent defeat at kwaGingindlovu, the Zulus in the coastal sector were no longer able to mount an effective resistance.

While the supplies of tinned beef – notoriously unpalatable when left in the sun for days on end, so that the gases expanded and the tin almost exploded on opening – may have been a contributory factor, there were other reasons why life in the coastal camps was potentially unhealthy. Although the Zulu dead closest to the British positions at kwaGingindlovu had been buried, many more lay out, unburied and putrefying, in the long grass, and in particular a large number were scattered in the long grass and bush of the Nyezane river, where they had been slaughtered during the retreat. The pollution of this river as a source of drinking water continued to haunt the British even after the camp at kwaGingindlovu was broken up and new fortified posts established nearby. Some weeks after the establishment of the supply depot at Fort Chelmsford the remains of several Zulu dead, by that time largely reduced to skeletons, were found in the Nyezane upstream from where the garrison drew its water supplies. Nor did the passage of supply convoys up the coastal road help; the shortage of draught oxen meant that those in harness were frequently over-worked, and dozens collapsed and died. Their bodies were dragged to the side of the track and left to rot, and the line of the road was marked by circling birds of prey and by the carcasses of dead animals scattered at regular intervals along it.

For the most part, of course, as Frances Colenso suggested, the Zulus were immune to the sorts of pressures which afflicted the British. As individuals, the Zulus were accustomed to life in their natural environment, and they were inured by regular exposure to many of the everyday complaints which struck down their British counterparts. They were better judges of good sources of water-supply and they carried no water with them, drinking instead from fresh streams along the line of march. They were not subject to the heavy fatigues imposed upon British soldiers, and they were familiar with the dramatic changes in temperature. Most importantly, however, their armies were never concentrated together for long; they came together for the duration of a particular campaign and were in the field for a week or perhaps two before dispersing again. In that time they moved frequently, covering perhaps 20 miles between each bivouac, seldom staying in one place for more than one night, and so sparing themselves exposure to the pollution their presence inevitably imposed on the environment.

Nevertheless, it must be presumed that some small proportion of Zulus became ill during the prosecution of the war, but with no statistics to remember them by their numbers, and their fate, will remain unknown.

In that too they are in telling contrast to the melancholy crop of graves which can still be found along the lines of the British advance.

Disembowelling

On 12 March 1879, roused from his bed in his tent at Luneburg by a distraught Lieutenant Henry Harward, Major Charles Tucker hurried out to the nearby Ntombe river where a convoy of his 80th Regiment had been attacked just a few hours before. What he found there was the typical aftermath of a Zulu attack:

As we approached the Intombe Drift a fearful and horrible sight presented itself, and the stillness of the spot was awful; there were our men lying all about the place, some naked and some only half-clad. On the opposite side of the drift I need not attempt to describe to you what I saw; all the bodies were full of assegai wounds and nearly all of them were disembowelled … I saw but one body that I could call unmutilated.[84]

The sense of shock which pervades this account mirrors the reaction of Lord Chelmsford's men, condemned to spend a night lying out on the fresh battlefield of iSandlwana. 'We saw the dead bodies of our men strewed about on every side and horribly mutilated',[85] wrote one, while another said 'the Zulus mutilated them and stuck them with the assegai all over the body',[86] and a third noted 'every white man that was killed was ripped up and their bowels torn out'.[87] It was a sight calculated to provoke those who saw it to a fury, of course, and indeed that vision of the aftermath of iSandlwana was to affect profoundly the character of the war thereafter.

The Zulu treatment of enemies killed in battle reflected three distinct post-combat rituals, all of which suggested the extent to which mortal combat was regarded as a powerful moment of interaction with the spirit world.

That the dead bore multiple stab wounds is a feature common to almost all eyewitness descriptions from every battle in which British dead fell into Zulu hands. Some of these were undoubtedly inflicted during combat itself; despite the Zulu warrior's fabled prowess with the stabbing spear, it is unlikely that death would always be caused by a single stab, especially if the opponent was blocking, defending himself and fighting back. On some occasions, when the fighting was fierce and confused, two or three Zulus might engage the same opponent, each trying to find an opening to deliver their blows: given the large wounds which were inflicted by spears, the act of killing itself was likely to be messy.

Once the opponent had fallen, however, it was a common practice to stab the body again, and indeed he was likely to be stabbed again by other Zulus passing over the field. Although Zulu attitudes towards courage in warfare stressed individual achievement, warfare itself was a communal act, and men were prepared for it by complex rituals which bound them together. The act of stabbing an enemy already killed by another was known as ukuhlomula, and it was intended to recognise the participation of the group as a whole in the effort. It was a practice which originated in the hunt, where each man in a hunting party was entitled to stab a fallen beast to affirm his particular stake in the glory of the

kill. The same practice was often followed in wartime, particularly when an enemy had fought well, and particular kudos therefore accrued to those who had overwhelmed him. As Mpatshana kaSodondo, who had fought with the uVe at iSandlwana, put it:

[our] numbers included those who had stabbed opponents who had already been stabbed by others (hlomula'd); then again those hlomula-ing became more numerous by reason of the fact that they had been fighting such formidable opponents, who were like lions ... This custom was observed in regard to Isandlwana because it was recognised that fighting against such a foe and killing some of them was of the same high-grade as lion-hunting. In regard to buffalo, too, anyone hlomula-ing first, second or third ... was looked on as responsible in some way for its death ...[88]

The second practice, the custom of disembowelling a fallen enemy – qaqa – was directly related to the Zulu view of the universe and its relationship with the world of the living. Prior to embarking on a campaign the warriors underwent a number of rituals which were designed to protect them from dark spiritual forces, known as mnyama, which were unleashed by the shedding of blood. To prevent them bringing harmful influences back into their everyday lives they were required to undergo a number of counterpart rituals at the end of the fighting. These rituals were particularly crucial for the abaqawe – the heroes who had killed an enemy in person. Men who had killed but not yet been cleansed were called izinxelera. They were a source of powerful spiritual contagion, and they were said to be 'wet with yesterday's blood'.

The first element in the cycle of cleansing rituals was a requirement to qaqa the body of the victim. In the hot African sun a corpse begins to putrefy quickly, the expanding gases in the body causing the stomach to swell. This the Zulus believed was the spirit of the dead man trying to escape to the afterworld, and it was necessary to ensure the safe passage of that spirit by opening the stomach. Depending on the circumstances, the clothes were partially removed and a cut made up the length of the abdomen. If this rite was not observed the spirit was likely to haunt the man who had done the killing with various unpleasant consequences; his own body might swell up, or he might be afflicted with visions and nightmares which drove him mad. Mehlokazulu kaSihayo explained that at iSandlwana 'all the dead bodies were cut open, because if that had not been done the Zulus would have become swollen like the dead bodies'.[89] There are suggestions that some Zulus touched the blades of their bloody spears lightly to their tongues, perhaps to symbolically 'eat up' the spirit of their victim.

The next act of cleansing was for the victor to wear some item of clothing taken from the man he had killed. This was worn until the full rituals were completed, and was an outward sign of both the man's state of spiritual contamination and his prowess as a warrior. The practice was called *zila*. Mpatshana again:

It is the custom for one killing another to take off the deceased's things and put them on, even the penis cover. He *zila*'s with them by so doing ... if he has killed two or more he will take articles from each and put them on. He will not put his own things on until the doctor has treated him and given him medicines. We took the Europeans' things at Isandlwana; they were all stripped. This was done to *zila* with.[90]

For the most part upper garments were taken from European bodies; red-coats were particularly popular. Trousers were often left because they were awkward to remove and most Zulus found wearing them constricting. If the upper garments were too bloody, they were left.

The act of disembowelling was a post-mortem ritual, and there was never any intention of inflicting it on a living enemy. Often the victims were disembowelled some time after death, when the fighting had finished and there was time to go back over the field. Sometimes, however, it was carried out immediately, in the heat of battle. Trooper Richard Stevens, a survivor of iSandl-

wana, noted with horror that the Zulus 'were not content with killing, but were ripping the men up afterwards',[91] while Kumbekha Qwabe, who fought with the uKhandempemvu, agreed that after stabbing one soldier 'as soon as he fell I pulled the assegai out and slit his stomach'.[92]

For the *izinxelera* the act of *qaqa* was the first stage in a process which would keep them isolated from ordinary society for many days, and which would entail prolonged cleansing ceremonies at the hands of specialist doctors.

The final act of mutilation, practised on only a small number of British dead, was the removal of body parts by the specialist *izinyanga* or war-doctors who accompanied the Zulu armies. Certain body parts removed from a fallen enemy – most of them associated with masculine vigour, such as facial hair, skin from the right arm, the penis – were regarded as an extremely potent means of assuring a future supernatural ascendancy over that enemy. From the descriptions of the British dead at iSandlwana, it seems likely that these items were removed from a number of corpses and were, in all probability, used in preparatory rituals before the subsequent battles. Body parts were certainly removed from men killed in the skirmish before oNdini on 3 July, and used in the 'doctoring' ceremonies performed on the Zulu army that night, prior to the battle of Ulundi the following day.

To the British, of course, the ideology behind the post-combat rituals, with their emphasis on the spirit world and an acknowledgment of the bravery of the fallen, was neither recognised nor understood, and provided little consolation to the comrades of the fallen. Instead, it merely emphasised the huge gulfs in cultural understanding between the two sides, and, once stories of the dreadful field at iSandlwana had been widely circulated, added a particularly bitter edge to the brutal fighting that followed.

Dixie, Lady Florence

When King Cetshwayo finally arrived in London in August 1882 to argue his case for restoration he attributed the success of the campaign to get him there to one person in particular. The person who had bullied, cajoled and lobbied the great and the good to gain Cetshwayo a fair hearing in the cause of his restoration was an influential Establishment figure who was neither English nor a man. She was an eccentric Scottish aristocrat, Lady Florence Dixie.

It was ironic that Lady Florence had proved such a champion of the Zulu cause for it was her natural support for British imperial causes which had led her to southern Africa in the first place. She was born Florence Caroline Douglas on 24 May 1855, and she and her twin James were the youngest children of the 8th Marquis of Queensberry. Her eldest brother John Sholto Douglas was a robust, quick-tempered sports enthusiast, whom Florence much resembled in character; later John would become the 9th Marquis of Queensberry, remembered today for the rules of conduct he prescribed for boxing, and as the nemesis of Oscar Wilde.[93]

Florence was something of a tomboy as a child, inheriting the family interest in sport and insisting on joining in as if she were a boy. She ran, climbed, swam and rode her horses like a boy. She was a person of strong enthusiasms, a Rationalist with a firm sense of fair play who none the less had a secret romantic side. In 1875 she married Sir Alexander Beaumont 'Beau' Dixie who was also sporty, steady and – fortunately – uncomplaining, since Florence's enthusiasms were destined to leave him trailing in her wake around the world. In 1878 she met an explorer who had just returned from Patagonia and decided on the spot to go there. She did so, dragging Beau and her brothers John and James with her. Before the adventure was out she would be compelled to wade through rivers and brave earthquakes, and the party only narrowly avoided a pampas fire. On her return she wrote a travelogue, *Across Patagonia*, and when it became a bestseller she determined upon a life of adventure and travel. She was considering a trip to Alaska at the end of 1880 when news broke of the Transvaal revolt in southern Africa; Alaska was dropped and instead she set sail for Africa with the faithful Beau in tow and a commission in her pocket to write for the *Morning Post*.

They arrived at the Cape in time to learn of the decisive British defeat at Majuba (27 February 1881) and the death of the British general, Sir George Colley. Pausing only to pay a fleeting visit to King Cetshwayo – then living in exile at the Oude Moulen farm, having become something of a fashionable tourist port of call – Florence sailed on to Durban, bristling with indignation at the British humiliation. By the time they arrived in Newcastle, however, the war was all but over, and Britain was preparing to hand back the Transvaal to the Boers – who had only themselves taken it from the indigenous population a generation before. Florence visited the scenes of the recent defeats, and accompanied the Imperial Commission to Pretoria where peace was signed. The whole experience had been a bitter disappointment to her, both because of the war's outcome and because she had missed out on the action. Nothing daunted, she organised a quick whistle-stop tour to see the diamond diggings at Kimberley, and on her return to Ladysmith found that Sir Evelyn Wood – who had presided over the Transvaal peace negotiations – was about to visit Zululand. The post-war settlement there was beginning to collapse under the strain of growing tensions between the royalists who wanted Cetshwayo back and the anti-royalists who did not. Wood was about to meet Zulu *amakhosi* to inquire into the unrest; her meeting with Cetshwayo fresh in her mind, Florence decided to go along for the ride. She visited most of the battlefields, and undertook a long excursion to Ulundi where Buller, who was guiding her, got lost, and had to tip a Zulu to put them on the right track. Most importantly of all, she attended Wood's meeting with the *amakhosi* at Nhlazatshe mountain on 31 August.

The Nhlazatshe meeting was a critical moment in Zululand's collapse into civil war. Representatives of both the British-imposed new order and the old attended, the former to be reassured and the latter to complain. But even to a die-hard imperialist like Lady Florence, who sat close to Wood among the British dignitaries, it soon became apparent that the genuine grievances of the royalists were being ignored. Wood was there to reiterate the status quo; the complaints of mistreatment by their enemies from the royalists, and their requests for the return of Cetshwayo, were stifled. The meeting ended, wrote Florence, having 'accomplished no end but to disappoint many a loyal and hopeful heart, which, coming filled with the latter, returned home angry and discontented'.[94] Indeed they did, for the meeting is widely held to have heralded the true start of the Zulu civil war.

The meeting had offended Florence's sense of fair play. Increasingly convinced that Cetshwayo commanded far more support in Zululand than British propagandists before the war had insisted, she visited Bishop Colenso in Pietermaritzburg, and on her return to England stopped off once more to visit Cetshwayo at Oude Moulen. Where before she had seen him as no more than a curious figure, languishing under his righteous punishment, she now saw him as the victim of an intolerable injustice. On her return to London she took up his cause with gusto in the press – seeing off return salvoes from, among others, Lord Chelmsford and Rider Haggard – and badgered every person of influence she knew. A visit by the king to London had been mooted, and Florence was determined it would happen. There were casualties along the way in her campaign; when it transpired that she was in touch with Cetshwayo's interpreter at the Cape, R.C. Samuelson, a scandal blew up that revolved around alleged tampering with Cetshwayo's correspondence – and to Florence's dismay Samuelson was sacked. And yet she won, for Cetshwayo at last to London came, and Florence's energy and enthusiasm had contributed much to the decision to allow his visit.

The outcome, however, was not as she had hoped. Florence had advocated all along that the king must be restored to all his former territory, yet the government felt this was impractical, not least because it would mean abandoning those whom the British had set in power in 1879. The king returned, but to a portion of his old kingdom only, and the rest was confirmed in the hands of his enemies. The result was an acceleration of the civil war, the destruction of the king's rebuilt

oNdini homestead by Zibhebhu in July 1883, and ultimately the death of Cetshwayo himself.

To Florence the king's fate was a bitter disappointment, and she blamed it on the consistent weakness of British policy in Zululand. She had, however, already moved on, adopting new causes to fight for with equal determination. She became interested in Irish politics; a believer in Home Rule, she none the less opposed the Land League agitation of the 1880s, a stance which earned her an assassination attempt. She turned her back on her former passion for blood sports and became an opponent of cruelty to animals. She organised seaside holiday camps for poor children, became a firm advocate of women's rights, and she continued to write. She died in Scotland on 7 November 1905.

Dogs

Soldiers, it seems, love a pet, and certainly the British Army in the 1870s was no different. In a male-dominated environment, pets offer a reminder of finer feelings rarely displayed in an often harsh existence, reflecting a touch of humanity in contrast to the stresses of campaign life. Hounds were, of course, a feature of the life of the gentry in Victorian times, particularly those with country houses who indulged an interest in field sports, and many officers kept dogs of one sort or another, and often took them to war with them. Other ranks were seldom in a position to enjoy such luxuries, but often accumulated strays who were attracted by the smells of the cook-house and who were then seduced away by proffered scraps of food. Certainly the 2/24th had found its fair share of pets during its time on the Eastern Cape Frontier, but to the men's disappointment they were ordered to leave them behind when moving to Natal. Only Colonel H.J. Degacher's dog, a Dalmation named Flip, was excepted:

Orders were issued that no dogs could be taken, because by this time many had been collected by the men as pets.

We entrained and left for East London on the new railway, with perhaps forty dogs of all breeds, sizes and colours galloping alongside the train, encouraged by the men shouting, calling and cheering them on, and the dogs all barking and whining at being left behind. The dogs gradually fell out or they became tired, until after a few miles the only one left was Kreli the yellow dog, who continued to keep up with the train 'midst the cheers of the men [and] the barking of his chum Flip, who was on the train.

At last the Colonel ordered the train to be stopped for Kreli, and he was helped on to rejoin Flip. The Colonel's kind act was loudly cheered by everyone.[95]

Both Flip and Kreli remained with the battalion as it marched to join the Centre Column at Helpmekaar, and no doubt a few others were picked up along the way; and there is no reason to suppose that the 2/24th were any different to any other unit about to go to war. Certainly Surgeon Reynolds of Rorke's Drift fame had his terrier Dick[96] with him, and by the time the Centre Column crossed into Zululand there were many other dogs with it.

The events of 22 January fell harshly on animals as well as men. In the fury of the close-quarter fighting at iSandlwana, the Zulus stabbed at anything that moved and men, oxen, horses, mules and dogs were all killed. At Rorke's Drift later that day Surgeon Reynolds tended the wounded with Dick barking at his side.

After the fighting some of the dogs who had been in the camp at iSandlwana managed to make their way back to Rorke's Drift:

A few hours later Flip came into camp with a rope tied to his neck, and a severe spear wound in the shoulder. Everyone crowded to see and to cheer Flip, the only living thing [sic] to survive the battle where we lost a thousand killed that day.

Apparently after being wounded a Zulu led Flip off, and the dog broke away and returned to his master. The yellow dog Kreli was not seen again. In the regiment Kreli was not forgotten, we spoke of him affectionately

for many years, this kindly common Kaffir dog that we found in one war and lost in another.[97]

Flip was not the only canine survivor of the battle. *The Graphic* published a picture of

a splendid animal, who was in the thick of the fight on January 22, and was fortunate enough to escape from the carnage [and] belonged to the late Lieutenant Daly of the 24th Regiment, who was one of the victims of that disaster. 'Don' is still suffering from two large assegai wounds inflicted by the Zulus, and he will probably carry his honourable scars to the end of his life.[98]

There is a distinct possibility that 'Don' is a mis-transcription of 'Lion', the 1/24th's dog, a known survivor of iSandlwana who today has an impressive memorial in County Kilkenny in Ireland.[99]

Other survivors were not so lucky. Many ran away, terrified no doubt by the sound of battle, and returned to iSandlwana to find their masters dead. With no one to feed them, they survived by eating the carrion left on the field. According to Lieutenant Maxwell of the NNC, their end was a sorry one:

About half a mile from the camp [Rorke's Drift] I was attacked by a pack of dogs about 20, consisting of various breeds. Newfoundlands, pointers, setters, terriers etc., a few with collars. These were the dogs that had belonged to the camp at Isandhlwana and having lost their masters, and been in the fighting, had become wild and although I tried, by calling them and whistling, could not quiet them, they followed still barking and howling some 300 or 400 yards, when they left me. These were shot at different times with very few exceptions afterwards.[100]

Indeed, the luckless Army dogs were destined to share their masters' fortunes throughout the war. Arriving at the site of the Ntombe disaster on 12 March, Major Tucker of the 80th Regiment noted that in addition to the soldiers the Zulus had 'killed all the dogs save one, and that we found with an assegai wound right through its neck'.[101] When the Prince Imperial rode out on his last fatal patrol from the Thelezeni camp on 1 June the party was accompanied by a pet belonging to Bettington's Horse; the dog, too, was killed alongside the Prince in the skirmish later that day. At the battle of Ulundi on 4 July the regimental mascot of the 17th Lancers, a big cross-breed, distinguished itself at the end of the battle by running around in the long grass, sniffing out wounded Zulus and barking at them, drawing them to the attention of parties of auxiliaries who were killing any who showed signs of life.

Dogs appear in many of the photos of British troops taken on campaign, particularly officer groups. An unnamed dog sits at the feet of a study of officers of HMS *Active*, another beside officers of the 91st Regiment; another nestles on the lap of an officer of the 90th, while no fewer than three appear in a photograph of D Company of the 1/13th Regiment. Commandant Pieter Raaff was photographed standing beside his horse, with two impressive hounds.

One question about the 'dogs of war' in Zulu-land remains: who is the dog in the famous photo-graph of B Company, 2/24th, taken at Pinetown at the end of the war? It has often been identified as Pip, a terrier belonging to Lieutenant Brom-head's senior officer in B Company, Captain A.G. Godwin-Austen. Godwin-Austen was wounded on the Cape Frontier and when he returned to England apparently left Pip with Bromhead. Yet the dog in the photo appears to be a spaniel, not a terrier, and he sits beside a private soldier, not Bromhead. Pip, indeed, was probably left at the Eastern Cape, when only Flip and the ill-fated Kreli were allowed to accompany the battalion to Natal. Whoever the dog in the photo is, he was probably picked up by the company along the way of its travels after Rorke's Drift.

Eclipse

According to a warrior of the uNokhenke *ibutho*, at the height of the battle of iSandlwana

the sun turned black in the middle of the battle; we could still see it over us, or we

should have thought we had been fighting til evening. Then we got into the camp and there was a great deal of smoke and firing. Afterwards the sun came out bright again ... [102]

Of the many descriptions from Zulu sources of the eclipse which took place on 22 January 1879, this is perhaps the best. With startling symbolism the moon had passed across the face of the sun, drawing a veil of darkness over some of the blackest hours in the history of Queen Victoria's empire.

Yet the eclipse was by no means total. It began about 1pm local time (11am GMT), was at its height at about 2.30pm and ended at about 4pm. The full eclipse was visible further north, however, and even at its height the sun was only about 65 per cent obscured. Although this might have been the more noticeable on a hot, cloud-less African day, it is probable that the eclipse would not have aroused much interest had it not been for the battle. Out with Lord Chelmsford's forces at Mangeni Trooper Symons of the Natal Carbineers merely noted that the middle of the day was characterised by a heavy dullness in the air – no doubt due to a diminution of the light – and he only discovered later that an eclipse had taken place.

The event was undoubtedly more significant to the Zulus, however. Not only were they more in tune with the natural world around them but the movement of bodies in the sky was considered to reflect the attitude of the ancestral spirits with regard to important events:

It would be thought likely that the Zulus in times of war or other serious trouble should be on the look-out for changes in the sky which are supposed to foretell success or failure, and it is generally to the spirits of their ancestors that their attention is specially directed at such times ... during the Zulu war of 1879 we heard that the men were daily watching the sun to see whether it had a ring around it, whether the ring was a wide or narrow one, whether it was a perfect circle or whether it had an opening at one side ... An eclipse or an earthquake foretells a great calamity and the natives are terrified whenever an eclipse takes place.[103]

That an eclipse should take place at a time of extraordinary destruction was therefore entirely in accord with the Zulu view of the universe. The eclipse was noted, too, by men who had been skirmishing with Colonel Wood's troops around the Hlobane and Zungwini mountains, and here it was thought to augur badly for Prince Mbilini waMswati, who was already emerging as the best Zulu guerrilla leader. Curiously, according to H.W. Struben, Theophilus Shepstone also took the eclipse as a sign of impending doom:

A strange thing happened at this time. I was walking with Sir Theophilus Shepstone outside Utrecht, discussing the situation, when suddenly it became dark, and for a moment neither of us realised it was a total [sic] eclipse of the sun. When we did he said 'Struben, this may have a strange effect on the Zulus, who are superstitious.' Next day we heard of the disaster at Isandhlwana and he said to some old Kaffirs who came to hear the news, 'Umtwanami u fele, George ugwazile.' 'My child is dead, George is stabbed,' and he was quite overcome.[104]

It is possible, too, that the darkness seemed greater at iSandlwana because the air was already full of smoke and dust thrown up by the fierce hand-to-hand fighting which took place in the final stages of the battle. One warrior of the uMbonambi recalled significantly that 'the tumult and the firing was wonderful, every warrior shouted "Usutu!" as he killed anyone, and the sun got very dark like night with the smoke'.[105]

Certainly, it seems that many veterans of the war took the eclipse as a sign of catastrophe, and indeed it proved to be so; for the British on the day, certainly, but ultimately for the Zulu people for whom the long-term consequences of their victory spelt ruin and dispossession.

Ernest Grandier, Prisoner of War

On 16 April 1879, three weeks after the battle of Hlobane, the Landdrost of the Transvaal border town of Utrecht, Gerhardus Rudolph, was leading a patrol near the Zungwini mountain when he made a startling discovery. Staggering towards them in the veldt was a solitary white man. A tall, wiry, dark man in his late 20s, he was wearing a ripped and torn Irregular's jacket and a pair of infantry trousers cut off at the knee. He was battered, bruised and scratched all over, and so incoherent that Rudolph could hardly make sense of what he was saying. Rudolph's men took him to Evelyn Wood's camp at Khambula where 'Colonel Wood ordered him some brandy, but the poor man could eat nothing, he was so overjoyed at being rescued from the jaws of death'.[106]

Gradually his story emerged. His name was Ernest Grandier and he was French, a native of Bordeaux where he had once been a stonecutter; he had come to Africa, presumably to make his fortune, but like so many itinerant adventurers he had failed to do so, and on the outbreak of war he had enlisted as a trooper in Weatherley's Border Horse. He had fought with them at Hlobane on 28 March, and at the height of the battle had been captured as the Border Horse were driven across the Ityenka Nek:

We fell back across the neck assailed on all sides. I was about the last, having put a comrade on my horse and was running alongside, when a Kaffir caught me by the legs and I was made prisoner. I was taken to Mbelini's kraal, on the south side and about half way up the Inhlobane. He asked me where Shepstone was and who was the leader of this commando. I passed the night tied to a tree. Next day Umbelini riding with two or three companies took me into the middle of a large *impi*. They all threatened to kill me, but Manyanyana, the leader, a large stout man, said he would send me to Cetywayo. I was taken back to the Inhlobana and remained there until next day, when I started in charge of four men riding for Ulundi. I was walking, carrying their food.

They had previously taken all my clothes from me.[107]

When the party arrived at oNdini Cetshwayo sent for him and interrogated him, asking whether Theophilus Shepstone was present with Wood's column (it was commonly believed by the Zulus that he was, as the column had started out from the Transvaal). The king asked too after the whereabouts of Prince Hamu kaNzibe, who had recently defected, and Grandier was shown the guns taken at iSandlwana, and asked if he could work them. When it became clear that he had little intelligence to offer, Grandier was consigned to a hut under guard where 'I was fed on mealies ... being frequently beaten'.

After a few days messengers arrived to report to the king that Prince Mbilini had been killed in a skirmish. According to Grandier,

Cetywayo, on hearing of it, said he would send me to Umbelini's Kaffirs to kill. On the 13th inst., I started in charge of two Kaffirs, one armed with a muzzle-loading gun, both with assegais. About midday we were lying down, the Kaffirs being sleepy. I seized an assegai and killed the man with the gun, the other ran off. I walked all night by the stars; the next day, the 14th, I had to lie still, as I met a large *impi* driving cattle towards Ulundi; they took all the morning passing. After this I saw no Kaffirs, and walked each night. This morning (April 16th) I was trying to recognise some of the hills when I met our own people, and was brought into camp.[108]

Grandier's story spread throughout the camp at Khambula and caused a sensation. Journalists in the camp eagerly sought him out and accounts of his adventures, suitably embellished, appeared in the Natal press. In England he was the subject of several sensational engravings in the popular illustrated papers, imagined either as a heroic representative of muscular Christianity, striking down his heathen guards, or as a defiant volunteer, refusing before a savage mob to unspike the guns, or simply tied to a tree, a vulnerable white

man imperilled by darkest Africa while King Cetshwayo pondered how best to dispose of him.

Yet Grandier's time in the spotlight was short enough. Like many in the Irregular corps, his life had been largely anonymous before the war began, and even before it ended he sank back into obscurity. Whether he returned to civilian society or remained to take part in the closing stages is as unclear as his ultimate fate.

It was only after the campaign that doubts about his story began to emerge. As early as October 1879 a correspondent writing for the *Natal Mercury* had the opportunity to interview *inkosi* Mnyamana kaNgqengelele Buthelezi, King Cetshwayo's most senior adviser. Mnyamana had accompanied the force which attacked Khambula camp on 29 March, and was presumably the 'Manyanyana' referred to by Grandier. Asked about the Frenchman, however, he

contradicted the story told by Grandier. His version is that Cetshwayo handed Grandier over to the Zulus to conduct him as near as possible to the British lines, and there let him go – that there was no intention of harming him. By a curious coincidence one of these very guards was Klaas (who found the Prince Imperial's uniform) and he confirms Mnyamana's story.[109]

There were, indeed, several improbable aspects to Grandier's story, as the traveller Bertram Mitford noted:

His escape was avowedly made during the halt after the first march, to wit, within a few miles of Ulundi. But in that case it would not take long for the surviving guard to return at full speed and raise the country on the fugitive's heels, whose recapture would be but a question of a very few hours. Then, again, from Ulundi to the Zunguin, where Grandier was picked up, is a little matter of 50 miles as the crow flies, and a good deal more by any known track; further, it is extremely rugged and mountainous ... How, then, could this man, on foot and without food, find his way across unknown wilderness, exposed, as he would be, to the glance of Zulu scouting parties patrolling the hills?[110]

Mitford had his own answer to that:

[The Zulus] said that a white man had been taken prisoner and brought to Ulundi; that Cetywayo had questioned him, and had then sent him back under escort, with orders that he should be let go near Hlobane, so that he could find his way to the English camp, but they knew nothing about the killing of the guard. Their statement agreed with that of other Zulus I interrogated on the subject in various parts of the country ...[111]

Moreover, Cornelius Vijn, a young Dutch trader who had been caught up in Zululand when the war broke out, and who spent much of it under Cetshwayo's protection at one royal homestead or another, was of the opinion that Grandier's treatment was by no means as harsh during his imprisonment as he claimed: 'When they arrived, tobacco and gin (or rum) were supplied to the Whiteman by the King. Further the King ordered that no harm should be done to the prisoner, but, at the end of the war, he should return to the land of his own people.'[112]

Nor was such behaviour inconsistent with the king's known attitude towards potential white prisoners. After iSandlwana he had complained to his *izinduna* that they had failed to bring him any captured British officers, who would have been a valuable source of intelligence and useful hostages against the fortunes of war. Especially in the aftermath of the defeats at Khambula and kwaGingindlovu, the king needed bargaining counters in his dealings with the whites – and a prisoner well-treated and safely released had greater political and propaganda potential than one killed as a reprisal.

Indeed, the king's request for prisoners probably accounted for Grandier's capture in the first place, and raised questions about his story in that respect, too. As late as the 1930s Zulu veterans of the war knew of the story, but understood that Grandier had been captured not at the height of

the battle on Ityenka Nek, but afterwards, hiding among the rocks somewhere near the western end of the mountain. A prominent *induna* named Sitshitshili kaMnqandi was mentioned in connection with the capture – a significant point since by his own account Sitshitshili was aware of the king's need for prisoners, and had tried unsuccessfully to take Captain Robert Barton prisoner earlier in the day.[113]

Grandier, it seemed, had made the most of his adventures. Presumably in an attempt to deflect any criticism for allowing himself to be captured, he had portrayed himself in a heroic light during the battle – wrestled to the ground after selflessly giving up his horse – and had told his listeners largely what they wanted to hear about his time at oNdini. His story of his escape was apparently a pure fabrication. The truth, as far as can be ascertained, was more prosaic. He had apparently become separated from his unit during the rout across Ityenka Nek and, probably hiding among the rocks, had worked his way across the foot of the mountain after the battle until at last Zulus under Sitshitshili's command had found him and captured him. Sent to oNdini, he had been comparatively well treated, and when, under interrogation, it had become clear that he had no useful information, he had been sent back under Cetshwayo's orders to the vicinity of Hlobane, and there let go. He had then made his way towards Khambula and Rudolph's party had found him.

And yet his was still an extraordinary story, for Ernest Grandier would remain the only white prisoner of war captured by the Zulus during the entire campaign.

False Alarms

On the night of 6 June 1879 the war correspondent Melton Prior

was in my tent working in Zangweni camp when I heard a distant shot from our pickets, followed by another, and then two more. Instantly there was a commotion in our laager as everyone rushed off to the tents to obtain firearms or came out of them ready for eventualities, and then a volley from one of the picket's supports was distinctly heard. At the same moment our alarm bugle sounded, the tents were struck ... and we all rushed to take up our positions near the wagons ...

Suddenly some of our officers imagined they could see a black mass approaching, and gave word to fire, and instantly a most terrific fire was going on all round the laager. For some ten minutes or so the most deafening noise of musketry was kept up; horses got loose and careered about among us. Our natives appeared almost mad with fear, and the danger we ran of being shot by our own men was horrible; as it was five of our men were wounded by our own fire.

I went up to the edge of the laager, and looking over a wagon tried to see if I could catch sight of the enemy, and as I turned round I saw any number of our natives with their muskets pointing straight towards me.

I need scarcely say that I soon cleared out of that position. The brutes were firing all over the camp, and I could hear the bullets whiz through the air, from one point of the laager to another. A more disgraceful scene I have never witnessed, more particularly when we realised that six rounds of cannister were actually fired by the artillery without having seen one single enemy ...[114]

That particular scare was one of the worst of the war – among other things it nearly ended the career of John Chard, of Rorke's Drift fame, who had been on picket duty and spent an uncomfortable few minutes lying in one of the outer ditches as British bullets whistled over his head – but it was by no means a unique occurrence. The British had begun the war with an over-inflated sense of self-confidence but iSandlwana had dramatically dispelled that, converting their impression of the Zulus at a stroke from an army of despised savages to a disciplined horde of almost super-human capabilities. Exaggerated stories of the horrors of iSandlwana passed round among the reinforcements sent out from England – many of them raw recruits hurriedly drafted in

to bring the battalions up to war establishment – as soon as they reached Durban, and while these seemed implausible enough during the daytime, surrounded by the full might of the British columns, they became suddenly all too credible in the strangeness of the African night. As one of Chelmsford's ADCs, Captain Molyneux, observed, under such circumstances the panic which can suddenly take hold of even steady troops became quite irrational:

> No one can account for the madness which seizes upon bodies of men at times. It is no use saying it is only young troops who are thus affected; old ones may be less liable but they are not impervious to it.
>
> This was a rather disreputable affair, as showing what exaggerated ideas the new troops from home had of their foes, and how easily panic increases at night. There was a bright moon with fleeting clouds; so there was really no excuse for a stray bullock, or even the shadow of a cloud, being mistaken for an *impi*.[115]

Such false alarms became a feature of life in the invading army during the latter part of the war. At Eshowe – where there was a real threat of Zulu attack – the garrison frequently stood-to ready to repel an imagined assault. On one occasion troops opened fire on what they thought were white Zulu shields moving in the darkness; the following morning they found a pair of white sailor's trousers, draped over a bush by a dying fire to dry out and forgotten about. They were riddled with bullet-holes. Far more seriously, early on the morning of 6 April, during the withdrawal following the relief of Eshowe, a bad scare in Lord Chelmsford's camp cost one man his life and wounded 15 others. Pickets of the 3/60th had been posted around the camp with John Dunn's scouts beyond them; one of the pickets mistook the scouts for Zulus, fired a shot and the 60th ran back towards the camp. Dunn's scouts followed them and in the darkness were met with shots and bayonets in the belief that they were Zulu. One of Dunn's men was killed and eight more wounded, together with five men of the 60th. Chelmsford was furious and a sergeant of the 60th was court-martialled, reduced to the ranks and sentenced to five years' penal servitude.[116]

Despite such stern reactions from senior officers, false alarms were destined to continue right to the very end of the war. Another alarm took place on the night of 1 July in the British camps in the White Mfolozi, close to oNdini, just days before the battle of Ulundi, although by that time Molyneux, for one, had come to tell the difference between the sounds of a panic and of an attack. 'The rush of panic-stricken feet requires to be heard once to be remembered;' he observed ruefully, 'no enemy attacks with such velocity as the frightened attain in running away.'[117]

Flogging

On 25 February 1879 Private Woodman of the 2/3rd Regiment was given 50 lashes at the Fort Pearson camp for leaving his post while on sentry duty. A watching officer of his regiment observed the proceedings with some disdain. 'Drummers Reilly and White flogged him,' wrote Lieutenant Julius Backhouse, 'they never hurt him at all.'[118] Neither Woodman's crime nor his punishment were at all unusual in the Zulu campaign; indeed, so many were flogged during the course of it that it provoked an outcry in Parliament and led to the final abolition of flogging as a military punishment.

Flogging had been an almost universal punishment in the Napoleonic Wars, where the various levels of court-martial had virtually unlimited powers to dictate the number of lashes. The Duke of Wellington, who had decidedly fixed views of the qualities of the ordinary soldiers under his command, was a firm believer in it, and declared that men would never fight unless they were flogged to it. Traditionally the miscreant was tied to a triangle of poles – made originally from sergeants' spontoons, or pikes – and lashed with a whip consisting of nine knotted leather strips, the infamous 'cat o'nine tails'. Flogging was a public spectacle, intended to deter others as well as punish the guilty, and it was carried out before

the entire regiment drawn up in a square while drummers beat their drums to drown out the screams. It was usually a bloody business for the cat, when laid well on, stripped away the skin after a few blows, bruising and lacerating the flesh underneath. Sentences of up to 500 lashes were not uncommon; men often died under it, while hardened veterans were known to faint among the spectators. After the punishment was over – if the man survived – he was doused with salt-water which served as a crude antiseptic but did little to alleviate the pain.

By the time of Queen Victoria's accession the number of strokes had been limited to 50, and following the much-publicised failings of the Crimean War there was a widespread movement to ban it entirely. In 1867 it was limited to serious offences such as mutiny, and shortly afterwards was banned on home service. It remained as a punishment in the field, however, and during the course of the Zulu campaign a staggering 545 men were flogged for various offences including drunkenness, dereliction of duty, theft, insubordination or deserting a post. The latter was a fairly common crime, particularly among those on sentry duty at night who faced long boring hours pacing about in the cold, or in freezing rain, or simply in the inexpressibly strange African night; it was, however, regarded as a serious offence, particularly in the aftermath of iSandlwana. Deserting a post might lead to a surprise attack by the enemy, or to the more insidious evil of undermining the discipline and resolve of men already made nervous by exaggerated tales of enemy prowess. The punishment itself varied only slightly from Napoleonic days; men were stripped to the waist and tied to the wheel of a wagon or gun-carriage, and the lash laid on by battalion drummers (who were mature men, not 'boys'). The most common punishment was a dozen lashes, with two dozen or 25 for more serious offences. Although the maximum of 50 was only awarded in the face of the most serious misdemeanours, many officers, like Lieutenant Backhouse, firmly believed that flogging was an essential tool for maintaining discipline while on active service.

The frequency with which 'the cat was let out of the bag' in Zululand did arouse the notice of Parliament, however, and led to fierce debates which ultimately outlawed the practice in 1881. Flogging's direct replacement as a punishment was Field Punishment no. 1, in which the defaulter was tied to the wheel of a gun carriage for a specified length of time. Gradually, however, the Army moved away from more physical forms of punishment and towards a greater reliance on custodial sentences.

Food (British)

In theory, the allotted ration for an ordinary soldier in Zululand in 1879 offered as much by way of a varied diet as could be hoped for, given the realities of life on campaign. The daily allowance consisted of:

Beef or mutton	1.25lb
Biscuit or flour	1lb
Bread	1.5lb
Coffee	0.3oz
Or tea	0.15oz
Sugar	2oz
Lime juice	1oz
Sugar for lime juice	0.5oz
Preserved vegetables	2oz
Salt	0.5oz
Pepper	0.25oz
Preserved meat (if any)	1lb

At the very beginning of the war, Lieutenant C.E. Commeline of the 5th Company, Royal Engineers, then en route from Greytown to Helpmekaar and the border, expressed the hope that such rations were likely to prove more than sufficient:

Our dinner in camp is the same as the men's. Between Durban and Pietermaritzburg we carried tins of Australian and Chicago beef, which, with dry biscuits and coffee, makes up the repast. The beef is very good and there is a liberal allowance of it – a 2lb tin between two men per day. There is also a ration of sugar and salt, and lime juice, instead of vegetables. Altogether, the meal

is not luxurious, but it is wonderful how nice a tremendous appetite, gained by a long day's work, makes it.[119]

It is interesting to wonder whether Commeline still shared that view eight months later, at the war's end; if he did, very few of his colleagues would have agreed with him.

Food, of course, is always a major concern with any army, and the fact that the British were the invaders in 1879 meant that they could not rely on any sort of local provisioning and thus all their supplies had to be carried with them. Hundreds of tons of basic foodstuffs had to be dragged great distances across country on ox-wagons and delivered to the troops on a daily basis. This in itself had posed a logistical nightmare which had materially affected Lord Chelmsford's plan of campaign, and it meant in reality that by the time food reached the troops it was seldom as varied, or as appetising, as the ration allotment suggested. Another Engineer officer, Captain Warren Wynne, certainly found the monotony of the diet trying:

How one longs for butter, milk, and fresh vegetables, and good bread. Biscuits (sometimes very musty), and the heaviest of doughy flat-cakes or loaves, without any lubrication, are not a good substitute for home bread and butter. We get rice sometimes, which I enjoy, and compressed carrots and onions; sometimes dried beans. These, with tea, coffee, pepper, salt and lime juice, constitute our food and drink (and the tough ox we get for rations) ...[120]

Tough oxen, indeed, became the staple for officers and other ranks alike. After weeks of being bumped about in wagons, the packaging exposed alternately to heat and rain, tinned beef lost something of its appeal – it often turned to liquid sludge in the can and sometimes exploded on opening – and meat slaughtered 'on the hoof' was at least a fresh alternative. It was seldom palatable, however, for although slaughter animals did accompany the columns, the more usual solution was to consume the tough transport oxen that died along the roadside from over-work. According to Captain Montague of the 94th,

As to eating, beef – everlasting beef – was our sole support. We got to hate the sight of an ox. All day we had to witness his invincible dislike to go with us in the wagons; and every night we had to see him again, boiled, roasted, or stewed, for dinner. We baked him in pies, we boiled him in puddings, we chopped him fine as mince, we mixed him in stews; but all with the same result. The ox revenged his sufferings on us even when cut into steak.

No wonder one's thoughts turned sometimes to the dinners we should order when we got home again. Alas! When our anticipations would be realised, our appetites would no longer remain as they were then. Of all things provocative of a good dinner, the Zulu air was the best; pity 'twas we got so much of it, while obtaining so little with which to satisfy its demands.[121]

Even for an officer, life in the field was very different to that imagined by the British public at home reading about their adventures:

We ragged ones used to look with envy on the pictures in the *Illustrated London News* about the Afghan War. There the mess-tent of some regiment was shown, wherein was an officer digging into a plump ham; several servants handing round 'Simpkin';[122] and most striking of all, a tablecloth on the table. Why, there was not a mess in Zululand, unless it were the General's; our waiters were 'Tommy Atkins', simple and fairly pure; a ham would have commanded the price of a dinner for six at the Club if it had put in an appearance; and as for liquor, well – it was spoken under one's breath that Wood drank champagne every night, only we did not believe it. Lucky the man who had a little bad rum; he will have many friends, and will not go, as we did go so often, wet, cold and cheerless to bed.

The craving for jam was insatiable, and rather expensive. The few tins which remained after Ulundi were beyond price. It must be remembered that we [officers] had entered the land more than a month ago with an allowance of twenty pounds apiece for stores and cooking pots, and the latter weigh heavily. Men at home who 'never touch sweets', in Zululand treasured up a pot of jam as a miser does gold.

'Jam!' cried a well-known correspondent, 'I have not tasted it for weeks; don't bring it out, or I shall finish the pot!' It came out of the want of vegetable food. Beef, nothing but beef. We catch our ox by day, kill and eat him on the next, and repeat the operation on every succeeding day.[123]

The quality of the beef, even that distributed to the officers, usually reflected the tough life of the ox. At Eshowe Captain Pelly Clarke grumbled that there was no fat on it, and that 'our "pound of flesh" would not fry without it'.[124] And the officers, of course, were in a much better position than the men to take advantage of the rare opportunities to vary their diet. Now and then a few luxuries would appear in camp – squirrelled away since their purchase from a store or passing trader on the border – and would be consumed with naked relish. Captain Wynne recalled that a wagon left behind at Eshowe after the departure of the Natal Volunteers was found to contain a windfall of edible delights:

Lieut. Main, of course, and I grub together, i.e. join rations, but we all four, i.e. Courtney and Willock as well, sit at one table for meals under a pleasant shady tree, which we monopolised from the first. There we chew the generally very tough, much stewed ox, with, as a rule, about a tablespoon of preserved carrots, sometimes some large haricot beans. These, and either biscuit, or a kind of 'fadge', manufactured by my servant out of Boer's meal, a sort of oatmeal, is our daily food at breakfast, lunch and dinner; in fact, every meal is the same, except that we have coffee at breakfast and tea at dinner. I really do not mind it but most fellows get very tired of it and complain of insufficiency. Yesterday, there was a sale of the private effects found in the wagons left behind by the Mounted Volunteers who came with us, but returned to Natal when the news of the disaster reached us, on 28th January. The following is a sample of the prices which the articles fetched. The auction was open to both officers and men. One ham (12lb) £6 5s. Tins of condensed milk, 26s each. Small tin of cocoa, 11s 6d. Bottle of curry powder (small) 23s. Boxes of matches (½d boxes) 6s per dozen. I need scarcely tell you that this child bought nothing on this occasion.[125]

Nor, presumably, did many of the men, for whom these prices were well beyond the reach of their daily pay of a shilling (minus deductions). Indeed, as Trooper Mossop of the Frontier Light Horse commented, the daily ration for the men was even less appealing than that enjoyed by the officers:

> when the tea was ready we would have our dinner, composed of half a small tin of bully and a couple of hard, thick, round biscuits, which could be boiled all day, the only result being that the outer skin blistered, leaving the inside as hard and dry as ever.[126]

Evelyn Wood, who was generally careful of the welfare of his men, attempted to vary the monotony of the 'biscuit and beef' diet by baking bread. His column was accompanied by a field bakery throughout the war and produced a daily quota of fresh bread made largely from ground mealies. While it no doubt provided some welcome variety, the evidence suggests it was not always of the highest quality: 'I should like you to see the bread we have served out to us,' grumbled a private of the 90th Regiment in a letter home to his parents, 'made of Indian corn, or, what we call it, mealies, and half of it sand'.[127] Some of the Irregulars or Volunteer units, when issued with coarse flour or mealies

instead of bread or biscuit, attempted to make something of it by the old Voortrekker practice of baking it in an oven made from a termite-heap. Ant-heaps were a feature of the open grassland in Zululand, and the tough mound could be broken open and hollowed out near the base, and a fire stoked in the hole.

For the most part the men received a lump of meat, roughly hewn from the carcass and often still on the bone, which regimental cooks had to make as palatable as possible, often by boiling it in a tin on an open fire. And while coffee and tea were a prop of military life in the field, they too were an unpleasant shadow of their equivalents in civilian life. There was usually too little of each to go round, the tea was full of dust and the coffee beans hard, and the water itself, drawn from the nearest stream, was often muddy and contaminated.

Where possible, the troops attempted to vary their rations with food procured by foraging. Now and then the officers might have been able to shoot the odd bird or buck, while Zulu homesteads were diligently searched for foodstuffs; often to little avail, since most Zulu civilians retired before the British advance, driving away their cattle and hiding their grain supplies.

At Eshowe, during its three-month investment by the Zulus, the situation was further exacerbated by the shortage of rations. With 1,700 men to feed from the supplies he first brought with him, Pearson was keen to eke them out as much as possible, and minor forays against nearby Zulu villages became a feature of life among the garrison. 'Occasionally,' wrote Lieutenant Lloyd RA, 'when our troops made a raid on the Zulu mealie fields, a large supply was brought into camp, we then had an entrée of roast mealies.'[128] Most prized of all was an occasional crop of pumpkins which fell into the garrison's hands – to be enjoyed, of course, primarily by the officers. According to Captain Pelly Clarke the pumpkin was a thing of wonder: 'Boiled as a vegetable or cut into stews! Frittered pumpkins! Pumpkin-pie! (just like a good apple tart). Pumpkin squash! There is no end to the variety of dishes you can make with it. Its tops make a nice green vegetable, too.'[129]

Some, of course, were better able to take advantage of their limited rations than others, and at Eshowe many a soldier turned his head enviously towards that section of the fort occupied by the Naval Brigade:

The resource and handiness of the blue-jackets was a considerable cause of amusement and wonder to the rest of the garrison. No matter how short the supply of food, nor the time of day, Jack always seemed to have something to cook, and small parties of men were preparing little snacks of some dainty-smelling dish at all hours.[130]

There was, however, one last trial to be endured before cooked food could be enjoyed, wherever the soldiers were – flies. Clouds of them followed the British columns, buzzing around the men, settling on sweaty faces in search of the moisture and descending on food wherever it was prepared. 'To get a cup of tea or coffee one had to cover the tea-cup with one's hand,' wrote one officer, 'leaving only enough room for the spout of the kettle while someone else poured the tea in – and even then they got in.'

But in the final analysis, if the food issued to the British troops in Zululand was unappealing, it was never entirely inadequate. Even by the end of the siege of Eshowe – where troops faced the most prolonged hardship of the war – the garrison had managed to eat enough to keep themselves fit and active. 'Many in our relief expected to find a lot of skeletons in the fort,' commented Gunner Carroll of the Royal Marine Artillery, 'but thank God we were not so bad off as all that.'[131] Indeed, as Lieutenant Lloyd RA explained, they were actually in a position to offer some comfort to their rescuers:

The relief column had marched up on the shortest possible rations. They therefore informed us that they had suffered very much from the pangs of hunger, and felt they undoubtedly had come to the worst place for assuaging their appetites. However, as luck would have it, much to their surprise, we managed to assist them, for we had carefully put aside three days' full provisions, in case we should be forced at any time to cut our way back to British territory. These rations were produced, and our gallant 'relievers' enjoyed a hearty meal after their exertions of the past five days.

But it was remarked that most of the newspaper correspondents reported that the garrison of Ekowe had suffered but little from the scarcity of food, that they found the place well-stocked with provisions, and one of them went so far as to say that he never enjoyed a better meal in his life than that supplied by the starved-out heroes of Ekowe. The real truth being that they were gloating over these three days' provisions which we had treasured for so many days, and had longed to 'be at' on so many occasions.[132]

In that, although they were an invading army on foreign territory, the British – curiously – held something of an advantage over the Zulus.

Food (Zulu)
After the battle of Khambula on 28 March, Trooper George Mossop went over some of the British positions overrun temporarily by the Zulus during the battle, and noticed a curious fact:

The next morning I went into the cattle laager where a number of Zulus were killed, and I found several with their mouths full of stiff ... porridge which they had taken from the wagon natives' pots; they had been shot before swallowing it. They could not resist the sight of food even in the midst of the battle.

Some years later I spoke to many Zulus who had taken part in the fight, and they all told the same story: 'We had no strength; for three days we knew no food!'[133]

While this impression is undoubtedly exaggerated, there is no doubt that provisioning their troops in the field in 1879 remained problematic for the Zulus. Unlike the British, they had no extensive logistical support system, and no allotment of daily rations; they obtained food where they could, and if they could not find it, they went hungry. In fact, it was impossible to sustain a Zulu army in the field for a long period of time partly because of the problems of feeding it, and in 1879 the difficulty was compounded by the fact that the army was operating on its home ground.

When a Zulu army was assembled and dispatched on campaign, it was the usual practice for the king to provide a number of cattle for slaughter. These were driven alongside the army and slaughtered on a daily basis, the meat being butchered and distributed to the men in groups, who then cooked it as best they could over an open fire, often managing to do little more than scorch the outside leaving the middle raw and bloody. It was also common for non-combatants to accompany the army for the first two or three days of the march. These were principally young boys, *izindibi*, who had not yet been mustered into an *ibutho*, and whose duties in civilian life included carrying food, sleeping-mats and shields for their fathers or elder brothers on long journeys. They performed this same service for their elders when on campaign, wrapping up roasted mealie cobs inside the mats, and on the first day of march they might even be accompanied by a few girls, walking at a safe distance to the rear, carrying pumpkins or pots of drinking water on their heads. To prevent them being exposed to the risks of combat, however, these carriers were supposed to return home after a day or two, once the food they carried had been consumed. While some of the boys often made excuses to stay with the army in the hope of seeing something of the coming action, the fact was that their provisions were soon exhausted. Water was procured by the simple expedient of bivouacking close to a river or stream each night.

In the early days of the kingdom, a march of two or three days had often been sufficient to take the army beyond the country's borders, where it might then legitimately live by foraging.

Even in January 1879, however, the army moved slowly to the front, following Cetshwayo's directive that they should not tire themselves, with the result that even before they drew within reach of the British many of the Zulus were hungry. Foraging parties were sent out to round up grain supplies or cattle, but as they were on Zulu soil this created some tension with the very civilian population on whose behalf they were supposed to be fighting. A Zulu boy named Muziwento described an encounter with foragers from the main army on the eve of iSandlwana.

in the afternoon there appeared in the fog the Bongoza regiment. They saw the many sheep belonging to our father and other people. Up [they came] and said 'A bit of food for us this, master!' They stabbed some of the sheep; they drained our calabashes; they took the sheep away with them. Suddenly one of the warriors espied an exceedingly fine kid. He seized it. Our father seized it, and the warrior seized it too. The next moment up came the induna and scolded the regiment. The men ran off and continued their march.[134]

While the Zulu commanders were undoubtedly aware of the delicate situation in which they found themselves, the fact remained that an army in the region of 25,000 men had to be fed. Foragers continued to operate, and indeed it was the discovery of one of these parties by British patrols that precipitated the battle at iSandlwana on 22 January.

It was the usual Zulu habit to eat two meals a day, one in mid-morning and the other in the evening, and this undoubtedly contributed to the hunger that Zulu veterans complained of in the field, for they were often sent into battle before eating. At iSandlwana one warrior grumbled that he had to abandon his breakfast of a roasted mealie-cob when a false alarm brought some of the *amabutho* out of their bivouac in the Ngwebeni valley, and up on to the iNyoni heights overlooking iSandlwana; he had only just returned to the valley and begun to think of his breakfast again when the battle began in earnest.

During the Khambula campaign, towards the end of March, the Zulu army had moved north-west from oNdini, passing through country that was sparsely populated. Fifty years before, the white trader Henry Francis Fynn had noticed Shaka's army break discipline and rush for water in the same area; in 1879 it is probably true that food had been scarce for days before the army reached its objective. And on the day of the battle the *amabutho* had formed up early at their bivouac, and marched straight towards the British camp at Khambula; there had certainly been no time to eat before the battle began, and the aban-doned porridge-pots of the black wagon-drivers in the British camp had proved too tempting to ignore. There was worse to come, for the battle was a catastrophic defeat for the Zulus, and their men were faced with a harrowing flight to escape the British pursuit, and for the survivors there was a long walk home. It is unlikely that any of them ate properly until days afterwards.

During the second invasion Lord Chelmsford realised that food was a potential Zulu weak-ness, and he authorised his men to wage a war of attrition, deliberately burning grain stores in ordinary homesteads they encountered during the march to oNdini, and carrying away what-ever cattle they could find. This undoubtedly caused some hardship to the non-combatant Zulu population, though not perhaps as much as Chelmsford hoped – most Zulus simply went into hiding before the British advance, taking whatever food and cattle they could carry to safety, and secreting much of the rest. While it may have contributed to the gradual erosion of the will of the population at large to resist, such a policy did little to materially damage the operations of the main Zulu army, for as the war progressed further and further into Zululand the army by definition operated increasingly on its own turf. When the final battle took place at Ulundi on 4 July, the *amabutho* were scattered within sight of the very royal homesteads which served them as barracks.

Nevertheless, it is interesting to note that as British troops patrolled the country in the after-math of the victory, they were met with a number of expressions of relief from ordinary Zulus who welcomed the return to peace 'that we may now plough again'.

Forts

In 1882, travelling through the Zulu battlefields in turn, Bertram Mitford had the opportunity to discuss the tactical lessons of the war with many Zulu veterans he met. On one occasion he was offered a succinct insight into the difficulties faced by the Zulus at Rorke's Drift:

'But at Rorke's Drift – there were no big guns there, and the English could have stood here (making my hand into a hollow) while the Zulus were everywhere; how is it that you didn't make a better fight of it?'

'The soldiers were behind a *schaans* (breastwork), and,' added the narrator signi-ficantly, showing all his ivories, 'they were in a corner.'[135]

The British success at Rorke's Drift, in sharp contrast to iSandlwana that same day, starkly illuminated the respective strengths and weak-nesses of the opposing armies, and by so doing transformed the nature of the war. Although the Zulus were well organised and disciplined, an army of courageous individuals, possessed of an aggressive ethic and led by experienced and intuitive officers, they relied essentially for their hope of victory on their ability to come to close quarters as quickly as possible, in order to maximise the advantages afforded by their numbers and by their hand-to-hand weapons. It was this aspect which Lord Chelmsford had so woefully underestimated at the beginning of the war, trusting to his superior firepower to disrupt Zulu attacks long before they struck home. The shortcomings of the open-order tactics he had initially advocated were painfully exposed at iSandlwana, but Rorke's Drift, just a few hours later, proved that the Zulus could be put at a severe disadvantage by even the flimsiest of improvised barricades. It was a lesson which local settlers had tried in vain to convince Chelmsford of before the war began; at the battle of Ncome ('Bloedrivier') in December 1838 an outnumbered Boer force had been able to inflict heavy casualties on a much larger Zulu force at a cost of just a few men wounded. Although the nature of Zulu weapons had to some extent changed by 1879 – they possessed many more firearms – the fact remained that merely by keeping the Zulus beyond arm's reach their effectiveness in battle could be largely blunted.

This realisation turned the Anglo-Zulu War from one initially visualised by the British as one of free strategic movement to one increasingly dominated by fortification.

Fortifications had, in fact, been a mainstay of colonial Natal's programme of civilian defence even before the war began. In 1861, during a brief political crisis with the Zulu kingdom – the result of the colony harbouring rival members of the Zulu Royal House in the aftermath of Prince Cetshwayo's victory in 'the war of the princes' – the Natal authorities had constructed a number of fortifications along the border. Known as laagers, an Afrikaans word which technically referred to fortifications made by encircling wagons, these were intended to provide a secure place of refuge for the settler population in the event of a Zulu attack. Fort Durnford outside Ladysmith, designed by Major Anthony Durnford RE and begun in 1874 as a response to the 'rebellion' of *inkosi* Langalibalele kaMthimkhulu, was an impressive stone bastion and had been kept in good repair, but most of the rest were simple earthworks, and although there were some hopes that they might prove serviceable as tension mounted again in late 1878, in fact they had fallen into such disrepair as to be useless. With war imminent, the colonial administration again authorised the creation of a number of civilian laagers. The most impressive of these was Fort Pine, built on the Biggarsberg ridge above the Mzinyathi not far from Helpmekaar. This had been started in 1879 and was planned as a stone fort with barracks to house local volunteers. Although it became a bastion of border defence in the aftermath of iSandlwana – and a refuge for local settlers – it was by no means complete, only the outside walls having been built. At the height of the invasion scare following the British defeat,

both civilians and garrisons alike lived out of tents and wagons crammed unhygienically into the muddy interior. Other smaller laagers were built near or close to settler villages along the length of the frontier. Their exact size and design depended on the number of settlers they were expected to shelter, and many incorporated existing structures. The most popular design was simply a large oblong with one or more projecting bastions at the corners to provide flanking fire. Most were made of dry stone, and the more sophisticated included high loop-holes to fire through with raised firing-steps inside. In some areas border farmers considered the public fortifications inadequate and erected their own on their private land. After iSandlwana, such was the panic at the prospect of a Zulu counter-invasion that large towns many miles from the border were hastily put into a state of defence. In Pietermaritzburg the Court House was fortified and loop-holed, while at Durban plans were drawn up to defend key buildings and a wooden palisade was built across the Point – a narrow spit of land at the mouth of the harbour – with a view to protecting women and children.

It is worth noting that these plans were only for the benefit of the settler population. No provision was made to defend Natal's African population; indeed, despite the fact that the African population had historical grievances against the Zulu kings, and had been heavily pressurised into providing auxiliary troops, they were not only left to fend for themselves but there was a widespread suspicion that they would side with the Zulus.

In the event, although the civilian laagers provided secure bases along the borders – from which colonial troops sometimes made forays into Zululand – they were never attacked by the Zulus, and their effectiveness in action therefore went untested. Their very existence, however, was undoubtedly encouraging to the settler population, and to that extent they must be judged a success as Natal's first line of psychological as well as practical defence.

When the invasion began in January 1879, both Lord Chelmsford and the Zulus had hoped for a rapid war of manoeuvre (or as rapid as

Chelmsford's cumbersome baggage trains would allow). Both needed to bring the war to a decisive conclusion as quickly as possible, Chelmsford in pursuit of Frere's political objectives, and to head off potential objections from London, and Cetshwayo because the Zulu army could not be maintained for long in the field, and the war took place at harvest-time. Chelmsford, in the standing orders issued before the campaign began, instructed that permanent camps should be at least partially constructed for their own protection. Over-confident as he was in the first week of the war, he clearly had a very specific interpretation of that in mind – he meant not halts on the line of invasion, but depots that were constructed with the intent of remaining in use for a significant period. Thus he did not consider iSandlwana a permanent camp because he intended to advance within days and abandon it, and so did not entrench it; on the other hand, both Evelyn Wood and Charles Pearson entrenched their bases on the Zulu border (Forts Thinta and Tenedos respectively) because they intended to use them as the anchor for their future advance.

After the failures of January, Chelmsford became the subject of considerable criticism for not entrenching the camp at iSandlwana. In response he pointed out that his transport wagons could not be used to form a Boer-style laager because they were in constant use (he occupied iSandlwana on 20 January, unloaded the supply wagons on the 21st, and had intended to send them back to Rorke's Drift on the 22nd before advancing the entire column to Mangeni), while the camp was too extended, and the ground too hard, to entrench it. These were, of course, perfectly legitimate judgements at the time, although their shortcomings in hindsight are obvious enough. It is also worth noting that at his base near Thinta's Kop – also a hard and stony landscape – Evelyn Wood had opted not to protect his entire perimeter but to build small stone bastions at key points around it.

Some idea of how a permanent camp might be protected is afforded by the complex at the Lower Thukela drift. One of the old 1861 forts, Fort Williamson, lay nearby but with the arrival of the first British troops in November 1878 it

was decided that rather than repair it a new bastion should be built on a high knoll directly overlooking the crossing. This was built by men of the 3rd Regiment ('The Buffs') with a solitary Engineer, Lieutenant T.R. Main, to advise them, and it was named Fort Pearson after their commanding officer. It was simple but effective in design – a series of trenches with inner ramparts which followed the contours of the knoll. With artillery mounted in the centre on top, and a sheer cliff-face dropping into the river, it was virtually impregnable. As Pearson's troops assembled close by they camped in the shadow of the fort, and some threw up simple entrenchments around their tents.

After Pearson had crossed into Zululand, another fort was built on the opposite (Zulu) bank to secure the bridgehead. By this time the column had been joined by a company of Engineers under Captain Warren R.C. Wynne, who would prove to be one of the most hard-worked Engineer officers throughout the campaign. It fell to Wynne to design the new fort. Built, as he admitted, on indifferent ground, it was a large earthwork, roughly hexagonal in shape, the sides being of different lengths (giving the impression of a rather 'squashed up' symmetry), and with one projecting bastion. Since the soil was rather softer in the coastal theatre, Wynne was able to dig an outer trench up to 6 feet deep, with the soil piled up inside to form a rampart. Firing-steps were built inside to enable the defenders to fire over the top of the rampart. In due course the ramparts were revetted – reinforced with stakes and gabions (wicker baskets filled with soil) – and an internal partition was constructed to prevent dropping fire sweeping across the interior. The approaches were screened with *trous-de-loup* or 'wolf pits' – holes with sharpened stakes set in them – and with wire entanglements. The wire was not barbed but was simply strung zig-zag fashion between stakes driven into the ground among the long grass to provide a mesh that was largely hidden by the grass and was intended to trip up any attackers.

Fort Tenedos established something of a precedent for the design of fortifications in Zululand. It was extremely simple by contemporary military standards, but although British military engineers in the 1870s were well versed in the theories of the day, the practical need in Zululand was modest. The Zulus did not possess artillery of any sort, so the complex defences constructed in the American Civil War and the Franco-Prussian War were unnecessary; all that was needed was something that would physically stop a close-quarter rush while at the same time protecting the defenders from rudimentary return fire. Wynne's design also reflected the fundamental principle that would so dominate war on the Western Front in Europe a generation later – the idea that an enemy should be delayed close to the works in a position which exposed them to maximum damage from the garrison's fire.

Wynne had scarcely completed Fort Tenedos when Pearson began his advance, taking the Engineers with him. On 23 January Pearson occupied the deserted Norwegian mission-station at Eshowe. Chelmsford had originally intended that this should be a forward supply depot and Pearson had already begun plans to fortify the post before he received news of iSandlwana. Obviously, however, the Zulu victory on the 22nd had destroyed Chelmsford's integrated plans and Pearson was instructed to act on his own initiative. He decided to retain much of his column at Eshowe but sent back his mounted troops and auxiliaries to reduce the strain on supplies – a decision which inevitably made Wynne's task more challenging. Some 1,700 men – plus the column's transport wagons and oxen – had to be secured in a position constructed around the existing structures.

The Eshowe fort would prove to be the most sophisticated built in Zululand by the British throughout the entire campaign. The mission station consisted of a church with a bell-tower and several outbuildings. The church was loop-holed and a field hospital placed there, and the tower turned into a look-out post. The other buildings were used to store supplies. Since Pearson believed a Zulu attack might be imminent, Wynne quickly threw a trench and rampart around the perimeter, enclosing an area about 150 yards long by 50 wide. The column's wagons were drawn into the interior and incorporated into the ramparts, both strengthening the defences and – since there was no room to erect tents inside the fort at night – providing basic shelter for the men, who slept on the ground under the wagon-beds. When no Zulu attack materialised, Wynne was able to improve his basic design and the fort continued to develop throughout the period of occupation. A small wagon-laager was constructed to contain the draught oxen at night, and the approaches were screened with wire and *trous-de-loup*. A wooden drawbridge was built over the trench at the main entrance and was raised every night. At one end, where a natural slope created 'dead ground' dangerously close by, Wynne constructed a stockade. This was built between the trunks of existing trees, which were reinforced with bags of earth, and it included a double-tier of firing platforms. A caponnier – a covered way with loop-holes to fire through – was built jutting out into the longest line of the trench to enable a handful of defenders to fire down the length of it. The trenches themselves were heavily revetted.

The fort at the Eshowe mission was destined to be occupied for three months before Chelmsford at last relieved it. During that time it was an uncomfortable place to live – at night the entire garrison slept within the walls, on ground churned to mud by the frequent rainfall and fouled by the column's animals – but always a secure one. Although the Zulus constantly harassed the column's outlying patrols, ambushing vedettes and sniping at work-parties, they never mounted a direct assault on the fort itself; both they and the garrison appreciated that it would have been an extremely difficult position to take. Wynne himself remained indefatigable throughout the siege, constantly working to improve the position and the garrison's lot. Pearson had no signalling equipment with him, and it was Wynne who tried to rectify this, his improvisations ranging from a hot-air balloon to a paper screen intended as a backdrop for semaphore. When the Zulus attempted to disrupt the work of a fatigue party improving the road to the fort – they came down at night and pulled up the marker stakes – Wynne improvised a 'torpedo' booby-trap to discourage them. He buried an explosive charge, set a friction detonator and tied the lanyard to the stake; when the Zulus pulled up the stake, they set off the charge.

Sadly, the constant pressure of his duties and the strain of his responsibilities affected Wynne's health; by the time Eshowe was relieved he was suffering from the dysentery which afflicted the garrison in general, and he died at Fort Pearson on 19 April, his 36th birthday. The fort he created at Eshowe was abandoned and the surrounding trenches can still be seen to this day, a fitting tribute to his endeavours.

In the Centre Column – famously – no attempt was made by Lord Chelmsford or his column commander, Glyn, to fortify the depots at either Helpmekaar or Rorke's Drift. The overrunning of the camp at iSandlwana on 22 January left these bases exposed, and indeed that at Rorke's Drift came under sustained attack later that day. The presence of the mission buildings and up-wards of thirty wagon-loads of supplies – due to go forward to iSandlwana that day – enabled the garrison to improvise an effective fortification behind which they withstood more than ten hours of Zulu attacks. The fortifications at Rorke's Drift were hardly sophisticated – there was no time to dig entrenchments or to make earth-work ramparts, and they consisted of nothing more than barricades of mealie-bags and biscuit boxes – but they were sufficient to confirm the fundamental weakness of Zulu attacks. Along the front of the post the barricades were piled along the top of a natural ledge, giving the defenders a significant height advantage; against it the Zulus were no more able to penetrate the British lines, and were just as exposed to a terrible killing zone, than if they had been attacking Wynne's ramparts at Eshowe.

In the aftermath of iSandlwana and Rorke's Drift British garrisons hurried to secure them-selves behind even the most basic of fortifications. The post at Helpmekaar was protected much as Eshowe would be, by a surrounding ditch and rampart, reinforced with supply wagons barri-caded with mealie-bags. Further down the line of communication, once the initial panic had passed, a battalion of NNC built an impressive dry-stone

fort, named Fort Bengough, on top of a knoll beside the Msinga road.

Rorke's Drift itself, after the battle, was properly fortified. The ruins of the hospital build-ing – gutted during the battle – were torn down and the remaining storehouse protected by a high stone wall with raised firing platforms and loop-holes. This post – known as Fort Brom-head – was home to the survivors of the Centre Column for over two months. And a very un-comfortable home it was too, for the fear of a Zulu attack was a real one and false alarms were common, particularly among men whose nerves had been damaged by the sights of the iSandl-wana battlefield. It was cramped and insanitary, too, for there was no room for tents and the men slept in the open at night, often in the rain – although B Company was allowed a post of honour, sleeping under the eaves of the store-house, protected by tarpaulins. When by March the Zulu attacks had failed to materialise, it was decided to construct a new purpose-built fort closer to the river – the first one on the central border designed for the purpose. It was con-structed on a knoll commanding the river crossing and consisted of an outer trench and inner dry-stone walls. It was oblong in shape with bastions at the corners and included a covered area inside to shelter the sleeping garrison at night. Empty bottles were thrown into the trenches to smash to provide a further obstacle and aloes – which have sharp spiky leaves – were planted on the approaches to form an *abattis*. The new fort assumed the name Fort Revenge among the troops but Lord Chelmsford, uncomfortable at the association, directed that it be called Fort Melvill instead, and early in April the garrison at the mission station was at last moved down from the old battlefield.

In response to the iSandlwana disaster Evelyn Wood, too, had moved his camp. Deciding that his first camp at Fort Thinta left the Transvaal border village at Utrecht too exposed he selected a new position at Khambula, a few miles to the west of Zungwini mountain. This position he also fortified. The camp itself was laid out on a ridge top and consisted of two large permanent wagon-laagers and a small earthwork fort cresting a high point. The fort itself was small – 30 yards long and less than 10 wide – and followed the usual pattern of an outside trench and inner rampart. As at Fort Thinta, however, it was primarily intended as an anchor-point for the defence, and the laagers themselves were entrenched by the simple expedient of cutting a shallow trench around them and piling the sods up between the wagon wheels.

On 29 March Wood's camp at Khambula was the subject of a sustained attack by the same Zulu army that had triumphed at iSandlwana. The battle proved to be the turning-point of the war, and vindicated the growing British reliance on fortifications. Despite determined attacks on all sides, the Zulus only managed to drive the British out of the smaller of their two laagers, although their firepower during the battle was greatly improved by the addition of Martini-Henry rifles captured at iSandlwana. Moreover the effort necessary to achieve even this limited success proved hugely costly; nearly 800 men were shot down close to the British positions, among them many of their most experienced and courageous *izinduna* who had conspicuously led the attacks.

Within days, at kwaGingindlovu in the coastal sector, Lord Chelmsford himself had won a second victory, again relying on an element of fortification by the simple expediency of entrenching his laager.

It was the second invasion, however, which was truly the war of fortification. Politically and militarily Chelmsford could not afford another iSandlwana, and he amended his standing orders to insist that every temporary halt on the line of advance be protected by a work of some description. In the coastal sector the newly created 1st Division built a number of quite major earthworks, notably Fort Crealock, guarding a drift on the amaTigulu river, Fort Chelmsford, on the Nyezane, and Fort Napoleon on the Mlalazi. Surviving evidence suggests that the designs of those forts was broadly similar, consisting of a roughly square profile with one or two projecting bastions. In each case the work consisted of an outer trench and inner rampart, and Fort Chelmsford at least included sheds inside to

protect a stockpile of supplies. In the event the 1st Division was never attacked and its war consisted largely of an endless round of convoy duty. Nevertheless, its contribution to the British victory should not be underestimated since its presence served to intimidate and discourage the *amakhosi* living in the coastal districts.

The forts built by the combined 2nd Division and Flying Column during their advance on oNdini were smaller but no less important. The two columns advanced in tandem, keeping within sight of each other, and pausing now and then to bring up supplies. At each stage they fortified their halts – the fort at Landman's Drift, Fort Whitehead, Fort Newdigate, Fort Marshall, Fort Evelyn and finally, on the banks of the White Mfolozi opposite oNdini, Fort Nolela. In each case the actual works were tiny, and usually consisted of two earthworks sometimes no more than 10 yards square. The redoubts were situated at some distance apart with a view to screening a camp in between. At Fort Newdigate the redoubts were actually designed to provide 'anchors' at the opposite corners of a large diamond-shaped wagon-laager which, with the arrival of each new supply convoy, was then constructed around it. When the supplies were unloaded, the boxes were apparently stacked between the forts to provide a walkway which was then covered over with tarpaulins. Fort Nolela, on the other hand, was simply a square dry-stone redoubt built on a high point above the camp.

Even after Chelmsford's victory at Ulundi on 4 July the British continued to build small forts during the pacification operations, either to protect withdrawing columns, to serve as bases for the pursuit of the king, or to intimidate recalcitrant *amakhosi*.

The fact that none of the forts built during the second invasion was ever attacked has robbed them of the glamour which has historically been associated with the great battles of January and March, or even of the dogged defence of Eshowe. For their garrisons, indeed, life there was monotonous and often uncomfortable. Nevertheless, they were undeniably a major factor in the ultimate British victory for they provided tangible proof of the inexorable British advance and were, for the Zulus, a disturbing reminder of their own tactical limitations.

As King Cetshwayo himself put it, advising his army against attacking British entrenchments, 'Do not put your faces into the lair of the wild beasts; you are sure to get clawed'.

Gallantry Awards (British)

In 1879 the means by which exceptional gallantry in battle might be recognised within the British Army were limited. Both officers and other ranks might be promoted – brevet ranks were often awarded to officers for distinction in the field – but only two decorations then existed to honour extreme courage. Both were comparatively new awards – the Victoria Cross had been instituted in 1857 and the Distinguished Conduct Medal in 1854. The Victoria Cross, with its deliberately and conspicuously egalitarian design – a plain Maltese cross in bronze with the words 'For Valour', suspended from its characteristic crimson ribbon – had been specifically intended as a recognition for gallantry across the ranks and has remained Britain's senior gallantry award. The silver Distinguished Conduct Medal was intended to recognise gallantry among the other ranks, and was not available to officers.[136] A total of twenty-three Victoria Crosses were awarded for the Zulu campaign (two of them posthumously in 1907) along with fifteen Distinguished Conduct Medals. Of the VCs, three were awarded for iSandlwana, eleven for Rorke's Drift, one for Ntombe, four for Hlobane,[137] one for Khambula and three for the action at oNdini on 3 July. Five DCMs were awarded for Rorke's Drift, three for Hlobane,[138] three for Khambula, one for the action on 3 July and three for Ulundi.

A number of factors limited eligibility for the Victoria Cross. No provision existed at that time for it to be awarded to men killed in action; it was only available to those who had survived their own acts of extraordinary bravery. Not until the rules were changed in 1907 were the first posthumous awards granted, including awards to Lieutenants Teignmouth Melvill and Neville Coghill of the 1/24th, killed while attempting to save the Colour at iSandlwana. Also, the act of courage itself was supposed to be witnessed and

validated by an officer – a limitation which itself disqualified many acts of heroism.[139]

There was undoubtedly courage aplenty in Zululand in 1879 but its recognition remained something of a lottery, often influenced by the patronage or opposition of senior officers. Of the VCs awarded at Rorke's Drift – the largest number ever for a single action[140] – the first eight to be announced in the *London Gazette* were to the senior commander, Lieutenant Chard RE, and to Lieutenant Bromhead and six men of the 24th. To both Lord Chelmsford and the Disraeli administration, however, Rorke's Drift represented a piece of good news at the end of an otherwise bleak day, and they were undoubtedly responsive to recommendations for further awards. Many of these were the result of regimental lobbying by those keen that the participation of their corps be recognised. A further four awards were duly gazetted – honouring the medical and commissariat services and the colonials – and at least one more was under consideration when the Commander-in-Chief, the Duke of Cambridge, called a halt, largely for fear that the award might become discredited. By contrast only one survivor of iSandlwana – Private Samuel Wassall of the 80th Regiment, attached to the Mounted Infantry, who had saved the life of a colleague during the retreat across the Mzinyathi river – was awarded the VC. Of course it is likely that there were many acts of desperate courage performed at iSandlwana but these either went unwitnessed by survivors, or were carried out by men who were afterwards killed. None the less there is a distinct impression that the authorities had little interest in drawing attention to what was an embarrassing defeat; at least one survivor, Lieutenant Horace Smith-Dorrien, had hoped to be nominated for the award, but felt his opportunity was blocked by an unsympathetic senior.

Even so, not everyone approved of the awards at Rorke's Drift. Sir Garnet Wolseley felt it was inappropriate to shower awards on men who had been trapped and fought to save their lives; he was also unimpressed by the popular acclaim accorded to Melvill and Coghill, disapproving of the example they had set in leaving their men. Although Wolseley was undoubtedly influenced by resentment of the approbation given to officers who served under Chelmsford, his attitude also reflects a genuine debate about the sort of deed eligible for the award. To Wolseley, and many like him, it was necessary for a man to deliberately seek to place himself in danger in the performance of his deed; having no choice largely invalidated it, in Wolseley's eyes. This view was common to many officers who came from an equestrian background, and who remained influenced by romantic ideas of knightly conduct; it is interesting to note that no fewer than seven of the awards in Zululand were made to men who had ridden on horseback into the face of a Zulu attack to rescue a fallen comrade. Indeed, towards the end of the war this seems to have been the most widely recognised opportunity to gain a VC, and a number of men – mostly officers – accomplished such deeds in the hope of receiving one.

Whether they did or not often depended on the attitude of their senior commander. Evelyn Wood, for example, was widely rumoured to encourage applications by his favourites and to dismiss those by outsiders. He was, for example, scathing about the award to Lieutenant Chard – over which he had no influence – and was largely responsible for the whispering campaign which has coloured Chard's reputation to this day. On the other hand Wood's support for his friends and personal staff ensured that both Buller and two of Wood's staff received the VC at Hlobane and that Captain Lord Beresford, Captain Cecil D'Arcy and Sergeant Edmund O'Toole received it for the action on 3 July.

At least one officer – Lieutenant Frederick Hutchinson of the 4th (serving with the MI) – had performed a similarly gallant deed on 3 July. He had been mentioned in despatches and his case was taken up by a former Colonel of the 4th, who was keen to see his regiment honoured. Yet Wood opposed the nomination, and Hutchinson, embarrassed, withdrew all claim to it. Wood had also opposed the award to Major W.K. Leet of the 13th, who had saved the life of an officer during the retreat from Hlobane; Leet was equal to the challenge, however, and appealed over

Wood's head to friends in the War Office. Leet got his award.

That the patronage of a senior officer was crucial to the granting of an award is also clear from the case of Captain Charles St Leger Shervington of the 2nd NNC who commanded a scratch force of mounted men, wryly known as the Uhlans, throughout the siege of Eshowe. On one occasion Shervington rescued a private in the Mounted Infantry who had been unhorsed during a Zulu ambush, placing his own horse between the man and the Zulus, driving them back with his revolver. After the war Shervington's mother had written to Colonel Pearson to suggest he might be recommended for the VC; Pearson was full of praise for Shervington and passed the idea to Lord Chelmsford, but it foundered on the basis that no other officer had witnessed the deed – a technical difficulty which, in the light of public indifference about the Eshowe campaign, neither Pearson or Chelmsford had the will to resolve.

For those who were lucky enough to receive the award it guaranteed both royal approval and public recognition – and a small annuity, which was particularly useful to ordinary soldiers – but its lasting advantages could be decidedly mixed. For many officers it offered a unique opportunity to secure patronage at the highest level, and an unparalleled degree of public profile which could only accelerate the pace of their careers. Some rankers were lucky enough to find themselves in a similar position – Alfred Henry Hook, for example, who had won the award as a private in B Company, 2/24th, at Rorke's Drift, became in civilian life an attendant at the British Museum, where the distinctive crimson ribbon on his coat secured him the attention of many of the museum's visitors. Even so, he died in decidedly straightened circumstances – and several VC winners from the Zulu campaign, ordinary soldiers like Hook, would experience such hard times that they were forced to pawn or sell their awards before they died.

Gallantry Awards (Zulu)

As a citizen militia, Zulu men fought for their king and country out of a sense of duty which was largely unrecognised by reward. Nevertheless, victory in battle was not without the possibility of practical recompense; in particular loot captured in battle – chiefly livestock, but also important military materiel, such as firearms – was expected to be given over to the king who redistributed it, under advice from his *izinduna*, to those who had distinguished themselves.

Courage in battle was regarded as an admirable quality, and it was recognised too by the award of a distinctive necklace made from small blocks of willow-wood and known as an *iziqu*. Although popularly referred to as the Zulu equivalent of the Victoria Cross, however, award of the *iziqu* was not confined to a handful of individuals throughout the army but to men within a specified *ibutho* who had played a decisive part in an action, thus reflecting a degree of both individual and corporate distinction which in many ways typified the Zulu approach to warfare.

In the aftermath of battle those who had killed an enemy were considered tainted by the supernatural forces the killing had unleashed, and they were separated off from the rest of the army. They could not report to the king or return to their civilian lives until they had been ritually cleansed. As part of the cleansing ceremonies, each man cut a wand of willow-wood, and when they were at last reviewed by the king – formed up according to their *amabutho* – the king would discuss with his *izinduna* which had been the first *ibutho* to 'stab' the enemy – to bring the fight to close quarters. Those men who belonged to that *ibutho* who had actually killed in battle were accorded the title *abaqawe*, heroes or warriors of distinction, and they were permitted to use their willow wands to make *iziqu*. Those who had killed but belonged to *amabutho* that had played a less prominent part had simply to discard their sticks. After the battle of iSandlwana, following fierce debate between the commanders and *amabutho*, King Cetshwayo awarded the coveted distinction to the uMbonambi *ibutho*, whose *abaqawe* were therefore granted the right to cut *iziqu*.

The necklaces themselves were intricately made, the willow stick cut into small, neat wooden beads, shaped at the sides so as to interlock.[141] The edges of the blocks were often scorched – presumably as part of a ritual doctoring process – and often the necklaces included segments with projecting twigs still intact, like thorns. Generally the necklace was worn slung once around the body, bandolier fashion, or looped around the neck. Although white settlers often suggested that each block represented a man killed, this was not the case – indeed, a single necklace would represent an improbable degree of slaughter, even for a dedicated hero – but if a man again distinguished himself in battle he might add the blocks cut from a second willow stick, doubling the length of the *iziqu*.

If, on the other hand, a man who wore the *iziqu* disgraced himself in a subsequent action and was accused of cowardice the king might order the string of his necklace to be cut as a very public sign of his humiliation. Indeed, while men who had fought well in battle could expect to enjoy an enhanced reputation in the community at large, cowards could expect to be the butt of mockery and taunts. In the early days of the kingdom, King Shaka would make a public example of a few cowards after each campaign, ordering them to be executed in front of the assembled army; his successors were not so harsh. By 1879 it was common for cowards to be publicly identified in the post-battle review before the king. When the *amabutho* were fed, the girls bringing food on platters to the men would dip the meat of the cowards in water before serving it, and often dashed the water over them, taunting them for their lack of manliness. Yet, as the glory of heroism could be wiped out by a future lapse, so might a coward redeem himself in a future battle, his reward being the praise of the king and the right to sit with his *ibutho* as a man again.

Another reward granted by the king was a heavy brass armband known as an *ingxotha*. This was not, however, a purely military distinction but was granted by the king to his favourites as a sign of their dedication to his service; it was a rare and treasured item largely confined to those in the king's inner circle. It was considered appropriate to wear the *ingxotha* on all state occasions and royal audiences; on bright days the metal would become uncomfortably hot, and many *amakhosi* who had been so honoured would keep an attendant close by to pour water on the arm-band at intervals to cool it down.

Men who had won the right to wear either *iziqu* or the *ingxotha* would treasure them throughout their lives and they remained a tangible sign of their distinction and the respect they enjoyed within the community as a result – so much so that it was usual for the items themselves to be buried with their owner on his death.

Gatling Gun

In 1861 Richard Gatling, an American doctor living in Indianapolis, noted the dreary spectacle of troops marching regularly out of town to fight in defence of the Union – and the corresponding daily return of the wounded and sick. It struck Gatling that if a weapon could be invented which could greatly increase firepower on the battle-field it would do away with the need to field so many men, and thus the corresponding losses through combat and disease would be greatly reduced. From this humanitarian concern sprang the idea of the world's first practical machine-gun – the Gatling.

Gatling patented his idea in 1862. The design worked by rotating a number of barrels around a fixed central axis. Cartridges were fed into the breech by gravity from a hopper which slotted on to the top, and the gun was operated by turning a handle. At each turn the barrels moved round in sequence and individual bolts pushed the cartridges into them, fired them and extracted them by turn. Gatling's early prototype had six barrels and was beset with technical problems which caused jamming and affected its accuracy, and it met with a lukewarm response from the Union army. The US Government refused to purchase any of Gatling's guns, judging them expensive and unreliable, but several were bought privately by Union generals and the weapon saw service at the siege of Petersburg and elsewhere.

After the Civil War Gatling was able to improve on his initial concept and found a ready market in Europe, beset as it was at the time by political rivalries. The British Government bought the weapon from 1871 onwards and it was produced under licence by the Armstrong company in Birmingham. The British version had ten barrels, fired .450 calibre Boxer ammunition and was sighted up to 1,830 metres (2,000 yards).

Because the machine-gun was a new concept tactical theorists struggled to adapt it to existing doctrines. Throughout the 1870s it was generally regarded as a light artillery weapon, to be de-ployed in batteries like cannon; it was only after the practical experience of a number of colonial campaigns, where it was usually deployed to augment infantry fire-power, that it came to be regarded increasingly as an infantry support weapon. Indeed, the Royal Navy appreciated the advantages of the Gatling rather earlier than the British Army. At a time when steam had begun to radically change the old naval tactics of the Napoleonic era, the Gatling was seen as a perfect weapon to combat the new phenomenon of fast steam torpedo-boats. Gatlings bracketed to the side of a ship could be used to sweep the decks of an enemy at close range, usurping the traditional on-board role of the Marines, or they could even be hauled up and fitted on platforms on the masts to spray the enemy below. They could, more-over, be easily dismantled and taken ashore on light land carriages and used as a ready means of adding weight to raids by landing parties.

Gatlings were first used by British troops during Sir Garnet Wolseley's campaign against the Asante in West Africa in 1873–74. Mounted on artillery-style carriages, they proved impractical for offensive operations – they were too wide for the narrow tracks through the rainforest by which the British advanced – but they were left to guard lines of supply along the river Pra, the border of the Asante kingdom. Although they were never employed in action, they were used to intimidate a group of Asante envoys, who were given a demonstration of the Gatling's awe-some firepower. Afterwards one of the Asante ambassadors hanged himself; at first this was taken as proof of the weapon's terrifying effect, but it was later discovered that the man had disgraced himself before his fellow envoys and dared not return to face his king.

It was with the Navy that the Gatling first saw action in Zululand. On 19 November 1879 HMS *Active* had landed a contingent of 230 sailors and Marines at Durban to support Lord Chelmsford's preparations for the invasion. With them were two 12-pdr Armstrong guns, two 24-pdr rocket tubes and a Gatling mounted on a light field carriage. *Active*'s contingent marched up to join the troops assembling on the Zulu border at the Lower Thukela Drift. Here, on 12 December, they provided a guard for the meeting with Zulu representatives at which Sir Bartle Frere's ultimatum to King Cetshwayo was read out; a Durban photographer, James Lloyd, took a picture of the Naval Brigade lined up, their Gatling proudly to the fore.

With the beginning of hostilities a detachment of *Active*'s men accompanied Pearson's advance to Eshowe. Early on the morning of 22 January, as the column struggled to cross the Nyezane river, scouts working ahead of the advance blundered into a Zulu army concealed behind the Wombane hill. The encounter provoked an immediate Zulu attack, and Pearson was forced to hurry his men forward to take up a position on a spur facing the hill. When the battle began the Gatling, commanded by a young Midshipman, Lewis Coker, was being pulled behind a cart at the rear of a long column of wagons, and Coker urged the crew to manhandle it forward. At first they took up a position beside the nearest company of infantry but here the bush was so thick that Coker decided their fire would be wasted, and that he should advance further still up the slope towards the head of the British position. As he did so, his sweating crewmen broke the pole of the cart, much to their commander's irritation, and it had to be hastily repaired. That done, they hurried it up the slope towards the summit of the spur where Pearson had anchored his command.

By the time it came into action, then, the crisis of the battle had already passed. The Zulu advance down the slopes of Wombane had stalled in the face of Pearson's fire, and the Zulus had occupied a chain of bush which lay in the bottom of a hollow separating them from the British. From here they had opened a heavy, but largely ineffectual, fire. Coker directed his men to point the Gatling at a clump of bush which seemed to be sheltering several Zulu snipers. They opened fire with a noisy clatter which immediately suppressed the Zulu fire. In fact, this opening burst – the first ever by a Gatling in action in British service – must have been very short; Coker later reported that he had fired 300 rounds. The nominal rate of fire was 600 rounds per minute, although in battlefield conditions, allowing for jamming, for changing the hopper and for pauses to allow the smoke to clear, a rate of 200–300 rounds was typical.

At Nyezane, then, the brutal fanfare which heralded the arrival of the machine-gun on a British battlefield can have lasted scarcely more than a minute.

After the battle, Coker reported himself delighted with the weapon's performance. Pearson buried his dead and resumed his march, occupying the deserted mission station at Eshowe the following day. Within days he heard the news of the defeat at iSandlwana and, realising he was unsupported, decided to dig himself in. Eshowe was surrounded by an impressive earthwork fort, and the Gatling was raised on a platform inside to fire over the walls. And there, since the post was never attacked, it remained for three months until Eshowe was relieved. By that time young Coker was dead, a victim of the dysentery which plagued the command during its investment.

In the aftermath of iSandlwana large numbers of reinforcements were hurried to Natal. Among these was a detachment of naval personnel landed by HMS *Boadicea* in Durban on 15 March, which included another Gatling gun. These reinforcements were added to a column which Lord Chelmsford had assembled on the Thukela and which crossed into Zululand at the end of the month to relieve Eshowe. On 1 April Chelmsford's column camped for the night on a rise near the ruins of the kwaGingindlovu royal homestead. The column's wagons were drawn up in a square and surrounded by a trench and a protective rampart; the *Boadicea*'s Gatling was placed to command the front right corner.

As dawn broke on the morning of the 2nd, long columns of Zulus could be seen advancing from the valley of the Nyezane ahead. The Zulus had assembled to contest Chelmsford's advance, and they advanced rapidly to surround the British square. Most of Chelmsford's troops were new to Zululand and had heard the stories of iSandlwana on their way up, and as they waited for the Zulus to come within easy rifle range the strain began to play on their nerves. According to Major William Molyneux, one of Chelmsford's ADCs, it was the Gatling from HMS *Boadicea* that broke the tension. The sight was one which Molyneux rightly saw as prophetic:

'Beg your pardon, sir', he [the officer in charge of the gun] said, 'last night I stepped the distance to that bush where those blacks are, and it's just 800 yards. This "no firing" seems like throwing a chance away. I've got her laid true for them; may I give her half a turn of the handle?' The Chief who was close by did not object to the range being tested, providing he stopped at once. A final sight and, I am sure, quite two turns of the handle was the response, and there was a clear lane cut quite through the body of men. The effect of the fire of a machinegun is awful if it is served by a cool hand; the gun has no nerves, and, provided the man is steady and the cartridges do not jam, nothing can live in front of it. The captain of this gun was a veteran, and afterwards during the fight his exhortation to his crew would have made, when carefully expurgated, an admirable essay on behaviour under fire.[142]

Nevertheless, the Zulu attack was able to use the ground to good advantage to approach close to the corner where the Gatling stood. A young Volunteer, Jack Royston, saw one Zulu run right up to the gun, touching it with his arm before he was cut down. Behind him was an *induna* 'haranguing them "as to what the Zulu maidens would say when they heard the Zulus had fled before the British dogs"', the force came on again, and was literally mown down'.[143] The Zulus were not able to penetrate the curtain of fire around the square and were driven off.

There can be little doubt that the Gatling made a significant contribution to the British victory at kwaGingindlovu. Although there are no records to suggest how many rounds it fired or men it killed, it undoubtedly caused great destruction in short bursts whenever a target presented itself, while its moral effect was equally important. Not only did it discourage the Zulu, but it gave heart to the British troops lined up beside it, most of whom had never been in action before and some of whom were raw recruits who had displayed distinct signs of nervousness when the Zulus attacked.

By the time the battle of kwaGingindlovu took place, the Army, too, had sent Gatlings to Zululand. Four guns from 10 Battery 7 Brigade under the commands of Captains Maclean and Evans arrived at Durban from Mauritius, where they had been part of the fixed garrison, on 26 March. Major J.F. Owen arrived from Malta shortly afterwards to take command and organised the guns into a field battery – the first machine-gun battery in the British Army. The Army's guns – always intended for land use – were mounted on a heavier carriage than their Navy counterparts, the difference being most apparent in the ammunition boxes attached to the axletrees. The guns were marched up-country to join the troops Lord Chelmsford was assembling for the second invasion of Zululand. They were attached to the Flying Column – as Wood's old column was by then called – and took part in the advance on oNdini. Two of the guns, under the command of Maclean and Evans, were left to guard the supply depot built at Fort Newdigate while the remaining two, commanded by Owen and Lieutenant H.M.L. Rundle, continued the advance.

These two guns played a prominent part in the battle of Ulundi on 4 July. They were placed just forward of the front line of the British square, facing towards oNdini, and were therefore engaged in the battle from the moment the Zulu attack began. This was a position that required longer and more sustained bursts of firing than the Navy had experienced at either Nyezane or kwaGingindlovu and the stresses which affected the guns after prolonged use were therefore more apparent. As the barrels became hot, so the cartridges thrust into them by the mechanism became soft with the result that the retractor grip sometimes pulled the base off the cartridge, leaving the remainder in the breech. Sometimes, too, the bolts slipped out and were lost for a moment in the long grass until the crew could find them again. In both cases the only solution was to cease firing until the gun could be repaired or cleaned. This happened six times throughout the course of the battle until in the end they 'jammed and were out of action'.[144]

Nevertheless, when they worked the guns were terribly effective, chopping great swathes through the Zulus in front of them. At one point one of Chelmsford's ADCs, Lord Grenfell, saw a Zulu *induna* lead a knot of men to within less than 20 yards of the guns before they were all suddenly cut down. After the battle was over, Evelyn Wood counted sixty Zulu bodies within seventy paces of the Gatlings.

The Gatlings were not used in action again after Ulundi. When, following Chelmsford's resignation, Sir Garnet Wolseley reorganised the British forces, Owen's battery was attached to Lieutenant-Colonel Clarke's column. This column took part in the last pacification operations, retreating from Zululand by way of Middle Drift so as to intimidate the Zulu *amakhosi* living on the central border; his passage was not opposed, however, and Owen had no further need to deploy his guns in anger.

As a baptism of fire for the Gatling the Zulu campaign had proved problematic, highlighting the weapons' failings as much as their advantages. Perhaps the last word should go to a Zulu veteran of Ulundi, however, who left a vivid account of just how terrifying it was to be on the receiving end of the hail of bullets they could dispense:

What could we do against you English? You stand still, and only by turning something round make the bodies of our warriors fly to pieces; legs here, arms there, heads, everything. Whouw! What can we do against that?[145]

Haggard, H. Rider

In 1914, visiting Zululand for the first time, the novelist H. Rider Haggard addressed a meeting of some 70 or 80 *amakhosi* from the Nkandla district. For the Zulus – as Haggard himself recognised – these were difficult times. They had suffered decades of impoverishment at the hands of the colonial and Union governments and much of their best land had been appropriated by whites. The horrors of the savage repression of the Bhambatha Rebellion, which had fallen heavily on Nkandla just eight years before, were fresh in their minds. Several times throughout his travels, Haggard had heard expressions of concern, of regret for things lost and anxiety as to what might come, from the Zulus he met. On this occasion, however, he was quick to steer the conversation away from contentious issues, and instead gave an account of himself, since the assembled Zulu dignitaries not unnaturally wondered who he was. He told them

I had spent my youth in this country, when I was a child of Sompseu (Sir T. Shepstone) and of Mali-mati (Sir M. Osborn), their late heads and chiefs. That then I had heard all their history from the lips of those Great Ones and had learned to love them with a love that, although since those days I had wandered far across the black seas and up and down the earth, I had never forgotten through the falling years. That I had written of them in books and striven to make their name known about the world.[146]

And written he had indeed. Henry Rider Haggard was born, the son of a country squire, in Norfolk on 22 June 1856. The eighth of ten children, he failed to shine at school and when he failed to pass the Army entrance exams, his future seemed problematic. In 1875, however, his father chanced to hear that a family friend and neighbour, Sir Henry Bulwer, had been appointed Lieutenant-Governor of Natal, and prevailed upon him to take young Rider on to his staff. Bulwer, of course, was being sent to southern Africa as part of the Colonial Office's plans to confederate the region. Haggard arrived in Natal in August in the role of Bulwer's lowly and unpaid catering manager. Bulwer undertook a tour of the colony which introduced Haggard not only to its extraordinary landscapes and people – the first piece he wrote for publication was a description of a welcome dance staged by *inkosi* Pakhade of the amaChunu people (whose followers later fought with the NNC at iSandlwana) – but also to prominent figures in settler society. Among these was Theophilus Shepstone, with whom Haggard, although many years the younger, struck up a lasting friendship. When Shepstone embarked on the expedition to annex the Transvaal Republic in January 1877, Haggard was permitted to join his staff in a private capacity. Among his colleagues was Melmoth Osborn, later to be British Resident in post-war Zululand. From these men Haggard, as he admitted later, heard many of the stories of the history of the Boers and the Zulus which fired his imagination. It was at this time, too, that Haggard met a Swazi who had attached himself to Shepstone, a tall man with an impressive battle-scar on his forehead and who carried a large axe. His real name was Mhlophekazi, and Haggard was later to immortalise him as the fictional Umslopogaas.

The Transvaal expedition made a lasting impression on Haggard. Being close to Shepstone he was at the centre of events, and when Osborn froze during the reading of the annexation proclamation in Pretoria it was Haggard who took over from him. It was Haggard, too, who helped run up the Union flag in a ceremony there on Queen Victoria's birthday, 24 May 1877. At the age of just 21, he found himself offered important positions within Shepstone's administration. Haggard was still living in Pretoria when the Zulu campaign began – he heard the news of iSandlwana from his African servants the day after it happened – but with the collapse of the confederation policy and the eclipse of Shepstone's reputation he resigned his posts there and bought a share in a farm in Newcastle, Natal. He returned briefly to England in late 1879 and in August 1880 married Louisa Margitson, the daughter of a Norfolk landowner. The couple returned to Africa at the end of 1880 only to be greeted by the news that a Boer rising had taken place in the Transvaal with the hope of throwing off British rule and restoring the Republic. Within days of Haggard's return to his Newcastle farm fighting had broken out across the nearby Laing's Nek pass. On 27 February Rider heard the sound of guns firing in the distance and later learned that General Sir George Colley had been killed and his troops defeated on the summit of Majuba hill. Ironically, given his own role in the annexation, the Commission which assembled to discuss the retrocession of the Transvaal met on Haggard's farm. Disillusioned, Haggard and his partners decided to sell the Newcastle farm and return to England. Haggard left Natal in August 1881, and did not return until 1914.

Back in England Haggard trained to enter the legal profession and began writing. His first book, *Cetywayo and His White Neighbours* (1882) was essentially a defence of Shepstone's policies. He also tried his hand at fiction, writing *Dawn* and *The Witch's Head* in 1884. It was a chance remark by one of his brothers, however, which was to shape the rest of his career. Discussing Robert Louis Stevenson's recently published *Treasure Island*, his brother challenged Rider to produce anything 'half as good'. The result was *King Solomon's Mines*, published in 1885.

King Solomon's Mines has remained Haggard's most enduring work, and it draws heavily on the camp-fire gossip of his days in Natal and the Transvaal, meshing travellers' tales of events in the interior – particularly the succession crisis in the amaNdebele ('Matabele') kingdom in 1868–77 – with Haggard's intense and rather brooding imagination. It also established the relationship between Haggard's fictional world and Zulu history, hinting that Haggard's main character, the hunter Alan Quartermain, had been present at the battle of iSandlwana and elsewhere. The book was a huge commercial success, at least in part because of Haggard's successful evocation of its African setting.

Haggard followed *King Solomon's Mines* with a succession of bestsellers, many of them with an African setting. While the Zulus appear in many of the books as a backdrop to increasingly exotic adventures, Haggard brought them to the fore in a trilogy that encompassed the rise and fall of the Zulu kingdom: *Marie* (1912), *Child of the Storm* (1913) and *Finished* (1917). Drawing on stories of Shaka and Cetshwayo which he had heard from Shepstone and Osborn, Haggard wove a complex, bloody, deliberately epic and sometimes fantastic tale of revenge which incorporated the early history of his two best-known characters, Umslopogaas and Alan Quartermain. In so doing, writing in the aftermath of the impact of the Anglo-Zulu War on British popular consciousness, he was largely responsible for shaping the image of the Zulu people as an archetypal 'warrior nation', at once bold, proud and – by British standards – savage. This impression, shot through with the powerful allure of adventure and the exotic 'otherness' of Africa, has continued to influence films, novels and popular histories to this day.

The success of Haggard's novels made him a celebrity, something which he was able to exploit in pursuit of his interests in the British Empire and the well-being of its subjects. Through the management of his Norfolk estate he became a champion of the agricultural community and served on several government commissions which required him to travel abroad. He was knighted in January 1912, and shortly afterwards was asked to join a Royal Commission to report on the state of Britain's overseas dominions.

It was in this capacity, in 1914, that Haggard finally returned to South Africa. He had no official duties in Zululand but he was keen to visit the historic sites which he had so often written about but never seen. He found that times had changed in more ways than one; in an attempt to reprise the happy memories of his youth, he asked if the tour could be accomplished by ox-drawn wagonette, but was told one could no longer be found. Instead, he travelled with Stuart and Gibson in an American-made Overland car.

Haggard's 1914 journey makes for an extraordinary travelogue, a fascinating precursor to today's battlefield tourism. The party travelled 400 miles in a week, staying at hotels or with local officials, driving on bad dirt roads and through river-drifts. In many places the evidence

of past conflict was still visible on the ground – at the site of King Dingane's eMgungundlovu royal homestead Haggard's party found human bones protruding from cairns, which may have been the remains of Piet Retief's party, killed in 1838 – and Haggard met many Zulus who had taken part in the 1879 campaign. Perhaps more tellingly, he found the Zulus generally to be in a fragile state, unsettled by the gradual destruction of their political institutions, by the appropriation of their land, and by the harshness of the government response to the recent (1906) disturbances:

I had an interesting conversation with Sir Charles [Saunders] about the Zulus, a race in which he takes the deepest and most sympathetic interest. He spoke feelingly of the harsh treatment they have received and are receiving and declared that the 'constant pin-pricks', such as land-snatching and the poll-tax, were the direct cause of the 1906 'Rebellion'. He added that this was suppressed with great cruelty notably in the last affair in the Insimba valley – Mome I think the place was called,[147] where all quarter seems to have been refused even to those who threw down their arms and pleaded for mercy, as did the old chief Mehlokazulu, who held up his hands and said 'please' before they shot him. In that fight, if so it can be called, 547 Zulus were slain and one white man received a scratch on the wrist ... somewhat significant figures ... Some natives I am told were finished who had taken refuge in caves and up trees. Well, cruelty bred of fear is no new story in South Africa. The white man neglects or oppresses the native and slights his needs until something happens; then in panic he sets to work and butchers him.[148]

Haggard left Zululand at the end of his journey more sympathetic than ever towards the Zulu people, yet despite grave reservations about the nature of Union Government rule he failed to grasp that the conditions he witnessed were the end result of the policies in which he had participated more than thirty years before. Although he recognised that the British invasion had been 'unnecessary', his understanding of the issues which had brought it about remained shaped by his faith in Shepstone and by Shepstone's suspicion of King Cetshwayo. Instead, he interpreted what he saw in Zululand in 1914 as a failure to fulfil the ideals and aspirations of the British Empire rather than as a criticism of imperialism itself – a shortcoming which typified the limitations of British liberalism at the time.

Haggard had not long returned to England when the First World War broke out and the Royal Commission was suspended; Haggard's reservations about the state of South Africa were destined to have little political impact. He continued to serve on government committees throughout the war and after, travelling again around the world. His health, however, began to deteriorate; he had suffered from bronchitis since his youth and from occasional bouts of depression which had undoubtedly influenced some of the darker aspects of his more imaginative fiction. He died on 14 May 1925 and was buried in Ditchingham, Norfolk.

Today Haggard is largely remembered for his novels *King Solomon's Mines* and *She* (1887). Yet his impact on the international reputation of the Zulu people should not be overlooked; it was he, more than anyone in his day, who created in the public mind the image of Zulu history as one of 'superstitious madness and blood-stained grandeur'.[149] As alluring as that image may be in fiction, it remains a stereotype from which the Zulus have never fully escaped.

Horses (British)

Not long after his arrival in Natal, the war correspondent Melton Prior suffered an unfortunate loss:

Our animals were a terrible trouble to us ... because of all those horrible ticks, while I lost one of my best horses with that vile sickness called Red Water. He had been ill for two days, when I found him lying on the ground apparently in awful agony. The veterinary surgeon assured me he could not live, and the officers begged me to shoot him and put him out of his misery.

I went to my tent to fetch my revolver to do so, when someone called out to me, 'Never mind, Prior, the poor brute is dead.' He must have suffered terribly, for he had pulled up the ground with his teeth and feet, and his mouth was full of earth. I was awfully sorry, for he was my best horse; but oxen as well as horses were dying all round.[150]

Red-water – or equine babeosis, a disease spread by ticks that were endemic across Natal and Zululand in the long grass where African cattle roamed – was but one of a number of complaints which plagued horses in southern Africa. Even more damaging was Horse Sickness, another disease spread by insects, particularly during the hot, wet, summer months. Mortality among the infected was above 50 per cent and animals died of chronic respiratory or cardiac failure.

The presence of such diseases was widely known but veterinary science in 1879 could offer few cures. Given the extent to which European armies – Boer or British – were reliant upon animal-drawn transport, strategic decisions were often made on the prevalence or otherwise of Horse Sickness in a given area. While Lord Chelmsford's decision to invade Zululand by way of Rorke's Drift in January 1879 was shaped by the presence of an existing track, for example, one factor which influenced his choice of Helpmekaar as the point of assembly for the Centre Column was that the high, windy Biggarsberg ridge was believed to be free of the insects which caused Horse Sickness.

Although many British officers had transferred their favourite chargers to Natal with them, many came to prefer the local horses which were the mainstay of the Volunteer and Irregular units. The Cape Horse – also known as the *Boerperd*, literally 'farmer's horse' – was a distinct breed, a cross between European animals and horses imported to the Cape from Indonesia by the Dutch East India Company from the mid-seventeenth century. The Cape Horse earned a good reputation early in its existence as a military horse because of its stamina and intelligence, and of course it was fully accustomed to the difficulties of the local terrain. The Cape Horse had produced an even hardier local variant, the result of early dealings between Cape settlers and the southern Sotho. Raised in a tough, cold, high-altitude environment, the 'BaSotho Pony' was renowned for its ability to pick its way carefully through the most corrugated boulder-strewn landscape. Although the British tended to use the term BaSotho Pony rather loosely, often to include any locally raised Cape horses, the true BaSotho Pony was undeniably in high demand, particularly among the Irregular units for whose long-range patrolling and skirmishing duties it was ideally suited.

Horses which were 'salted' i.e., had been exposed to Horse Sickness or Red-water and survived – were particularly highly prized simply because they were immune to the risk of further contagion.

When the British regular cavalry – the 1st (King's) Dragoons and 17th Lancers – arrived in Natal after iSandlwana they brought with them their magnificent English horses. These were, of course, fully trained for the particular duties the British cavalry required of them but their initial showing in Natal was disappointing. The horses had to be unloaded from the transports at Durban – each horse being lowered into a tender by means of a sling – and it took some time before they had recovered from the journey. The cavalry deliberately took their time marching to the border, to join the columns being formed for a fresh invasion, in order to allow the horses to acclimatise. Even so, the horses refused to forage from local grasses, as Cape horses of course did, and had to be fed, as they had been used to at home, from imported forage offered in nose-bags. They struggled, too, to cope with the difficulties of the terrain, and in particular were vulnerable to the traps set by *aardvarks* – 'ant-bears' – which, in breaking open termite hills and digging deep inside to feed, left holes scattered dangerously across the veldt, often concealed in the long grass.

In the charge at Ulundi, however, the Lancers and their English chargers proved their worth,

driving into the retreating Zulus in a practised way which astonished young George Mossop of the Frontier Light Horse, used as he was to the skirmishing tactics of the Irregulars:

> ... the Lancers rode out. On their great imported horses they sat bolt upright, their long lances held perfectly erect, the lance heads glistening in the sunshine.
>
> They formed into line. In one movement the lances dropped to the right side of the horses' necks, a long level line of poles, stretching out a distance in front of the horses, the steel heads pointing straight at the retreating mass of Zulus. As the big horses bounded forward and thundered into them, each lance point pierced the Zulu in front of it; the man fell, and as the horse passed on beyond him the lance was withdrawn, lifted, and thrust forward into another Zulu in front.
>
> The movement of withdrawing the lance and again getting it into position was very rapid; I could not quite understand how it was done. It was such a mix up for us riding behind the Lancers, with our horses jumping over dead Zulus, and having to deal with those who were knocked down by the Lancer horses but not pierced, that we did not have the opportunity to study the work ...[151]

Horses (Zulu)

In 1880 Captain W.R. Ludlow, who had just embarked upon a tour of Zululand to examine the scenes of the recent fighting and to investigate its sporting opportunities, had just crossed the Lower Thukela Drift in the company of the trader, Charlie Adams, when

> We met two of Dunn's white people coming down to the colony, one of them riding a wretched, rough, scarecrow-looking pony. Adams said, 'That's the best pony in this part of South Africa. Dubulumanzi, Cetewayo's brother, rode it all through the war, and owed his life to its speed in carrying him away from the battle of Ulundi.'[152]

Wretched or not, many *amakhosi* had acquired horses before the invasion of Zululand and prized them not so much according to their looks but for their endurance and hardiness. Throughout the 1860s white traders had plied their trade across Zululand, exchanging blankets, beads, brass wire and trinkets for cattle. Other items were in greater demand – including firearms – while the price of horses was such that only men of considerable stature could afford them. Nevertheless, they were considerably prized – the more so if they were 'salted', or immune by previous exposure to Horse Sickness – partly because their possession implied a sophisticated association with the exotic world of the *abelungu*. White horses were particularly popular, apparently because the colour white was associated with status and seniority; likewise white cattle were especially valued. And if the horses themselves were sometimes unprepossessing, those prominent Zulus who had cultivated links with the whites, like the *amakhosi* Zibhebhu and Sihayo and Prince Dabulamanzi, could at least afford good saddles and kit. Some *amakhosi* like Sihayo, who profited from their position astride the main entry points into the kingdom, maintained a small herd and their sons had learned to ride confidently as they grew up.

Many *amakhosi* rode their horses to war in 1879. In particular Zibhebhu kaMaphitha, who commanded the scouts in the iSandlwana campaign, had access to small parties of mounted men who screened the advance of the main army and watched British movements from a distance. Indeed, Zibhebhu exploited his own horsemanship to good tactical effect in the skirmish before oNdini on 3 July when he acted as a decoy in an attempt to draw Buller's mounted men into a carefully planned ambush. It is interesting to note, however, that when the main army set out for the central border from oNdini on 17 January the senior general, *inkosi* Ntshingwayo kaMahole, opted to walk so as to set a good example to his men, the vast majority of whom were of course on foot.

His decision hints at a conservatism which was as much a part of the Zulu reluctance to embrace the potential offered by the horse in the manner that other African groups – notably the baSotho – had done. Horses were not merely expensive and difficult to maintain but their practical use, among a people who walked miles on a daily basis and, during an attack, could cover the ground almost as quickly as a mounted man, was limited. Wedded to the tactical concept of an attack in mass on foot, the Zulu continued to regard the horse as an exotic but largely superfluous addition to military techniques to which past successes over the years had imparted an impressive weight of tradition.

inkatha yesizwe yakwaZulu

The *inkatha yesizwe yakwaZulu* – the sacred coil of the Zulu nation – was an object of great spiritual potency which was said to bind the Zulu kingdom together.

Many *amakhosi* in both Natal and Zululand possessed an *inkatha*, a coil made from plaited grass which embodied the history, traditions and unity of their people. During the rise of the Zulu kingdom in the 1820s King Shaka either captured or destroyed many of the *izinkatha* belonging to the groups he conquered. He added elements from their *izinkatha* to his own, thereby ensuring that they were subjugated to the Zulu Royal House. The *inkatha* was an item of such magical potency that it was housed in a special hut of its own within a royal homestead, and no commoners were allowed to see or touch it for fear of damaging its power. Shaka kept the *inkatha* at his royal homestead at kwaBulawayo, near Eshowe; after his assassination in September 1828 it passed to his successor, King Dingane, who housed it at kwaNobamba. After Dingane's death in 1840 it passed to his successor, King Mpande, who housed it at esiKlebheni. Following Mpande's death in 1872 it passed to King Cetshwayo.

Physically the *inkatha* was a circular coil about half a metre across, and about as thick as a man's leg below the knee. It was kept wrapped in a python skin and a piece of cloth. Bound into the coil were items collected over the years which represented the unity of the nation. These included hair clipped from the heads of *amakhosi* killed by Shaka, body dirt scraped during their ablutions from the persons of the kings, strands of grass which had been dipped in the collected vomit generated during the mass cleansing ceremonies of the *amabutho*, and shavings scraped from the gateposts worn smooth by the passage of thousands of people into the royal homesteads. These items were of such personal and collective intimacy that they were believed to carry with them something of the soul of the people who were then tied spiritually together by the *inkatha*. The *inkatha* was regularly 'topped up' over the years by the addition of new items. It had mystical powers to protect the nation from evil, to ensure that the Zulu army triumphed in battle, and to prevent fugitives from leaving the kingdom.

Cetshwayo kept the *inkatha* for some of his reign at least in the black *isigodlo*, the most private section of his quarters at oNdini. Since the king served as a powerful conduit through which to harness the power of the royal ancestral spirits, he alone could engage with the *inkatha* to harness its powers for the good of the nation. During important national ceremonies or at times of crisis he communed with the *inkatha*. It was big enough for him to squat upon, and he would sit holding an *inhlendla*, a staff with a crescent-shaped blade, rather like a sceptre. During such times he could not be disturbed for it was believed that he was radiating an awesome spiritual power which transcended physical distance and even the constraints of time. When, for example, runners first brought news that the battle of iSandlwana had begun, Cetshwayo retired to the *inkatha* to direct its power on behalf of the Zulu army. In fact, of course, the outcome of the battle had probably already been decided by the time the king first heard about it, but the power of the *inkatha* worked on a supernatural level and until news arrived of the result it was believed that it could still influence events. According to one of his female attendants,

As soon as Cetshwayo was apprised by his messengers that battle had been joined, he took his seat on the magic coil, the *inkatha*,

holding the crescent-shaped *nhlandla* in his hand. He did this to ensure that his warriors would fight with unity of purpose, that they should not waver, and that victory would be theirs. It was generally believed that if the king was sitting on the *inkatha* the influence of his personality would reach out to the people ensuring the unity of the nation. His mothers [i.e. King Mpande's widows] urged him not to get up from the magic coil to go to the cattle-kraal. They maintained that if he did, the battle could not possibly end in his favour.

Fleet-footed messengers kept coming in with hurried reports about the progress of the battle. When the king heard that his regiments were heading towards victory, he began to leave his seat on the *inkatha* every now and then. But the mothers scolded him on that account. In the end it did not help much; the warriors returned from battle carrying the fury of war on their backs. They were covered in blood and had tied up their wounds with grass.

When it became known that a large Zulu force had failed to overwhelm the small British garrison at Rorke's Drift, the mothers reproached Cetshwayo severely. They put the blame on the king for not having occupied the *inkatha* uninterruptedly.[153]

At some point during the war of 1879, perhaps to increase its potency, the *inkatha* appears to have been moved to esiKlebheni, one of a cluster of old royal homesteads which stood in the valley of the Mkhumbane stream, the home of the ancestors of the Zulu Royal House, and one of the most sacred spots in Zululand. On 25 June, however, British cavalry from the advancing 2nd Division and Flying Column descended into the valley from the Mthonjaneni heights and attacked and set fire to these royal homesteads. The *inkatha* itself was destroyed in the flames.

The British, of course, knew nothing of its whereabouts or its significance, and its destruction was in that respect accidental. The omens for the future unity of the Zulu kingdom resulting from the destruction of the *inkatha* were catastrophic, and within a fortnight the Zulu army had been defeated at the battle of Ulundi. The subsequent partition of Zululand by the British, and the civil war which followed, destroyed much of the unity Shaka had striven to create.

Ironically, from a Zulu viewpoint the capture of the *inkatha* intact would have been regarded as equally damaging, since it would have implied that the power of the Zulu kingdom was now subjugated by the British.

Even after the destruction of the independent Zulu kingdom, the *inkatha* continued to represent the idea of Zulu unity and tradition. In 1924 it inspired the name of a political organisation, Inkatha ka Zulu, an alliance of middle-class Africans from KwaZulu-Natal backed by white sugar-cane planters and headed by the then Zulu king, Solomon kaDinuzulu. The organisation was specifically rooted in the context of the times and aimed to raise the lot of the Zulus, two generations after their subjugation, by encouraging an awareness of tradition and involvement in commercial agriculture. Among other things it was responsible for the erection of a statue to the memory of King Shaka on his grave in Stanger/ kwaDukuza. This original Inkatha organisation was disbanded after King Solomon's death in 1933, but it served as the inspiration for the Inkatha Freedom Party which was formed in 1975 by (among others) Dr Mangosuthu Buthelezi, and which is still in existence.

A small grass ring, traditionally worn to support pots carried on the head, is also called *inkatha*.

Irregular Troops (British)

The Irregulars were raised under different terms of service from either the Regular imperial troops or the pre-existing Natal Volunteer corps. They were not part-time troops maintained by the Natal administration, like the Volunteers, but were rather specially raised full-time troops enlisted for a specific period of short-term service. When planning the invasion of Zululand, it was all too obvious to Lord Chelmsford that he lacked sufficient troops for the job, particularly mounted men. He therefore put pressure on the Natal administration to license the use of its Volunteers across the border in Zululand, and directed that a number of Irregular mounted corps be raised in both the Eastern Cape – where they had been particularly useful in the war against the Xhosa – and the Transvaal.

Unlike the Natal Volunteers, which attracted recruits who had a stake in the colony's future and who enjoyed the social aspects of the regular training camps, the Irregulars tended to attract adventurers who were looking for the short-term excitement of the campaign, or were down on their luck and needed the money. They were raised by regular or ex-regular officers but the men in the ranks came from all walks of settler society, from the proverbial 'gentlemen adventurers' to remission men (sent abroad by their families to escape some disgrace), wanderers, unsuccessful diamond diggers and itinerant labourers of all nations – French, Americans, Scandinavians and Germans as well as Englishmen, Irishmen and Scotsmen. Many simply enlisted, served their period of duty and then moved on, leaving nothing in history to remember them by except their names on the regimental rolls.

The British had made extensive use of Irregular units on the Cape Frontier. When these units were disbanded at the end of the hostilities, many of the men joined the new units being raised for the Zulu campaign. Perhaps the most famous of the Cape units – which remained in service until the end of the Sekhukhune campaign in late 1879 – was the Frontier Light Horse. The FLH was first raised by Lieutenant Fred Carrington of the 1/24th Regiment in 1877, recruiting in the King Williams Town area. Carrington moulded the men into a surprisingly effective mounted infantry force – known then as Carrington's Horse – as they served throughout the 9th Cape Frontier War. In April 1878 command of the FLH passed to Major Redvers Buller, who further enhanced the reputation established by Carrington. The unit served in the abortive first expedition against the baPedi of King Sekhukhune in November and December, and was then attached to Wood's column, with which it served throughout the Zulu campaign.

Further Irregular units were added to Wood's command, notably the Border Horse commanded by Lieutenant-Colonel Fred Weatherley and recruited in the Transvaal (these troops were sometimes known as 'Weatherley's Border Lances', the term 'lance' or 'freelance' being widely used to represent dashing irregular horsemen). Commandant F. Schermbrucker, who had also impressed Chelmsford on the Cape Frontier, raised a unit from predominantly German-speaking settlers, which was known as the Kaffrarian Riflemen; attached to Wood's column, it was initially formed as an infantry unit but became mounted shortly before the Hlobane expedition at the end of March. Commandant Pieter Raaf raised Raaf's Rangers from the Kimberley diamonds fields and from Pretoria. As the war progressed and Irregular and auxiliary units were reformed, further units were raised, such as Baker's Horse, Lonsdale's Horse and the Natal Light Horse.

The Irregulars were famous for their rough and ready appearance. Some, like the FLH, had affected smart uniforms when they were first mustered but as time went on and their uniforms became worn out they were seldom issued with replacements of the same pattern. The FLH started with smart black cotton uniforms with a red trim and a wide-brimmed hat with a red rag wound tightly around it. When the black trousers became worn they were replaced with hard-wearing yellow corduroy, which was in plentiful supply in the government stores. Yellow, indeed, became the colour most associated with the Irregulars, and those who aspired to nothing more were issued yellow jackets as well. By the time the FLH moved up to the Transvaal for the Sekhukhune campaign, it seems their regimental tailors had given up on black jackets, too, and were decorating the yellow cord ones with black braiding instead; by the time George Mossop joined the unit on the Zulu border, he formed the impression they were dressed entirely in civilian clothing – although his view may well have been coloured by the fact that he enlisted straight from a spell working with professional hunters in the Transvaal, most of whom wore yellow cord as a matter of course.

So ubiquitous was the universal yellow that some of the Irregular units were nicknamed 'the Canaries', but in fact the cord did not stay yellow for long; exposed to the sun and rain and engrained with dust, it turned to a variety of tobacco tones, as Captain Montague observed:

My escort were four Volunteer [i.e. Irregular] Horse, rough-looking men at first sight, in cord suits of warm brown faced with scarlet, mounted on little ponies that somehow or other managed to scramble along at a fine pace. On closer appearance the troopers proved to be gentlemen, unshaved, not likely unwashed too; was I not all but the same? There was an ex-captain of the line, a young draughtsman from an engineer's office, and a couple of medical students from Trinity College. All had come out for the fun of the thing; some had been promised commissions, others nothing; all had in the end to be content with berths in the Volunteer Horse, to be dressed in brown cords, and to carry the mails.[154]

On the Frontier most of the Irregular units were issued with Snider carbines, and there were still some of these in evidence in Zululand, although most were withdrawn and replaced with Swinburne-Henrys before the campaign began. The troopers carried their ammunition – 50 rounds – in loops on bandoliers slung over the shoulder. That, a blanket and perhaps a water-bottle over one shoulder and a haversack over the other, was the extent of their kit. With this, as Mossop observed, they were fully equipped for their duties of 'patrol, patrol, fatigue duty, outlying picket, horse-guard, cattle-guard – an endless round of duties and no leisure'. The strengths of the Irregular system – their mobility and flexibility – were ideally suited to the temperament of both Buller and Wood, and throughout the war they were fully employed to the best of their abilities. They took part in long-range reconnaissance work, kept up the pressure on the Zulu by raiding homesteads and carrying off cattle, and formed an ideal striking arm for punitive work. Mossop, again, summed up their way of life:

It was a hard life for the FLH at this time – always on patrol, wet to the skin for days on end. We had no overcoats or raincoats, only one blanket, strapped to the saddle, in which we wrapped ourselves; and in long rows, closely packed together for warmth, we would sleep, with the rain pouring down on us.

Awakened by a gentle kick on the foot by the corporal during the night, we would silently arise, leave our wet blankets behind, and, with several other shivering wretches, follow him into the darkness, in the teeth of driving rain, to relieve guard, and stand there for hours.

There was no grumbling. If we were lying in the mud and rain, so was Buller. If we were hungry, so was he. All the hardships he shared equally with his men. Never did Buller, as commander, have a patrol tent to sleep under, while his men were in the open.... Such a life soon hardened me, and I was able to endure it all as well as the toughest man in the corps.[155]

The Irregulars fought extensively in the major engagements of the war, too; indeed, they provided the majority of the troops employed in the disastrous expedition to Hlobane on 28 March. Despite the many casualties – Weatherley's Border Horse suffered particularly badly on that occasion, both Weatherley and his teenage son being killed – they fought again at Khambula the following day, at first provoking the Zulu right to an unsupported attack, then, at the end of the battle, driving the exhausted Zulus from the field. They were involved in numerous skirmishes throughout the second invasion, and again formed the majority of the troops who scouted across the White Mfolozi under Buller on 3 July. On that occasion two of the Frontier Light Horse, Captain Cecil D'Arcy and Sergeant Edmund O'Toole, were awarded the Victoria Cross for their efforts to save unhorsed men in the face of

the Zulu attack. The following day at Ulundi – as they had at Khambula – the Irregulars first drew on the Zulu army, and later joined the pursuit. Some of the Irregular units were employed during pacification operations right up to the end of hostilities, and indeed went on to serve in Sir Garnet Wolseley's decisive campaign against Sekhukhune in November 1879.

It is Mossop again – the most vivid chronicler of life in the ranks of the Irregulars – who describes what was, for many, the reality of the return to civilian life when the war was over and the Irregulars disbanded:

We then trekked to Landman's Drift, to the south of Utrecht – a disreputable-looking lot of men – where we were deprived of our horses by a grateful government, and told to walk to Maritzburg, a distance of some hundred miles, to be disbanded.

I applied for my discharge on the plea of having joined the force at Blood River, and living in the Transvaal. It was granted, and after receiving my pay – between seventy and eighty pounds – I bought a horse for seven pounds (I think the seller stole him) and rode off to Utrecht, where I arrived about nine o'clock that night. It was bitterly cold, the blanket I had been using belonged to the government and was handed over, therefore I had only the threadbare, torn clothes I was wearing. Proceeding to the hotel, I was told by the proprietor that he did not cater for my class; he not only refused me accommodation, but would not even sell me a bundle of forage for my horse.

Going to the open Church Square, I hobbled the horse and returned to the hotel kitchen, thinking I could perhaps pick up a snack of food, and get warm near the fire, but the [Indian] cook turned me out.

The stores were all closed, and no blanket to be bought. I returned to my saddle, using it as a pillow, curled myself up and slept until about two in the morning, when I awoke with my clothes stiff with frost. I did sentry-go until sunrise. Such was my reception in Utrecht, and all my boyish dreams of returning 'a warrior bold' melted with the frost on my clothes.[156]

Irregular Troops (Zulu)

Since the Zulu military system was essentially a citizen militia, in theory every man in the kingdom was enrolled in his turn in one of the king's *amabutho*. One of the few exceptions to this rule concerned those who were training to become *izangoma* – spirit diviners – and who were considered to have a higher calling; nevertheless, the high incidence of young men wishing to claim immunity from national service on the grounds that they had been called to serve the ancestral spirits instead had aroused some suspicion in King Mpande's time, and his successor King Cetshwayo had restricted the practice.

Despite an almost universal degree of enlistment, however, it was unlikely that at any given time an *ibutho* was assembled in its entirety. Some men were always held back from the king's musters to tend cattle and protect noncombatants, even at a time of national emergency such as the British invasion. Indeed, when he assembled his *amabutho* in January 1879 to prepare them to contest the British advance, the king none the less instructed *amakhosi* living in the border regions to hold back enough of their men to watch the British movements and potentially harass them. Although these were men who individually were members of the *amabutho* they functioned on these occasions as local irregulars, commanded by *izinduna* appointed by their *amakhosi*. In some areas this tradition was particularly strong; the men of the abaQulusi section in northern Zululand, who were particularly loyal to the Royal House, were not enrolled in age-based *amabutho* but instead fought throughout as irregulars.

Often, when the *amabutho* marched through Zululand on their way to the enemy, they would be joined by groups of men who had hitherto remained with those *amakhosi* who lived along the way. The Sithole *inkosi* Matshana kaMondise, for example, had retained his men along the central Mzinyathi border and had sheltered them in the Qudeni bush when the Centre Column pressed forward to iSandlwana, in Sithole territory. When the main Zulu army reached iSiphezi mountain on 20 January, King Cetshwayo's appointed *izinduna* sent instructions for Matshana's Sithole to join them. It was their journey, up the Mangeni towards iSiphezi and across the front of Chelmsford's column, that the British reconnaissance had interrupted on the evening of 21 January, and which the British so fatally misinterpreted. It is not clear whether these groups dispersed when they joined a large army, to allow the men to seek out their own *amabutho*; if so, they must have fought with their own shields, having missed the distribution of shields at the central muster.

After the Zulu success at iSandlwana the *amabutho* dispersed. As the war progressed, the regional *amakhosi*, especially those threatened by the British advance, tended to keep back more men each time from the subsequent musters. As a result, particularly after the mid-period battles at Khambula and kwaGingindlovu, the British noticed an increase in activity by locally directed Zulu forces. In the north, where the war was essentially a local affair punctuated by occasional activity from the *amabutho*, the attack on the 80th convoy at Ntombe Drift was carried out by a mixed force drawn from the followers of Prince Mbilini and Manyanyoba Khubeka, the abaQulusi, and members of the *amabutho* who were then living locally at home. The action at the Zungeni mountain on 5 June – when the adjutant of the 17th Lancers was killed – seems to have been carried out in defence of *inkosi* Sihayo's eZulaneni homestead by members of his own amaQungebeni people. Similarly, the Zulu raid across the Thukela at Middle Drift on 25 June was carried out by members of the Ntuli, Magwaza and Cube people, who lived on the Zulu bank.

iSandlwana: 'Ancient, Stern and Grand'

In 1914 the novelist Sir Henry Rider Haggard visited Zululand for the first time. At iSandlwana he found himself deeply affected by the atmosphere of the battlefield, the more so because

King Cetshwayo kaMpande, photographed in captivity at Cape Castle. (*Ron Sheeley Collection*)

Lieutenant-General Lord Chelmsford, the commander of British forces in southern Africa in 1879. (*Ron Sheeley Collection*)

Royal Artillery: two 9-pdr RML guns in Zululand. (*Private Collection*)

Burying the dead. A wooden headboard made by members of the garrison of Eshowe and afterwards placed upon the British graves at Nyezane. (*Campbell Collections, University of Natal*)

n battlefields where they were defeated, the Zulu dead in contrast were left where they fell. At undi . . .

and kwaGingindlovu.

Irregulars under Redvers Buller capturing abaQulusi cattle during the attack on the ebaQulusini homestead on 1 February 1879. The swords carried by the troopers are a romantic flourish by the engraver.

Lady Florence Dixie, seated among the British officers at the Nhlazatshe meeting on 31 August 1881. The failure of the British representative, Evelyn Wood, to address the grievances of Zulu royalists led to the start of a bitter Zulu civil war – and led Lady Florence to champion the cause of King Cetshwayo.

False alarm. The nervousness generated by the Zulu success at iSandlwana meant that panics like this were common in the British camps at night during the final advance on oNdini.

The high incidence of flogging as a field punishment in Zululand – for regulars and auxiliaries alike – led to a parliamentary debate in London and contributed to the abandonment of the practice.

Gatling guns. Major J.F. Owen (in front of gun, left) and the two Gatlings of 10/7 Battery RA he commanded at Ulundi. (*Private Collection*)

A Zulu *inyanga* or herbalist, draped in the gourds and horns containing his medicines. (*Private Collection*)

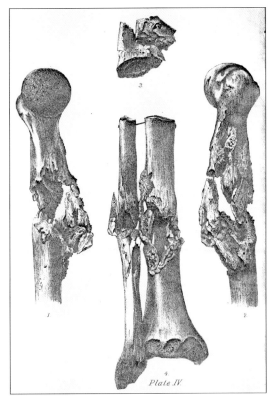

Limb bones shattered by the impact of Martini-Henry bullets, as sketched by British surgeons. Such injuries were beyond the skills of Zulu *izinyanga*.

Auxiliary troops. A white officer – thought to be Henry Francis Fynn Jnr – and some of his men, photographed on their return from the war. (*Private Collection*)

Natal Volunteer troops. Two men of the Victoria Mounted Rifles in typical field uniforms.

The Last of the 24th, Isandula. R.T. Moynan's 1883 painting of one of the last British soldiers to die in the battle is loaded with heavy imperial symbolism. (*Private Collection*)

Ernest Grandier, the only white man captured alive by the Zulus during the war, represented as a classic hero smiting the heathen in this engraving from *Pictorial World* magazine.

The assault on the hospital at Rorke's Drift, represented for once from the Zulu side in this remarkably accurate contemporary study.

A dramatic rendition of British troops looting and burning the royal homestead at oNdini; note the man (centre) carrying away a shield as a trophy.

The efficiency of Zulu rifle fire at Khambula was greatly improved by the capture of British Martini-Henrys at iSandlwana.

A striking studio portrait of a Zulu man, his stabbing spear and his wife. (*Private Collection*)

These Swazi men attached to Wood's Irregulars fought with Wood's column; unlike the Zulus, the Swazi retained a good deal of their ceremonial costume in the field. (*Private Collection*)

'We are soldiers; we have shown you how we can fight, and I'll show you how we can die' runs the original caption to this surprisingly honest contemporary engraving.

The novelist Rider Haggard examining British graves on the Ulundi battlefield in April 1913, guided by a Zulu named Simpofu (centre) who had fought in the battle with the iNgobamakhosi.

Travelling shows: 'The Great Farini' (centre) and some of the Zulu troupe he brought to Europe. The costume of the men is undeniably authentic, that of the woman and boy rather more suspect. (*Private Collection*)

Zulu prisoners under guard by men of the Buffs at the Lower Thukela in the aftermath of the kwaGingindlovu campaign.

A Zulu man in the full ceremonial regalia of his *ibutho*; the shield and the headdress are consistent with the appearance of the uKhandempemvu. (*Private Collection*)

Captain F. Glennie and men of the 2nd Battalion, 24th Regiment, photographed at the end of the campaign. (*Private Collection*)

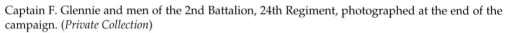

roops unloading supply wagons at 'Dunn's camp', a temporary halt on the line of advance of the st Division. (*Private Collection*)

The war correspondent Melton Prior, doyen of the Victorian 'special artists', has a narrow escape at oNdini, according to his own sketch of the incident.

Zibhebhu kaMaphitha, *inkosi* of the Mandlakazi branch of the Zulu Royal House; a skilful general in 1879, he bitterly opposed the return of King Cetshwayo in the 1880s. (*Private Collection*)

Changing times in Zululand: Hlubi kaMota, the Tlokoa *inkosi* who fought for the British in 1879 and was rewarded with a slice of Zulu territory opposite Rorke's Drift, photographed in about 1883 alongside representatives of the old order, the Princes Ndabuko kaMpande (left) and Shingana kaMpande (right). (*Private Collection*)

he had known in life many of the officers whose bones lay there in death:

When I had gone some way I turned and looked back at this lonesome, formidable hill standing there, a fit monument for the multitude of dead; immemorially ancient, stern and grand. The twilight was closing in, the sky was red, fading into grey. Over that savage crest trembled one star ... the stark mount had become very black and solemn ... This must be a quiet place for a man's eternal sleep. But the scene which went before that sleep![157]

While the sweep of historical events inevitably moves on, dramatic incidents in human history often imprint themselves on the landscape, and not merely in the detritus they leave behind – the fragments of bone or rusty metal – but, by their effect on the imagination, shaping future human interaction with the site. Rider Haggard was not the first to feel the emotive pull of iSandlwana, and the subsequent history of the site has largely been shaped by the battle which took place there.

In 1880 an Anglican mission was established on the battlefield, at the foot of the iNyoni ridge over which the Zulu attack had developed. The site was chosen because *inkosi* Hlubi kaMota of the Tlokoa – who had fought in the battle with the British, and had been rewarded by them with a chieftainship in the post-war settlement – had requested a mission presence to cement his relationship with settler Natal, and because of the mournful associations of the site. The mission was built by the Revd Charles Johnson, and one of his first tasks was to clear the prospective site of the bones of Zulu dead which still lay there. The name of the mission reflects the association with the battle – it is called St Vincent's because 22 January is St Vincent's Day.

The existence of the mission inevitably facilitated the casual trickle of visitors who passed the site in the last decades of the century and drew this otherwise remote area slowly but inexorably into the process by which Zululand was penetrated and dominated by the settler way of life. By the

beginning of the twentieth century trader Charles Parr had established a store on the outskirts of the battlefield, between the iNyogane donga and the 'Conical Koppie'. Mr Parr apparently took a passing interest in the relics of the battlefield which turned up frequently enough in those days, and amassed a small collection.

The process of burying the dead had continued even after the arrival of the mission, and it was not until 1883 that the shallow graves of the fallen British soldiers – hitherto haphazardly piled up with stones – were marked with properly constructed cairns. In 1913 the South Wales Borderers – successors to the old 24th – erected an impressive memorial on the nek below iSandlwana hill. They chose a spot which had been noted during the burial expeditions conducted by Major C.J. Bromhead in September 1879 as marking a place where a large concentration of British dead had been found. Bromhead had built a high cairn – one of three he had supervised on the battlefield – on the spot, and the stones from this were used in the construction of the base of the new memorial.[158] It was probably during the construction of this memorial that A.W. Lee, who had replaced Charles Johnson at St Vincent's, witnessed a meeting between men of the SWBs and Zulu veterans of the battle:

The British NCOs stood fresh, clean, alert, and with every button and buckle shining, over against the huddle of old, wrinkled Zulu men in their *mutshas* and skins. 'How the devil, padre,' one of the sergeants asked me, 'could these old rapscallions kill men of ours?' He forgot that in their day those same old rapscallions had been as upstanding and bold as the sergeant was then. They were terrible in war – those fine, athletic boys, with their waving plumes and their shining assegais. They had discipline, they had the *elan* which comes with a record of unblemished victory, and they were fighting for King and country.[159]

The 24th memorial was dedicated on 4 March 1914 by General Sir Reginald Hart VC.

In preparation for the 50th anniversary of the battle in 1929 an area containing the greatest number of monuments and cairns on the nek was fenced off to protect it – a decision which, ironically, left many of the outlying cairns to the ravages of neglect. The anniversary itself was attended by a large number of veterans of the battle, including Dugald MacPhail, who had been present as Quartermaster of the Buffalo Border Guard, and Richard Stevens, who had been a Trumpeter in the Natal Mounted Police. A large number of Zulu veterans also attended, and men who had fought on opposing sides talked over the stories of the battle. Sadly, watching journalists only recorded the names and reminiscences of a small number of the Zulu participants. The commemoration service was conducted by the Revd Lee, and the senior military representative was General Sir Duncan McKenzie, who had been responsible for the suppression of the Poll Tax rebellion in 1906.

Occasional gatherings on the site seem to have taken place to mark significant anniversaries thereafter, but following the victory of the Nationalist Party in the whites-only election of 1948, with its ideological commitment to Afrikaner history, a number of British historical sites were left uncared for, including iSandlwana. That the site was protected at all at this time was largely due to the efforts of George Chadwick of the Natal branch of the National Monuments Council:

During 1958 a graves curator, in ignorance, flattened many cairns to make them look like ordinary graves. This exposed some remains. The writer was requested to rebuild the cairns, and after studying all available old photographs and relying on his own memory, work was commenced. However, many of the grave-like structures made by the curator were simply covered with stones and are clearly recognisable as incompletely restored cairns. The opportunity was taken to search for neglected cairns. Some forty of these were found, carefully examined for remains, fully documented, photographed, and marked on a plan and rebuilt. These cairns included those out on the ridge where the British companies were stationed and along the route of the fugitives. In view of recent statements that very few British were killed at the advanced positions, it is interesting to note that buttons, boot protectors and bones were found when the neglected cairns were dismantled and documented. This is, of course, not evidence that the casualties in these positions were very heavy.[160]

The extensive network of cairns that characterise the site today is therefore the result of George Chadwick's efforts, although it is interesting to note that the placing of some of these cairns was based purely on his memory alone.

In order to prepare for the 1979 centenary, access to the site was improved. An existing track leading on to the battlefield was widened and a car-park bulldozed on the nek. Although undoubtedly pragmatic, these works have caused considerable damage to the site, destroying archaeological evidence in the top-soil in the area of the fiercest close-quarter fighting. The road has also encouraged the rapid spread of erosion dongas below it, which have scarred the area of the British camp.

The centenary commemorations took place in May 1979 – a date chosen to reflect the chronology of the war as a whole and to avoid stressing the significance of one incident to the detriment of others. At that time there were no tourist facilities near the site and visitors had to be located in Dundee or Vryheid and bussed to the site. Given the fragile nature of South Africa's relationships internationally during the apartheid era, it was not possible for the British Army to be officially represented but the Royal Regiment of Wales (successors to the SWBs) attended in the private capacity of its Old Comrades Association.[161] The senior dignitary was *inkosi* Mangosuthu Buthelezi, then Chief Executive of the KwaZulu Homeland.

Since the centenary tourist facilities in the region of the battlefield have significantly improved. With the opening of Fugitives' Drift Lodge in 1989 and Isandlwana Lodge in 1999 it is now possible for visitors, following the trail first opened by the likes of Bertram Mitford and Rider Haggard, to stay in luxurious accommodation within sight of iSandlwana itself, although the infrastructure built to support these Lodges has of course had its own impact upon the landscape. In 1993 iSandlwana was declared a National Historic Reserve and part of the battlefield – extending from the British firing positions to the Mzinyathi river – was fenced off to ensure its preservation. Although a number of monuments have been added to the site since 1914, particularly around the time of the centenary, the first monument to the Zulu dead was not unveiled until 1999, some 120 years after the battle. That same year the first limited-scale re-enactment of the battle took place on the anniversary, and this has become a feature of subsequent commemorations.[162]

iSandlwana: 'A Portion of Bovine Intestinal Anatomy'

One of the minor but enduring controversies surrounding the events at iSandlwana concerns the meaning – and even the spelling – of the name itself. The word *iSandlwana* has historically presented problems of pronunciation for those not used to the isiZulu language, particularly the fluid sound represented by the middle '*dl*'. As a result, the word was initially rendered phonetically in British reports in various ways from the garbled *Isandlalana* to the simplified *Isandula*, which remained popular with the British press throughout the war. Lord Chelmsford himself wrote of his intention on 16 January 1879 to advance 'to the Isanblana hill', but on the 21st he dated his despatches with marginally more accuracy from 'Insalwana Hill'. His reports of the 23rd, breaking the terrible news of the battle's outcome, referred to 'Isandlana Hill', and by May he had added a 'd', rendering the name 'Insandhlwana'; he retained this version, with occasional lapses, as late as his memorandum of May 1880 defending his conduct during the campaign. Most reports, official or unofficial, from British sources reflect a similar lack of consistency although the colonial press, with rather

more awareness of local language, generally preferred the form *Isandhlwana*. This became the most popular version used in histories of the battle until the 1970s, although in fact linguistic studies of isiZulu as early as the 1940s declared that the combination '*dhl*' was unsound. The early revisionist studies of the battle, about the time of the centenary, therefore adopted the version *Isandlwana*. More recently, in respect to the technicalities of isiZulu (the first 'I' is in fact a locative prefix), it has become common to render the name *iSandlwana*.

The meaning of the word has also been the subject of some confusion. When the novelist Rider Haggard visited the site in 1914 he grumbled that two of the great colonial experts on Zulu history could not agree on the meaning of the name: 'Mr Gibson[163] declares that this name means "Like a little house"; Stuart[164] on the contrary says that the true interpretation thereof is "the second stomach of an ox". When such learned doctors disagree, as they did with vigour, I may be pardoned if I cling to the old rendering of "the place of the little hand".'[165]

Ironically, while both Gibson and Stuart may be said to be right, Haggard was not. It is true that the word *isandla* means hand, but the diminutive form ('little hand') is more correctly given as *Isandlana* not *iSandlwana*. In fact, the word iSandlwana literally means 'like a little hut' (from *indlu*, hut) but in this form it has a very specific reference. It refers to a 'little hut', raised upon stilts to keep it clear of damp and away from rats, used as a grain store in an ordinary family homestead, but the comparison is not to the hut itself but rather reflects the Zulu habit of identifying features in relation to their cattle. The 'little grain hut' is in fact a term used as an analogy to the second honeycombed stomach of a cow. The hill *iSandlwana* is therefore believed to resemble 'the second stomach of a cow'.

A number of expert isiZulu linguists, both contemporary and modern, concur with this translation. Henry Francis Fynn Jnr – son of the 1824 pioneer and friend of King Shaka, Henry Francis Fynn – who was the magistrate at Msinga at the time of the war and was present with Lord

Chelmsford's troops at Mangeni on 22 January, attempted to further explain the analogy:

> Sandhlwana is the honey-combed smaller paunch. Sandhlwana is an abrupt conical hill, precipitous rock on the eastern, southern and western sides, and much honeycombed. On the northern side its continuous ridge extends northwards and forms a spur or thumb, as it were, of the Nqutu range, Zululand, thus representing the Sandlwana store to its relative hut.[166]

The traveller Bertram Mitford noted rather testily in 1883 that the word meant 'neither "little hand" nor "little house"', nor any other of the hundred and one interpretations which were devised at the time of the disaster, but refers to a portion of bovine intestinal anatomy'.[167]

Colonel H.C. Lugg, whose father Harry Lugg had fought at Rorke's Drift with the Natal Mounted Police, and who was himself a Zulu linguist and a Native Commissioner, added further linguistic details:

> Sandhlwana is the Native form for the second or honeycomb stomach of a cow, and the hill was named, some say by Sihayo, *because of its resemblance to this organ.* The word itself is the diminutive form of *isandhlu*, the upper portion of a corn crib, or even a native watch-hut (*ixiba*), and as the second stomach of a beast serves as a storehouse, and is similar in appearance to a corn crib, or *isandhlwana*. A small corn crib is often referred to as an *isandhlwana*.[168]

He added, rather optimistically, that 'this explanation should dispose of the controversy which has arisen over this word'.

There are indeed a number of traditions that the hill was named by *inkosi* Sihayo kaXongo whose amaQungebeni people lived locally. While this may be apocryphal – a case of a significant name attaching itself to the memory of an important man who was involved in the events concerned – it is not inconceivable.

Sihayo's family had originally lived close to the White Mfolozi river but were appointed guardians of the Mzinyathi border region by King Mpande in the 1850s; as newcomers it is possible they therefore applied names to geographical features which caught their attention.

iSandlwana: 'Arguments ... Prolonged and at Times Rather Hot'

In 1914 the novelist H. Rider Haggard was about to visit Zululand for the first time, and would be shown round the historic sites by two of the great colonial experts on Zulu history, James Stuart and James Gibson.[169] After dining with them one evening at the start of his adventure, Haggard noted in his diary:

> Stuart dined here last night and the arguments between him and Mr Gibson on obscure points of Zulu history were prolonged and at times rather hot. Rival experts are apt to grow fierce about their own subjects, especially when both have written books thereon.[170]

Of all the many words Haggard wrote about the Zulu people, those contain perhaps the most enduring truth.

The fiercest debates largely centre on the battle of iSandlwana. As one of the survivors, Trooper Richard Stevens of the Natal Mounted Police, observed in a letter to his family at the time, 'there will be an awful row at home about this'.[171] He was right, of course, and the controversy which greeted the news of the disaster in both Natal and the United Kingdom still finds an echo among historians to this day.

It is not hard to see why. The sheer scale of the defeat, largely unparalleled in British military expeditions during the heyday of the empire, inevitably raises questions about the handling of the campaign and the tactics employed. The fact that none of the senior British officers present during the battle survived to justify their actions – indeed, only one regular officer holding a front-line command, Lieutenant Curling RA, survived at all – has meant that from the British perspective there is an almost total absence of first-hand evidence regarding crucial command decisions. Equally, because of the subsequent history of the Zulu kingdom (many of the senior Zulu commanders at iSandlwana were killed during the civil war of 1884) there is a similar absence of testimony from most of the major Zulu players. While accounts from participants on both sides remain the mainstay for interpreting and reinterpreting the battle, they originate for the most part from men who were peripheral to command decisions, or who were not party to them at all. Most survivors' accounts, furthermore, are naturally preoccupied with personal impressions of the horrific experiences they endured.

The battle of iSandlwana has remained, therefore, like a monumental crime scene from which huge swathes of vital evidence are simply missing, while much of what remains is fragmentary and sometimes contradictory. This of course has added to the enduring air of mystery which surrounds the battle – and the unanswered questions have been given further twists by the process of historical revisionism that has accompanied the dramatic political changes in South Africa in recent years.

Initial reaction in the immediate aftermath was one of disbelief and shock, which soon gave way to a search for scapegoats and a desire among those directly involved to salvage their personal reputations. This, with its implicit emphasis on British weaknesses and failings, remained the theme of most studies of the battle throughout the colonial period and into the 1960s. With the passing of the participants, their supporters and detractors, and with a growing interest in African perspectives of history, there has since been a gradual moving away from the concept of the battle as a 'British defeat', considering it instead as a 'Zulu victory'. The latter view stresses the central role of the Zulu generalship, of their success in manoeuvring so close to the British camp without being discovered, the way the Zulu commanders seized and retained the initiative throughout the battle, the leadership displayed by officers at regimental level and the courage and endurance displayed

by ordinary warriors. This change in perception has broadened as the battle has gradually achieved an iconic status; no longer seen merely as an isolated incident in the triumphal progress of British imperialism across southern Africa, it is now interpreted as a defining moment in both local and imperial history. In that respect the ideological and historiographical shifts reflect a similar process to that undergone by the Battle of Little Big Horn in America. The battle of iSandlwana encapsulates many of the choices imposed upon African communities by the fact of European conquest – whether to opt for violent resistance or complicity and collaboration – and exposes the over-confidence of imperial power. It also reveals many of the underlying attitudes and assumptions of settler society, and cuts to the heart of contested notions of Zulu identity and nationality. Some indication of the battle's importance can be deduced from the fact that C.E. Fripp's famous painting – largely ignored by the public at the time – is now widely reproduced beyond the context of the literature of the Anglo-Zulu War as an emblem of the period of high Empire in general.

Initial controversies largely revolved around the question of blame. The British military, for the most part, was convinced that its troops were technologically and morally superior to the Zulus, and underpinning the search for scapegoats was the assumption that the British must have won the battle, had something not 'gone wrong'. Certainly this framed Lord Chelmsford's response. Although his reputation has suffered lasting damage from his transparent efforts to distance himself from responsibility for the disaster, there is no doubt that he genuinely did not think himself culpable. As far as he was concerned he had left adequate troops at iSandlwana to defend the camp; its loss must therefore have been due to errors committed by its commanders during his absence. The tenor of the famous court of inquiry held at Helpmekaar in February 1879 reflects this. This was in no sense an impartial investigation into the conduct of the campaign as a whole; it was convened by Chelmsford's orders for the specific purpose of trying to find out, for Chelmsford's information, why the defence had failed so disastrously. As a result, the officer in charge, Colonel Arthur Harness RA, deliberately took a narrow view of his remit, and while a good deal of evidence was taken from survivors much of it went unrecorded because Harness considered that it was not relevant to the central issue.

Nevertheless the court's findings were extremely influential in shaping early impressions of the battle. They provided the basis of a report by Lieutenant Walter James RE in March 1879 which in turn later greatly influenced the account in the official *Narrative of Field Operations* (London, 1880). These not only institutionalised a number of questionable interpretations of the battle itself but also laid the framework for attempts to apportion blame. In particular, responsibility for the command decisions which led to defeat was laid at the feet of Anthony Durnford, while any implication of poor performance by troops on the ground was deflected to the black auxiliary troops of the Natal Native Contingent. Both were perfectly positioned to be scapegoats; Durnford was not only the senior officer present in the action but something of an outsider, isolated from the Natal settler society among whom he worked by the events of Bushman's Pass six years before, and by his sympathetic views towards Africans. He was also of course dead, and in no position to defend himself. The implication in James's report that the 24th Regiment had deployed in two sections, with the NNC placed between, seems to have been based on a misunderstanding of survivors' evidence and is not supported by any impartial study now; it did, however, allow British apologists to suggest that the collapse of the NNC was therefore responsible for the disintegration of the British line. Being black, the voices of the NNC survivors in their own defence also carried little weight among the British.

The limitations of these judgements were apparent even at the time and continue to influence debates about the battle. The attempts by Lord Chelmsford's staff to cement Durnford's guilt by insisting that Chelmsford, when he told Durnford to advance to the camp on the morning of the 22nd, ordered him to 'take command'

were undermined when Durnford's body was found and the orders recovered – and proved to contain no such directive. Many contemporary critics also came to argue that the defeat was not merely due to tactical errors committed during the battle but was due to the wider failings of Lord Chelmsford's leadership. Critics such as the journalist Archibald Forbes questioned the wisdom of Chelmsford dividing his army when he knew an enemy to be in the vicinity and his failure to insist that the camp at iSandlwana was fortified. Whatever culpability accrues to Durnford, it also falls within the ambiguity of Lord Chelmsford's orders, and in particular his failure to specify a role for Durnford to fulfil on his arrival in the camp. Lord Chelmsford himself must bear the principal responsibility for the extended formations adopted by the troops during the battle; his Standing Orders issued to column commanders specified these tactics as standard and copies belonging to both Durnford and (presumably) Pulleine were recovered among the dead.[172] In refuting these accusations in the years after the war, Chelmsford clung determinedly to his position that he had done all that was practicable for the defence of the camp before his departure, and that he could not be held responsible for decisions made during his absence. These issues still remain the basis of many modern debates about the battle.

The court of inquiry also highlighted divisions between the British Army professionals and the colonial troops from Natal. Differences had existed before the battle but were largely unstated – the professionals tended to be disdainful of the presumptions of the 'amateur' colonials, while the colonials felt that their experience of local conditions should have carried greater weight. In the fraught days after the battle, particularly during the court of inquiry, these differences were openly expressed. They, too, influenced early histories of the war; W.H. Clements' *The Glamour and Tragedy of the Zulu War* (London, 1936), which drew on stories gleaned from colonial survivors, largely articulated the colonial perspective, while Major Gerald French's *Lord Chelmsford and the Zulu War* (London, 1939) attempted to defend the reputation of both Lord

Chelmsford and the British military. Both points of view can still be found in modern interpretations of the battle.

In an effort to protect the reputation of the 24th Regiment, Captain William Penn Symons compiled an account of the battle based largely on survivors' evidence. His first draft – to be seen now in the regimental museum in Brecon – contained a number of implicit criticisms of the conduct of the campaign and was moderated for publication in the *Historical Records of the 24th Regiment* (London, 1892), which Penn Symons compiled with Colonels Paton and Glennie. Increasingly central to the regiment's understanding of the battle was the opinion of the survivor Horace Smith-Dorrien, first articulated on its behalf early in the twentieth century and later expounded in his autobiography, *Memories of Forty-Eight Years' Service* (London 1925), that the 24th had been overrun due to a failure of ammunition supply. A careful study of Smith-Dorrien's surviving accounts suggest, however, that his mature reflections on the battle – in which he participated as a young lieutenant – differ considerably in emphasis from his first impressions; a letter written to his father in the immediate aftermath in fact highlighted his own role in distributing ammunition.

All of these elements largely shaped the first analysis of the battle by a professional historian, Sir Reginald Coupland's *Zulu Battle Piece* (London, 1948). Coupland met with Zulu veterans of the battle on the battlefield but his account remains firmly rooted in British sources. He did, however, establish a pattern of events during the battle which was expanded and popularised by one of the most influential studies of the Anglo-Zulu War, Donald R. Morris's *The Washing of the Spears* (London, 1966).

Morris, a former United States Navy officer, wrote *The Washing of the Spears* while based in Berlin as a CIA operative during the Cold War. A confessed admirer of Hemingway, he tackled the subject with a literary flair that has made the book an enduring classic. In particular he took up and expanded the idea that certain British tactical failings were responsible for the outcome of the battle, notably a failure of ammunition

supply and the collapse of the NNC. His account has remained hugely popular and remarkably resilient to studied criticism.

Even as Morris's book was published, however, F.W.D. Jackson produced a dense, highly analytical account of the battle based entirely on a close reading of primary sources. It appeared first as a series of articles – 'Isandhlwana 1879; The Sources Re-examined' in the *Journal of the Society of Army Historical Research* in 1965 – and was reworked and expanded as *The Hill of the Sphinx* (Bexleyheath, 2002). Jackson effectively challenged many of the principal elements of Morris's version – including the ammunition question and the role of the NNC – and his study has gained a wide following and has formed the basis of most subsequent revisionist histories of the battle.

Other scholarship, much of it utilising sources unavailable to pioneers like Morris, has filled in missing parts of the jigsaw. From the 1970s many South African historians began to reassess the impact of European settlement on indigenous societies from the African perspective. A groundbreaking work in this regard was Jeff Guy's *The Destruction of the Zulu Kingdom* (London, 1979), which offered a profound insight into the nature of the Zulu political economy, and in particular the way it fractured in the aftermath of the post-war settlement imposed by the British. John Laband and Paul Thompson, both then at the University of Natal, made major contributions to the study of the war as a whole and iSandlwana in particular, initially by giving it a firm geographical basis through rigorous mapping of the sites (*A Field Guide to the War in Zululand 1879*, first published in 1979 and revised and expanded several times). John Laband went on to offer a penetrating analysis of the war from the Zulu perspective which was incorporated into his broader history of the nineteenth-century Zulu kingdom, *Rope of Sand* (Johannesburg, 1995). Paul Thompson's *The Natal Native Contingent in the Anglo-Zulu War 1879* (Pietermaritzburg, 1997) is invaluable in disentangling the intricacies of the auxiliaries' role at iSandlwana. Ian Castle's *Zulu War Volunteers, Auxiliaries and Irregulars* (London,

2003) provides an excellent concise study of the colonial units who fought at iSandlwana and elsewhere. My own *Zulu; The Battles of Isandlwana and Rorke's Drift* (London, 1992) was an attempt to describe the battle itself within the context of the Centre Column's wider campaign and through the perspective of various participants.

Since the 1990s popular interest in the Anglo-Zulu War, stimulated by television documentaries and a growth in battlefield tourism, has given rise to a small publishing industry and both iSandlwana and Rorke's Drift remain popular subjects for dissection. The value of some of these books is questionable – many merely rework existing themes, while others simply displace old myths with new ones – although others have sought to explore new theories or re-invent old ones by radically reinterpreting the surviving evidence. Ron Lock and Peter Quantrill's *Zulu Victory; The Epic of Isandlwana and the Cover-Up* (London, 2002) questioned the accepted wisdom regarding the movements of the Zulu army on the morning of the battle, argued again in favour of the ammunition failure theory, and explored the attempts by the Victorian Establishment to protect Lord Chelmsford's reputation. Lieutenant-Colonel Mike's Snook's *How Can Man Die Better? The Secrets of Isandlwana Revealed* (London, 2005) offered a strong defence of the 24th's role – he was at the time a serving officer in the 24th's successor regiment – and fresh condemnation of Durnford. Both books are further proof that the controversies which began as soon as the last shots were fired on the battlefield remain potent today, and that, even after the passage of nearly 130 years, historians are unlikely to reach a consensus in many important areas of debate.

A partial archaeological investigation of the battlefield was carried out in 2000 by a team from Glasgow University led by the pioneering battlefield archaeologist Dr Tony Pollard. While the site is undoubtedly degraded – the removal of battlefield debris across more than a century and the increase in levels of local population, with the attendant surface damage and detritus, both make it difficult to present definitive con-

clusions from the findings – the survey was highly suggestive in a number of areas. In particular there were clear suggestions that the 24th's positions were initially further forward than had been supposed, and that a significant level of re-supply of ammunition had been achieved during the battle.

In a field of study which has often been characterised by strong passions, entrenched opinions and ideological conviction rather than by a firm grasp of the evidence, however, it seems unlikely that the survey's findings will prove persuasive. In many respects the battles surrounding iSandlwana still continue.

iSandlwana: 'Such A Bloody Mess'

The battle of iSandlwana was one of the bloodiest defeats inflicted on the British Army during the Victorian era. According to the official statistics – which are not entirely reliable – some 52 white officers (regular and colonial) were killed in the battle, and 806 white NCOs and men. The number of African auxiliaries killed was officially recorded as 471, but was probably significantly higher. In addition, of course, there were a number of civilian wagon-drivers and leaders killed who did not appear on military statistics.

The only comparable disaster in terms of slaughter was during the infamous 'retreat from Kabul' in 1842, when British and East India Company forces were forced to retreat through the Afghan passes in the depths of winter and were mercilessly attacked by the Afghans. Apart from a few Europeans taken prisoner as hostages, and one man who managed to escape, the entire command was destroyed. A total of 690 regular British soldiers, 2,840 East India Co. Indian troops, and 12,000 camp followers – including women and children – were slaughtered over a period of a week (6–13 January 1842).

In terms of loss of life, particularly if civilians are included, the retreat from Kabul positively dwarfs iSandlwana, and politically the disaster was arguably greater. Yet the two events are not entirely comparable in that the retreat was spread over a longer period, and the greater loss of life fell to the Company's Indian troops. In terms of purely British military losses, iSandlwana was marginally greater; the (Queen's) 44th Regiment lost 22 officers and 645 men through action, exposure, or captured during the retreat, a figure which is broadly comparable to the losses of the two 24th Battalions alone at iSandlwana – 21 officers and 578 NCOs and men. A further 6 regular officers (Artillery, Engineers, medical staff, etc.) were killed at iSandlwana and 105 regular other ranks. Total British regular losses at iSandlwana were in the region of 710 men, making it the British Army's single bloodiest day in the Victorian period. In addition, 24 colonial officers and 121 (white) other ranks were killed as well as over 400 of the auxiliaries' rank and file.

Surprisingly, other military disasters of the period were by no means as costly as iSandlwana. At the battle of Chillianwallah (13 January 1849), when the 24th had also suffered heavily during a frontal attack on a Sikh artillery battery, they had lost 14 officers and 241 killed but a further 10 officers and 266 men wounded. Total British killed in the battle numbered about 300, although EIC casualties numbered over 300 killed and wounded – still fewer than iSandlwana. During the famous 'Charge of the Light Brigade' at the battle of Balaclava (25 October 1854) just 118 men were killed and 127 wounded. At the battle of Maiwand (27 July 1880) in the 2nd Afghan War – an action which has much in common with iSandlwana – total British and Indian Army losses were 21 officers and 948 men killed (compared to iSandlwana's grand – and probably underestimated – total of 52 officers and 1,277 men). Of the casualties at Maiwand 328 were men of the 66th Regiment – a significantly smaller total than the 1/24th's losses at iSandlwana.

At Majuba in February 1881 British losses were just 92 dead, 134 wounded and 59 captured. During the disasters of 'Black Week' in the Anglo-Boer War the British lost 135 killed and wounded and a further 600 captured at Stormberg (9 December 1899), 205 dead, 690 wounded and 76 missing or captured at Magersfontein (11 December 1899) and 143 killed, 755 wounded and 240 captured at Colenso (15 December 1899).

At Spioenkop (23/4 January 1900) British losses were 383 dead, of whom 243 were killed in Churchill's famous 'acre of massacre' on top of the mountain – far fewer than were killed in a comparably small area at the foot of iSandlwana – and 1,000 wounded and 300 captured.

One of the distinctive elements which made iSandlwana so costly is that most of those wounded in the fighting were unable to escape, and nearly all were killed, so that the proportion of killed to wounded was disproportionately high. Nor did the Zulus take any prisoners. In the Anglo-Boer War, moreover, the numbers of troops involved were much greater and the proportion of casualties therefore small; at Spioenkop, for example, the British killed amounted to only about 3 per cent of the total forces engaged. Even at the battle of Maiwand British casualties were just 44 per cent of the troops actually engaged; at iSandlwana the casualty rate was in the region of 75 per cent.

Liars, Fakes and Rogues

In December 1896, at the close of the Ndebele and Shona rebellions against British South Africa Company rule in (then) Rhodesia, Robert Baden-Powell, who had served through the fighting as a staff officer attached to the Company forces, spent an entertaining evening in the officers' mess in Umtali:

To-night we had to dinner 'Maori' B., who was with me with the Native Levy in Zululand in 1888. Celebrated over Africa for his yarns of fighting and adventure. Originally of a fine old Irish family – arrested, while a schoolboy from Cheltenham on his way to shoot at Wimbledon, on suspicion of being a Fenian; enlisted as a gunner; blew up his father with a squib cigar; shot his man in a duel in Germany; biked into the Lake of Geneva; went to New Zealand, where for twelve years he fought the Maoris; ate a child when starving, and afterwards hunted bushrangers in Australia; took a schooner in search of copper island, or anything else of value; next, a Papal Zouave; under Col.

Dodge in America he fought the Sioux. When with Pullein's corps in South Africa his men shot at him while bathing; he beat them with an ox-yoke; they stole an ostrich and hid it; a row among themselves followed, begun by a Kentish navvy, who complained he did not get his fair share of the 'duck'. B. denies that in the Maori war the Maoris displayed a flag of truce for more ammunition but to ask the troops to stop firing shells into town, so as to let them have water, 'else how can you expect us to fight?' they said. Then became a gold-digger; later, fought in the Galeka war, then the Zulu, Dinuzulu, first Matabele campaigns, and lastly the present operations, in which he is a major in the Umtali forces.[173]

George Hamilton Browne was indeed a great teller of yarns, and it must have been a particularly convivial evening for him to have repeated quite so many. Browne (the name was not originally hyphenated) was born on 22 December 1844 in Cheltenham, the son of a major serving in the 35th Regiment. From an early age George displayed an adventurous disposition and a keen interest in the military life, and – by his own account at least – his early life was much as Baden-Powell relates. He arrived in New Zealand, he said, in 1866, hoping to take part in the last of the cycle of wars which had deprived the Maori there of their land. He talked much about those adventures in later life – they earned him his nickname – and in 1911 wrote a book about them, *With the Lost Legion in New Zealand*. Drifting eventually to southern Africa he had served in Pulleine's Rangers – an Irregular unit raised by Colonel H.B. Pulleine of the 1/24th – on the Eastern Cape Frontier, and at the beginning of the Zulu campaign he joined the 1st Battalion 3rd Natal Native Contingent as a major. He took part in the early stages of the war, and crossed the Mzinyathi with the Centre Column on 11 January; he was in the thick of the fighting at *inkosi* Sihayo's stronghold on the 12th, and on 21 January he accompanied his battalion in the sweep through the Hlazakazi and Malakatha hills. The following day, sent back with his battalion to camp by Lord Chelmsford, he had watched the attack on iSandlwana unfold from a ridge a few miles away. He later took part in the Eshowe relief expedition and was present at the battle of kwaGingindlovu on 2 April; he missed the end of the war after he was crushed and injured by a mule. He had then knocked about Africa for most of the rest of his career, though he ended his days in a nursing home in Jamaica in February 1916. George Hamilton Browne married twice – first in June 1879 to Dolphina Spolander who bore him six children but died in 1904, and secondly to Sarah Wilkerson, a lady of independent means whom he married in 1909. As Sarah Browne was to discover, however, her husband's career was not all it seemed. Their days in Jamaica cleared her out financially and after George's death Sarah returned to England where she was soon reduced to working in a munitions depot, repairing soldiers' worn-out clothing. A friend appealed on her behalf to the New Zealand government, asking if Sarah might be given a pension, in view of 'Maori' Browne's long and distinguished service there. The reply she received was surprising; the government refused point-blank. So far from being a great hero of the Maori campaigns, the government had no record of any service by Browne before 1872 – when the shooting was all but over.

So was Hamilton Browne merely a fraud who had fabricated the stories of his early career to impress the military men among whom he moved in later life? Perhaps. There is no doubt that many of the adventures he describes in *With the Lost Legion in New Zealand* were not his own. He was a man who revelled in his reputation as a story-teller – and the true claim to that story did not bother him over-much. It bothered those in New Zealand whose records were entirely credible, however; when Browne's book reached the islands it was greeted with howls of indignation from former officers in the various volunteer corps – some of whom found their own adventures described inside. Yet the issue is not entirely clear-cut. A second book, this time describing his exploits in Africa (*A Lost*

Legionary in South Africa, London, *c*. 1913) – although it describes many incidents and attitudes which are uncomfortable to modern sensibilities – can largely be confirmed by independent sources. It is significant that in the first book he wrote of his involvement in New Zealand under a pseudonym; in the second he writes under his own name. The Maori War stories, it seems, were intended as just that – a succession of stirring true tales, attributed to a single fictitious character to make for a more exciting read. Browne had undoubtedly heard many of these incidents at first hand from those who participated in them, and he saw no reason to exclude them simply because they had not happened to him; if nothing else, he was broke at the time, and needed the money a best-seller would generate. So did George Hamilton Browne deserve his universal nickname of 'Maori' at all? The truth is never likely now to be known. Certainly he did not see action in the wars of the 1860s under his own name, but it was a common enough practice in the nineteenth century for men to enlist in both regular and colonial units under a false name. Intended to grant a degree of anonymity to those wishing to escape the attention of the authorities or their families, it was a habit which has left many men untraceable to history.

So of whatever George Hamilton Browne actually did in New Zealand only his own unreliable stories have remained. That he fought in Zululand and elsewhere in southern Africa, however, cannot be denied.

Hamilton Browne was not the only colourful character whose adventures in Zululand grew in the telling. In 1901 an Englishman, one 'Captain' Godolphin Finney Burslem, was tried in New York for fraud, found guilty and sentenced to imprisonment. He had pleaded for clemency before the judge on the grounds that he was a badly wounded veteran of Britain's colonial wars, and indeed his left leg had been amputated below the knee and he wore a false foot made of cork. On reviewing his case, however, the authorities found that he had a long and distinctly chequered history. Although he was clearly a 'gentleman', a member of a distinguished military

and naval family, he was very much a black sheep. He may have been born in India but his family returned to England in 1855, when he was very young, and he was christened in Portsmouth. His claim to a military rank dated to a spell in the Army in the 1870s during which he lost his leg, but by 1881 he had pitched up in New York. Almost as soon as he arrived he was causing trouble, for he insulted a lady at his hotel and refused to apologise; when he saw the same lady at a ball at West Point Academy a few days later he languidly blew cigar smoke in her face, much to the outrage of a cadet who threw him out. A year later he was arrested for fraud along with his father, but the case collapsed owing to his father's timely death. With America proving too hot for him, Burslem set sail for Egypt, hoping to join the gendarmerie then being recruited by Valentine Baker Pasha. On his arrival, however, he was turned down, presumably because of his false leg. He went, instead, to London where he was again arrested for attempted fraud. This time he was tried and convicted and spent four years in prison. On his release he returned to New York and became an American citizen but petty skirmishes with the law continued. Burslem was, apparently, a plausible charmer – with his family background, he knew of course how officers behaved. Newspaper accounts speak of his distinguished looks – and many of his victims were women.

In the end his life of crime caught up with him. When confronted by New York police officials with careful descriptions of his physical injuries compiled by the authorities during his incarceration in England – which included not only his false lower limb but gunshot wounds in the right thigh – Burslem remained game enough to insist it was a case of mistaken identity. His appeal for clemency was rejected.

Throughout his career Burslem had exploited his injuries to ingratiate himself with his victims. He was, he said, a cruelly wounded veteran of the Zulu campaign. In some versions of the story he described himself as a survivor of iSandlwana, while in another he had been present with the patrol when the Prince Imperial was killed. Needless to say no Captain Godolphin Finney

Burslem is recorded as being present on either occasion. Yet, barefaced liar though he undoubtedly was, a careful study of the military records shows that he had indeed been present in Zululand during the war – as a gunner with 11/7 Battery, Royal Artillery. He had been discharged on 9 August 1879 as unfit for duty. The reasons for this are scored through on his service papers, although one final version of the story, which he gave at the time of his last conviction, may be the closest he ever came to telling the truth – that he fell under a gun-carriage, and the wheels crushed his foot. Being Burslem, he of course claimed that he was going into action at the time; ironically, he may have been a genuine veteran of the battle of Ulundi, but if his injuries occurred there, he is not listed on the casualty returns.

Oddly, there is a Burslem family connection with another tale of the disgrace which befell a rather more genuinely heroic veteran of the Zulu campaign. Thomas Lane was born in Cork in Ireland in May 1836 and joined the Army to escape the potato famines. He served with the 47th Regiment in the Crimea and later transferred to the 67th, with whom he fought in the China campaign of 1860. During an attack on the Dagu Forts Lane and Lieutenant Nathaniel Burslem managed to crawl through flooded ditches under fire and tear a breach in the Chinese defences through which the British troops then stormed and carried the fort. Both men were badly wounded but survived, and both were later awarded the Victoria Cross. Like Hamilton Browne, Lane claimed to have fought the Maori in the 1860s, and by 1879 he was in southern Africa. Some accounts suggest he joined the 3rd Regiment, Natal Native Contingent, and if so may have been present during the iSandlwana campaign (although most of the NNC were out with Chelmsford rather than in the camp at the time it was attacked, so he was unlikely to have participated in the battle). Certainly he later joined the Natal Horse, and took part in the closing stages of the war.

In 1881 Lane joined another Irregular unit, Landry's Horse, to take part in the BaSotho 'Gun War'. From this he deserted, however, compounding his crime by absconding with his government-issue weapon and horse kit. He was caught and tried in Ladysmith and sentenced to four months' hard labour – and his VC was apparently forfeited. He was later in trouble again following the retrocession of the British annexation of the Transvaal, where he was arrested for tearing down the Republican flag. He then joined the Cape Police in Kimberley, but died there shortly afterwards in 1889.

Only eight VCs have ever been forfeited owing to subsequent misbehaviour by the recipients, and the practice was discontinued in 1920 because King George V was of the opinion that nothing should detract from a gallant deed once recognised. Some mystery surrounds Lane's medal, however, for it seems that he later applied to have it re-issued; the official records on the point are obscure, but the Royal Hampshire Regiment now holds two VCs bearing Lane's name, while a third was for a time believed to be in a private collection in southern Africa.

For others who maintained perfectly respectable records of service and were never guilty of anything more than telling a few old soldiers' yarns, a degree of genuine confusion has sometimes played havoc with the historical record. Men who served with the 2nd Battalion, 24th Regiment, were particularly vulnerable in this regard; many of them were of course present with Lord Chelmsford's command during the reconnaissance to the Mangeni on 22 January, and returned to spend a night on the devastated field of iSandlwana. They then marched back to Rorke's Drift, where they were destined to remain camped in uncomfortable circumstances for many weeks. Inevitably, on their return they regaled their families with anecdotes from their experiences, often rich with vivid detail of the aftermath of the two battles – and, wittingly or otherwise, sometimes gave rise to distinctly false assumptions. This presumably explains why Private 1195 R.A. Smyth of the 2/24th is described on his memorial stone in Anfield cemetery, Liverpool, as a 'hero of Rorke's Drift'; in fact he was a member of C Company, and his name appears on none of the authenticated Rorke's Drift rolls. Similarly, Private George

Hudd was wont to tell a story in later life that was strongly reminiscent of both iSandlwana and Rorke's Drift – that he was one of the few survivors of an action in which a small number of the 24th were attacked by an overwhelming number of Zulus. He had, he said, been badly wounded in the leg, and had survived by crawling away and hiding in the bush. But George Hudd's name does not appear on the survivors' rolls for either action, nor on any casualty returns.

For others events in the war cast aspersions on their reputations which do not, at this distance, seem to be justified. The Revd Otto Witt, the Swedish incumbent at the Rorke's Drift mission who left the battle shortly before the attack commenced, was scorned in Natal in respect of an interview he gave to the British press. It was suggested that he had claimed to have been present at both iSandlwana and Rorke's Drift. In fact, Witt said nothing of the sort; he had watched iSandlwana from the top of the Shiyane hill, overlooking the mission, and his description of what he saw – of British movements on the fringes of the battle, and of long lines of Zulus moving across country towards the Mzinyathi – is entirely credible. Realising that the garrison was about to be attacked, Witt and a friend rode away from Rorke's Drift shortly before the attack, and Witt merely remarks that he had looked back to see the first Zulu attack rushing up to the British barricades. What really seems to have provoked the ire of the colonial press, however, and led them to heap scorn on Witt's veracity, were some disparaging comments he had made upon the settlers' attitude towards, and treatment of, Natal's African population.

Another man whose name seems to have been unfairly tarnished is Gert Wilhelm Adendorff. Adendorff was born in Graaff Reinet in the Eastern Cape on 10 July 1848 to a German father and French mother. During the 9th Frontier War against the amaXhosa, an Irregular unit called the Kaffrarian Rifles was raised among the German-speaking settlers on the Cape frontier, and Gert Wilhelm volunteered. With the end of that campaign and the prospect of a fresh one in Zululand Adendorff again volunteered and was made a lieutenant in the 3rd Regiment, Natal Native Contingent. As such he served throughout the iSandlwana campaign.

Rumours doubting his conduct during the events of 22 January seem to have begun circulating almost immediately afterwards. Yet Adendorff left his own account of his movements – and there is a surprising amount of independent evidence to support his veracity. He was certainly in the camp on the morning of the battle, for he is noted as having brought in reports from the outlying NNC pickets on the iNyoni ridge. By his own account he remained with his men until they broke in the face of the final determined Zulu attack when he too – like most of the NNC officers – fled. When his own horse was killed under him he commandeered another from a mounted auxiliary and escaped in company with *inkosi* Hlubi's mounted Sotho troop. Hlubi did not go by way of Sothondose's Drift but instead his men broke through the encircling right 'horn' and followed the Mzinyathi river upstream. When they stopped to rest their horses just below Rorke's Drift, Adendorff and another survivor rode ahead to warn the garrison, crossing by way of the pont commanded by Lieutenant Chard. Chard, in his official report, went out of his way to state that Adendorff was the only one of the iSandlwana survivors who stayed to assist in the defence. Adendorff's participation was not generally noticed because he took up a position inside the storehouse and remained there throughout the battle; nevertheless, his presence was remarked upon by two further witnesses the following morning, and later another iSandlwana survivor supported his statement.

Despite this, Adendorff has been subject to this day to the persistent criticism that he in fact left iSandlwana unconscionably early, and that he again abandoned the garrison at Rorke's Drift. The Zulu campaign was the graveyard of many a military reputation, and Adendorff's seems destined to be among them – which is particularly ironic since in fact he has a very good case to claim that he was the only man on the British side to have fought in both battles.

Medical Facilities (British)

For the first two decades of Queen Victoria's reign the medical facilities of the British Army – like so many aspects of military practice – had remained largely unchanged since the days of the Napoleonic Wars. There was no common structure of medical care across the Army; civilian surgeons were employed by individual regiments and the standards of medical care and knowledge varied considerably as a result. Many Army doctors were conscientious men who struggled to do their best for their patients with the facilities available to them; others were unimaginative, ignorant or brutalised by years of exposure to floggings and casual injury.

Even among the best of them the level of understanding of basic survival and surgery techniques was limited. It was an important element of tactical doctrine that in battle an attack should not be allowed to lose impetus under pressure from its own casualties. Officers in an attack kept their men moving; the wounded were left where they fell and only after the battle was over were soldiers – and the lot usually fell to bandsmen – allowed to undertake the grim duty of picking over the battlefield to sort the dead from the living. Bandsmen themselves were given no medical training; it was merely their job to carry the injured as best they could to field hospitals for treatment. By that stage many men who might have been saved by a basic application of first aid had already died from loss of blood or shock.

Nor were conditions at the hospitals enticing. A major action, such as that at the Alma in the Crimea, simply swamped the available services, and wounded men were left in agony to take their turn, fully exposed to the suffering of their comrades around them. Faced with a ghastly array of injuries, most surgeons resorted freely to amputation, cutting off badly damaged limbs with as much speed and efficiency as they could muster. While some believed in the anaesthetic effect of alcohol – a slug of brandy or rum – others recognised that this merely excited the patient further and facilitated blood-loss and so offered nothing except a wad to bite on. Flesh was cut through in a matter of seconds with a sharp knife; sawing through the bone took a little longer. Bleeding arteries were sewn up or cauterised – sealed by burning – with carbolic acid. The severed limbs were thrown in a pile outside the hospital tent, in plain view of those waiting their turn, and were later buried by fatigue parties, a duty that was particularly hated. Other injuries were probed – the bullet needed to be extracted from gunshot wounds, together with any fragments of material from clothing driven into the wound, which were a notorious source of infection – and sewn up. Particularly skilful surgeons might try to treat head injuries by rearranging pieces of shattered skull, but the prognosis was never good – and indeed a high proportion of injured survived their wounds only to die under the surgeon's knife, or from shock and infection afterwards, since the basic principles of post-operative hygiene were only dimly understood.

The much-publicised shambles of the Crimean expedition – which differed from early campaigns not in the degree of shamble-ness but in the degree of publicity it was afforded – had led to a far-ranging review of Army medical facilities. As with so much contemporary reform, much of it was carried out in the face of determined conservative opposition, and many Army doctors were not only unconvinced by attempts to introduce common practice but also resented the erosion of regimental privileges. In 1873, however, the regimental system was finally abolished as part of Minister of War Cardwell's reforms, and all existing military doctors were brought under the control of the Army Medical Department which was given its own command structure. And while the AMD provided surgeons of officer rank, to be trained to a common standard of practice, the Army Hospital Corps was formed to provide trained orderlies and bearers.

Although the new system created a greater level of infrastructure for medical support, it was inevitably tested to the full by the realities of colonial warfare. In 1877, for example, when the 9th Cape Frontier War broke out in southern Africa, there were just two AMD surgeons at the Cape who could be spared to join the troops in the field, together with a handful of AHC personnel. Since the resulting campaign was fought by troops spread in small garrisons or widely spaced offensive columns across a wide swathe of difficult terrain the strain on the medical services was immense. That they did not collapse completely under the pressure was due to the energies of the senior medical officer in southern Africa, Surgeon-General John Woolfreys. An experienced officer, who had faced the challenges of evacuating the sick and injured down forest tracks in the Asante campaign in West Africa in 1873, Woolfreys struggled to impose as efficient a system on the frontier campaign as the facilities would allow. He augmented the number of AMD surgeons with civilian volunteers from the settler community, and established field hospitals near the forward positions which fed injured men down a line of communication to secure hospitals in the rear. In earlier frontier wars the injured had faced long and agonising journeys away from the front line in springless ox-wagons; anxious lest this be repeated Woolfreys had applied to the War Office for an issue of purpose-built ambulance wagons, but this request had been flatly refused. Nothing daunted, he organised the hire of a number of light carts and wagonettes at the Cape which at least improved the speed of casualty evacuation.

Woolfreys' experiences were fresh in his mind when Chelmsford began planning for the invasion of Zululand in late 1878. The War Office in London had been similarly reluctant to support Frere's aggressive stance against King Cetshwayo, and Chelmsford was faced with launching his invasion with too few resources – a common enough complaint among Victorian military commanders. There were still only a handful of AMD surgeons and just 120 AHC staff available to support the invasion, but Woolfreys drew up a thorough set of Field Hospital Regulations in an attempt to use them efficiently. The standard peace-time concept envisioned by the AMD was a Field Hospital of 200 beds. Clearly, given the widely separated nature of the British forces – three offensive columns and two defensive ones – such a unit was both impractical and unnecessary and Woolfreys broke it down instead

to eight units each capable of supporting 25 beds, which were then dispersed among the columns. Two of these units were attached to Chelmsford's offensive columns. Each unit consisted of an AMD surgeon and a small detachment of AHC orderlies. To increase the resources available to him, Woolfreys accepted the services of a number of civilian volunteer doctors while frontline casualty evacuation fell – as it traditionally did – to regimental personnel. A number of base hospitals were established at towns in Natal and the Transvaal – Durban, Pietermaritzburg, Ladysmith, Newcastle and Utrecht – to provide convalescent facilities for men sent down from the front. To assist in this task Woolfreys established a bearer corps, manned by African auxiliaries, who were equipped with 'Asante cots' – covered hammocks slung between poles, carried over the shoulder by two bearers. Anticipating the same lack of ambulances as had prevailed on the Cape Frontier, Woolfreys authorised the conversion of a number of Ordnance Department 'General Service' wagons. These were lighter than ox-wagons, had springs, and were drawn by mules; Woolfreys suggested that they be adapted by the addition of a second floor – to hold men lying on stretchers in tiers, to double the capacity – and by the addition of extra seats at the front for the walking wounded.

Woolfreys' system was largely in place by the time the invasion began on 11 January 1879, but it was stressed almost to the limit by the events of 22 January. The medical staff attached to the Centre Column were commanded by Surgeon-Major Peter Shepherd, a conscientious Scot who was an acknowledged expert on first aid, and who had produced a pamphlet on it for the use of troops under his command. Shepherd attached a forward hospital unit to the Centre Column itself and established another in the house at Rorke's Drift which the missionary Otto Witt had leased to the military. The Rorke's Drift detachment was commanded by Surgeon James Reynolds and was primarily intended to treat men passed down the line from the column who were suffering from wounds, accidental injury or – most commonly – the sort of ailments that were endemic among British troops operating in Africa, such as stomach complaints and blisters.

On the 22nd Shepherd's detachment had been left with the camp at iSandlwana and when the Zulus attacked Shepherd established a field hospital among the tents, to where men were brought from the firing line by the bandsmen of the 24th. Once it became clear, however, that the British position was on the verge of collapse Shepherd loaded the wounded into an ambulance and tried to evacuate them to Rorke's Drift. He was, however, overtaken by the speed of the Zulu attack: the wagon was intercepted and the wounded dragged out and killed. Shepherd himself was killed during the retreat, struck by a thrown spear after he had stopped to tend a wounded man in the Manzimnyama valley. Elements of the Zulu army then went on to attack Rorke's Drift, and the staff of Reynolds' detachment found themselves in the front line of a sustained attack which lasted intermittently for ten hours. The sick who were already in the makeshift hospital building were evacuated under fire; Reynolds himself would later be awarded the Victoria Cross for not merely tending to freshly wounded men but also carrying ammunition to isolated positions.

In addition to Shepherd, Lieutenant of Orderlies A.W. Hall and ten other men of the AHC were killed at iSandlwana, together with Surgeon F.W. Buee and Hospital Sergeant Cane of the NNC; at the same time most of the column's medical supplies were destroyed. While iSandlwana produced almost no wounded – the Zulus killed them all – many in the garrison at Rorke's Drift required medical treatment, while the fact that the remainder of the column was directed to remain at Rorke's Drift, in cramped and insanitary conditions fouled by the lingering presence of the Zulu dead, added to the strain on the surviving medical facilities. As soon as they were able, the surviving wounded were evacuated to Helpmekaar where a new field hospital was established. Even there, however, conditions were far from ideal, and sick men were often required to lie on improvised beds supported by sacks of supplies which had been exposed to the elements and were steadily rotting.

Nevertheless, the actions of the 22nd had at least indicated how far the standards of medical care and knowledge had advanced since the Crimean War. Even under the most trying circumstances the wounded had been treated promptly, their injuries debrided of damaged material and dressed. At Rorke's Drift Reynolds managed to locate and extract Zulu musket balls despite the often erratic injuries they inflicted, slewing through muscle and bouncing off bone, while a generation before it is unlikely that an injury like that inflicted on Private Fred Hitch – whose shoulder-blade was shattered by a musket-ball fired at close range – could have been treated without recourse to potentially fatal amputation.

The disaster at iSandlwana did at least galvanise the authorities in London, and Chelmsford was sent extensive reinforcements. These included a number of AMD personnel and AHC drafts. When newspaper reports began to appear describing the rise in sickness which prevailed among Chelmsford's static camps between February and April, a number of civilian volunteers also offered their services. Seven trained nurses from the Royal Hospital at Netley, under the leadership of Superintendent of Nurses Jane Deeble, were dispatched to Durban, along with a doctor and seven nurses from the privately funded Stafford House South African Aid Society. In Natal itself the Bishop of Natal, William Colenso, offered the services of six nuns to act as nurses. All of these volunteer personnel were employed in the base hospitals rather than in field hospitals at the front.

By the end of May Lord Chelmsford was ready to begin a new invasion of Zululand and Woolfreys had reorganised his medical staff to meet the challenge. Although the number of columns was reduced, Chelmsford still intended to invade on two fronts and the columns would be operating at the heads of long lines of communication. Woolfreys established field hospitals at the base of each column but decided to allocate AMD personnel at the front to particular units or brigades of units – ironically mimicking the old and controversial regimental system. It was, however, the most practical use of the resources available, and it coped remarkably well with the fighting during the last stages of the war. Early on the morning of 4 July Lord Chelmsford left his camp on the White Mfolozi and crossed the river with a large part of the troops under his command, intending a final confrontation with the Zulu army within sight of the royal homestead at oNdini. With him was a field hospital commanded by Surgeon-Major Patrick Stafford, which was positioned inside the left rear of the square formation adopted by Chelmsford. After the subsequent Zulu attack, the wounded were brought from the ranks to be treated by Stafford's surgeons, despite the fact that due to the undulations in the ground the dressing station found itself exposed to a heavy Zulu cross-fire.

The battle of Ulundi was the last major test in action for the AMD, and its personnel coped well. Although skirmishing continued during the pacification operations until September, by far the greater challenge remaining to Woolfreys' staff was the ever-growing number of sick in the British camps, most of them suffering from dysentery brought about by a reliance on polluted water-supplies. Although iSandlwana distorted the statistics – producing a great many British dead but no wounded survivors – it is none the less significant that throughout the war some 37 officers and 206 European troops were otherwise wounded in action, together with 57 African auxiliaries,[174] while almost an equivalent number – 17 officers and 330 men – died of disease. A further 99 officers and 1,286 other ranks were invalided from the campaign as a result of sickness and accidents, reflecting a universal truth of Victorian colonial warfare – that disease presented the medical services with by far the greatest challenge during the campaigns in Africa.

Medical Facilities (Zulu)

A few days after the battle of Ulundi, one of Lord Chelmsford's staff officers, Captain William Molyneux, was returning to Natal when he marked a distinct change in the Zulus he encountered along the way. Men who had been enemies just a few days before, fighting in defence of their country, now seemed accustomed to the reality of defeat, and were prepared to meet with the invaders without apparent animosity. Molyneux noted, however, the high price they had paid for their defiance:

> There were a lot of wounded, all as merry as could be. One had lost two brothers at Isandhlwana, and had been wounded at Ulundi himself; his regiment was the Nkobamakosi ... How he had got home in a fortnight he scarcely knew; it was very hard work, for he had been wounded in the thigh, but the other boys had helped him ...
>
> An old man, who had lost half his right arm ... had fought in the district, at Inyezane and Ginghilovo, and at the latter place the bone of his arm had been smashed by a bullet below the elbow; but he had cut the loose part off, and the wound had healed now. The many little mounds outside, covered with stones, told how many poor fellows had crawled home merely to die.[175]

As this account suggests, the chances of survival among Zulus wounded in action in 1879 was something of a lottery. Unlike their British counterparts, the Zulus had no organised medical facilities. The treatment of wounded was left to individual *izinyanga* who fulfilled the role of both herbalists and surgeons, and no attempt seems to have been made by the Zulu high command to ensure that *izinyanga* accompanied a military expedition, although of course some may have chosen to do so. Most medical care seems to have been provided to injured men after their return to their homesteads, however.

As Molyneux noted, it therefore fell to relatives and friends of the wounded to provide the first line of medical support. After a victorious battle – in which the Zulu were left in possession of the field – men sought out their injured comrades, stuffing moss or other vegetable matter into open wounds and binding them up with grass. After iSandlwana it is said that many in the Zulu army remained in the vicinity of the Ngwebeni valley – where they had bivouacked the night before the battle – until the injured had either recovered sufficiently to be moved, or had simply died. They were then faced with long and agonising journeys across country, over rocky hills and through streams and rivers, to reach their homes. If they did not succumb to loss of blood or infection along the way they could expect there a surprisingly sophisticated level of medical assistance, all of it carried out, however, without the aid of anaesthetic. Most *izinyanga* understood the importance of debriding wounds – of removing damaged or mortified parts with a sharp spear-blade – and of washing wounds regularly with clean water. Exposed organs were washed and replaced and the wound sewn up with sinew, broken limbs were supported with wooden splints, and poultices and herbal infusions were used to reduce infection and bring down fever. Some particularly admired *izinyanga* were reputedly able to replace broken skull fragments and treat serious head injuries. Certainly, British observers noted some remarkable examples of men who had survived a terrifying array of injuries. Henry Harford met a young veteran of iSandlwana at the close of the war who seems to have been on the receiving end of a veritable hailstorm of bullets:

> One ... had gone through his hand, three had gone through his shoulder and smashed his shoulder-blade, two had cut the skin and slightly into the flesh right down the chest and stomach, and one had gone clean through the fleshy part of the thigh. The others were mere scratches in comparison with these, but there he was, after about eight months, as well as ever and ready for another set-to.[176]

In 1902 Harry Lugg, who had fought at Rorke's Drift as a trooper in the Natal Mounted Police, met a Zulu who had stood on the opposite side of the barricade during the same battle. This man, too, had been injured several times – one bullet had creased his scalp, another had hit his left shoulder, and two had passed through the calf of his leg.

Yet these men were the lucky ones. If the *inzinyanga* were familiar with the wide array of natural injuries that resulted from living in the open air in a dangerous environment, and with the sort of penetrative or impact injuries that resulted from fighting with traditional weapons, few were able to cope with the ghastly injuries inflicted by British artillery and shell fire. Shells and shrapnel knocked off limbs and shattered torsos, rockets sprayed men with burning propellant, and Martini-Henry bullets, while they clipped neatly through muscle and flesh, shattered long-bones into fragments or left dreadful exit wounds. Faced with such devastating tissue damage, most *izinyanga* could do little but bind up the injury – and hope.

One major element affecting the survival of Zulu wounded was the ability of their comrades to evacuate them quickly and safely from the battlefield. Even after a victory this was problematic – men lying hidden in long grass or gullies, or unconscious, could easily be overlooked – and after a defeat it could be almost impossible to retrieve them. At best the wounded might be abandoned by their fleeing colleagues; at worst they were likely to be overtaken by pursuing enemies and killed. After Khambula some British observers noted large numbers of wounded Zulus being supported away by one or two of their comrades; most were too slow to escape from the particularly rigorous pursuit on that occasion. After kwaGingindlovu Captain Hutton of the 3/60th noted that,

> Many dead bodies were found by the mounted men, so Barrow told me, on the following day close to the Inyezane, and all along the banks of the stream, half concealed in the long grass, the dead lay thick. The bodies were presumably those of men who had crawled or been supported by their friends from the field of battle, and then been abandoned when it was found impossible to carry them across the swollen river.[177]

On his return to Rorke's Drift on the morning of 23 January, Lord Chelmsford and his command found large numbers of bloodied Zulu shields on the Natal bank, which the Zulu retreating from the battle had used to drag away wounded comrades. Given that the water-level in the river was high, it is unlikely that many of the badly wounded were safely carried across. Later, when his men reached the battlefield itself, they passed over it, killing those wounded Zulus who still lay there.

For those individuals left injured on a battlefield who were lucky enough to escape the pursuit the only option was to try to stagger or crawl to the nearest homestead and seek help. This was all the more difficult in 1879 because, although the fighting took place on Zulu soil, the majority of non-combatants had abandoned their homesteads as the armies drew near. At Nyezane, British troops passing through the battlefield *en route* from Eshowe to the Thukela a few days after the battle heard wounded Zulus calling out to them; while they stopped to help a few lying close to the road, there was no time to assist others lying further off. Wounded men, some of whom had managed to cover remarkable distances despite their injuries, were a feature of Zulu battlefields for days afterwards as Guy Dawnay noted at kwaGingindlovu four days after the battle:

Found a prisoner, a poor wretch who had been shot through the foot and heel at Gingindhlone, and had crawled miles on his hands and knees till the latter were swollen in the most horrible way and all the flesh worn off.[178]

That anyone survived the ordeal of being injured, and the journey back home, was, as George Mossop recognised after Khambula, largely a tribute to the general level of fitness and stamina enjoyed by a people who had lived healthy out-door lives and were inured to a degree of physical hardship as a matter of routine:

For some days many wagons were employed in carting away the dead. This I am sure of, that for every one picked up five died in the surrounding country. For months we found them when on patrol – some considerable distances from Khambula. A native will travel for many miles with a

wound which would prevent a white man taking one step.[179]

And as Molyneux had recognised, many of those who succeeded in reaching the succour and support offered by their families were by no means safe. Bertram Mitford came to the conclusion that their chances were altogether slim:

I was surprised at the fewness of wounded men I fell in with during my progress through the country. Whether, owing to rude surgery, numbers died whom the most ordinary skill could easily have saved, I cannot say, but considering that every man with whom I conversed had taken part in one or more of the battles, the fewness of those who had wounds to show *was* rather remarkable.[180]

Military Organisation (British)

In 1879 the standing of the British Army in Victorian society was so low that it was said that even in the labouring classes – for whom work was hard to find and the struggle to survive intense – many mothers would prefer to see their sons lost to prison than to an Army career. Even the educated middle classes, who thrilled to the dramatic illustrations in the weekly press of their red-coated heroes' adventures on the far-flung borders of empire, were rather less enamoured of the examples they saw brawling and whoring in garrison towns at home.

Many of these attitudes dated back to the Napoleonic era when to 'go for a soldier' was indeed the last resort of the desperate or the degenerate, and the great Duke of Wellington had no very high opinion of the men under his command – 'scum of the earth', he characterised them taciturnly, 'fellows who have enlisted for drink'. And, in the days when the Army supplied huge quantities of cheap alcohol to its men to dull the boredom of the crushing daily routine there may have been some truth in this – although the grim reality was that hard times, 'Jack Frost and unemployment', were the best recruiting sergeants. In the early nineteenth century men enlisted for a remarkably long time – twenty-one years in the infantry and twenty-four in the cavalry. To some extent the length of service was part of the attraction – it meant at least twenty-one years of regular food – but given the extent to which the hardships of service aged them it meant few men could look forward to the prospect of meaningful employment afterwards – and thus their service was in effect for life.

The attitude towards the welfare of the men in the ranks began to change, as with so much in Army experience, in the aftermath of the Crimean campaign. In particular, Edward Cardwell, the Minister of War in Gladstone's 1868–74 administration, undertook a programme to both improve the lot of ordinary soldiers and make service more attractive. Cardwell introduced a 'short service' system in which a recruit signed up for a minimum of six years. At the end of that time he could enlist for a further six years' active service – 'with the Colours', as it was known – or pass back into civilian life with no more than a commitment to serve as a reservist for six years. The change made enlistment less of a life-time's commitment, making it attractive to a better class of recruit,[181] while at the same time creating a large trained reserve against the possibility of a conventional war in Europe.

This change was not entirely welcomed by Army traditionalists who argued that it loaded the ranks with young and inexperienced men at the expense of steadier old salts. The debate was at its height in 1879 and conservatives saw much in the behaviour of the young battalions, sent out fresh from England after iSandlwana, to support their arguments.

There were subtle changes in the demographics of recruiting across the period too. Most men were still drawn from that great Victorian underclass, the unemployed labourer – for whom work could be painfully intermittent and the only alternative the cold charity of the workhouse – but whereas in 1800 the Army had recruited most heavily in Ireland, the potato famines of the 1840s and the subsequent exodus

from the Irish countryside had meant that by 1870 no more than 13 per cent of the men in the ranks were Irish. Whereas, too, a large proportion of recruits had come from the English countryside early in the century, the population shifts that came with industrial expansion meant that by 1870 the Army, against its preferences, was recruiting more among the urban than the rural poor. Similarly, the ties of patronage which bound Highland lairds in Scotland to their tenants, and which greatly influenced the pattern of recruiting there, had to some extent been undermined by the decisions of many landowners to replace uneconomic crofters with sheep.

Most recruits were seduced into service by recruiting sergeants who frequented public houses and tempted the unwary with exaggerated promises of regular pay and military glory. Recruits were entitled to a bounty – 'the Queen's shilling' – on enlisting and once they had accepted this they were considered to have entered into a legally binding contract. They were then taken before a magistrate to be sworn in; a few who had sobered up in the meantime could escape the obligation by the payment of a penalty fee, wryly known as 'smart money'. They were then taken before a doctor and given a cursory examination before being marched to their regiments; some took the opportunity to desert along the way, no doubt congratulating themselves on the fact that they had cheated the Queen of her shilling. Although another of Cardwell's reforms was to link regimental titles to districts within the UK, this meant little in terms of recruitment and men from recruiting depots across the country were liable to be drafted into battalions with no connection with the district.

In theory the Army was choosy about the men it accepted. From 1871 the minimum age for a recruit was 18 and the maximum 25, although men enlisting often lied about their ages, and much else besides. The minimum height preferred was generally 5ft 6in for the infantry and an inch or two higher for the cavalry. Rural recruits were in greater demand than urban ones since it was felt they were more wholesome and likely to be fitter than their slum-living counter-parts. Although in times of national shortage the Army was occasionally flexible in its require-ments, it never again sank to the depths plumbed during the eighteenth century when the diseased and the decrepit were accepted simply to bolster the numbers.

Since there were, outside the India garrisons, no permanently constituted brigade structures – brigades were improvised on an *ad hoc* basis in the field according to circumstance – the principal infantry battlefield unit remained the battalion. British infantry battalions were identi-fied by number according to precedence and most had originally been constituted as single battalions. Following the crisis of the Indian Mutiny in 1857, however, when the reliability of auxiliary troops to protect the empire had been called into question and with it the capacity of the Line regiments, a second battalion had been raised for the first twenty-five regiments. In theory, one battalion was always supposed to be on home garrison duty while the other was posted overseas, but in practice the demands of policing an expanding empire meant that at any given time more battalions were needed for over-seas service than was ideal. Thus both battalions of the 24th Regiment had come to southern Africa – the 1st to garrison the Cape in 1876 and the 2nd to take part in the Frontier War of 1877–78 – separately, and they were to enjoy the highly unusual experience of serving together when they were both attached in November 1878 to the Centre Column assembling for the invasion of Zululand at Helpmekaar.

A battalion, as Kipling put it, consisted at peace-time establishment of 'Eight 'undred fightin' Englishmen, the Colonel, and the Band'.[182] At full strength it comprised 30 officers and 866 men making up a headquarters establishment, a band and eight companies identified by letter. Each company consisted of 3 officers – a cap-tain, lieutenant and second lieutenant – and 107 men. In the field, however, battalions were often drastically under-strength; men might be sick, or detached for other duties, while others who had finished their time had not yet been replaced by new drafts from home. This sort of

natural attrition tended to occur at a higher rate among battalions which had been overseas for a long time, and it was not unusual for experienced battalions such as the 1/24th to go into action with as few as sixty men in a company.

A regular cavalry regiment consisted of a nominal total of 653 officers and men, making up a headquarters and four squadrons, each squadron consisting of 6 officers, 22 NCOs and 120 privates. Each squadron was divided into two troops of 3 officers, 11 NCOs and 60 privates. Lord Chelmsford had no regular cavalry at his disposal at the beginning of the war, but two regiments – the 1st (King's) Dragoon Guards and the 17th (Duke of Cambridge's Own) Lancers – were dispatched as reinforcements after iSandl-wana. Coming straight from England, they were largely up to strength, the Dragoons with 27 offi-cers and 622 men and the Lancers with 28 officers and 594 men.

A Royal Artillery Field Battery consisted of 6 guns with their limbers, 6 ammunition wagons, 3 supply wagons and a forge, commanded by a major and 6 other officers and manned by 167 men. These included not only gunners and drivers but also the full range of specialist artificers who were necessary to keep any service dependent on horse-drawn transport functioning effectively, such as farriers, shoeing smiths, collar-makers and wheelers. Because of the limited number of batteries available in southern Africa, it was com-mon practice to break up batteries temporarily and employ guns in multiples of sections (two guns); thus one section of N/5 battery was left in the camp at iSandlwana on 22 January while the remaining two sections accompanied Lord Chelmsford's advance to Mangeni.

The standard unit of the Royal Engineers in the 1870s was the Field Company, which was commanded by a major and 5 officers and con-sisted of 196 men. The Sappers were designated by their specialist skills and included carpenters and masons, smiths, clerks, bricklayers, painters, tailors, miners, wheelwrights, coopers, collar-makers and telegraphists. It is interesting to note that when the 2nd Field Company was dispatched to Natal from Shorncliffe camp in November 1878 – the War Office's token support for Lord

Chelmsford's looming Zulu difficulty – it was under-strength at 125 all ranks, despite recent recruiting. The CO, Captain Richard Warren Wynne, was himself below the specified rank of command.

Military Organisation (Zulu)

There were profound differences in the nature of the two armies which faced each other in 1879. While the British Army was a full-time professional institution, whose members were largely isolated from civilian society and were governed by self-contained rules and regulations, the Zulu army was no more than a part-time citizen militia – the manpower of the Zulu kingdom, mobilised temporarily for military purposes.

The basis of the Zulu system comprised guilds enrolled from men of a common age and called *amabutho* (sing. *ibutho*). *Amabutho* had existed before the rise of the Zulu kingdom in the early nineteenth century, and they were by no means unique to the Zulus since many neighbouring groups also maintained them; it is probably true, however, that they were most highly developed under the Zulu system. They played a very significant role in the formation of the kingdom and remained the most crucial structure for the maintenance of state authority thereafter, since they were a means of temporarily removing the most powerful resource in the country – its young men – from the control of the local interests and placing it instead directly under the king.

The enrolment of an *ibutho* was a straightforward process. Every three or four years the king would issue a directive that all young men who had reached their late teens since the last call-up should be mustered. Initially, the youths reported to one of the king's local *izinduna* and then were taken to the nearest royal homestead where they underwent a period of cadetship, learning to work together under an *induna ye'zinsizwa*, an 'officer of the young men'. After a few months they would be called together from across the country to one of the king's principal homesteads where they would be formally enrolled as an *ibutho*. They would be given a name and directed to provide themselves with a particular style of headdress for ceremonial

occasions; if this consisted of rare pelts of feathers, the king himself might give a bundle of such items to the leading men in the group as a token of support – the rest were expected to provide for themselves. They were also appointed cattle from the royal herds matched according to the colour of the hides; these would provide the basis for their war-shields. War-shields remained the property of the state rather than the individual and were kept in stores in royal homesteads and were only issued when an *ibutho* assembled. Other weapons – spears, sticks, firearms – remained the property of the individuals themselves and were brought to muster when an *ibutho* was assembled for war.

The young men would either be attached to one of the existing *amakhanda* – the large royal homesteads that served as barracks for the army when it was assembled – or be directed to build a new one themselves. Thus the iNgobamakhosi *ibutho* was initially attached to oNdini while the uKhandempemvu *ibutho* (also known as the uMcijo) built an *ikhanda* called kwaKhandempemvu at the foot of the amaBedlana hills near oNdini. This would serve as their headquarters whenever they were assembled.

While they were acting under the king's orders, the *amabutho* expected to be fed by him, chiefly on beef and sorghum beer. Large numbers of cattle had to be slaughtered every day for the purpose but there was seldom enough food to go round and it was common for individuals to top up their rations with food parcels, in the form of maize and vegetables, brought to the royal homesteads by younger family members. Also, the *amabutho* became notoriously boisterous when assembled for any length of time, and potentially difficult to control. For these reasons, they were seldom assembled for long. After settling in to their barracks, the men of a new *ibutho* were allowed to disperse to their homes where they resumed their everyday lives. The king would simply call up *amabutho* when he had need of their services, and it is unlikely that many Zulu men spent more than two or three months a year in such service.

This had important political and social consequences. The young men, of course, carried the burden of everyday work at home, chiefly in herding the family cattle, and the part-time nature of the *amabutho* left them free to carry this out. They were also required to serve their local *amakhosi*, to act as his police force and take part in occasional hunts and rituals. Nevertheless, by imposing a greater obligation to serve the king over and above the local requirements the system mitigated against localised dissent, taking young men away from their regional affiliations and giving them instead a greater sense of national identity and belonging.

There was no ideal size for the strength of an *ibutho*; it depended upon the birth-rate over a given period, and upon the determination of the king to enforce the obligation to serve. Throughout the kingdom's history many of the powerful regional *amakhosi* were reluctant to give up all their prerogatives to the king and found excuses to keep some of their young men back from the musters. In times of national stress, when the king needed to rely upon the support of the *amakhosi*, it was sometimes impolitic to insist on strict observance of the musters; in the aftermath of King Dingane's disastrous war against the Voortrekkers in 1838, and the subsequent rift between Dingane and his brother Mpande, many *amakhosi* traded a degree of independence as the price for their allegiance to either party. Although King Mpande patiently rebuilt the apparatus of state control throughout his long reign, a similar process occurred during the succession dispute of the 1850s. Mpande therefore found it difficult to enrol large *amabutho*. His son Cetshwayo – who had begun to assume day-to-day power long before his father's death in 1872 – was younger and more vigorous and was determined to revive the system; as a result, *amabutho* enrolled under his influence were much larger.

Sometimes, when an *ibutho* was particularly large, groups of men who had enrolled in the same area were formed into a section which was given a separate identity within the *ibutho*; some *amabutho* might have a dozen or more such sections. One single *ibutho* might therefore have a number of names associated with it, much to the confusion of modern historians. Each *ibutho* had a properly constituted internal organisation and command structure. It was divided into 'wings' – left and right – and further subdivided into companies. The size of each company (*iviyo*; pl. *amaviyo*) also varied between about 50 and 70 men. One reason why historians have struggled to obtain an accurate picture of the Zulu strength in particular battles was the habit of participants to assess their strength in companies rather than as a grand total. Each company had an officer – *induna* – picked from within the ranks and chosen from among those who showed a degree of initiative during cadetship. Senior officers were appointed from older men picked by the king and his councillors. Groups of companies had such officers, as did each wing, while a colonel was appointed to command the *ibutho* as a whole.

The duties of the *amabutho* were by no means confined to warfare. They were essentially a national-service state labour gang, and the king called them up whenever he needed manpower. The *amabutho* built and maintained the royal homesteads, tilled the king's fields, herded the royal cattle, acted as the national police force and took part in mass hunts and ceremonies. Although the period of service was open-ended, the greater burden of the duty fell upon the younger men, and it was in this context that the role of marriage was so crucial.

Marriage was a hugely important rite of passage within Zulu society for it marked the onset of the full status and responsibilities of adulthood. Before marriage a Zulu male, whatever his age, was regarded as an *insizwa*, a youth; after marriage he was an *indoda*, a man. The change in social standing was so great that it was marked by a physical change; on the eve of their first marriage Zulu men put on a head-ring, known as *isicoco*. A cord of animal sinew was carefully bound into the hair to form a circle, plastered with gum blackened with charcoal, then polished with beeswax; some fashionable men carefully shaved their heads around the ring so as to enhance its appearance still further.

With marriage came a new series of responsibilities, and in practice it was difficult for a Zulu man to provide for his own family while at the same time giving service to the king.

Successive Zulu kings recognised this, and as a result married men were considered free of the more pressing burdens of service. They still retained their allegiance to their *amabutho* but they only mustered for the great national ceremonies or for a major military expedition; the everyday work fell to the unmarried men who were free to perform it. To prevent the gradual erosion of their control over the national manpower, however, the Zulu kings took to themselves the right to give permission for men to marry. Except under exceptional circumstances, it was never given to individuals but to an entire *ibutho* en masse. In order to prolong the period of active service, *amabutho* were seldom allowed to marry until the first flush of youth – and with it their greatest usefulness – had passed, and many were in their mid-30s when permission was granted. It is not true, as the British supposed, that an *ibutho* had to be blooded in battle as a prerequisite to marriage; in practice, however, since *amabutho* were not given the right to marry until they had completed years of service, they had usually by that time notched up some military experience.

This was an aspect of the system which both fascinated and horrified white observers, who imagined the Zulu army seething with a collected sexual frustration somehow transmuted to blood-lust, though the image of dark warriors yearning to sink their spears into quivering white flesh owes more to contemporary British sexual inhibition than it does to Zulu custom. In fact, bachelorhood did not equate to celibacy, and it was perfectly acceptable for the young men to have girlfriends and to indulge in limited sexual activity providing they did not make their partners pregnant before marriage.

In choosing a time to allow an *ibutho* to marry the king was influenced by public opinion. His councillors, the regional *amakhosi* and the parents of both young men and women, all of whom had a vested interest in the changes which accompanied marriage, all lobbied the king when they thought the time had come for a particular *ibutho* to be released from service. The king usually delayed permission for as long as possible, but it was the custom to publicly

announce his decision at the end of the annual harvest ceremonies each year. An *ibutho* allowed to marry on such an occasion then gleefully dispersed to put on their head-rings and tell their girlfriends; the marriages then took place according to ordinary custom across the country. Their *ibutho* might not be assembled again until the next harvest ceremony while the luckless unmarried ones continued with their duties.

There was considerable rivalry between the *amabutho*; those who were recently married tended to lord it over the unfortunate *amabutho* younger than themselves who had not yet achieved the prized distinction, while *amabutho* of a similar age strove for supremacy. To some extent this rivalry was institutionalised, for the kings recognised that it honed esprit de corps and enhanced performance on the battlefield. In particular, in the ceremonies which preceded an imminent campaign, *amabutho* were called out to challenge one another as to the feats they would perform in the coming fight. Such rivalry could not always be contained, however, and when several *amabutho* were assembled together friction could sometimes spill over into violence. Stick-fights were common, and on one famous occasion at the harvest ceremony at the end of 1877 the married uThulwana *ibutho* clashed with the younger iNgobamakhosi and over 70 men were killed. That clash was the result of simmering tensions arising from the airs adopted by newly married sections incorporated into the uThulwana, and by the fact that both *amabutho* were quartered in the same royal homestead, oNdini.

Discipline during such musters was vigorously enforced by *izinduna* wielding sticks like batons; those guilty of severe infringements could expect to be fined in cattle by the king.

Although every Zulu man was nominally a member of an *ibutho* – a strong tie which he retained throughout his life, sometimes to the point of adopting his *ibutho* name as his own – it was unusual for *amabutho* to assemble in their entirety, even in time of war. Many *amakhosi* even then held a few men back to guard their homes and crops or to perform everyday tasks; over a protracted campaign, such as the war of

1879, the number of these rose in proportion to public support for the war and a growing sense of war-weariness. Indeed, at the beginning of the war King Cetshwayo specifically directed *amakhosi* living in the border regions to keep some men back from the muster to serve as scouts, watching and harassing the British movements; sometimes, when the army passed through these areas en route to attack the enemy, these men would join with it to fight. As the war progressed, however, and the army endured a succession of defeats in the field the need to protect homes and property became more pressing, leading to an increase in locally based armed groups at the expense of the *amabutho* in general.

Before the army was dispatched on campaign it was necessary to ritually prepare it in ceremonies designed to bind the men together in a common purpose and ensure their protection against evil influence. After these ceremonies it was then dispatched towards the enemy; the order of march was decided by the king and his councillors beforehand, for the right to be in the vanguard was jealously guarded. Initially the army moved off in one long column, but after a day or two's march – as it drew near the Zulu borders – it split into two columns marching a mile or two apart, and screened by scouts to prevent detection. When the army drew near the enemy it was necessary to perform a final round of rituals before the *amabutho* took up their attack formations. The exact position of the *amabutho* in their lines seems to have been determined by the order of march. In battle, although junior and regimental commanders were expected to lead from the front, the senior general usually took up a commanding position to the rear which allowed him to exercise command and control more effectively.

The Zulu army could not remain in the field for long, if only because of the difficulty of provisioning it over an extended period; indeed, throughout the war of 1879 it was never assembled at any one time for longer than a fortnight. After a battle – successful or otherwise – it tended to disperse. Even when victorious, such as after the iSandlwana campaign, the temptation was for the men simply to go home,

despite the dictates of custom which insisted they should return to the king to report their progress. In general only the senior *izinduna* and those most keen attended the king. Cleansing ceremonies were performed and the king listened to his officers' reports on their men's performance, and praise and blame were apportioned. Those members of the first *ibutho* to penetrate the enemy lines who had actually killed an enemy were allowed to cut and wear a wooden *iziqu* bravery-bead necklace. Other individual heroes were rewarded with spoils or with gifts of cattle. In King Shaka's time, those accused of cowardice were liable to be picked out and executed in front of the assembled men; by Cetshwayo's day the punishment was less drastic and consisted instead of public 'naming and shaming'. When an army was defeated in the field, such as after kwaGingindlovu or Khambula, it simply fell apart, the survivors escaping as best they could to their homes.

The British never really understood the *amabutho* system in 1879. For them, it was an expression of a tyranny they perceived in the rule of the Zulu kings; they could not – or would not – understand its essentially part-time nature and the subtle complexities of the marriage restrictions, and they tended to equate the *amabutho* with professional European regiments. As such, they made the destruction of the system a central theme of both the ultimatum of December 1878 and of the war itself. In that they were undeniably successful. The final defeat at the battle of Ulundi on 4 July 1879 effectively broke the *amabutho*. Not only had thousands of men died during the course of the war in defence of their home country, but the king was deposed, the great *amakhanda* – which served as barracks – were destroyed, and thousands of head of the cattle that sustained them were looted by the invaders. So deep-rooted was the custom, of course, that many men continued to think of themselves in terms of their *amabutho* allegiances for the rest of their lives, but it was no longer possible to assemble or sustain them in royal service. Indeed, when Cetshwayo was restored to the Zulu throne in 1883, he was specifically prohibited under the terms of that restoration from reviving the *amabutho* system. Nevertheless, when the Zulu civil war subsequently broke out, many of his supporters still rallied to the king under the umbrella of their old *amabutho*. They had to carry their own shields, however, since the British had destroyed their old stocks when the *amakhanda* went up in smoke, and their ranks had been thinned by the heavy losses of *izinduna* and brave men in 1879. More to the point, many did not join them because they had given their allegiance instead to the king's enemies. Many had taken advantage of the post-war conditions to marry freely, and the Zulu kings were never again able to regain their control over the right to marry. Nevertheless, the names of the old *amabutho* still surfaced in the battles of the 1880s, and indeed new *amabutho* continued to be enrolled by Cetshwayo's successor Dinuzulu, and into the twentieth century by his son Solomon Nkayishana. Allegiance to these later *amabutho* was largely notional, however, and they consisted of no more than a few hundred of the king's direct supporters, for the tragic truth is that the British invasion had irrevocably shattered both the material and the administrative bases of the institution, and weakened the universal allegiance to the Royal House.

Missionaries

'First', King Cetshwayo is said to have observed, commenting wryly on the progress of British imperialism across southern Africa, 'comes the trader. Then the missionary. Then the Red Soldier.'

It was an acute and perceptive observation charting not merely the history of his own people's interaction with the white world but highlighting the role of the missionary within the colonial process. With much of Africa unexplored by Europe until the middle of the nineteenth century, and made hostile to interlopers by prevalent diseases, difficult terrain, wild animals and suspicious people, southern Africa – and in particular Natal, with its ready access by sea to the outside world – was the focus of considerable and often competitive missionary endeavour. Rival mission groups from different nationalities and denominations vied with each other to proselytise, their zeal encouraged by a mistaken perception that southern African indigenous societies had no strong pre-existing religious faiths. Yet the lives of most southern Africans were defined by their relationship with their ancestors, and they would find room for Christianity only when it proved flexible enough to incorporate aspects of their belief. Mission endeavour inevitably brought a good deal of cultural baggage with it, requiring as a proof of conversion the acceptance of many aspects of a European lifestyle, and often of the essentially colonial and subservient role of the African within it. For the Zulus, in particular, the appeal of a foreign religion which required them to break with their ancestors, set aside their multiple wives, wear clothes, assume the manners and customs of a second-class white man and give up tending their own cattle and crops to work as menials for outsiders was particularly limited at a time when their confidence in their own religious and political institutions was high. The truth of this dawned slowly upon the mission community and the frustration it engendered inexorably forced many among them to align themselves with the forces of British political intervention in Zululand. And, ironically, this was the perception of the Zulu kings who seem to have regarded the missionary presence in a political light from the early days of their interaction with the British Empire.

The first missionary, an ex-Royal Navy captain named Alan Gardiner, arrived at the settlement at Port Natal in 1835, scarcely a decade after it had been founded. Gardiner's initial intention was to preach among the settler community – in whose anarchic lifestyle he saw a good deal to prove the need for salvation – but the positive reception he gained from King Dingane soon encouraged him to hope that the Zulu kingdom as a whole might be converted. In fact, however, he found himself thrust into the centre of a growing wrangle between the settlers, who were keen to establish a degree of independence from Dingane, and for whom Gardiner offered a hint of imperial protection, and the king himself, who regarded the settlement, in the light of past atronage, as a client chiefdom. It was an early int of the complex role missionaries would often e called upon to play, and which they embraced with various degrees of enthusiasm. Gardiner ccepted the role Dingane offered him as a egulator of the settlement's affairs and won the ight for a fellow missionary to attend the Zulu ourt. The apparent willingness of the Zulus o accept a mission presence brought rival American missionaries hurrying to Natal too, ut the inability of the mission community o distance itself from the process of colonial nteraction brought with it early disasters. At Gardiner's suggestion the Revd William Owen stablished a station within sight of Dingane's esidence at eMgungundlovu in 1837, only to ind himself within months a witness to Dingane's laughter of the Voortrekker leader Piet Retief. The subsequent war between the Trekkers and Dingane almost destroyed mission endeavour in he region, nor did it prosper in Natal in the afternath of the Trekker victory, since many Trekkers vere suspicious of the effect of mission teachngs on the African population. Following his lefeat of Dingane in 1840 Mpande allowed an American missionary, Aldin Grout, to settle in Zululand but Grout's attempts to lure the Zulu to nlightenment with the promise that they need not obey Mpande's laws if they converted led to Mpande revoking his permission and closing the mission down.

In 1848 the Norwegian Lutheran missionary Hans Schreuder established a mission at Ntumambili on the Natal bank at Middle Drift and from there he began to encourage in Mpande a more positive view of missionaries, largely by offering the king medical assistance. In the aftermath of the succession dispute of 1856 and the devastating battle of 'Ndondakusuka Mpande began to regard missionaries – with their implicit connections with the white world – as a means of protecting his own position against the ambitions of his son Cetshwayo. Mpande gave Schreuder permission to establish further missions on Zulu soil and, when his own Norwegian resources proved inadequate, Schreuder invited German Lutherans to take up the offer on his behalf. In 1868 the German Hermmansburg Mission Society

established a settlement, with Mpande's blessing, at Luneburg on the Phongolo frontier. The Anglicans also established a foothold in the country when, in 1860, following further tensions between Mpande and Cetshwayo, the Bishop of Natal, John William Colenso, was invited to contribute two missionaries to Zululand. The Revd Robert Robertson established a station at kwaMagwaza and S.M. Samuelson at St Paul's.

For the most part, however, the missionary impact on Zulu life was temporal rather than spiritual. The missionaries offered practical goods and services to the Zulu kings and to their local communities but they made little progress in the work of conversion. The heir apparent, Cetshwayo, was suspicious of their motives – their presence coloured in his mind by Mpande's agenda – while most ordinary Zulus remained hostile to converts. By abandoning their forefathers and adopting a new religion converts were believed by many traditionalists to have risked bringing the wrath of the ancestors upon the community as a whole and assaults upon converts were not unknown. On 9 March 1877 Maqhumasela Kanyile, a convert from the Revd Ommund Oftebro's kwaMondi mission at Eshowe, was waylaid and killed by a small *impi* which included members of his own family. The mission community reacted to such incidents with horror and remained convinced that Cetshwayo's opposition lay behind them. With no more than 450 Christian converts in Zululand by the mid-1870s, the missionaries' frustration led to their increasingly vociferous support for British intervention. The Revd Robertson, in particular, while enjoying the benefits his Zulu host had granted him, campaigned surreptitiously in Natal, pressuring Shepstone and other colonial officials and feeding exaggerated stories of the horrors of Cetshwayo's administration to the settler press.

As political tension grew throughout 1878, the Zululand missionaries eventually realised the vulnerability of their position and abandoned the country for Natal. When war broke out in January 1879, many of them none the less found themselves – and their property – in the front line. With very few permanent buildings in Zululand, the abandoned missions that lay astride the country's under-developed road network assumed a strategic importance to the British as potential supply depots. Lord Chelmsford planned that his Centre Column should cross into Zululand from mission property at Rorke's Drift, and the Revd Otto Witt, the Church of Sweden's first mission representative in Natal, was happy to lease his buildings to the military for use as a store and hospital. On the coast British troops occupied the St Andrew's mission close to the border, and then advanced on Oftebro's kwaMondi station. The Revd Robertson accompanied Pearson's advance, and during the subsequent siege of Eshowe not only held regular church services for the defenders but also lectured on Zulu history and acted as Pearson's adviser on Zulu affairs. At kwaNtumjambili on the border Schreuder exploited his network of contacts inside Zululand to provide intelligence for the British. The Luneburg settlement was at the centre of constant skirmishing throughout the war. Ironically, however, abandoned missions, where they were not occupied by British troops, were largely ignored by the Zulu and were more at risk of looting and vandalism from passing soldiers.

One major exception to the prevailing missionary climate of support for the invasion was Colenso. A Cornishman, born in 1814, Colenso had trained as an Anglican minister and had accepted the post of Bishop of Natal in 1853. His time in the colony had been dogged by controversy – the questions posed by one of his African converts had led Colenso to challenge the validity of elements of the Old Testament and the resulting furore had seen him deposed for a while as bishop; it also split the Anglican community in Natal into rival camps – and the harsh repression of the 'rebellion' of the amaHlubi people in 1873 had caused Colenso to question the morality of British policies in the region. No stranger to controversy, he had challenged many of Frere's assertions in the run-up to the war, a stance which had widened his rift not only with settler society but with the Anglican missionaries of Zululand. Throughout the war he continued to denounce the injustice of the invasion, and afterwards he became one of the few steadfast and influential allies enjoyed by the Zulu

Royal House in Natal. He was ably assisted by his daughters Frances ('Nel') – who had been a friend of Anthony Durnford's, and who defended his reputation after his death at iSandlwana – Harriette and Agnes. After Bishop Colenso's death in 1883 his daughters continued to champion the Royal House throughout the dark years of civil war and rebellion in the 1880s.

After the war was over the mission community largely returned to Zululand. The British had entrenched their right to work there in the post-war settlement but it was many years before the pace of conversions accelerated. For many Zulus the war had merely confirmed their initial judgement: that behind his preaching the missionary was as much an agent of imperialism as the trader and the red-coated soldier.

Mnyamana Buthelezi, *inkosi*

Throughout the 1879 war *inkosi* Mnyamana Buthelezi remained the most trusted of King Cetshwayo's councillors, and in his capacity as the nation's senior military *induna* was responsible for shaping the strategies that attempted to resist the British invasion.

Mnyamana was born about 1813, the son of Ngqengelele kaPungashe, a junior son of the *inkosi* of the Buthelezi people who lived on the upper Black Mfolozi river. Just a few years later the Zulu king Shaka kaSenzangakhona defeated *inkosi* Pungashe and extended his control over the Buthelezi, raising up to rule as his representative the junior line of Ngqengelele. Ngqengelele became a trusted servant and confidant of Shaka, and after Shaka's death Ngqengelele's son Klwana assumed a similar role to King Dingane. When Dingane was duly driven out by his brother Mpande, the latter remained wary of Klwana's loyalties and he was killed. Instead Mpande raised up another of Ngqengelele's sons, Mnyamana. He became one of Mpande's senior councillors and was given command of the uThulwana *ibutho*, a position which brought him into contact with the young Prince Cetshwayo. Mnyamana assumed something of a paternalistic role to Cetshwayo, and his support for Cetshwayo's claims during the bitter succession dispute of 1856 cemented their friendship. When King Mpande died in 1872 it was Mnyamana who was largely responsible for Cetshwayo's smooth transition to power, and Cetshwayo rewarded him by appointing him *induna'nkhulu*, his most senior official. Only girls from the Buthelezi people were allowed to cut thatch for Cetshwayo's new oNdini homestead, while two of Mnyanama's sons served among Cetshwayo's most trusted body-servants.

A tall, spare man with a neat moustache and pointed beard, Mnyamana was a traditionalist who resented the increasing influence of whites upon Zulu affairs. He was, however, a cautious man who weighed his advice carefully and who gave great thought to the well-being of the nation as a whole. As a result, during the political crisis which led to war with Britain, Mnyamana advocated appeasing British demands where possible; when this proved impossible he committed himself to resisting the invasion. Although he did not take to the field during the early phase of the war – any more than did the British commander-in-chief, the Duke of Cambridge – Mnyamana was largely responsible for the strategic decision to attack the British Centre Column, and command of the troops dispatched to achieve this was given to his personal friend *inkosi* Ntshingwayo kaMahole. During the battle at iSandlwana one of Mnyamana's sons, Mtumengana, was killed.

Although the Zulu victory at iSandlwana checked the British invasion, it largely exhausted the Zulu army, giving rise thereby to a lull which allowed the British to reinforce their positions on the Zulu border. By the middle of March it had become clear that a new wave of fighting was imminent, and Cetshwayo reassembled his army, directing it north, against Wood's column, to support the beleaguered abaQulusi. On this occasion, although field command was again entrusted to Ntshingwayo, Mnyamana accompanied the army as the king's personal representative. This was a measure of the importance the Zulu high command placed on the campaign, and on the morning of 29 March Mnyamana addressed the assembled *amabutho*, encouraging them with his oratory, before they attacked the British camp. Although the Zulu fought well, however, they were heavily defeated, and two

more of Mnyamana's sons were among the dead. Mnyamana himself apparently tried to stem the Zulu rout but the army was demoralised and exhausted and he could do no more than lead some of the survivors dolefully back to report to the king.

The defeat at Khambula left the Zulu with few military options. No longer able to resist fresh British thrusts into his territory, King Cetshwayo could do little more than assemble his army for a final defence of the royal homesteads around oNdini. On 4 July, however, the British dispersed the last Zulu concentration in the battle of Ulundi. *Inkosi* Mnyamana had been among the senior Zulus who watched the fight as the king's representatives; Cetshwayo himself did not wait to see the final humiliation of his army, but instead retired to Mnyamana's ekuShumayeleni homestead on the Black Mfolozi. From here he attempted to negotiate his surrender, and both Mnyamana and Ntshingwayo attempted to intervene with the British on his behalf. The British were unwilling to make concessions, however, and Cetshwayo went on the run in northern Zululand but was captured by British dragoons on 28 August.

With the king captured, the British disposed of his kingdom. Both Mnyamana and Ntshingwayo were offered chiefdoms but Mnyamana refused, partly out of loyalty to the king and partly out of concern for his supporters, many of whom were placed under the control of Prince Hamu kaNzibe. Cetshwayo had given his heir Dinuzulu into the care of *inkosi* Zibhebhu of the Mandlakazi, but as Zibhebhu's relationship with other members of the Royal House deteriorated it was Mnyamana who smuggled Dinuzulu out of Mandlakazi territory and into the care of Prince Ndabuko kaMpande. Over the next few years Mnyamana remained a determined advocate of the king's return to Zululand and when Cetshwayo was finally restored in February 1883 Mnyamana hurried to join him and to resume his old position.

The king's return merely provoked a direct confrontation with Zibhebhu, however. Embittered royalists, led by Ndabuko and Mnyamana's principal son Tshanibezwe, assembled at ekuShumayeleni amd marched on Zibhebhu. Zibhebhu met them in a skilfully planned ambush in the Msebe valley on 30 March and routed them. Both sides promptly assembled their followers but Zibhebhu struck first, launching a surprise attack on Cetshwayo's rebuilt oNdini complex on 21 July. The royalists were again scattered, Cetshwayo himself was wounded and many of the senior councillors and commanders of his administration were killed.

Cetshwayo fled to take sanctuary under British protection at Eshowe where he lived until his sudden death in February 1884. His passing allowed control of the royalist fortunes to pass to his young son Dinuzulu and to a younger, more vigorous generation. *Inkosi* Mnyamana argued against the involvement of outsiders in Zulu affairs but Dinuzulu appealed to volunteers from the Transvaal republic to support him. A combined Boer and royalist force defeated Zibhebhu at Tshaneni mountain on 5 June 1884 but the claims in land made by the Boers as payment were so severe that the British were provoked to intervene. In 1887 Zululand was partitioned between Britain and the Boer 'New Republic', to the intense frustration of Dinuzulu and his supporters. In 1888 Dinuzulu orchestrated a brief rebellion against British authority. By that time *inkosi* Mnyamana was an old man in his 70s and wary of the damage which might be inflicted in further fighting against the whites. He tried to remain aloof from the rebellion, although some of his sons joined the 'rebels', but he was pressured to supply a contingent of auxiliaries to support the British.

Dinuzulu's rebellion failed and he and his uncles, the Princes Ndabuko and Tshingana, were tried by the British and exiled to St Helena. *inkosi* Mnyamana did not live long enough to see much of the erosion of the traditional Zulu way of life – for which he had fought all his life – which came with conquest. He died on 29 July 1892.

Mnyamana's son Tshanibezwe remained a close adviser to King Dinuzulu after his return to Zululand in 1897. Tshanibezwe's son Mathole continued the tradition of the close alliance of the Buthelezi *amakhosi* with the Royal House when he was appointed a councillor to Dinuzulu's heir, Solomon Nkayishana. *Inkosi* Mathole married King Solomon's sister Princess Constance Magogo; their son, *inkosi* Mangosuthu Gatsha Buthelezi, became a prominent politician, leader of the Inkatha Freedom Party and a Minister of the Interior of the South African Government.

Natal Auxiliary Troops

Once it became clear, in the middle of 1878, that armed intervention in Zululand was likely, Lord Chelmsford was forced to the realisation that he had insufficient regular troops for the job. Given the reluctance of the government in London to wholeheartedly support a campaign against the Zulus, it was clear that he would have to augment his imperial troops with volunteers, irregulars and auxiliaries raised from the British colonies. These included the part-time Volunteer corps maintained by the Natal administration and the Irregulars, recruited on the Eastern Cape and in the Transvaal, and raised by the Crown for a limited period of service. By far the largest source of manpower, however, was the African population of Natal.

The African population of Natal was tied to the Zulu kingdom by a shared – and sometimes antagonistic – history dating back to the early years of the century. During the 1820s King Shaka had attempted to extend the influence of the Zulu Royal House south of the Thukela, with mixed results. Some groups had allied themselves with him, some resisted him and some were simply displaced and Zulu satellite chiefdoms installed on their vacant land. The arrival of the whites in the 1830s and 1840s had confined the direct influence of the Zulu kingdom to the territory north of the Thukela and Mzinyathi rivers but the imposition of an international boundary had further complicated the existing relationships between those groups who straddled it. Some former allies of the Zulu kingdom found themselves stranded in colonial territory – at least one, the Sithole, found this situation untenable and moved back to Zululand after a clash with the Natal authorities – while others, who had never been a part of the kingdom, were freed from the fear of it. In the 1850s, moreover, political opponents of the emerging power of Prince Cetshwayo – including members of his family – were able to remove themselves from his authority by the simple expedient of moving across the border, creating a small but significant party of émigré Zulus living in Natal who were keen to reassert their influence in Zululand proper.

To Lord Chelmsford these factors offered an opportunity not merely to increase the manpower available to assist the invasion but also to legitimise British intervention in Zululand on the pretext that it had the support of members of the Royal House. Chelmsford instructed Anthony Durnford – a regular officer with more experience of working with, and sympathy for, African auxiliaries than most of his colleagues – to draw up plans for the raising of an auxiliary force to be known as the Natal Native Contingent. To Chelmsford's irritation the plans met with opposition from Natal's senior administrator, the Lieutenant-Governor Sir Henry Bulwer. Bulwer was concerned that by arming a significant number of Natal's Africans he might not only compromise the safety of the white settler population but also poison the relationship between the black population and the Zulus for generations to come. In the event Frere and Chelmsford bullied Bulwer into setting aside his objections but the authority to raise the Contingent was not granted until early November 1878, and regulations for it were not issued before 23 November. Most of its subsequent failings can be attributed to the fact that the NNC was raised, trained, equipped and pitched into war against a powerful enemy – of whose qualities it was only too well aware – at just a few weeks' notice.

The Contingent was raised by a similar system to the existing *isibhalo* forced-labour scheme by which white magistrates in African locations imposed upon local *amakhosi* the requirement to submit a levy of young men in proportion to the size of their followers. Although an attempt was made to keep men from the same groups and areas within the same unit, the Contingent was created along British organisational lines rather than according to the *amabutho* system. Initially the Contingent consisted of three regi-

ments, the 1st comprising three battalions and the 2nd and 3rd two. Each battalion comprised a headquarters section consisting of white officers – a commandant, officer interpreter, adjutant, quartermaster/bugler and paymaster – and 10 companies. Each company was commanded by white officers – a captain, 2 lieutenants and 6 NCOs – and consisted of an African officer, 10 African NCOs and 90 men. Initial plans to uniform and equip the Contingent along British lines were abandoned because of the expense. The men were required to attend muster with their own weapons – shields and spears – while each company was allotted ten firearms. These were distributed to the black NCOs and were mostly obsolete Sniders or Enfields.

In addition to the NNC, Chelmsford persuaded Bulwer to authorise the raising of a defensive body to be known as the Border Guard. Natal was divided up into defensive districts, and the *amakhosi* who lived in those areas abutting the borders were required to provide groups of three or four hundred men to watch the crossing points. These camped near their allocated posts and were regularly rotated; should the Zulus attempt a crossing the *amakhosi* were directed to support the Border Guard with all available manpower, a temporary mustering rather grandly designated the Border Guard Reserve. The troops of the Border Guard were armed and dressed in the traditional manner and led by white officers, mostly from the settler community, although from April they were issued Enfield rifles in some quantity.

To assist with an anticipated shortfall of trained Engineers, Chelmsford also authorised the raising of the Natal Native Pioneers. Three companies were raised with a nominal strength of 5 European officers, 4 African officers, and 96 Pioneers – although only one company achieved full strength – and the men were issued with loose knee-length white canvas trousers, old infantry scarlet frocks with the collar torn out, and a blue forage cap with a yellow band. Among the Africans only the NCOs were issued with firearms, the pioneers being given either an axe, a pickaxe, a shovel or a crowbar.

Because Evelyn Wood's column was based in the Transvaal rather than Natal, he was given no allotment of NNC troops. Instead, he was instructed to raise a force of 2,000 auxiliaries from among the Africans living on Boer-owned border farms. Two battalions were formed; the officers were inevitably white, and many of the men were of Swazi origin, and appeared at muster wearing full regalia, after the Swazi fashion. After the defection of the Zulu prince Hamu kaNzibe a number of Zulus from among his followers were drafted into the unit – known as Wood's Irregulars – but in fact it seldom achieved a strength of more than half the intended total, and during the fighting in March the two battalions in fact fielded fewer than 300 men each.

Undoubtedly the best of the auxiliary units were those initially known as the Natal Native Contingent (Mounted), but popularly known as the Native Horse. Initially six troops were raised, each of roughly fifty men apiece under white officers. They were raised among groups who had a history of loyalty to the colonial administration, and included men who had served under Anthony Durnford during the Langalibalele crisis in 1873. Three troops were raised among the amaNgwane in the Khahlamba foothills; the amaNgwane had an historic grievance against the Zulu kings after their *inkosi* Matiwane kaMasumpha had been killed by King Dingane in the 1830s. In 1879 the amaNgwane were ruled by Matiwane's son Zikhali, and their contingent was generally known as the Zikhali (or Sikhali) Horse. One troop was raised from the Tlokoa Sotho of *inkosi* Hlubi kaMota, who also lived in the mountain foothills and had fought beside Durnford at Bushman's Pass. Of the others, one was drawn from the Christian community at the mission settlement at Edendale, outside Pietermaritzburg – many of whom were Swazi speakers by descent – and the other from the followers of *inkosi* Jantze of the Ixopo district in southern Natal. The mounted units wore a practical uniform of yellow corduroy jacket and trousers, and a hat with a distinguishing red band. They were issued with Swinburne-Henry carbines and 50 rounds of ammunition in leather bandoliers. The Edendale men wore boots; most of their traditionally minded comrades went barefoot.

The circumstances of the first few weeks of the invasion saw the auxiliary units pitched into some of the fiercest fighting of the war long before they were properly trained or had developed a sense of spirit and belonging. Severely criticised by the white troops, and generally blamed for the debacle at iSandlwana, their performance has often been judged unfairly. The 2nd Regiment performed useful scouting duties on the advance to Eshowe, although the battle of Nyezane revealed their limitations as front-line troops; poor communication between European NCOs and the rank-and-file led to the unnecessary deaths of several NCOs. During the iSandlwana campaign the 3rd Regiment, together with elements of the 1st attached to Durnford's command, proved excellent at reconnaissance and during the attack on the Zulu camp their morale generally held all the while they were supported by white troops. The mounted contingent in particular performed extremely well. Once the British line collapsed, however, the Contingent broke, a act which both destroyed their own confidence and undermined the faith that the rest of the army had in them. On 23 January Lord Chelmsford disbanded the remnants of the 3rd NNC at Rorke's Drift.

In May 1879, as Chelmsford prepared to mount a fresh invasion of Zululand, he authorised a complete overhaul of the auxiliary units. The NNC was reconstituted in five separate battalions, many of them drawn from the original regiments, and to bolster their confidence many of the men were issued with obsolete pattern infantry tunics. They were also issued a much higher proportion of firearms, mostly Sniders or Enfields. The changes undoubtedly led to a significant improvement in the performance of the auxiliaries. The 4th and 5th battalions took part in the Eshowe relief operations and in the battle of kwaGingindlovu, while the 2nd battalion accompanied the final advance to oNdini.

The auxiliaries were disbanded at the end of the fighting. Reaction to them had been mixed, and they had attracted criticism both from regular British officers and colonial Volunteers alike. In return, some *amakhosi* expressed disillusion with the treatment and rewards meted out to them. For the most part, however, they had been an essential element in the British victory, and when used as they had originally been intended – as scouts and in pursuit – they had proved highly effective.

Natal Volunteer Troops

In addition to the raising of auxiliary troops among Natal's African population, Chelmsford needed the services of the part-time white Volunteer Corps maintained by the Natal colonial authorities.

Natal had become a British colony in 1844. For years its white population remained small, and only from 1849 did a series of sponsored immigration schemes bring settlers out from the United Kingdom in any significant numbers. From the first, the colony was garrisoned by detachments of regular troops but their numbers were usually small, and with the outbreak of the Crimean War in 1853 it seemed to the colonial administration that they might be yet smaller as troops were withdrawn from outposts around the Empire to fight in the war against Russia. As a result it introduced an order in 1854 which allowed for the establishment of Volunteer units to be raised from among the white settler population for the colony's defence. The establishment of each unit had to be confirmed by the Lieutenant-Governor – the colony's senior administrator – but beyond that the workings of each unit were largely democratic, reflecting their part-time nature. Members of a unit chose their own name, selected a headquarters, elected their officers and drew up their regulations. They paid for their uniforms and equipment and, in the case of mounted units, their own horses and saddlery; the colonial government provided them with firearms and ammunition. The Volunteers were required to attend a training camp four times a year and were liable to be called out when the colony was under threat, either from external attack or by the internal rebellion of the African population, the possibility of which was a feature of the colonial mind-set. The government recognised that the limited settler population meant that numbers in each unit were likely to be small but reserved the right to disband any unit whose numbers fell below twenty.

Service in these units was generally popular among the young men of the settler elite who not only had a stake in the colony's success, but also the wherewithal to cover the necessary expenses. Most of the units affected smart uniforms of dark colours – blue, black or green, often with bright facings and distinctive badges – with imperial-style foreign service helmets. The quarterly camps were something of a social event affording an opportunity to demonstrate a smart appearance and show off riding and shooting skills.

The so-called 'rebellion' of the amaHlubi *inkosi* Langalibalele kaMthimkhulu in 1873 underscored the settlers' sense of vulnerability and led to the formation of further units. It also led to the establishment of the only professional armed body permanently maintained by the colony, the Natal Mounted Police.

The Police were not part of the Volunteer movement, although in 1879 they served together. The Police were raised in 1874 by Major John G. Dartnell, a former regular soldier who had distinguished himself in the Indian Mutiny. Unlike the Volunteers, they were a full-time body who lived in barracks and performed regular policing duties; these aspects of the service did not much appeal to the settlers, who generally preferred the more glamorous and less onerous duties of the Volunteers, and as a result many members of the NMP were recruited directly from England. They wore a practical uniform of black corduroy.

With war looming against the Zulus, the Volunteers were an obvious source of manpower to Lord Chelmsford, the more so because they could ride and shoot and knew the country well, and he was chronically short of cavalry. Nevertheless, by the terms of their service neither the Police nor the Volunteers were required to serve outside the borders of Natal, and the Lieutenant Governor, Sir Henry Bulwer, was reluctant to give up the prerogative of the colonial authorities and place them under imperial military control. Both Chelmsford and Frere pressured him to do so, however, and in the event Bulwer agreed, providing the Volunteers were allowed to express their willingness to serve in Zululand by a ballot. The majority did so, and were placed under military orders in November 1878.

Their numbers remained tiny – just 753 men in all, serving in 15 separate units consisting of 11 mounted, 3 infantry and an artillery corps. Of these, 8 mounted units were ordered into Zululand – a total of 370 men – together with the regular Police. The remaining units were employed in defensive duties in Natal. The strength of some of the individual units was very small – the Police were the strongest at 100 officers and men, while the oldest of the Volunteer corps, the Natal Carbineers, entered Zululand with 3 officers and 57 men. At the other end of the scale the Buffalo Border Guard, recruited among the settlers in the Mzinyathi valley, mustered scarcely more than 30 men, of whom half a dozen had refused to enter Zululand. Of the 36 men of the Newcastle Mounted Rifles, 4 elected to stay on the border. The men were all armed with Swinburne-Henry carbines – issued shortly before the war began – and Webley's Irish Constabulary pattern revolver, while the officers carried swords.

These units were attached initially to either Colonel Pearson's coastal column (the Victoria Mounted Rifles, Stanger Mounted Rifles, Durban Mounted Rifles, Natal Hussars and Alexandra Mounted Rifles) or Colonel Glyn's Centre Column (Natal Mounted Police, Natal Carbineers, Buffalo Border Guard and Newcastle Mounted Rifles); the cavalry attached to Colonel Wood's Left Flank Column consisted of Irregulars. Because the Volunteer Corps had limited battle experience and would be required to work alongside the regulars, Lord Chelmsford directed that they should be placed under the command of regular officers. These were Lieutenant-Colonel J.C. Russell for the Centre Column and Major Percy Barrow for the Coastal Column.

The appointment of Russell caused some concern to the Centre Column men, however. They had agreed to serve in Zululand on the basis that they would be led by Major Dartnell, who was Natal's Commandant of Volunteers, and who had accompanied them to the front. They were disappointed to be told that Dartnell would not be leading them, and their frustration increased when they found that Russell – a 12th Lancer – had decided views on how cavalry troops should be handled which did not match their own. Faced with the possibility that the Volunteers might flatly refuse to cross the border after all, Chelmsford agreed to a compromise; Russell was left in field command, but Dartnell was made a member of the Staff with special responsibilities for the Volunteers.

In fact, from the beginning the Volunteers found themselves engaged in a much more intense warfare than their experience or training had prepared them for, although they coped remarkably well. Both the Centre and Coastal Columns were engaged on 22 January. On the 21st Chelmsford had ordered a strong probe to investigate the Zulu presence in the Mangeni hills ahead of iSandlwana; the command of this was given to Dartnell and most of the mounted troops were included. Small detachments of each unit were left in the camp, however, and when it was attacked on the 22nd over fifty of them were killed. On the same day Pearson's column was attacked at Nyezane, and a picket of Volunteers played a crucial role in deterring the attack of the Zulu right horn.

The intensity of these battles came as something of a shock to both Lord Chelmsford and the Volunteers themselves. Dartnell's men returned to Natal on the morning of the 23rd, and when news of iSandlwana reached Pearson – who had by then occupied Eshowe – he decided to reduce the strain on his provisions by also sending Barrow's men back to the border. For the most part the Police and Volunteers were employed on garrison duty along the border thereafter, although a scratch force from Barrow's men was assembled to support the Eshowe Relief Expedition in late March. Called the Natal Volunteer Guides, this consisted of 3 officers and 59 men of the Victoria, Durban, Alexandra, Stanger and Isipingo Mounted Rifles (the latter had not entered Zululand in January). The Guides were present at the battle of kwaGingindlovu on 2 April and later accompanied the 1st Division during the second invasion. Some of the other Volunteer units took part in raids across the border, notably at Middle Drift on 20 May.

The Volunteers were all ordered to stand down at the end of the war and the Police returned to their normal duties. They had seen out a degree of service and proved themselves useful out of all proportion to their numbers.

Naval Brigades

Throughout the nineteenth century Britain's supremacy as a naval power was a major factor in the growth and maintenance of the Empire. Although the sharp end of Britain's international policies traditionally fell to the Army, it was the Navy which maintained the safety of the maritime highways which serviced the Empire and enabled troops to be shipped in safety all round the world. Nor was the Navy's active participation in the many wars of Queen Victoria's reign limited to offshore bombardments and support for amphibious landings; British generals on land regarded it as a ready source of manpower to support land operations, and both sailors and Royal Marines were regularly put ashore.

And so it was in Zululand. Required by Bartle Frere to assemble a sufficient force to invade Zululand in January 1879, but deprived by-and-large of reinforcement from London by an unsympathetic government, Lord Chelmsford appealed for Navy support. The Commander-in-Chief of the Royal Navy's Cape of Good Hope squadron, Commodore F.W. Sullivan, agreed to land a detachment from the warship HMS *Active* – rather to the irritation of the Admiralty, which complained that the squadron's strategic role had been weakened as a result. *Active*'s party landed at Durban on 19 November 1878 and consisted of 10 officers and 163 men together with two 12-pdr guns, two rocket tubes and a Gatling, all under the command of Commander H.J. Fletcher Campbell. Among them were a detachment of men recruited in West Africa, known as 'Kroomen', and a detachment of Royal Marines. The sailors were armed with Martini-Henry rifles with an impressive cutlass bayonet.

Active's contingent was attached to Colonel Pearson's Right Flank Column which was then assembling at the Lower Thukela Drift, although as a courtesy to acknowledge their support Chelmsford took Lieutenant Archibald Berkely Milne on to his staff. Soon after they arrived at the Drift they were joined by 3 officers and 58 men from HMS *Tenedos*, which had arrived at Durban on 1 January. *Active*'s men provided a guard of honour at the reading of Frere's ultimatum to the Zulu representatives on 11 December, and the sailors were also heavily involved in preparing for the invasion.

Pearson's first task, once war began, would be to transport his column across the Thukela, which at that point was some 300 yards wide and, after the onset of the seasonal rains, fast-flowing and dangerous. The Navy's expertise on water was in great demand, and the sailors were required to ferry parties across the river in small boats, while an anchor belonging to HMS *Tenedos* was used to anchor the flat-bottomed pont (a flat-bottomed ferry). On 6 January 1879 – five days before the ultimatum expired – *Tenedos*'s anchor was rowed across and fixed on the Zulu bank and a steel hawser slung across the river. The following day it rained heavily, however, so that by the 8th the river had risen to a torrent. That evening the sheer force of water on the hawser 'wrenched the anchor to which it was secured on the opposite bank out of the ground, and all our work for the last week was destroyed in a few minutes; away went all our hawsers out into the middle of the stream, the anchor being dragged like a feather'.[183]

The following day, when the river had abated, the anchor had to be dragged slowly on to the Natal bank by the hawser, still firmly attached on that side. A further attempt was made to ferry it across to Zululand on a barrel raft but midstream the hawser tipped over the raft, spilling Lieutenant Craigie and Able Seaman Dan Martin of *Active* into the water. Craigie struggled to the surface and was rescued by a boat but, despite the efforts of two of his comrades who dived in to save him, Dan Martin was never seen again – the first of many lives lost in the cause of the Anglo-Zulu War.

Pearson was not ready to begin his advance on 11 January – the day the ultimatum expired – but the following day proved to be an exhausting one for the men of the Naval Brigade who found themselves in charge of the ponts, boats and rafts employed to ferry the troops across into Zululand. The men of *Tenedos* were, to their chagrin, deputed to guard the Drift[184] but *Active*'s men were attached to the advance. It took several days to move the transport across the river, and it was not until the 18th that Pearson pushed forward into Zululand. His advance was painfully slow, made worse by the heavy rains which had swollen the rivers across his path and turned the track into a quagmire.

On 21 January Pearson detached a strong reconnaissance party to investigate the royal homestead of kwaGingindlovu, which lay a few miles east of his line of advance. It was found to be deserted and *Active*'s men fired rockets into it to set it on fire. The following morning Pearson had just crossed the Nyezane river when his scouts blundered into the vanguard of a Zulu army bivouacked behind Wombane hill beyond. As the Zulus streamed into view, deploying into their traditional encircling movement, Pearson hurried his men up from the river and took up a position on a spur facing Wombane. *Active*'s Gatling, commanded by 18-year-old Midshipman Lewis Coker, had been at the back of the first column of wagons, and Coker ordered his men to manhandle it up the slopes of the spur. At one point the pole of the cart to which it was attached broke, much to Coker's annoyance, but at last the gun was brought into action, firing a short burst to suppress Zulu snipers hidden in the bush. By this time the battle was at its height and the Zulu centre had occupied a deserted homestead directly up the slope from Pearson's position. From here they opened a heavy but badly directed fire which enfiladed Pearson's line. To drive them out Pearson ordered up *Active*'s 24-pdr rocket detachment and the first shell, skilfully directed by Boatswain Cotter, passed right through the homestead, setting it on fire and driving the Zulus out. A small group of NCOs from the Natal Native Contingent advanced to take advantage of the Zulus' discomfort and at

Commander Campbell's suggestion the sailors and a company of infantry were sent after them in support. For the Navy men it was certainly an exciting moment:

> The Jack Tars seemed mad for blood, for they charged up the hill in any formation, banging away right and left, driving the Zulus before them. The company of the Buffs did their best to keep up with the sailors, but were not equal to the occasion, as they had been 'doubled up' from the rear in order to take part in the attack.[185]

For a few minutes the Zulus held their ground and there was a brief fire-fight at close quarters and a hand-to-hand tussle before the Zulus reluctantly gave way. Afterwards a Zulu prisoner admitted that he thought his men were winning the battle until 'those horrible men in white trousers rushed up and showered lead on them'.[186]

The Zulu attack was repulsed and later that day Pearson continued his advance. The following day he occupied his first objective, the deserted Norwegian mission station at Eshowe. Within days, however, he received the news which would throw Lord Chelmsford's strategy into disarray; the Centre Column had suffered a disastrous setback at iSandlwana. Left to his own devices, Pearson was reluctant to retreat and, while sending his mounted men and auxiliaries back to the border to reduce the strain on his supplies, he ordered the column to dig in. Eshowe was turned into the biggest field fortification built by the British during the war, and 1,700 men were destined to remain cooped up there for three months.

Active's men were given command of one sector of the fort, and their Gatling was dug in so as to fire over the ramparts. There was no room inside the perimeter to erect tents, and all the men were required to sleep on the ground under the wagons which had been incorporated into the defences. It rained frequently, and life inside the fort was muddy and miserable for everybody. As the weeks went by, food became in short supply and was monotonous. During one night of particularly heavy rain the water streamed

[146]

down a slight slope inside the fort towards *Active*'s sector, washing the sailors out of their camp and destroying part of their ramparts. Nevertheless, the practicalities of daily life aboard ship had left the Navy men far more practical and adaptable than their Army counterparts, and they simply made the best of things, often to the envy of the rest of the garrison:

> The resource and handiness of the bluejackets was a considerable cause of amusement and wonder to the rest of the garrison. No matter how short the supply of food, nor the time of day, Jack always seemed to have something to cook, and small parties of men were preparing little snacks of some dainty-smelling dish at all hours.[187]

Nevertheless, *Active*'s men were equally at the mercy of the sickness which gradually took hold among the garrison. Four of them would die before the post was relieved, among them Midshipman Coker, who died on 16 March. Coker's cheery disposition had made him popular throughout the garrison, and his death was keenly felt; ironically the cause of his death was attributed to his habit of sleeping in the open in all weathers next to his treasured Gatling gun.

While Pearson's command was invested at Eshowe the wider war moved on. The Navy had played a small but significant part in the iSandlwana campaign. When Lord Chelmsford had divided his command early on the morning of 22 January, his staff had of course ridden out of the camp with him, including Lieutenant Milne of *Active*. Milne's servant, Signaller 1st Class W.H. Aynsley, had been left in charge of Milne's tent and kit. Early on the afternoon of 22 January, in response to curious reports that something was happening at the camp, Chelmsford sent Milne up on to the slopes of the Magogo hill to look back at iSandlwana with his telescope. Milne's view was obstructed by a shoulder of a neighbouring hill, Silutshana, and iSandlwana was in any case sunk below the horizon and partly obscured by the haze. Milne could see little to suggest anything wrong as the tents of the camp were still standing. He reported as much to Lord Chelmsford. Milne had noted dark smudges at the foot of the hill which he took to be cattle; he was later forced to admit that he may have been wrong in that judgement.

Signaller Aynsley, meanwhile, had the misfortune to be the only Royal Navy man present at iSandlwana during the battle. He seems to have stuck to his charge throughout, and when the British position collapsed and the Zulus overran the camp Aynsley was seen standing with his back to a wagon, defending himself with his cutlass. As late as the 1950s an elderly Zulu who had been a mat-carrier at the battle, and who earned a few pennies from passing travellers by telling the story of the battle, recalled how a man dressed in blue had set his back to a wagon, and, shouting defiantly, had dared the Zulus to come and attack him, cutting down each in his turn until one warrior crawled under the wagon and stabbed him through the spokes of the wheel.[188] That night, one of Chelmsford's officers recognised Aynsley's body on the battlefield.

In the aftermath of iSandlwana, reinforcements were hurried to Natal. Two more Naval contingents were landed – on 16 March 16 officers and 378 men had been landed from HMS *Shah* and on the 18th 10 officers and 218 men from HMS *Boadicea*. Both were marched to the Lower Thukela, where Chelmsford was assembling a new column to march to Pearson's relief. Large detachments from both parties, together with some of the *Tenedos* men whom Pearson had left at the border, were attached to the column. On 2 April the column defeated a Zulu concentration which had assembled to block their path near the ruins of the kwaGingindlovu *ikhanda*. *Boadicea*'s Gatling gun held one corner of the British square with the rest of the Naval detachments fighting as infantry alongside. George Hamilton Browne was particularly impressed by the Navy's steadiness, and considered it a significant factor in the battle's result:

> Comparisons are, I know, odious, but no impartial onlooker that day could have been present without being strongly impressed with the difference between the conduct of

the mature blue-jacket together with that of the stalwart jolly and the half-baked nervous boys in whose company they were fighting.

[The Gatling] fortunately not jamming and being backed up by the steady fire of the blue-jackets and jollies, in my humble opinion, saved the whole outfit from being cut up both physically and morally.[189]

Hamilton Browne also noticed a curious incident during the battle:

The Zulus' rush was only checked when they were within twenty yards of the laager, some of them falling shot dead even at a closer distance, while one small boy, a mat-carrier, crossing by a miracle the fire zone, reached the Naval Brigade bastion, where one of the blue-jackets spotting him, leaned over, grabbed him by the nape of the neck and collected him, kicking and squirming, inside the work, where after he had been cuffed into a state of quietude his captor kept him prisoner by sitting on him until the end of the engagement. This youthful corner-man, preserved alive as a *spolia opima*,[190] was adopted by the crew of HMS *Boadicea* as a mascot and, if I remember rightly, was subsequently entered into the Royal Navy, a proceeding that reflects great credit on the handy men, although I have sometimes thought that considering the manner in which he was first of all captured and detained, that the Exeter Hall gang [i.e. the Aborigines' Protection Society] would have wailed over him as a brutally pressed boy.[191]

Which, of course, he was.

After the battle an officer of the 60th Rifles deputed to bury the Zulu bodies noted that the sailors were particularly proud of their contribution to the victory:

We buried sixty-one Zulus who had been killed within 500 yards of our line, more we had not time to bury. The bluejackets on either flank were very jealous about their bag, and some little tact had to be shown when Jack claimed his 'birds'. The Marines made no extravagant claims.[192]

The battle of Gingindlovu broke the Zulu cordon around Eshowe. Chelmsford left part of his force to camp on the battlefield and marched the rest as quickly as he could up to the mission. Since there was no strategic advantage to holding it, the garrison was then withdrawn. Most of the graves in the small cemetery nearby had been marked with simple crosses, but *Active*'s men had carved out a rough stone cross for Coker; before they left, they garlanded it with flowers.

After Eshowe had been relieved Chelmsford reorganised his columns. Pearson's old column was brigaded together with the Eshowe relief column to form the 1st Division. The new unit's objectives were to continue the advance to pacify the coastal districts, and if possible to establish a base on the coast where supplies might be landed by sea. A chain of supply depots was to be built to provision the advance, and it was at one such depot, Fort Chelmsford on the lower reaches of the Nyezane, that the Naval brigades were destined to spend much of the war.

In pursuit of this strategy ships attached to the Cape squadron were sent to survey the Zulu-land coast in search of a viable landing place. A spot was selected on the open beach a few miles south of the mouth of the Mhlatuze river, and optimistically christened Port Durnford. The movements of ships offshore had not gone unnoticed by the Zulus, however, and led to one of the more bizarre incidents of the war. On 24 April HMS *Forester* had anchored close inshore and dispatched boats to take soundings to test the viability of a landing. To their surprise, they saw a large herd of cattle being driven down to the water's edge. The cattle were a decoy, for a force of several hundred Zulus had collected in the bush beyond the sand-dunes in expectation of repelling an amphibious landing. When the boats were not tempted to put ashore, the Zulus emerged from cover and moved on to the beach where they opened a heavy but inaccurate fire on the boats. In response HMS *Forester* opened fire with her guns, and the shells landed on the beach, scattering the Zulus and killing a number of the cattle. A few days later, on 6 May, when *Forester* again came close inshore another Zulu force gathered on the beach, but by the time the first steamers arrived at Port Durnford with supplies for the 1st Division at the end of the month the Zulus had apparently abandoned any hope of defending their beaches.

Forester's adventures were the last excitement to be had by the Navy in Zululand. The shore parties spent the remaining weeks of the war in garrison duty or in facilitating the operations at Port Durnford, where at least they were by the sea again. After Chelmsford's victory at Ulundi on 4 July – where Lieutenant Milne was again present to represent the Navy – they were gradually broken up. Their guns and equipment were shipped first down to Durban by steamer, and by the end of July most of them had been disembarked at Port Durnford and returned to their ships.

On the whole the Navy's contribution to the war was out of all proportion to their numbers. The campaign was not one which had enhanced many military reputations, but Bartle Frere summed up the general consensus when he commented that 'composed as they were of seasoned and hardy, well trained and disciplined men, accustomed to turn their hands at any sort of employment, and to work in small detachments; these were far more serviceable than unseasoned troops, and immature recruits'.[193]

'No Quarter': Total War in Zululand?

At about 9.30 on the morning of 22 January, shortly after the last shots had been fired at the battle of Nyezane, Lieutenant William Roberts of the Victoria Mounted Rifles was struck by the plight of the Zulu wounded:

We then had leisure to look after the wounded men, and very pitiful it was to see the poor fellows lying with fearful wounds. They were very quiet, and seemed to bear pain well, no groaning or crying out. We could not do anything for them except give them water to drink.[194]

Some of the Volunteers took the trouble to drag a number of the injured men out of the direct sunlight and into the shade.

Yet this compassion was in stark contrast to the reaction of Lord Chelmsford's command on returning to iSandlwana, elsewhere in the country, later that same day. The rumour had spread among Chelmsford's men during their march that the camp had fallen, and his command was tense with the anticipation of what they might find there. According to Lieutenant John Maxwell of the 3rd NNC,

> ... we made a rush and got in among some waggons. On a buck waggon we came across some of the enemy drunk, about eight or ten. Some of the 24th being close by then, I shouted to them. They mounted the waggons and put the bayonet through them ...[195]

This was the first manifestation of a ruthlessness that would profoundly affect the attitude of British troops towards the Zulus throughout the rest of the war. The following morning, on the march back down to Rorke's Drift, Chelmsford's men encountered a number of exhausted Zulu stragglers making their way back up the Manzimnyama valley, returning from the pursuit to the Mzinyathi – the British shot them. A number of prisoners had been taken by the Natal Volunteers during Chelmsford's skirmishing at the Mangeni hills; once the column was back safely on the Natal bank at Rorke's Drift the men were given their freedom – but as they ran towards the river they were shot down.[196] There was worse to come at Rorke's Drift itself; the post had been attacked throughout the previous night, the hospital gutted, and piles of Zulu bodies lay heaped against the improvised barricades. And there were many Zulus still lying out in the bush nearby, where they had been missed in the darkness when their comrades withdrew; according to George Hamilton Browne of the NNC,

> During the afternoon it was discovered that a large number of wounded and worn-out

Zulus had taken refuge or hidden in the mealie fields near the laager. My two companies ... with some of my non-comms, and a few of the 24th quickly drew these fields and killed them with bayonet, butt and assegai.

It was beastly but there was nothing else to do. War is war and savage war is worse than the lot. Moreover our men were worked up to a pitch by the sights they had seen in the morning and the mutilated bodies of the poor fellows lying in front of the burned hospital.[197]

It is interesting to note that Lord Chelmsford was still present when some of these incidents occurred; there are no references to any attempts on his part to stop them. Yet Browne's comment that 'there was nothing else to do' also reflects the desperate plight of Chelmsford's men, whose food and medical supplies had been lost at iSandlwana; they were in no position to care for prisoners, even had they wanted to.

It was the slaughter at iSandlwana which, of course, immediately transformed the nature of the war. It was all too painfully obvious that the Zulus themselves had taken no prisoners; the dead, both black and white, lay jumbled up together among the carcasses of slaughtered animals. Most of the British dead – at both iSandlwana and Rorke's Drift – had also been disembowelled, and the sight of their torn corpses had an electrifying effect on those who saw them, inculcating a desire for revenge that spread throughout the columns, sweeping up those who had not themselves witnessed it, and growing in strength with each telling of the story. Many of the reinforcements sent out from England heard the story long before they reached Natal, often coloured by exaggerated stories of Zulu atrocities. At the Cape Guy Dawnay

went to the Club, saw Commandant Lonsdale who escaped from Isandhlwana and is now raising some cavalry volunteers ... The slaughter was far greater than we first stated ... A great number of the dead ripped

open, and the poor little band boys stuck up on meat hooks.[198]

Years later, referring to the slaughter which took place in the 1906 rebellion, the author H. Rider Haggard summed up the practical effect that fear and horror induced among the British towards the Zulus:

Well, cruelty bred of fear is no new story in South Africa. The white men neglects or oppresses the native and slights his needs until something happens; then in a panic he sets to work and butchers them.[199]

And along the Mzinyathi border in the aftermath of iSandlwana a very real fear of a further Zulu attack led to a significant degree of butchery. At Rorke's Drift Hamilton Browne captured a Zulu scout who had tied a red rag – the badge of the NNC – around his head in an attempt to deflect British suspicions; Browne had him hanged as a spy, later excusing the incident with the comment that he had been caught in a moment of temper when an NCO asked for orders seconds after Browne had barked his shin. That Zulu was probably not alone, for most eyewitness accounts draw a discreet veil over the fate of the Zulu wounded who were discovered by British patrols some distance away from the battlefield in the days afterwards.

At Helpmekaar, during the rest of January and much of February, any African who could not account for himself was shot as a spy; according to Civil Surgeon L.W. Reynolds:

A prisoner who was taken yesterday was tried by court-martial today, and found to be a spy, and was shot by 10 Basutos. He jumped into his grave to try and escape the bullets, but without avail.[200]

Although the feared Zulu counter-attack did not materialise, the further Zulu successes at Ntombe on 12 March and Hlobane on 28 March added to the lurid reputation they enjoyed among their enemy. As a result, in the battles which followed, the British unleashed upon the Zulus, when they were able, the full fury of their fear and loathing. At Khambula on 28 March the British pursuit of the defeated *amabutho* was particularly ruthless. In truth there was some military justification for this, since it was necessary to inflict a decisive defeat upon the Zulu army to counter the lingering strategic effects of iSandlwana. More to the point, however, the men who conducted the pursuit were the same Irregulars who had suffered so heavily at Hlobane the day before. Cecil D'Arcy of the Frontier Light Horse 'told his men "No quarter, boys, and remember yesterday," and we did knock them about, killing them all over the place'.[201]

Frederick Schermbrucker, commanding the Kaffrarian Rifles, noted with some enthusiasm that

For fully seven miles I chased two columns of the enemy. They fairly ran like bucks, but I was after them like the whirlwind, and shooting incessantly into the thick column, which could not have been less than 5,000 strong. They became exhausted, and shooting them down would have taken too much time; so we took the assegais from the dead men, and rushed among the living ones, stabbing them right and left with fearful revenge for the misfortunes of the 28th ... No quarter was given.[202]

A private soldier of the 1/13th, John Snook, wrote a letter to his family back home:

On March 30th, about eight miles from camp, we found about 500 wounded, most of them mortally, and begging us for mercy's sake not to kill them; but they got no chance after what they had done to our comrades at Isandhlwana.[203]

When Snook's family released his letter to the press it caused a furore among humanitarian groups in England and Wood himself was prompted to intervene, issuing a denial that wounded Zulus had been slaughtered and persuading Snook to publicly recant. Yet in the light of the heavy casualties inflicted on the Zulus in the battle, and the number of wounded who lay out miles from the battlefield, the small numbers of prisoners taken by the British belie Wood's protestations. Certainly the experience of one Mgelija Ngema, who was a teenager in the uVe at the time of the battle, suggests that, where there were no senior officers on hand to prevent them, most British patrols quietly shot any wounded they came across. Wounded three times during the battle Ngema had crawled several miles before a patrol found him several days later;

They said, 'What is your regiment?' They saw the gun I had with me I had taken from the soldier I had killed [at Hlobane], and all I know I was shot by one of them here in my head and left for dead. I came round in the evening and crawled to a kraal where I was looked after and my wound washed.[204]

The pursuit at kwaGingindlovu a few days later was no less vigorous. Private Edwin Powis of the 2/24th, serving with the Mounted Infantry, wrote home in a style calculated to impress a lady-friend,

We went about seven miles, but they had got clean away with the exception of three that we caught, who had been wounded, trying to make for the bush. We cut off their heads, the three of them, and let them lay.[205]

Other reports confirm that large numbers of Zulu wounded had been killed, either by mounted men or by auxiliaries, when they were unable to cross the Nyezane river. The following day Jack Royston – then a young trooper in the Natal Volunteers – was involved in an incident which would affect him for the rest of his life. He had found two Zulus lying with chest wounds in a donga. Both men were able to walk and Royston persuaded them to accompany him to the British camp. Before they reached it, however, they encountered a colonial officer who roundly cursed Royston for a fool, pulled out his revolver and shot both Zulus dead. 'I was at an age when such things leave impressions', recalled Royston – who would go on to enjoy a distinguished career in the Anglo-Boer and First World Wars – 'it took me a long time to get over it. The man was much older than I, and I was powerless to prevent his action, though I knew it was wrong.'[206]

The British victories of March and April did little to disperse the underlying fear of the Zulus, however, and when Chelmsford renewed his offensive it was plagued by false alarms. In particular, troops fresh out from England were highly susceptible to panic when the dark nights on the open veldt were alive with the cries of strange animals and the sound of wind hissing through the grass. When the chance came to finally lay the ghosts of iSandlwana to rest by inflicting a crushing defeat on the Zulus for the last time at the battle of Ulundi, the British took it. Again, the pursuit of the defeated *amabutho* was punitive. Once the Zulus began to withdraw, auxiliary troops were dispatched to sweep through the grass around the British square, killing any wounded Zulus who lay there; the regimental dog of the 17th Lancers distinguished itself by searching out and barking at any among the bodies who showed signs of life. A colonial war correspondent witnessed an incident which summed up the prevailing mood:

> The Basutos took three prisoners, the only prisoners taken. During the chase one of the Basutos shot a Zulu in the leg, and then interviewed the man with all the thirst for news which distinguishes a New York reporter. It was a singular time, and a dangerous spot, in which to interview a man, especially a wounded man, but the questioner went to work seriously, and got all the news of the week. Then he gently asked the Zulu if he had got nothing more to tell, and on being assured that there was no more information to be had, he quietly shot the man, mounted his horse, and joined again in the chase. If this was cruel, and deeds which appear cruel in times of peace

are regarded in a totally different light in times of war, then there was much cruelty that day, for every wounded man was killed.[207]

When one wounded Zulu appealed to an Irregular for a doctor, the man tapped his carbine and replied 'This is the only doctor for you today,' – and shot the Zulu dead.

And yet the very ruthlessness of that final victory served to dissipate the latent fear among the British which had produced such a brutal response. Whereas the Zulu army had seemed a very real danger on the night of 3 July – when the songs of the *amabutho*, ritually preparing for battle, drifted across the White Mfolozi to Chelmsford's camp – it was equally clear on the night of the 4th that it no longer was. The old Zulu military system had been damaged beyond repair, and the British mood lightened immediately. Even so, in September, during the last skirmishes of the war, when groups of Zulus in the Ntombe valley refused to emerge from their caves to surrender, the exasperated British simply blew up the mouths of the caves with the Zulus still inside.

Yet even at its most extreme the war in Zululand never reached the proportions of a true 'total war'. Although during the second invasion Lord Chelmsford deliberately targeted ordinary Zulu homesteads, destroying huts and food stores in the hope of eroding the Zulu will to resist, these incidents were largely confined to the close proximity of the British columns, while non-combatants themselves were never regarded as legitimate military targets. British wrath fell discriminately enough upon fighting men and within the context of recent campaigning. And although, by contrast, the Zulus traditionally regarded all enemy personnel – civilians and military – as targets during a time of war, they refrained at King Cetshwayo's order from attacking vulnerable settlements across the border in Natal, while only in the northern sector, around Luneburg, were the civilian families of Africans who supported the invasion attacked.

After Ulundi, moreover, both sides quickly drew back from the fierce animosities which had characterised the fighting itself, and individual British and Zulu men were able to meet to discuss their experiences for the most part without rancour. With victory, indeed, the British began the process of recasting their image of the Zulus, transforming them in their collective imagination from bloodthirsty savages to noble warriors, their courage a thing of nostalgic respect, their military skills safe to be admired once they were no longer a threat.

Yet in this process lay the true tragedy for the Zulu people, for the common ground sought by the veterans of the war was largely illusory, the product in fact of an undeniable British dominance and of the utter destruction of any Zulu capacity to resist the resulting erosion of their political and economic independence.

Paintings

Although the outbreak of the Anglo-Zulu War went almost unremarked in the British press – one of the side-effects of Frere's efforts to out-manoeuvre the government in London meant that only one of the mainstream British newspapers had a representative in Natal when it broke out – the reverse at iSandlwana soon catapulted it on to the front pages. From the moment the news first broke in the second week of February it was to prove a hugely popular theme among the readers of the illustrated papers, all of which produced dramatic representations of the battle. Initially, given the paucity of information, these reflected the prevailing air of sensation rather than strict representational accuracy but as the war progressed and the experienced 'war artists' of the day hurried to southern Africa the quality steadily improved. The *Illustrated London News* sent Melton Prior, its leading artist, to cover the war, while the *Graphic* sent the equally experienced Charles Fripp. The work produced by both artists – even in engraved form, allowing for unintentional errors introduced by the engravers – has remained an important source of historical information. These two papers were not alone, however, for the *Pictorial World* also produced a dramatic series of engravings and some of Prior's

work appeared in the rather more down-market *Penny Illustrated*.

The coverage of the war in these papers stimulated the prevailing interest in battle paintings. At a time when access by the majority of the public to photographs of current events was limited, paintings were a way of conveying images on newsworthy events to a wider audience. Paintings by popular artists often created great excitement when they were first displayed in galleries and queues to see them were not uncommon. Such pictures were also, of course, a way for the Victorian world to impose a sense of order on its actions, and the way in which contemporary battle pictures, in particular, were presented reveals a great deal about the way the events themselves were perceived.

The first artist to tackle a Zulu War scene was W.H. Dugan, a Hampshire artist, whose *The Defence of Rorke's Drift* was exhibited as early as May 1879. The painting was viewed by Prince Edward of Saxe-Weimar and Colonel Stanley, the Secretary of State for War, both of whom applauded Dugan for producing the work at a time when accurate information about the battle was still scarce. Lack of good reference material perhaps explains the composition of Dugan's picture – now in the Royal Welsh Museum in Brecon – which avoids any representation of landscape or buildings and concentrates entirely on a section of the British barricades with the Zulus rushing up on one side to attack the British on the other. Although the picture includes a number of errors in Zulu weapons and dress – based as the figures are on early press engravings – it is none the less one of the few Victorian paintings of the battle which give equal attention to both participants. The picture was well received and Dugan apparently painted a further picture of the fighting at Rorke's Drift during the night, and a study of the death of Melvill and Coghill. These pictures went on tour as part of a travelling 'diorama' depicting the battles, although the whereabouts of the second two paintings is currently unknown.

In response to popular interest in Rorke's Drift, the Fine Art Society of New Bond Street, London, commissioned the French military artist

Alphonse de Neuville to paint the battle. De Neuville already enjoyed a reputation as a painter of striking scenes from the Franco-Prussian War, and to ensure the accuracy of his new project the Society advertised in search of photographs, artefacts and eyewitness accounts of the battle. Among those who contributed notes as sketches was Trooper Harry Lugg of the Natal Mounted Police, a veteran of the battle, while de Neuville was also able to work up preliminary sketches from life of Chard and the dog Dick. The result was *The Defence of Rorke's Drift*, exhibited in March. The painting was executed with great skill and a verve lacking in most of the other early Zulu War pictures. In a manner common to narrative paintings of the time it telescopes several well-known incidents from the battle, presenting them within a single time-frame. De Neuville took great care to include most of the individuals who had distinguished themselves in the battle – whose names were already well known to the public – and a leaflet was available at the viewing identifying them. Unlike Dugan's picture, however, the perspective is very much a British one, with the viewer placed squarely within the British perimeter, and the Zulus squeezed out and reduced to a threatening anonymous mass beyond the barricades. One reason for this was that de Neuville was apparently unable to find Zulu models from which to work but he unwittingly established a precedent which has affected representations through art and cinema into recent times.

De Neuville's work was such a popular success that the Fine Art Society produced a large commercial engraving of the picture and the artist was commissioned to produce two more Zulu War scenes. These were conceived as a pair and represented the attempts of Lieutenants Melvill and Coghill to save the Queen's Colour at iSandlwana. *Saving the Queen's Colours* depicted the two on horseback with Melvill holding the Colour in one hand and pistolling a Zulu with the other, with the reins looped over his arm. *Last Sleep of the Brave* depicted the discovery of the pair lying dead beside the Mzinyathi river, still clutching the Colour. Both pictures have a similar *elan* to the artist's early Rorke's Drift

picture but otherwise represent a triumph of iconography over authenticity, since almost every important detail is inaccurate. Melvill is depicted clutching a 24th Regimental – not Queen's – Colour, while the bodies were not in fact found draped across each other, nor by the river, nor was the Colour present – and nor, indeed, were the 17th Lancers yet then in Africa. Both scenes had in effect been largely reinvented to fuel the growing public fascination with the incident, and de Neuville's imagery has continued to influence representations of iSandlwana; the Melvill and Coghill scenes in Douglas Hickox's 1979 film *Zulu Dawn* owe much to these paintings. De Neuville was also criticised in some quarters for his obvious lack of realism – for painting Zulu War scenes in his Paris studio without having been to Africa, and for using models found in Paris to represent both the British officers and the Zulus. None of these criticisms has affected the enduring appeal of his pictures, however.

The news of the death of the Prince Imperial, coming just a few months after iSandlwana burst upon the British public, also created an intense demand for images which the dramatic and often inaccurate representations in the illustrated press could not entirely fulfil. The Empress Eugenie – Louis's mother – commissioned a French artist then living in England, Paul Alexandre Protais, to paint a series of pictures representing her son's time in Zululand. One, *An Attack on a Kraal*, depicted the Prince at the head of a column of mounted troops emerging from a donga to attack a Zulu homestead. The second, *The Death of the Prince Imperial* (which has apparently remained in private hands), depicted Louis reaching for his sword as the Zulus attacked, while the third showed him lying dead on the veldt with the skyline of Paris traced in the clouds above. On seeing these pictures Queen Victoria herself, whose personal interest in the Prince had largely influenced the decision to allow him to go to Natal, commissioned another by the same artist, *Finding the Body of the Prince Imperial*. A typically Victorian and elegiac piece, full of hints of mourning and regret, this depicts the body of the Prince being carried to an ambulance wagon past rows of lancers and dragoons. French artist Paul Jamin painted a scene of the Prince's death which is notable for its historical accuracy rather than its symbolism – although the criticism implicit in the fleeing British troops in the background, and the artfully posed Zulus, about to strike the death blows, is clear enough.

The Queen also took a keen interest in Rorke's Drift, and indeed had invited Chard to Balmoral in October 1879 to explain the details of the battle to her. Perhaps rather irked by the fact that a Frenchman, de Neuville, had been commissioned to paint what seemed likely to be the defining image of the battle, the Queen commissioned Lady Elizabeth Butler to paint the battle. Butler – who, as Elizabeth Thompson had enjoyed huge success as a military painter since the exhibition of her Crimean painting, *The Roll Call* in 1874 – was married to Sir William Butler, who had served in Zululand on Wolseley's staff. In researching her picture Butler was able to call upon a number of men from the 1/24th, and invalids of the 2/24th, who had recently returned to England. She also drew Chard and Bromhead from life. Although the Queen herself, when she later asked for a private viewing of both the Butler and de Neuville paintings, declared herself emphatically more impressed by Butler's, it has the same limitations as her rival's but without his sense of fluid movement. Like de Neuville's, Butler's *The Defence of Rorke's Drift* includes a number of famous incidents from the battle, telescoping them into a single time-frame, and concentrates on recognisable British personalities. Butler was uncomfortable, however, at depicting figures actually struggling in combat, and despite an attempt to represent figures frozen in moments of intense action the poses of too many of the central figures seem stilted and artificial.

Both Lady Butler and de Neuville clearly struggled with the physical and ideological constraints imposed by the British barricades at Rorke's Drift. It was perhaps inevitable that the viewer in each case was invited to sympathise with the British perspective, but the presence of the barricades meant that the Zulus were squeezed awkwardly out of the frame, physically and sym-bolically marginalised. Although de Neuville, at least, was certainly capable of painting striking studies of figures assaulting barricades – such as his 1883 picture, *Tel-el-Kebir* – only one contemporary painting attempted to depict Rorke's Drift from the other side of the barricade. Reproduced on the cover of this book, it is a large watercolour which has only recently come to light. Painted about 1890 by an artist as yet unidentified, possibly with the collaboration of Chard himself – who features in the centre of the composition, and whose sketches prepared for Queen Victoria's personal reference were the obvious source of topographical information – the picture is remarkable in a number of respects. Its viewpoint suggests a rare degree of sympathy for the difficulties faced by the Zulus in assaulting the position, and its depiction of Zulu dress and weapons, together with the representation of the buildings, are unusually accurate. In this case the artist uses the barrier of the barricades to good effect, quite literally underlying the struggles of the defenders who still remain central to the composition, streaked across the middle of the painting.

Other incidents in the war – the siege of Eshowe, the disasters at Ntombe and Hlobane, and the crucial victory at Khambula – aroused little interest among the public and artists alike. Only Orlando Norrie – a prolific painter of precise military watercolours – was moved to paint *The Battle of Kambula*, a composition inspired largely by an engraving, based on a Melton Prior sketch, which had appeared in the *Illustrated London News*. Norrie also painted studies of the 13th Light Infantry and 60th Rifles on the march in Zululand, a view of the interior of Chelmsford's square at Ulundi, and a spirited study of the 17th Lancers' charge.

Ulundi, indeed, was greeted by a sudden flurry of pictures keen to celebrate the sense of vindication felt by the victorious British public, and the role of the Lancers in particular lent itself to the Victorian ideals of courage and dash in battle. In 1880 a little-known artist, B. Fayel, exhibited *The Charge of the 17th Lancers at Ulundi*, which depicted the incident in stirring style as a head-on clash between the charging cavalry and attacking Zulus. Fayel's understanding of African geography was clearly worse than de Neuville's, for he added a few palm trees in the background just to labour the scene's exotic location. Rather more romantic in tone was John Charlton's *After the Charge; The 17th Lancers at Ulundi*, which was exhibited in 1888, nearly a decade after the battle. Charlton was a popular painter of equestrian scenes who had depicted a number of cavalry charges in his earlier work and his picture eschews the blood-letting of conflict in favour of the symbolism of riderless horses and wounded men following in the wake of the reforming Lancers. Technically excellent, the mood enhanced by the extremes of the dawn light, the painting is none the less otherwise remarkable for not depicting a single Zulu figure within the context of the battle.

Adolphe Yvon, another established French artist who specialised in epic military scenes, produced *The Battle of Ulundi* at the request of the Empress of Austria. The picture was intended to be displayed as a panorama, on an almost circular stretcher, so that the viewers stepped into it and studied the battle as if in the middle of it. Yvon's scene depicted the battle from the centre of the British square, with baggage carts and hospital wagons in the foreground and the Lancers charging beyond the lines of British infantry. The painting – minus one section which surfaced recently in South Africa – is now on display in the National Army Museum in London, where the constraints of space have meant that it is exhibited flat. As a result the British positions seem far more extended than the artist intended, while the smoke of battle at either end drifts in opposite directions.

The battle of iSandlwana was, of course, a highly problematic subject for Victorian battle painters, not least because it was a British defeat, and because there were few incidents – beyond the much-publicised 'dash with the Colours', scooped by de Neuville – of recorded British heroism to celebrate. In 1883 a young Dublin-born painter, Richard T. Moynan, exhibited at the Royal Hibernian Gallery there a remarkable study, *The Last of the 24th Isandula*. Based on a Zulu account (published in Colenso and Durnford's *A History of the Zulu War*) it depicts a last survivor of the 24th, who had held out in a cave on the flanks of iSandlwana, falling to a volley of Zulu rifle-fire. Moynan had obviously researched his subject well for the cave, the soldier's uniform and equipment, and even the Zulus are all represented with considerable accuracy. What is more striking, however, is the painting's obvious symbolic content; the dying red-coat has a mystical look on his face, and his hand is raised as if in a blessing, while the Zulus draw back at his feet like Roman soldiers before the Crucifixion. It is a painting which effectively turns the dead soldiers of the 24th into Christian martyrs.

Undoubtedly the most interesting paintings of iSandlwana came from the brush of Charles Edwin Fripp. He was unusual among contemporary military painters of the war in that he had actually witnessed some of it; he was sent out as a 'special artist' for the *Graphic* after iSandlwana, and was present at Ulundi. In 1881 Fripp produced a large watercolour on the Melvill and Coghill theme, *Dying to Save the Queen's Colour*, which was reproduced as a supplement to the *Graphic*. Fripp's experience of Zululand is reflected in the overall accuracy of the scene – there are no Colours present, and Melvill and Coghill are clearly recognisable – and in the authentic studies of the Zulus. In 1885 Fripp exhibited at the Royal Academy a much more ambitious work, *The Last Stand at Isandula*. This attempted to meld an essentially conventional Victorian battle painting with some hidden insights into the true nature of the battle. At the centre of the composition is a tableau typical of the time – including the stalwart sergeant and young, and largely fictitious, 'drummer boy', facing their fate with quiet resolution – while behind, in the background, are vignettes of brutal slaughter. A soldier bayonets a Zulu through the throat while another Zulu attacks him from behind; wounded men are stabbed, and a fallen soldier is about to be disembowelled. Unusually for a heroic painting of the period, there are no officers in the composition, a subtle criticism of the failures of command which have brought the ordinary soldiers to their fate. Unfortunately,

Fripp's painting aroused little interest at the time owing to a growing sense of public unease about the justice of the invasion which followed upon the successful visit of King Cetshwayo to London in 1882. In recent years, however, the painting has achieved an iconic status and has been widely reproduced, not only in the context of the Anglo-Zulu War, but to represent the great age of Victorian military adventuring in general.

Indeed, the visit of Cetshwayo to London was an important moment in the process by which the British came to recast the Zulus from savage enemies to noble warriors. This process can be discerned in a wonderful portrait of Cetshwayo, commissioned from the German artist Carl Sohn Jnr by Queen Victoria to commemorate her meeting with the Zulu king. The portrait is an excellent likeness, and Cetshwayo's expression is both regal and faintly benign – yet, perhaps for the want of accurate traditional costume, the artist has draped his subject in what appears to be a decidedly un-African bear skin. It gives Cetshwayo the air of a Roman emperor, a touch of exoticism which cements his ideological transformation in the eyes of the viewer.

Although interest in the Zulu campaign quickly faded at the time, displaced in the public mind by a series of overseas entanglements, all to be commemorated or condemned, the upsurge in interest which followed the release of the film *Zulu* (1964) and the growth of tourism to the battlefields has been reflected in a new burst of artistic creativity. Artists such as Keith Rocco, Mark Churms, Simon Smith, Chris Collingwood, Steve Liptrot, Brian Palmer and Jason Askew – whose paintings suggest an edge of horror not always found in war art – have all found inspiration in the war, many of them reworking themes that were first popularised by their Victorian counterparts.

Pay

Throughout the Victorian era, the social standing of the British Army remained enduringly low. While members of the public were prepared to eulogise the soldiers as a thin red line of heroes when they were manning the far-flung outposts of Empire, they were less impressed by the reality of redcoats drinking, brawling and whoring in garrison towns at home. It was often said that to lose a son to the Army was a greater disgrace to a family than seeing him in prison. Despite determined efforts by the government – the introduction of the 'short service' system, which was designed to appeal to a 'better class of recruit' by reducing the period of commitment, and attempts to improve literacy and education levels within the Army – this perception did not begin to change until the advent of patriotically motivated mass volunteering in the Anglo-Boer War.

What then persuaded men to enlist? Usually the answer lay in a combination of desperate circumstances in civilian life – to escape unemployment, or the consequences of a crime, a family dispute or a romantic entanglement – and the appeal of regular food and regular pay. Recruiting sergeants promised their quarry basic pay of a shilling a day. Although this was considerably lower than a labourer's wages in civilian life – perhaps 3 shillings a day – it was at least regular, and from 1875 2d a day was deferred and paid in a lump sum at the end of the service. As most recruits soon ruefully discovered, however, that basic pay was subject to all manner of deductions or 'stoppages'. Although the first issue of uniform and equipment was free, as were subsequent official replacements, the men were responsible for the upkeep of military items and the replacement of any that were damaged or lost. The combined effect of the tailors' and shoemakers' bills, of 'regimental necessaries', of contributions to the repair of the barracks, of replacing deficiencies in clothing, of washing uniforms and clothes, of haircuts, of fines, of extra rations (beyond the daily allowance) and groceries was often so severe that Army regulations were forced to specify that soldiers should be allowed to retain at least 1d per day.

Extra wages could, however, be earned through extra duties, and those men who were up to the job could work as cooks, mess waiters, carpenters, shoemakers or tailors to supplement their pay. Officers employed men as servants at a fixed rate of 2s 6d in the cavalry and 1s 6d in the infantry. Good conduct also brought a reward – possession of a 'good conduct' badge brought an extra penny a day, as did promotion. In 1876 an infantry corporal earned 1s 4d a day and a sergeant 2s 1d.

Although officers' pay seems generous in comparison – it ranged from 5s 3d a day for the lowest infantry officer's rank, the ensign or second lieutenant, to 17s a day for a lieutenant colonel (slightly more among the cavalry to reflect the expense of maintaining horses), it was still based on rates which had been established during the Napoleonic era. Indeed, because being an officer in the Army was considered a gentlemanly profession, officers were often required to meet expensive mess and social bills from their private incomes. This was particularly true in the most fashionable cavalry regiments where expenses far outstripped pay and a considerable degree of private wealth was essential. Those who came from good social backgrounds but were poor tended to seek service in India where a good standard of living could be enjoyed at far less cost. As a result, many in the Army tended to look down upon officers who had spent much of their career in India.

Rates of pay among the Volunteer units who served in Zululand were markedly superior to their regular counterparts. The Natal Volunteer corps were required under the terms of their normal enlistment to serve for a total of 20 days a year in peacetime, for which they were paid at a rate of 6s a day plus rations and fodder. Service was comparatively well paid to reflect the fact that, as Volunteers, the men would have to give up civilian work for the duration of their service, and of course they provided their own horses. This rate applied equally to active service, but because of the protracted nature of the war in 1879 it was doubled to 12s a day. The quasi-military Natal Mounted Police, being regulars, were paid rather less than the Volunteers – 5s 6d a day for troopers – and horses were provided for them by the Natal Government.

Horses were generally provided for members of the Irregulars, too. Their rates had been fixed at 5s a day for a trooper, 6s for a corporal, 7s for a sergeant, 8s for a troop sergeant-major, 9s for a regimental sergeant-major, 11s for a lieutenant and 15s for a captain. Among the infantry auxiliary units there was a distinction between the rates paid to Europeans and to African members. Among the NNC white buglers and corporals were paid 6s a day, sergeants 7s, quartermaster sergeants 8s, sergeant-majors 9s, interpreters (second class) 10s, interpreters (first class) 20s, the adjutant and quartermaster 13s, lieutenants 11s, captains 15s and the Commandant 30s. An African officer, however, received £2 per month (slightly more than a shilling a day), an NCO 25s a month and a private 20s. In mounted auxiliary units – the 'Native Horse' – European captains received 20s a day, lieutenants 15s, African officers £4 10s a month and troopers £3 a month.

Zulus who served their king expected no payment in return – it was merely part of the duties of citizenship. While the *amabutho* were mustered – whether for war or to take part in a ceremony – they did, however, expect to be fed at the king's expense. When living at the royal homesteads this usually took the form of a daily issue of beef and beer although food was notoriously short over periods of longer service. Many men relied on food parcels – usually pumpkins and corn – brought to the *amakhanda* from home by younger relatives (male and female), or simply went hungry. On active service much the same situation prevailed – the king provided an *impi* with slaughter cattle while mat-carriers brought roasted mealies. Generally the supplied food was consumed within a few days and the warriors were then dependent upon forage. Victory in war might, however, bring rewards for the men were allowed to keep most of the items they looted from the fallen enemy. Cattle captured in battle were the property of the state, to be assessed and distributed by the king, and it was usual for some of them to be given to men who had particularly distinguished themselves. In 1879 captured British firearms were also supposed to be given to the king but these were so jealously prized that Cetshwayo wisely gave permission for those who had secured them to retain them.

Photographers

During the British expedition to Abyssinia in 1868 the Royal Engineers took with them a photographic detachment to record the incidents of the campaign. No such facility was available in Zululand in 1879, and it was left to civilian photographers to record what scenes they could. There were a surprising number of photographers working in Natal at the time of the invasion, no fewer than nine in Pietermaritzburg and six in Durban. Of these James Lloyd had been at Durban since 1859, J.W. Buchanan had accompanied Theophilus Shepstone's expedition to 'crown' King Cetshwayo in 1872, while the Kisch brothers, Benjamin and Henry, enjoyed a particularly good reputation and had studios in both towns. Natal's settler population provided their primary market, together with travelling colonial officials and soldiers, and while studio-based *cartes-de-visite* portraits were a stock-in-trade, a few of the more adventurous practitioners made occasional journeys into the countryside to photograph local landmarks or 'exotic' African life. The outbreak of the war had obvious commercial potential – photography was popular among those well-off enough to afford to collect commercially produced albums of topical or scenic studies, and passing officers could be relied upon to provide a ready market. Yet photographing the war would be problematic since not only was the photographic process slow and cumbersome but the war would take place in remote and inaccessible spots. It was, moreover, dangerous, as iSandlwana demonstrated during the first fortnight of the campaign, and most photographers had to be content to watch the build-up of troops on the comparatively safe Natal side of the border, or to visit the battle-fields months after the fighting had moved on. The slow exposure time, moreover, meant that action shots were impossible even had it been safe to take them, and most photographers could do little more than take static views of camp life, forts, landscapes, or posed individual or group studies. The enemy, moreover, was only likely to be photographed as a prisoner, after he had surrendered, or when he lay dead upon the ground.

Nevertheless, despite the difficulties they faced, Natal's photographers produced a remarkably rich and historic record of the war. James Lloyd had the foresight to travel up from Durban to photograph the presentation of the British ultimatum to Cetshwayo's envoys on 11 December 1878, and he returned a month later to capture Pearson's men in the act of crossing the border – two moments of the greatest historical significance. Although Lloyd's photographs were all taken from the Natal bank, he had stolen a march on his rivals, none of whom had felt able to cover the early advance of the other columns – perhaps wisely, as things turned out. Not until the war began to swing decidedly in Britain's favour did some of the photographers dare to join the advance into Zululand itself. Henry Kisch photographed some of the troops massing on Zululand's western border for the second invasion at the end of May, while George Ferneyhough of Pietermaritzburg attached himself to Wood's Flying Column. Ferneyhough, indeed, took another of the great historic photographs of the war – a view from the British camp on the White Mfolozi on the morning of 4 July, showing smoke rising from the burning oNdini homestead. Lloyd had photographed the 1st Division assembling at the Lower Thukela in May, and the Zulu dead lying on the field of kwaGingindlovu, and in June he made an extended tour of the central border, photographing the fortified storehouse at Rorke's Drift – recently abandoned in favour of camps closer to Fort Melvill and the river, which he also photographed – and British dragoons burying some of the remains which still lay exposed at iSandlwana.[208] Even King Cetshwayo himself was photographed on board the steamer *Natal* after his capture, a series of studies in which he looks – as well he might – uncomfortable and dejected; the smile he adopts in one, presumably at the photographer's suggestion, seems distinctly false. And they proved a commercial success, too, most photographers doing a brisk trade into 1880 and until the last of the troops departed.

The photographs taken in the war were undoubtedly limited in many ways – technically, geographically, even ideologically – yet they provide a glimpse behind the curtain of the passing years to reveal a literal reflection of the war which often conveys a reality, an enduring point of human connection with the generations that have come after, which is somehow lost in the huge and often more dramatic output of war-artists and engravers.

abaQulusi

In the early 1820s King Shaka brought a wide swathe of northern Zululand under Zulu control, from the upper reaches of the Mzinyathi valley eastwards towards the Phongolo river. In order to establish his control over the area he ordered that a royal homestead be built to the east of Hlobane mountain. This homestead was called ebaQulusini, and Shaka gave it into the control of his formidable aunt, his father's sister Mnkabayi. The homestead ruled over the remnants of the people who had remained in the area after the conquest – many of them Swazi speakers – and a version of ebaQulusini was still in existence in 1879 (Buller burned it down during a raid on 4 February). Over the next fifty years the descendants of those attached to that homestead, together with their adherents, came to be regarded as a distinct section of the Zulu Royal House. They were known by the name abaQulusi. Unlike traditional chiefdoms, they were not ruled over by hereditary *amakhosi* but by officials – *izinduna* – appointed directly by the king. Throughout their history the abaQulusi proved determinedly loyal to the Royal House, and in 1879 they were a bastion of loyalist support in the north. Their senior military commander was Sikhobobho kaMabhabhakazana.

Much of the military strength of the abaQulusi depended upon a chain of natural strongholds to which they could retire in times of stress, notably the Zungwini, Hlobane and Ityenka mountains. Hlobane, in the centre of the three, was largely impregnable since the gently undulating plateau summit was largely surrounded by impenetrable cliffs. Here and there paths meandered up through the boulders, and up these the abaQulusi drove their cattle to protect them from attack; the summit itself was too open and exposed to electrical storms to be permanently habitable. The paths themselves were then blocked with dry-stone walls. As soon as the British invasion began, Evelyn Wood recognised that the suppression of the abaQulusi would be essential to ensure that his lines of communication were not threatened on the advance to oNdini, and in the third week of January he led an extended foray from his camp at Fort Thinta to drive them off their strongholds. He successfully carried Zungwini but had failed to drive the abaQulusi off Hlobane when news of the disaster at iSandlwana caused him to break off the engagement. It was not until 28 March that he again attempted to capture Hlobane but his assault parties, having reached the top of the mountain, found their lines of retreat cut and were compelled to make an ignominious and costly withdrawal down a steep slope at the western end of the mountain. The abaQulusi attributed the Zulu victory to the tactics of Sikhobobho in combination with the timely arrival of the king's *amabutho* from oNdini. The following day some elements of the abaQulusi joined the main army's abortive attack on Wood's camp at Khambula, but arrived late, did not take much part in the fighting, and suffered heavily in the retreat.

The British victory at Hlobane greatly dis-couraged the abaQulusi. Hlobane was largely abandoned, although abaQulusi contingents con-tinued to support Zulu resistance in the area, and the group did not formally surrender until the beginning of September 1879. After the war they were deliberately placed under the control of the British appointee Prince Hamu kaNzibe, the only member of the Royal House who had defected to the British during the invasion. The abaQulusi not unnaturally regarded Prince Hamu as a traitor, and he in turn was vigilant for signs of dissent among them; the tension between the two pro-vided some of the first manifestations of the brewing civil war. Throughout the troubles of the 1880s the abaQulusi remained loyal to the Royal House, and an abaQulusi contingent played a decisive role in the defeat of *inkosi* Zibhebhu at Tshaneni on 5 June 1884. When Zululand was subsequently divided up into British and Boer zones, the abaQulusi found themselves subjects of the Boer 'New Republic', whose capital, Vryheid, was built close to Hlobane mountain.

Over the next decade the abaQulusi found their position steadily eroded, their land appropriated and their authority increasingly reduced.

Their resentment of Boer authority came to a head during the closing stages of the Anglo-Boer War. British troops had occupied Vryheid but the Afrikaner farming community remained sympathetic to the Boer cause and during the guerrilla war a commando operated in the vicinity, fed both by Boer supporters and by raiding cattle and crops from the abaQulusi. In May 1902 the abaQulusi appealed to the British to intervene to protect them but, with peace negotiations looming, the British were reluctant. When he heard of this the leader of the commando, Jan Potgeiter, issued a contemptuous challenge to the abaQulusi. Sikhobobho responded by assembling his forces and at dawn on 6 May attacked the commando camp at the foot of Holkrans hill. After a stiff fight the Boers were overrun, losing 56 of 73 men. Ironically, the action accelerated the Anglo-Boer peace process because it convinced influential Boer leaders that the African population was turning against them.

The battle of Holkrans proved to be the last military victory of the abaQulusi, but their descendants still live in the area between Hlobane and Paulpietersburg.

Regime Change, 1879

When British troops crossed into Zululand on 11 January 1879[209] they did so under the pretext of waging war not upon the Zulu people, but upon the administration of King Cetshwayo himself. In the propaganda prelude to the war, designed to convince the British Government in London, as much as anyone, of the righteousness of the invasion, Sir Bartle Frere and Theophilus Shepstone had been keen to portray the Zulu king as a despot, from whose excesses the Zulu people as a whole were yearning to be free. Indeed, the British also hoped that this stance would persuade significant numbers of Zulus to defect to them; it didn't work, and for the most part the Zulu people united behind their king in defence of their country.

Such a position begged the question of how the British would administer a 'liberated' Zululand after the conquest and who, if anyone, they would set up in place of Cetshwayo. This question was not resolved during the course of the war, partly because by keeping it unanswered the British were able to exploit the hopes of their various African allies.

There were, in fact, a number of significant members of the Zulu Royal House living in exile outside Zululand, and their potential participation on the British side reinforced the impression that the war was directed against Cetshwayo personally and appeared to legitimise the British intervention. They were by no means reluctant to support the British invasion because they harboured ambitions of their own, of varying degrees of legitimacy, to the Zulu throne. King Mpande, Cetshwayo's father, had raised a large number of sons and, towards the end of his life, had attempted to constrain their ambitions by playing their aspirations off against one another. Although as early as 1840 he had nominated Cetshwayo as his heir, he later came to favour his son Mbuyazi. This created bitter divisions between his sons which came to a head in a civil war in 1856 between Cetshwayo and Mbuyazi. The latter attempted to flee to Natal with thousands of his followers (known as the iziGqoza), but was trapped by the flooded state of the Thukela river. Caught by Cetshwayo's pursuing army, the iziGqoza were largely destroyed in one of the bloodiest battles in Zulu history and Mbuyazi himself was killed.

The death of Mbuyazi did not eliminate all opposition to Cetshwayo's succession within the Zulu Royal House, however, and over the next few years a number of royal princes who harboured ambitions of their own slipped across the borders to either Natal or the Transvaal. The most important of these were the Princes Mkhungo and Sikhotha, who took refuge in Natal, and Mthonga, who moved between Natal and the Transvaal. Mkhungo, the most senior, gradually accumulated a following from political refugees fleeing Zululand who placed themselves under his protection, and who took up the name of Mbuyazi's old faction, the iziGqoza. Natal's Secretary for African Affairs, Theophilus Shepstone, was quite prepared to use their presence to gain leverage over affairs within the Zulu kingdom, a factor which kept alive Cetshwayo's lingering resentment towards the princes.

With the outbreak of war, Lord Chelmsford was keen to achieve the active participation of the royal princes, both for their propaganda value and to add to the manpower available to the black auxiliary units. All three did so, largely in the hope of securing a place in the post-war settlement of Zululand. Although Mkhungo offered his support he did not take to the field himself, however, because he was middle-aged and overweight. Instead he was represented by his younger brother Prince Sikhotha, who joined the 3rd Regiment Natal Native Contingent with about 300 followers and, in recognition of his standing, was given a staff position. In the Transvaal Prince Mthonga joined Wood's column with a handful of his personal followers.

Their presence with the British columns undoubtedly shaped Cetshwayo's perception of the strategic threat once the war began; he regarded the Centre Column as the most dangerous. This was partly because the presence of Sikhotha and the iziGqoza with the Centre Column – together with hundreds of other NNC recruited from Natal chiefdoms who were historically antagonistic towards the Zulu Royal House – made that column look for all the world like a viable coalition of African groups opposed to Cetshwayo, supported by British troops.

Both Sikhotha and Mthonga were involved in the subsequent fighting. Sikhotha and some of the iziGqoza were among those NNC companies left in the camp at iSandlwana on 22 January; Sikhotha was present at the battle and narrowly escaped by way of Fugitives' Drift. Mthonga and his followers were attached to Colonel Wood's staff during the attack on the Hlobane mountain on 28 March; when two of Wood's staff, Campbell and Lloyd, were killed, it was Mthonga's followers who dug shallow graves for them with their spears. When Wood subsequently decided to retire to Khambula camp, Mthonga himself was the first to spot the main Zulu army approaching from oNdini.

Even before the battle of Hlobane, however, the British had succeeded in winning over to their side a far more influential member of the Royal House, whose defection made the support of the émigré princes largely superfluous. Prince Hamu kaNzibe was actually a son of King Mpande – and therefore another of Cetshwayo's brothers – although he had been raised as heir to the estate of Mpande's deceased brother Nzibe. As such, Hamu had no legitimate claim to the Zulu throne but he was an immensely powerful figure who ruled his own people, the Ngenetsheni, in northern Zululand with very little interference from oNdini. He was known to be ambivalent towards Cetshwayo's administration, and indeed in 1878 the two had quarrelled following a clash between two *amabutho* at the annual harvest ceremonies. He spent the early part of the war in his homestead at Ngome, being one of the few of the Zulu elite not to participate in the iSandlwana campaign, and from there opened secret negotiations with the British. In the middle of March he surrendered to Wood's column, fleeing with his followers and cattle in the face of pursuit from an irate royalist *impi*. He was temporarily relocated outside Utrecht, and some of his warriors fought with Wood's auxiliaries at Hlobane.

There is some evidence that Prince Hamu hoped that at the end of the war the British would make him king, and indeed the British rather lost interest in Mkhungo, Sikhotha and Mthonga following Hamu's defection. Whether Lord Chelmsford encouraged Hamu in this respect is not clear, but in any case the final decision would not be Chelmsford's to make. The post-war settlement in fact fell to Chelmsford's successor, Wolseley, who had already decided to partition Zululand and who did not take to Prince Hamu personally. Nevertheless, Hamu was made one of the thirteen *amakhosi* appointed to rule Zululand after Cetshwayo was deposed; none of the other émigré princes was rewarded in the settlement.

In fact, as the British came to realise, by fleeing Zululand those members of the Royal House who were living in Natal or the Transvaal at the beginning of the war had largely forfeited any significant degree of support within the country, and their use to the conquerors was therefore limited. Only Hamu had sufficient influence inside Zululand to make him a possible alternative to Cetshwayo; it is, however, very unlikely that the British would ever simply have replaced one king with another, since their main political objective was to weaken the unity of the country to prevent it offering a threat to white interests.

Ultimately the émigré princes were no more than pawns to be exploited while they were useful and their ambitions were expendable once that usefulness had passed.

Religious Belief and Ritual (British)

The British Army during the Victorian era enjoyed a complex – if rather distant – relationship with religious belief. In the sense that neither its ideology nor its practice were primarily motivated by religious doctrine, the Army was essentially a secular organisation; that said, it did of course reflect many of the religious attitudes of the society from which its personnel were drawn, and which was of course notionally Christian.

In the first half of Queen Victoria's reign the Army stood low in the opinion of British society as a whole. Because it had traditionally recruited the rank and file among the lowest sectors of civilian society – the majority of recruits were uneducated and unemployed labourers, for whom conditions in civilian society were desperate, and for whom hunger was often the main motivation for enlisting – service in the Army tended to be regarded as the last refuge of the lawless and godless. This contempt was not confined to the newly emergent middle classes; the opinion was often expressed among labouring families, too, that to lose a son to the Army was a greater disgrace than to see him imprisoned. While Army reformers sought across the period to improve the social and educational lot of the ordinary soldier – a process which was already beginning to produce results in the 1870s – religious evangelists also struggled to save his soul. And while much of this pressure came from civilian organisations with little understanding of the realities of Army life, the Army establishment was by no means unaware of the need to provide for the spiritual care of its troops. The Army Chaplains Department had been formed as early as 1796, initially reflecting the link between the Crown and the Anglican Church. By 1879, however, the proliferation of non-conformist religions which characterised the debates within the English Protestant Church during the nineteenth century had been gradually recognised by the Army; Presbyterians had been admitted to the ACD in 1827, and even Catholics – feared a generation before lest their religious beliefs incline them towards subversive sympathies – in 1836. Indeed, although the great age of recruitment among the Irish peasantry had passed, there was still a significant proportion of Irishmen in the ranks in 1879, most of whom were at least nominally Catholic. Wesleyans were on the brink of being officially recognised by the ADC, but would have to wait until 1881 – two years after the Anglo-Zulu War – and the first Jewish chaplain was not admitted until 1892.

Nevertheless, it is probably true that a serious commitment to religious belief was confined to a fairly small minority among the other ranks. Most ordinary soldiers were not, in Kipling's words, 'plaster saints', nor did 'plaster saints' feature unduly in their priorities. The situation was rather different among the officer class, however, where higher standards of education and close social connections with Church life in civilian society – many officers had relatives among the clergy; both Evelyn Wood and Lieutenant J.B. Carey, for example, were the sons of parsons, while John Chard's brother was a clergyman – made for a greater degree of religious commitment. The promulgation in the Public School education system of concepts of Christian virtue and of *noblesse oblige*, of a predominant sense of the righteousness of duty and self-sacrifice, had led to changing concepts of the role of a gentleman and to a greater reliance on a religious-based value system which was inevitably reflected by the Army's officers. Devotion to the Church and family were the cornerstones of middle- and upper-class Victorian society, and many officers took their commitments in this respect seriously. Most would have considered themselves to be practising – in the sense of committed and church-going – Christians, and many were openly conspicuous in their religious devotion. Indeed some, like General Sir Hope Grant and Charles 'Chinese' Gordon, regarded the spread of the British Empire, even by military means, as synonymous with the spread of Christian values. The sense that the Army acted in accordance with a Christian-inspired concept of a 'civilising mission' was widespread among officers in Zululand and elsewhere; Anthony Durnford was among those who, despite a sympathy for the African population of Natal and Zululand that was rare among his colleagues, broadly shared this view. While some outside the Army – like the controversial Bishop of Natal, John William Colenso – struggled to reconcile their Christian belief with the cynical reality of British policies in Zululand, most were prepared to judge the apparent injustices of the invasion as an aberration of British values, rather than make the enormous leap necessary to recognise that aggressive British colonial policies were essentially incompatible with Christian values. Indeed, many civilian Christian missionaries on the spot, frustrated at their failure to evangelise among the Zulus, went so far as to regard the invasion as morally justified. For them, the administration of King Cetshwayo – with its emphasis on Zulu traditional belief, suspicion of missionary activity and reluctance to embrace European economic values – was a bastion of heathenism from which the Zulus should be prised for the sake of their own spiritual and material well-being.

When the first invasion began in January 1879 Chelmsford's lack of resources was reflected, as in every other field, in a scarcity of Army Chaplains Department personnel. The Revd George Ritchie of the ACD was based at Fort Napier in Natal, and remained there throughout the first invasion, presumably because the war was not expected to last long. As a result, the spiritual care for the invading columns fell largely to volunteer local clerics. Thus Zululand's best-known Anglican missionary, the Revd Robert Robertson – who had abandoned his mission station at kwaMagwaza on the eve of war – accompanied Pearson's column, and would

find himself confined with the troops at Eshowe during the siege. The vicar of Escort in Natal, the Revd George Smith, was en route to take up a similar position with the Centre Column when events overtook him at Rorke's Drift.

Nevertheless, there is considerable evidence that the troops felt the need for spiritual care even at this stage of the war – the prospect of combat no doubt had an effect in this regard – and the writings of officers in the field are peppered with religious references. Evelyn Wood and his staff regularly offered up individual prayers most nights before retiring; the Prince Imperial (whose background, religious and otherwise, was admittedly rather different), a devout Catholic, prayed aloud. Church parades were held on Sundays unless circumstances prevented them. Pearson's chief engineer, Captain Warren Wynne RE, wrote home regularly to his wife and his letters suggest the extent to which his faith, at least, provided him with comfort during the difficult times of the siege:

We are to have Holy Communion next Sunday. How I am looking forward to it in the midst of all this work and anxiety. May our dear Lord make himself very fully known to me in the breaking of bread, and may I be enabled to realise the blessedness of the Communion of the mystic Body of Christ, even his Holy Church, His saints on earth and in Paradise.[210]

Indeed, at Eshowe a small but devout group took full advantage of the presence of the Revd Robertson to indulge in regular Bible readings throughout the siege, according to an anonymous staff officer:

Soon after coming here we began a Bible-meeting. We meet four times a week; between thirty and forty soldiers and blue-jackets attend. Indeed, we could not accommodate more, as the outhouse where we meet is nearly full of biscuit-boxes and corn. But they form capital seats, and the wooden logs a luxurious carpet. Sometimes, when we are much crowded, some of the blue-jackets clamber aloft, where they seem to be more at home. The men seem to enjoy our little meetings much, as they show by coming to them after very hard work in hot weather, and under circumstances not altogether comfortable.[211]

To put this observation in context, however, it should be noted that while 'thirty or forty' soldiers attended these readings, there were some 1,700 troops present at Eshowe throughout the siege.

The provision of religious support had increased significantly by the time the second invasion began in June 1879, since a number of Army Chaplains Department personnel were dispatched to Natal with the reinforcements sent out after iSandlwana. The medal roll confirms that a total of fourteen ACD chaplains had qualified for the South Africa campaign medal by the end of the war. There was certainly work for them to do; the Catholic chaplain Father J. Bellard read the first funeral service over the body of the Prince Imperial of France at Thelezeni camp on 2 June, while the Revd Ritchie was present during some of the burials at iSandlwana. Robert Robertson continued to serve with the 1st Division after Pearson's column was relieved and the forces on the coast reorganised. George Smith read the funeral service over some of those killed at the battle of Ulundi, alongside Senior Chaplain C.J. Coar – who had been attached to the Flying Column – and the Revd Bandy from Durban.

Most of the African troops who accompanied the British forces followed traditional beliefs and rituals broadly similar to those practised by the Zulus. An exception was the mounted unit drawn from the Edendale Wesleyan mission community outside Pietermaritzburg. These men were drawn from a variety of ethnic backgrounds – many were descended from Swazi or Sotho-speakers rather than from Natal African groups – and they were of course *amakholwa* – Christian believers. As such, they were accompanied throughout their time in the field by their spiritual leader, John Zulu Mtimkulu, who conducted regular religious services which were attended by the group as a whole. Indeed, their prayer meetings, and in particular their hymn-singing, brought favourable comment from many of the British troops serving alongside them.

Religious Belief and Ritual (Zulu)

For the Zulu, spiritual beliefs were of the greatest importance in the conduct of military campaigns, to the extent that the success or failure of particular actions was often attributed as much to the observation (or neglect) of relevant rituals as to more practical elements of leadership or strategy.

Traditional Zulu religious belief involved a reverence for deceased ancestors, who were thought to watch over the living from an alternative plane of existence, and who needed to be propitiated to ensure their support and goodwill. Almost every misfortune in daily life was regarded as a potential manifestation of discontent among the ancestral spirits, and it was the role of the spirit diviner – *izangoma* – to determine the cause and to suggest a remedy. The support of the ancestral spirits was sought before embarking on any major undertaking, and since the potential for disaster was obviously enormous should that support be withheld, this was particularly true in the case of events of great national importance, from the gathering of the year's first harvest to the launching of a military campaign. Should the nation or group be suffering from an unexpected disaster, similar rituals were performed to placate the spirits, cleanse and purify the group, and bind them to a common sense of purpose and belonging.

The rituals performed in these circumstances were broadly similar but varied in detail according to their specific purpose. It was necessary that all those involved performed the rituals fully and correctly, for any failure to do so might undermine their effectiveness.

King Cetshwayo assembled most of his *amabutho* in the second week of January 1879 to prepare them for the coming campaign against the British. The ceremonies were carried out not at oNdini itself but at Cetshwayo's kwaNodwengu homestead nearby. KwaNodwengu had been the principal homestead of King Mpande, and while the original homestead had been abandoned out of respect after the old king's death, Cetshwayo had rebuilt another one to honour his memory. The choice of kwaNodwengu as a venue is significant because it implied the need to secure the support of Mpande's spirit for the coming campaign. Indeed, the power of former Zulu kings, going back to the time of Shaka's grandfather, *inkosi* Jama, was believed to be immense, and it was particularly important that it was harnessed to the national cause.

We know a good deal about the nature of the ceremonies performed in 1879 because many Zulus involved later described them; however, in everything except scale, the rituals themselves were largely the same whenever any group mustered for war during the nineteenth century.[212] Indeed, those *amakhosi* living in Natal who supplied contingents to fight alongside British troops in the auxiliary units, against the Zulus, staged similar ceremonies before their men departed for the front.

The Zulu army did not muster in its entirety in January 1879 – men living in the border districts, and opposite the line of advance of the British flanking columns, were ordered to remain in their districts to watch the enemy's movements – but the *amabutho* assembled at kwaNodwengu still numbered some 29,000 men, and the ceremonies to prepare them lasted for several days. They were conducted by specialist herbalists – *izinyanga* – who provided the powerful medicinal concoctions needed. First, it was necessary to purify the entire army and cast out bad influences, and to do this every one of the men assembled was required to drink an emetic and to vomit into pits already prepared by the *izinyanga*. The medicines were applied to each *ibutho* in turn, men being called out to drink from clay pots which the *izinyanga* had filled with secret liquids. The men then ran in groups to the pits to vomit – 'there was naturally a desire to quickly finish, and have done with the vomiting',[213] as one young Zulu artlessly recalled – until the entire unit had been cleansed. To doctor the whole army in this way took the best part of a day, and when it was done the *izinyanga* dipped grass into the vomit, and – since it contained something of the essence of

the people – this was later bound into the sacred coil of the nation, the *inkatha yesizwe yakwa-Zulu*. After the vomiting ceremony, the troops were marched to kwaNodwengu, where men from the youngest *ibutho* were required to kill a specially selected black bull with their bare hands. Once the bull was dead, the *izinyanga* stripped off the hide, cut the flesh into strips, roasted it quickly over open fires, and sprinkled it with more medicines. The army was then formed into a large circle – an *umkhumbi* – and the *izinyanga* entered the centre carrying the meat. The strips were then tossed into the crowd, and each man attempted to seize one, bite off a strip then toss it back into the air. This ritual was intended both to pass something of the strength and courage of the bull on to the men, and to further bind them together by the application of the protective medicines. After the vomiting ceremony, many men were hungry and tried to swallow more than their share of the meat, although this was strictly forbidden. Indeed, the atmosphere was so excited, with so many men pressed together in the heat, grabbing for the strips, that it was not unknown for even experienced warriors to faint, and to have to be helped away by their friends to recover.

Once the men had undertaken these ceremonies, they were considered to have entered a very different state of spiritual being from that of their everyday lives. They were bound together in spiritual unity, and were prepared for the evil effects – known simply as *umnyama*, blackness – which would be unleashed by the shedding of blood in combat. They were, on the other hand, vulnerable to spiritual pollution themselves which might undermine the effect of the ceremonies, and they were therefore required to abstain from the normal activities of civilian life until they had returned from the campaign and undertaken the counterpart cleansing rituals.

Once these ceremonies were complete, the *amabutho* were paraded before the king, who had himself been ritually purified to greet them. The king called out *amabutho* in pairs, selecting those who were closest to each other in age, who therefore had a common bond and were thought to be *phalane*, linked. Members of each *ibutho* then challenged men known to them in the other, promising to outdo each other in the coming fight. In January 1879 the iNgobamakhosi first challenged the uKhandempemvu, then the uNokhenke challenged the uMbonambi. The purpose of this ritual was to build on existing loyalties and channel rivalries into battlefield aggression. According to Mpatshana kaSodondo, who was present with the youngest *ibutho*, the uVe:

A man of the Ngobamakosi got up and shouted 'I shall surpass you, son of So-and-so. If you stab a white man before mine has fallen, you may take the kraal of our people at such-and-such a place … You may take my sister So-and-so.' Having said this, he will then start leaping about (*giya*-ing) with his small dancing shield and a stick (for assegais are not carried on such occasions in the presence of the king, for it is feared that the troops may stab one another with them). The other who had been addressed may now get up and say 'Well, if you can do better than I do, you will take our kraal … and my sister.' He will then *giya* [dance a display of martial prowess].[214]

Such challenges were a matter of honour, and to refuse risked an imputation of cowardice. In fact, however, the wagers were largely symbolic, for while the king often called out the same *amabutho* after a campaign to see whether they had lived up to their boasts, no property actually changed hands. It was common, however, for these challenges to be evoked by *izinduna* in the heat of battle – as happened at iSandlwana – to spur the men on, sometimes with devastating effects.

In January 1879 the ceremonies had an extra element which reflected the gradual adoption by the Zulu army of European technology: the firearms possessed by the *amabutho* were also prepared to ensure that they were effective. A specialist doctor – imported from Basutoland – burnt medicinal herbs on a shard of broken pot, and the men filed past, holding their guns with the barrels pointing down so that the smoke drifted up the barrels.

With the ceremonies complete, the king then addressed the assembled army, giving a short speech outlining the reasons for the campaign, encouraging his men, and giving them limited advice, such as not to advance so quickly as to tire themselves, nor to attack defended concentrations. The specific details of his strategy he had already decided in conference with his councillors, while the tactical decisions were left to field commanders to make as circumstances dictated.

Once the army had been dispatched to the front, the king took no part in its direction, beyond adding his own spiritual power to its chances of success. As soon as messengers brought him news that the army was engaged with the enemy, it was customary for the king to retire to the private hut where the *inkatha* was kept and there sit upon it. This bound his own spiritual energy, and that of his forebears, with that of the nation as a whole, represented by the *inkatha*, and focused it in support of the army's endeavours.

One last ritual was necessary before the army left for the front; as the great columns of men filed away from kwaNodwengu, they headed towards the White Mfolozi river, beyond which lay the graves of the powerful ancestors from the time of Shaka's father, Senzangakhona. The *amabutho* would visit each significant grave in turn, chanting sacred songs and calling out ancient praises so that the ancestral spirits would be persuaded to lend their crucial support.

No further rituals were necessary until the moment of attack. None the less, the army was constantly on the look-out for signs and portents which might indicate the favour – or otherwise – of the spirits, and therefore affect the outcome of the campaign. Attacks were not generally launched at night – a time when the spirit world was closer to the living one (and troops were in any case difficult to control) – or on the day before the night of the new moon, which was considered a time of *umnyama*, of spiritual darkness. The untimely appearance of certain animals or birds might betoken ill omen, while any misfortune to a prominent commander might be taken as proof of a coming disaster. Sometimes, however, the quick-wittedness of a charismatic leader might save the day. In December 1856, for example, during the succession dispute between the rival princes Cetshwayo and Mbuyazi, a puff of wind lifted a crane-feather from the head-dress of Prince Mbuyazi as he stood observing his rival's forces advance; his watching commanders were awestruck and, convinced before they began that they were destined to lose, his troops showed little fight in the ensuing battle. A similar incident had occurred to King Shaka during a campaign against the Ndwandwe people in 1818, however – but Shaka had been sharp enough to cry out quickly that it was an omen of how his enemy would fall down before him! On that occasion, his men were successful.

Zulu *izinyanga* also used their skills to ensure supernatural ascendancy over their enemies in other regards too, and particularly powerful individuals were thought to be able to cause confusion by conjuring up mist or to render the enemy blind to troop movements. On 25 June a local Zulu force mounted a successful raid across the Thukela river at Middle Drift, concealed by mist which, it was widely held, their *izinyanga* created for the occasion; in June 1906, however, during the Bhambatha Rebellion, the success of colonial troops in trapping a large rebel concentration in the Mome Gorge under cover of darkness – and subsequently destroying it – was largely attributed by surviving rebels to the superior spiritual powers possessed on that occasion by the whites.

When the army was in the vicinity of the enemy, and about to be launched to the attack, it was necessary to undergo one final ritual. It was again formed into a circle, and this time the *izinyanga* strode among the men, splattering them with liquid medicines held in pots and using a wildebeest's tail. At the same time the commanders recited the praises of the king and his ancestors to catch their attention before the attack, and to focus the men's minds on their common heritage and loyalties. These ceremonies were absolutely crucial in order to counter any spiritual contamination which might have occurred since the first rituals were performed, and to top up their potency. Failure to observe them could lead to the *amabutho* fighting in a weakened spiritual state, with dire physical consequences ensuing as a result.

The exact content of the *izinyanga*'s medicines on this – and indeed the earlier – occasion is not known, although it was common for them to introduce human body parts into them at some point. These parts were taken from the bodies of enemies killed in action, which therefore had the power to ensure supernatural mastery over them in future. Certain body parts were preferred because they carried with them associations of strength and power; these included skin from the forehead, cartilage from below the breastbone, tissue from the anus, the penis, and in the case of fallen Europeans, facial hair – which was thought to represent their masculinity. By doctoring an *impi* with medicines made from these ingredients, it was thought that the enemy's courage would fail him in coming fights. It is unlikely that human tissue was included in the medicines of January 1879, since at that point no Europeans had been killed in combat. There are suggestions, however, that such items were removed from the British dead after iSandlwana, and would presumably have been used in the ceremonies preceding the renewed fighting of late March and early April. Certainly the bodies of troopers killed in the skirmish near oNdini on 3 July were mutilated to provide ingredients for the ceremonies which took place that night, preparing the *amabutho* for the great battle of the following day.

Finally, as the *amabutho* at last advanced to the attack, their *izinduna* gave the order for those who had privately procured protective medicines – which they wore in pouches around the neck or in snuff-containers in pierced ear-lobes – to administer them. Most of these were snorted up the nose. While their effect is generally held to be psychological, it has been argued that they included narcotic elements which would, for a short time at least, have stimulated the warriors' aggressive spirit and dulled their awareness of fatigue. Certainly cannabis was widely held to be an ingredient, and locally grown South African cannabis contains a high proportion of natural chemical stimulants.

After a battle, it was necessary to undergo cleansing ceremonies to free the men from the effects of the preparatory rituals before they could return to civilian society. This was particularly true of those who had actually killed in battle, and who were therefore believed to be in a state of powerful spiritual contamination unleashed by the shedding of human blood. They ran the risk of being haunted by the spirits of the enemy they had killed, and of spreading that spiritual taint among their families and into society at large. Their path to redemption began on the battlefield; it was for this reason that Zulu men cut the abdomen of their fallen victims, to allow safe passage of the spirit to the afterlife. A man was also required to wear part of the clothing of his victim until the ceremonies were complete – in 1879 the tunics of fallen red-coats were popular in this regard.

Those who had been so blooded were separated off during the army's return from the front, together with those who had themselves been injured, and who were therefore equally spiritually vulnerable. They were said to be 'wet with yesterday's blood', and could not report to the king or return home until they were cleansed. The king appointed homesteads where they could live and the cleansing was supervised, as usual, by *izinyanga*, and might take four or five days. Each day the affected men, still wearing the clothes of the dead and carrying their weapons with blood upon them, marched to a nearby stream where they stripped and bathed, while the *izinyanga* boiled medicines over fires on pot-sherds. The men were then required to dip their fingers into the warm solution, suck it off their finger-tips and spit it out, crying at the same time 'Come out, evil spirit, come out!' Only when the *izinyanga* judged the cleansing complete would these men – the *abaqawe* or heroes – be allowed to rejoin their *amabutho* to parade before the king for the review of their performance, and the apportion of praise or blame.

Since many of those who had not killed in battle simply returned home afterwards, it seems that the lesser ceremonies required to cleanse them were carried out privately.

The importance of these preparatory rituals cannot be overstated, and it is interesting to note, when debating Zulu intentions at iSandlwana on the morning of 22 January, that the final medicinal ceremonies were not carried out among the majority of the *amabutho* immediately prior to the attack. Since no Zulu commander would willingly engage in a battle on the day of the 'dead moon', and without having first completed these rituals, this strongly suggests that the attack was not begun deliberately, but was indeed precipitated by a chance encounter with British troops. It is also significant in this regard that, even as the situation developed rapidly with the majority of the *amabutho* hurrying towards the British camp, the Zulu commanders struggled to hold back the reserve units and administer the necessary rituals rather than let them also engage in battle in a spiritually weakened state.

After the battle, indeed, many Zulu blamed the heavy casualties suffered by the *amabutho* at iSandlwana on the failure by the senior commanders to ensure that the rituals were properly applied, while members of the Royal House criticised Cetshwayo for leaving the *inkatha* briefly while the battle was in progress. These lapses in spiritual procedure were seen to be every bit as responsible for the costly nature of the victory as the effects of British firepower.

Ironically, of course, on 22 January it was those elements who had been properly prepared – the reserve *amabutho* – who suffered the heaviest casualties of the day in the abortive attack on Rorke's Drift. For the most part the army entered the fray in the remaining major battles of the war – at Khambula, kwaGingindlovu and Ulundi – properly prepared, and the fact that it was repeatedly defeated led not so much to a loss of confidence in the power of Zulu ritual but to a growing sense of despair that the British seemed to be more powerful, not merely militarily but spiritually.

Rockets

After the battle of Nyezane on 22 January Lieutenant W. Lloyd RA expressed a rather dour professional opinion of the performance of the rockets which had formed part of his command:

> The rockets, as I expected, proved of little value; so much has been said of their moral effect on savages, but, to my mind, the Zulus displayed the utmost contempt for them. The enormous 24-pounder Hale's rocket fired from tubes by the Naval Brigade seemed to cause as much anxiety to our own men as to the enemy.[215]

And in truth, the record of rockets during the campaign was decidedly mixed, despite significant improvements in the technology of the weapon over the previous fifty years. The first practical war rocket had been designed for British use by Colonel William Congreve, who had apparently been inspired by the Indian use of rockets during the Anglo-Mysore wars of the 1780s. Congreve invented a rocket that was similar to a large modern firework – a metal shell full of explosive propellant, fixed to a stick to increase stability in flight. Congreve's rockets were introduced into the British Army during the Napoleonic Wars and achieved some notable successes, although the shortcomings of the design meant that they were generally unreliable, unpredictable and inaccurate.

In the 1840s William Hale invented a rocket system which considerably improved on Congreve's techniques. Hale's rocket did away with the need for a stick by making the rocket spin in flight. At first the British Army showed little interest in his design, and Hale sold manufacturing rights to the US, which employed his rockets in the Mexican–American War. The British Army subsequently agreed to try the Hale system on an experimental basis in the Crimean War. It was not until 1866, however, that the British Army declared the Congreve system obsolete and officially adopted the Hale type. Prior to 1879 Hale's rockets were employed in the Abyssinian campaign of 1868 and the Asante expedition of 1873–74.

Two sizes of rocket were used in Zululand in 1879, the 9-pdr, with which Royal Artillery detachments were equipped, and the 24-pdr, which was issued to the Royal Navy and was primarily intended for use at sea. The design of rocket was the same in each case but the launch apparatus was different.

The rocket itself was essentially a steel tube with a rounded head. The walls of the tube were strong enough to withstand the explosion of the black powder propellant with which it was filled, so that on being ignited the propellant burned away only through vents at the bottom, providing the thrust. On the base of the rocket were three such vents, and these were partly screened by steel flanges which directed the thrust at an angle, imparting a spinning motion.

The 9-pdr rocket was fired from a metal trough and required a crew of five – an NCO and four men – to operate it. Because the apparatus was less complex than the working of a field gun, it was usual in Zululand for the crew to consist of volunteers from an infantry battalion under the command of a Royal Artillery bombardier. Two troughs constituted a rocket section and were commanded by an artillery officer. Both the apparatus and the rockets themselves were carried in Zululand on mules. The rocket trough consisted of a V-sectioned length of steel fixed to a complex tripod of steel legs. A central elevating bar slid up and down on the legs to position the angle of the trough. The troughs were usually painted black and the rockets red.

The apparatus was loaded by first setting up the trough, then placing a rocket against a metal holder at the base of it. A friction tube (detonator) was then fitted into the upper-most vent of the rocket. According to the 1875 *Manual of Field Artillery Exercises*, a lanyard was then attached to the tube and discharged by the lanyard-man, 'bringing the lanyard up under the hollow of his left foot, which should be placed close to the hind rest of the trough, and by pulling upwards with his right hand with a steady pull'. The exploding friction tube then ignited the propellant and the rocket was fired.

There were, however, several unpredictable elements inherent in this procedure. For one thing, for the rocket trough to have any degree of accuracy it needed to be set up on flat ground;

such ground was seldom available in the field, and probably never in Zululand's boulder-strewn landscape. Secondly, the act of tugging on the lanyard inevitably jolted the apparatus, further upsetting the aim.

The much larger 24-pdr rockets carried by the Navy were potentially more effective, since they were designed to be fired from a long steel tube, fixed by a bracket to the side of a ship. For use on land the tube could be detached and mounted instead on legs; although the rockets were fired in the same way, the greater length of the enclosed tube, rather like a gun-barrel, gave them a greater velocity and steadier flight at the launch. In the field in 1879 the 24-pdr rocket apparatus was transported in light carts.

In fact, the technological limitations of the process meant that rockets were never likely to be either very accurate or greatly destructive. For one thing, they contained no detonating warhead, simply the compacted propellant in the shell; ideally, if they hit their target, they fizzed about in a spray of burning propellant, but just as frequently they simply went out. More often than not they missed the target anyway because once launched they were at the mercy of the wind, of obstacles in flight, and of the uneven burning of the propellant which often caused them to spin erratically and whizz off in odd directions. Rockets which had been stored in damp conditions or in the heat – both of which might be expected in Africa – were particularly liable to such problems. The 9-pdr rocket tended to dip briefly as it came off the trough, before it had built up sufficient velocity, and it was not unknown for it to strike the ground; on one occasion during the 1877–78 Cape Frontier War a rocket exploded on leaving the trough, and a fragment sliced off the ear of one of the crew! Melton Prior observed the typically erratic progress of one 9-pdr rocket at the battle of Ulundi:

I saw one fired, and watched its triumphal progress amongst the enemy, until, catching the corner of a hut, it suddenly altered its direction, then, striking the ground, it once more deviated from its proper course,

and came straight back at us, luckily missing our square by a quarter of a yard. My faith in rockets and tubes was considerably weakened on that occasion.[216]

None the less, despite their shortcomings – well known even at the time – rockets were considered to have three significant advantages. They were effective to a range of 2,000 metres, and often went much further (usually against the crew's wishes). They were lighter and much easier to transport than conventional artillery, making them ideal for use by mobile troops, and they had considerable value as an incendiary weapon – it was widely believed that the terrifying screech and spray of sparks and smoke they emitted would overawe enemies unacquainted with them.

As a result rockets played a significant part in almost every action of the Anglo-Zulu War. Colonel Pearson's Right Flank Column included two 24-pdr rockets with Navy crews and one 9-pdr trough from 11/7 Battery RA; all three were in action at the battle of Nyezane on 22 January and were later emplaced in the fortifications at Eshowe. Durnford's no. 2 column included two 9-pdr rockets commanded by Major Francis Russell RA – these were famously overwhelmed at iSandlwana. Two further 9-pdr troughs from 11/7 Battery were attached to Wood's column; during the assault on Hlobane mountain on 28 March each of the main assault parties (commanded by Colonels J.C. Russell and Redvers Buller) was accompanied by a single mule-borne trough, and at least one of them (presumably Buller's) came into action. The same rockets[217] were used the following day at Khambula and later – when Wood's column had been designated the Flying Column – at Ulundi. Two 24-pdr Naval rocket tubes were employed at the battle of kwaGingindlovu on 2 April, and a further 9-pdr tube was stationed at Fort Cherry, above Middle Drift, and employed during the British raid across the border on 20 May.

The actual performance of the rockets on these occasions was, as might be expected, variable. Although Lieutenant Lloyd was clearly unimpressed by the 9-pdr trough under his command, the Naval Brigade's 24-pdrs had some success at Nyezane. Under the command of the redoubtable Boatswain Cotter of HMS *Active*, they scored several hits against the Zulu centre, which was then sheltering in a deserted homestead uphill from the British position. One rocket, indeed, passed straight through the huts, setting them on fire, and thereby driving the Zulus out. After the battle was over, a clump of Zulu bodies was found on the spot, 'some of which were terribly burned' by rockets. After the war Captain W.R. Ludlow, travelling through Zululand, met 'a man who had been struck by a rocket, which, catching him on the breast, had literally melted the flesh off his chest, then taking a course down his side and leg, had cut a deep furrow down his thigh and calf, making the leg four inches shorter than the other'. [218]

At iSandlwana Russell's rocket battery, which had become separated from the rest of Durnford's command, only had time to fire one rocket before the vanguard of the iNgobamakhosi *ibutho* rushed up and fired a volley from close quarters, killing Russell himself and causing the mules to panic. The only apparent reference to rocket performance at Hlobane comes from an oral tradition which simply states that a rocket fired on top of the mountain passed absurdly high over the men at whom it was aimed. At Khambula, however, one Zulu recalled that rockets 'made a great noise and burnt natives so badly they couldn't recognise who they were'.

Yet if the British hoped to strike terror into the hearts of the Zulus with a demonstration of White Man's Magic, they were to be sorely disappointed for, as Lloyd noted, the Zulu response to them was entirely pragmatic. They recognised them for what they were – a noisy weapon which was only really dangerous to a few men directly in its path. One Zulu survivor of Nyezane, *inkosi* Zimema of the uMxapho *ibutho*, thought that rockets were simply 'a long pipe coming towards us'. [219] At iSandlwana the one rocket discharged by Russell's battery prompted a praise-singer in the ranks of the iNgobamakhosi to call out an improvised chant, taken up by the *ibutho* as a whole:

Mbane, mbane weZulu, kuyacwazimula;
Langa, langa amaZulu, liyashisa konke.
(Lightning, lightning of Heaven, it glitters and shines;
Sun, sun of the Zulus, it consumes all.) [220]

It was a wry comment on the rocket's ineffectiveness, for while the rocket glittered and shone, the 'sun of the Zulus', represented here as infinitely more powerful, did indeed on that occasion consume all.

The name *imbane weZulu* became a popular phrase to refer to rockets throughout the war. Others, less poetically but with perhaps rather more understanding, simply referred to rockets by the English word 'paraffin' – which explosive substance they were acquainted with through the pre-war activities of white traders.

Rorke, James

Seldom has a man's name been so closely associated with a war which he did not live to see as that of James Rorke of Rorke's Drift.

James Alfred Rorke was born in the Eastern Cape in 1827. His father, also James, was one of three brothers who emigrated from Ireland to the Cape in that year. James Alfred Rorke left the Cape Colony in 1849 to move to Natal, which had only recently become a British colony. He acquired a 1,000-acre farm on the middle Mzinyathi river around a distinctive hill known in Zulu as Shiyane (the property was officially registered by a corruption of this name). Rorke built a dwelling at the foot of the hill, looking out over the pleasant views upstream. Like many frontiersmen at this time, Rorke made his living by combining hunting with trading and running a store. He built a large barn-like structure next to his house where he stored his trade goods and which he operated as a part-time canteen for passing whites. He pioneered the use of a good crossing into Zululand from his property which became known as Rorke's Drift. Rorke married the daughter of a local Voortrekker family, Sara Johanna Strydom, and they had two children, James Michael and Louisa. In the aftermath of the 1873 'rebellion' of the amaHlubi *inkosi* Langalibalele kaMthimkhulu, a volunteer unit –

the Buffalo Border Guard – was formed from among the scattered settler population on the Mzinyathi. James Rorke became a lieutenant in the unit, and also a Border Agent for the colonial administration. He kept watch on and reported incidents along his stretch of the border. He was known to the Zulus as '*Jimu*' and his property as '*KwaJimu*' – *Jim's place*. Rorke died on 24 October 1875 at the age of only 48; local legend has it that he shot himself after a consignment of gin he had ordered was lost on the road from Greytown. Whether the gin was for his personal use, or whether it was stock and the loss had a business implication, is not clear.

Sara Rorke sold the property to a settler named John Surtees, who only enjoyed it briefly before selling it to the Swedish missionary Otto Witt.

James Rorke's son, James Michael Rorke, apparently crossed the border, even in his father's lifetime, and took a position as an adviser to Prince Hamu kaNzibe. He acted as Hamu's trading agent in his dealings with whites, and in 1879 Rorke signed several letters on Hamu's behalf during his negotiations to surrender to the British. When Hamu did defect early in the war, Rorke accompanied him to the British camp. He may have been present when Hamu's warriors accompanied the British foray against Hlobane mountain on 28 March. After the war Hamu was confirmed as one of the thirteen 'kinglets' appointed by the British to rule Zululand, and Rorke returned with Hamu to live in the Ngome district. Rorke adopted a semi-Zulu lifestyle and married a number of Zulu wives; he died in 1934 leaving at least three children.

Royal Homesteads (Zulu)

While the majority of ordinary Zulus lived throughout the nineteenth century in small family homesteads – known as *umuzi* (pl. *imizi*) – each of the Zulu kings maintained a number of royal homesteads. These were considered the property of the king, his palaces, as well as centres of state administration where officials, servants and young men providing service were housed. The largest of them were known as *amakhanda*, literally 'heads', meaning of authority.

The largest of these royal homesteads, and particularly the king's favourite – his *komkhulu*, or 'great place' – contained hundreds of huts; Cetshwayo's oNdini contained as many as 1,200 huts. The design of each was simply that of an ordinary family homestead writ large – a large circle of dome-shaped huts, arranged in rows, surrounding a central enclosure. The enclosure served as a corral for cattle and a parade-ground for the *amabutho*. Around the outside was a stout palisade of branches, set into two concentric trenches so that they pointed together and overlapped at the top. At the head of each homestead, where the ordinary homestead-head might live in an ordinary dwelling, were the private quarters of the king, his wives, officials, maidservants and attendants. This section was known as the *isigodlo* and entrance was by royal invitation only upon pain of death. The majority of the remaining huts were set aside for the *amabutho* attached to the homestead. Although most ordinary *amakhanda* were empty, apart from a caretaker staff, for much of the year while the *amabutho* were not assembled, successive kings tended to maintain large numbers of men in attendance at their *komkhulu*. Cetshwayo, for example, kept large numbers of men from the married uThulwana permanently in residence at oNdini, although individuals were allowed to come and go, and the men were allowed to entertain their wives there. As a result for most of the year there were probably some 3,000–4,000 people living at oNdini, although that number would increase significantly when the population was assembled for the annual harvest ceremonies.

Although each king had a preferred residence – Shaka his kwaBulawayo and kwaDukuza, Dingane eMgungundlovu, Mpande kwaNodwengu and Cetshwayo oNdini – each of the other royal homesteads was considered equally his, and it was common for the kings to move court and take up residence in a different *ikhanda* elsewhere in the country for a few months as the mood, climate or political considerations dictated. Although those *amakhanda* close to the *komkhulu* were also large, those in more outlying areas tended to be smaller. KwaSixepi, on the south bank of the White Mfolozi, consisted of some 338 huts, while kwaHlalangubo – an important homestead on the coast which was sometimes referred to as 'old oNdini', and where Cetshwayo had spent much of his youth – contained about 600 huts. Nearby emaNgweni had 300–400 huts, while ebaQulusini, near Hlobane mountain, some 250. In each case this represented, when they were occupied, housing for a significant number of men (three or four to a hut), usually one *ibutho*. KwaGingindlovu, near the coast, was smaller, boasting just 60 huts when the British destroyed it in January 1879.

Most of these *amakhanda* were given into the care of senior female members of the Royal House; when a king died his successor inherited a large number of royal widows who were usually dispersed among the royal homesteads throughout the country. Together with their attendants they occupied the *isigodlo* section of each one, keeping it in good order between the musterings of the *amabutho*.

Something of a king's spiritual essence was considered to rub off on the fabric of those homesteads where he spent much of his time, and as a result it was important that they should not be exploited by an enemy to bring supernatural harm on the nation as a whole. When a king died, his homestead was abandoned to fall into the veldt; rather than see an important homestead captured they were often burned by the Zulus themselves, as had happened with King Dingane's eMgungundlovu homestead in 1838, and with several of the homesteads in the emaKhosini valley in 1879. New homesteads might, however, be built as successors to the original, to maintain their spiritual links to the past, sometimes far from their original locations. Thus, although Shaka had abandoned his kwaBulawayo homestead, overlooking the Mhlatuze valley, when he moved to kwaDukuza in the 1820s, his successor Dingane had built a new kwaBulawayo to succeed it closer to his own homesteads in the Moflozi valley, and one still stood near oNdini in 1879. Similarly King Mpande had been buried at his original kwaNodwengu homestead in 1872 and the huts allowed to fall away, but Cetshwayo had rebuilt a new kwaNodwengu within sight of it.

The location of the *amakhanda* reflected the distribution of royal power within the kingdom. In 1879 most were clustered either in the old Zulu heartland, the emaKhosini valley, or around oNdini on the Mahlabathini plain, but there were others – ebaQulusini in the north, kwaGingindlovu near the Natal border, kwaHlalangubo, emaNgweni and kwaMbonambi along the northern coast – which served as provincial centres. And, in addition to the large *amakhanda*, there were many smaller homesteads, often no bigger than a family *umuzi*, which served as a base for royal *izinduna*. One of these, consisting of just a handful of huts, was built at Cetshwayo's order near the Luneburg settlement on the Phongolo in late 1878, to reiterate his claim to the area.

Although the British were not entirely correct in their insistence on referring to royal homesteads as 'military kraals', they instinctively understood the importance of the *amakhanda* as administrative centres and rallying points. As a result, wherever they could throughout the war of 1879 they destroyed them.

Shields (Zulu)

On 22 January 1879, shortly after the British incursion which had discovered the Zulu bivouac in the Ngwebeni valley and precipitated the battle, the senior *induna*, Ntshingwayo kaMahole, addressed those few *amabutho* that his commanders had been able to hold back from the general rush towards the British camp. These were the uThulwana and its associated *amabutho*, and they were to form the reserve at iSandlwana, and later went on to attack Rorke's Drift. In a pre-battle speech typical of Zulu commanders, Ntshingwayo began by calling out the praises of King Shaka and his father Senzangakhona, to remind the men of their heritage and the traditions which they were upholding. Then in a dramatic gesture he held up his great war-shield, calling out

This is the love charm of our people. You are always asking why this person is loved so much. It is caused by the love charm of our people. There is no going back home.

This is a complex piece of rhetoric which strikes not only at the perceived role of military success in the corporate identity of the Zulu people, but at the obligations of service due to the king from his people and the security and wealth he offered in return. It was to war in Shaka's time that the Zulu owed their prestige and wealth; the nation grew rich in cattle won in war, and the hides of those cattle were provided by the king to equip the men of the *amabutho* who owed him honour in return. The king held his shield over the people – protected them – and they in return fought for him. Without the king's permission *amabutho* could not marry, and the markings on a shield reflected the progress of a man's journey through adulthood. The Zulu shield was the love charm of the nation indeed.

Every Zulu man had a number of shields throughout his life, some of them owned concurrently. A medium-sized shield, about 24 inches by 12 and known as *ihawu*, was carried for personal protection against a chance encounter with an enemy or a wild animal on the road, or in local disputes. Young men carried smaller shields, about 12 inches by 8, called *amagqoka* when courting their girlfriends. These were used for display or in the ritual sparring of competitive lovers, as was a smaller shield, *ingabelomunye*, about 9 inches long.

The war-shields of the *amabutho* were not the property of the individual, however, but of the state. They were made from the hides of cattle supplied by the king and matched according to their natural patterns so that each *ibutho* therefore carried shields of the same colour. Shields were kept in special thatched stores, raised on stilts to keep them out of the way of rats and the damp, within each royal homestead. When the men of an *ibutho* assembled the shields were broken out and issued to them – and they were returned to the stores later when the men disbanded. War-shields were sometimes therefore referred to as 'the king's shield', and to carry one was regarded as a badge of service and of official commission. Since the shields did not last indefinitely, they were changed several times during an *ibutho*'s active lifetime; younger *amabutho* tended to carry dark shields and older

ones white ones. New shields were granted after some noted success and each issue reflected a shift in the patterns denoting experience.

In each case the methods of construction of shields were the same. Shields were oval-shaped and cut from the flanks of a hide (the centre being avoided because of the coarse hair which grows down an animal's spine). In King Shaka's time the largest war-shield, the *isihlangu*, from a verb meaning to brush aside, might be as large as 54 inches by 27, although smaller variants, cut to take account of the height of a more average warrior, were also common. Only two such shields could be cut from each hide, and any shield which bore the mark where the beast had been slaughtered was thought to possess greater properties (being the route by which the animal passed over to the ancestors). In 1856, during the civil war between then-Prince Cetshwayo and his brother Prince Mbuyazi, Cetshwayo introduced a smaller shield. Called *umbumbuluzo*, this was some 40 inches by 20 and was lighter to carry on the march and easier to wield in combat. Shields were secured to a wooden pole at the back by means of strips of hide threaded through parallel slits cut in two rows into the centre of the shield; these strips were threaded up one side, folded over the stick at the back, and threaded down the other. The stick projected a few inches at the bottom and perhaps a foot at the top, which was decorated with a strip of carefully bound-round genet skin.

On the march it was the practice to remove the stick, roll up the hide and tie it with a grass string. Sleeping mats, food and items of war-costume might be placed inside the bundle, which was usually carried on the head; most Zulu elders were accompanied on campaign by their sons of pre-service age to carry their shields and mats.

In Shaka's time men apparently advanced with their shields held horizontally, close to their sides, only displaying them during the final rush to contact. By 1879 several decades of warfare involving firearms had led to men advancing as much at a crouch as they could with their shields held up before them. In battle a shield was then used to deflect spears in flight, and in hand-to-hand combat in a combined and practised movement with the stabbing spear. A man blocked his enemy's movements with his shield and tried to batter him off-guard, exposing his body to the spear-thrust.

In 1879 both sizes of war-shield were carried in action, even within the same *ibutho*. On the whole, however, older, more conservative men preferred the large *isihlangu* while younger men used the *umbumbuluzo*.

In Shaka's time the distinctions between the patterns on the shields of the *amabutho* were precise and rigidly adhered to. It was considered a great disgrace if a man's *ibutho* could not be recognised when he was in ceremonial costume and carrying his shield. By 1879 the situation was more complex, however, partly due to a crisis in cattle resources which had characterised the latter years of Mpande's reign and the early years of Cetshwayo's. Cattle were being traded out of the country to Natal in huge quantities, while the spread of European-introduced bovine diseases had decimated the herds that remained. It was no longer possible to retain complete uniformity throughout an *ibutho*, particularly a large one which had been apportioned a less than common pattern. Zulu concepts of uniformity differed in any case from that of Europeans, causing some confusion in British accounts. Colours were apportioned according to the Zulu name for a particular pattern, and such names often only distinguished between dark and light rather than indicating particular patterns. Shields might therefore be considered of a uniform pattern whether they had dark brown or black markings. The exact position of spots might vary on the opposite sides of a hide, moreover, so that patterns considered by the Zulus to be identical might produce some significant differences in individual shields. In some cases, apparently because there were not enough uniform colours to go round, particular companies within an *ibutho* might have their own distinct and different patterns, leading casual observers to the mistaken conclusion that no particular patterns were carried.

It is difficult to be certain about the patterns of shields carried by the *amabutho* in 1879,

and research is on-going. Nevertheless, of the principal *amabutho* engaged in the war it seems that the youngest, the uVe and iNgobamakhosi (both large groupings), carried shields from the commonest patterns which were all-brown, ranging from a light golden colour to almost-black. The uKhandempemvu or uMcijo *ibutho* carried dark shields with a large white patch at the side, although some companies carried white shields with a broad dark swathe across the middle. The uMbonambi carried white shields mottled with a large number of distinct dark spots, while the uNokhenke carried black shields (perhaps with white spots). The uMxapho *ibutho* – who would probably have been allowed to marry in 1879 had war not intervened – carried white shields flecked all over with black or brown hairs, while the senior men of the uThulwana and iNdlondlo *amabutho* carried shields which were all white with small brown patches.

In the 1820s one of the early white visitors to Shaka's court recalled how the king debated the virtues of the shield and spear against the flint-locks then carried by the whites. Noting the limited range and penetrative power of the musket, and the time it took to reload, Shaka commented that his warriors might reduce the effectiveness of an enemy's first volley by dipping their shields in water to deaden the impact of the lead ball, then rushing upon them before they had time to reload. It was the tragedy of the Zulu kingdom that when this was put to the test in 1879, the balance of technology had swung decisively in favour of the British; even at long range the shield would not stop a Martini-Henry bullet, while reloading had been made infinitely easier.

Signalling

On 26 January 1879 British pickets from the Natal Volunteers, watching from the promontories, heard Zulu voices echoing across the open hill-tops. They were calling out in the crisp morning air, passing the news across the country that they had won a great victory over the invaders. It was the first hint the Eshowe garrison received of the events at iSandlwana; it was not until later that day that a runner arrived from the Thukela with a short and confusing note from Lord Chelmsford himself; a further note suggesting the true extent of the disaster only arrived on the 28th.

These incidents illustrate the difficulty in communicating vital information across large distances of Zululand's rugged countryside, and demonstrate that the Zulus were rather better at it, in the early stages of the war, than the British.

Communication by runner was an integral part of the Zulu administrative system. Royal decrees were carried by messengers whose duty it was to learn long communications verbatim, and in matters of regional management orders were carried first to local officials or provincial royal homesteads. From there fresh messengers would be sent out to spread the information throughout the local community. By this means a royal instruction could generally be sent to any part of the kingdom within a matter of two or three days. This method was used to summon the army, and as soon as men received the command they reported first to their nearest royal homestead, where they assembled in groups by *amabutho*, and then marched to the appointed meeting place. Popular news was generally shouted from one hill-top to another, and on several occasions in 1879 British observers marvelled at the ability of the Zulu to project their voices clearly across distances of several miles.

In battle, Zulu generals communicated orders by visual signals or by runner. Both methods were problematic, since the number and nature of orders that could be communicated visually was extremely limited and while runners were more reliable there was a significant danger of them being killed in action. At iSandlwana, for example, the Biyela *inkosi* Mkhosana kaMvundlana was sent by Ntshingwayo to order the pinned-down uKhandempemvu to renew their advance; he did so but was shot through the head and killed immediately afterwards. The Zulu high command was well aware of the difficulty of communicating orders once an assault was in progress and relied to some extent on command briefings for regimental *izinduna* beforehand, and trusted to individual field officers to be able to react to changing circumstances according to their knowledge of their role within an attack. With an *ibutho* in action commands were transmitted verbally.

At the beginning of the invasion the situation was not dissimilar among the British. In January 1879 Lord Chelmsford lacked any mechanical means of communicating across large distances. Although the Mance heliograph – an apparatus used to communicate Morse code messages through sun flashes directed by means of a movable mirror mounted on a tripod – had been used in the Afridi expedition on the North-West Frontier in 1878, there were none present in Natal at the start of the invasion.[221] Instead Chelmsford had to rely on riders or runners. During the iSandlwana campaign communication was kept up between the camp at iSandlwana and Chelmsford's forward positions at Mangeni by riders, but it was an imperfect system with inherent delays, due to the distances to be covered, and it was made more difficult on that occasion by Chelmsford's habit of roaming across the field to witness events for himself, which made his staff difficult to locate. During the early days of the siege of Eshowe communication was kept up between the fort and the garrisons on the Thukela by African runners. Although these men were better able to elude Zulu patrols than white troops they were still vulnerable; several were caught and killed and for a few weeks communication was cut completely.

The Eshowe garrison lay roughly 20 miles from the nearest British positions at the St Andrews mission on the Thukela. Such a distance was easily within the range of a heliograph, which could be seen to about 30 miles with the naked eye and over considerably greater distances with the help of field-glasses or a telescope. Since communication was important – not merely to understand the changing course of the war but to prevent a sense of isolation corroding the garrison's morale – Pearson's senior Royal Engineer, Captain Richard Warren Wynne, did his best to improvise some means of long-distance communication. With considerable ingenuity he first made a hot-air balloon of paper – the idea was to release it when the wind blew towards the border, but the plan was frustrated on the day by a sudden change of wind direction – and then a large screen made from a black tarpaulin. The tarpaulin was stretched over a wooden frame and fixed to a pivot, and Wynne's idea was provide a large moving object, which might be seen through a glass from the Thukela, and which he might use to spell out messages in Morse. Sadly on the day the screen was erected on a hillside which commanded a clear view of the fort it was caught by a sudden gust of wind and wrecked.

In the end communication was opened between the two garrisons through improvised heliographs. The Thukela camps had no proper signalling equipment either but on 3 March they began to transmit messages using a heliograph improvised by Lieutenant Haynes RE from a shaving mirror found in Smith's Hotel, situated by the Lower Drift. Working with Captain H.G. Macgregor of Pearson's staff and Captain G.K. Beddoes of the Natal Native Pioneers, Wynne eventually came up with his own equivalent using a mirror and a piece of lead piping from the mission church to direct the flashes. By this means, on 14 March, two-way communication between Eshowe and the Thukela was reopened – as long as the sun shone. It is interesting to note that the initial exchanges were confined to terse communications of military import; within a fortnight, however, the men at Eshowe had been given permission to pass private messages in return for a fee of 5 shillings.[222] Sergeant Sherer of the NNC, at Eshowe, asked if some of his pay might be transmitted to his wife in Cape Town, while the Thukela garrison asked if Colonel Forestier Walker wanted his clean flannel shirts sent up with the relief column. Even Pearson himself succumbed to this temptation; his pregnant wife was in Natal, and he inquired after her well-being. The message came back 'Mrs Pearson is …' before a cloud passed in front of the sun and no further communication was possible; Pearson had to wait several hours to receive at last the word 'well'. Eventually private messages were banned because they had begun to interfere with military communications.

The British communication situation improved considerably when C Telegraph Troop, Royal Engineers, was dispatched to Natal as reinforcements following iSandlwana. They were equipped with four heliographs sent out from the workshops of the Bengal Sappers and Miners in Roorkee, India. C Troop also brought telegraphs and cables and by the end of May had established a telegraph line extending from the Thukela border to the 1st Division supply depots at Forts Crealock and Chelmsford. A further telegraph cable was laid as far as the 2nd Division's base camp at Landman's Drift on the Ncome; from there, however, all communications had to be carried by riders or by heliograph to the advancing headquarters column. After Ulundi it took the journalist Archibald Forbes twenty hours – and six horses – to ride from oNdini to Landman's Drift with news of the battle, a distance of 110 miles by the tracks. This journey could be dangerous for those charged with delivering messages. On 30 June Lieutenant James Scott-Douglas and his orderly, Corporal W. Cotter of the 17th Lancers, set out from Fort Evelyn on the Mthonjaneni range to carry a message forward to Lord Chelmsford with the advancing column. Scott-Douglas delivered the message but was determined to return that same day, despite the onset of a heavy mist; the two missed the road and found themselves near the deserted kwa-Magwaza mission where they apparently spent the night. The following morning, however, they blundered into a party of Zulus making their way to oNdini, where the amabutho were mustering to make a last stand before the king's homestead, and after a desperate chase Scott-Douglas and Cotter were run down and killed.

The fate of Scott-Douglas and Cotter is an enduring reminder of the frailty of communicating by messenger during the Zulu campaign – and, indeed, throughout history. Yet mechanical means of communication had their limitations too, which could sometimes be exploited to political effect; by late June Lord Chelmsford knew Sir Garnet Wolseley was on his way to Zululand to supersede him, and Chelmsford exploited the delay in sending messages down the line to effectively place himself beyond Wolseley's control until after he had won the battle of Ulundi.

Small Arms (British)

In 1879 the standard small arm of the British Army – in use in southern Africa, Afghanistan and elsewhere – was the Martini-Henry rifle. Regarded as one of the most practical military arms of the day, being accurate, simple to use and robust, the Martini-Henry was a single-shot breech-loader which combined a falling-block mechanism invented by the Swiss gunsmith Frederich Martini with a seven-groove rifled barrel invented by the Scot Alexander Henry. It had been approved for manufacture for the British Army in June 1871, and the first rifles were issued in 1872. It replaced the Snider, which had been a hybrid breech-loading conversion of the earlier Enfield percussion rifle.

The Martini system was generally regarded as superior to the Snider in every respect. The rifle was loaded by depressing a lever behind the trigger-guard which dropped the breechblock, allowing a round to be inserted into the top of the breech. Raising the lever caused the cartridge to be pushed into the chamber, closed the breech and cocked the rifle ready to fire; after firing, the dropping of the lever again caused the breech to open, expelling the expended cartridge ready for loading again. The rifle fired a heavy unjacketed bullet with a charge to match; one virtue of the Snider was considered to be its 'stopping power' – its bullet was so heavy it could stop a charging target in his tracks – and the Martini-Henry was designed to facilitate an equally large .577 charge (85 grains of black powder). In a design perfected by Colonel Boxer, however, and taken into service from 1873, the round was stepped to fit a smaller .450 bullet. In Boxer's early design – standard issue in 1879 – the cartridge was made of soft rolled brass foil. Rounds were supplied in brown paper packages of ten tied round with twine and carried in the field in mahogany boxes of 600.

The military Martini-Henry measured 49 inches in length and weighed 8.9lbs. It was sighted from 100 to 1,500 yards, although it took a remarkably good shot on a windless day to achieve results at extreme range. Aiming was by means of a sliding back-sight which at ranges beyond 300–400 yards hinged upwards which required the firer to crane his neck at a rather unnatural angle to line up with the foresight; at shorter ranges, however, the back-sight was lowered, allowing the firer to nestle the rifle more comfortably into the shoulder. As a result accuracy in battlefield conditions improved significantly at ranges of less than 400 yards. The Field Exercise manual of 1884 gives some insight into the ranges at which a trained soldier might be expected to hit a target 'without wasting ammunition':

At 200 yards a man partly sheltered or lying down.
At 300 yards, a man standing or kneeling.
At 450 yards, a mounted man.
At 500 yards, fire may be opened on a thin line of skirmishers, with intervals of about 5 paces between each man.
At 600 yards, on a thicker line with 3 paces intervals.
At 800 yards, on skirmishers with less intervals, or on a company at 'open files'.

The same manual advocated fire of varying degrees of density up to 1,400 yards, where it might cause damage 'on Battalion Columns and on compact bodies of Artillery or Cavalry'.

This is not, of course, to imply that the majority of rounds would strike home at such distances; merely that the men had a realistic chance of scoring a proportion of hits at those ranges. Even in the ideal conditions of the training ranges, firing against static targets, a very high proportion of shots would miss; in battle conditions, with adrenalin pumping, shooting at men who were shooting back, and who might be moving rapidly, taking advantage of cover and obscured by dust and smoke, the proportion of hits to rounds expended was often remarkably low. At ranges between 700 and 1,400 yards, a hit rate of 2 per cent would be regarded as good; at 300 to 700 yards 5 per cent, at 100 to 300 yards 10 per cent and at 'point blank' – less than 100 yards – 15 per cent.

Smoke and adrenalin were, indeed, arguably the greatest factors influencing the inaccuracy of individual shooting. The black powder propellant of the Martini-Henry gave off a thin cough of white smoke on discharge which hung in the air on still days so that even a few rounds fired by a small unit of men soon produced enough smoke to completely obscure their view of the target. In a major battle troops could expect to enjoy an uninterrupted view of their targets for one or at best two volleys; after that they were largely firing blind, directing their shots to where their enemy had been seconds before, or where it was anticipated they were going. At kwaGingindlovu Captain Hutton of the 3/60th recalled that:

> After the first volley, which could hardly be expected to have done much execution, since there were but a number of darting figures at irregular intervals to aim at, I ordered my men to go on firing very steadily. A few men showed signs of firing wildly, but a smart rap with my stick soon helped a man recover his self-possession.[223]

In the excitement of an action, there is a natural tendency for men to fire faster and faster in the hope of discouraging an approaching enemy, with a consequent lack of care in aiming and thus inaccuracy. Largely for this reason – but also to allow some time for the smoke to clear – British training of the day placed great emphasis on slow and steady volley firing rather than rapid independent firing. Volley fire – in which a number of men fired at a specified target on command – might waste individual shots but it had a definite psychological impact on the target, for whom the sudden crash of a volley, and impact *en masse* of bullets, was arguably more demoralising than a slow but steady incidence of casualties. Volley fire might be inaccurate but it was terrifying to face, and the officers in command could control it sufficiently to cease firing when a target was obscured by smoke or cover. Independent fire, when performed by nervous men, wasted a greater proportion of shots and, by seeming to those on the receiving end to be ineffective, had the potential to encourage rather than discourage the resolve needed to face it. It also wasted ammunition at a far greater rate. Lieutenant E.O. Wilkinson of

the 3/60th summed up the point neatly when he noted that at kwaGingindlovu his men were 'firing volleys by sections in order to prevent the smoke obscuring the enemy, and we had repeatedly to cease fire to allow the smoke to clear off, as some young aspirants out of hand paid little attention to the section firing'.[224]

Even so, John Dunn, the professional hunter, noted in the same battle that the 3/60th – which included a high proportion of recruits – seemed uncertain as to how to adapt training procedures to the altogether more serious requirements of the battlefield:

> I noticed that the bullets of the volleys fired by the soldiers were striking the ground a long way beyond their mark, and on looking at their rifles I found that they still had their long-range sights up, and that they were firing wildly in any direction. I then called to Lord Chelmsford, asking him to give orders for lowering the sights. This was done, and the soldiers began to drop the enemy and consequently check the advance; but again, when I had my sights down to 100 yards, as the Zulus came nearer, I noticed that the soldiers had up the 300 yard sights.
> ... I was much disappointed in the shooting of the soldiers. Their sole object seemed to be to get rid of ammunition or firing so many rounds per minute at any-thing, it didn't matter what.[225]

These passages make it clear why the emphasis in tactical manuals was upon a slow and steady rate of expenditure. Under ideal conditions on the range, with rounds laid out before-hand, a modern marksman might fire between 18 and 20 rounds in a single minute; under battlefield conditions in the nineteenth century, however, the rates were far lower. Instead the emphasis lay upon firing evenly paced volleys at longer ranges, allowing time to observe the fall of the shot and the movements of the enemy, rising to three or four volleys a minute during the climax of an attack. The rate of expenditure in battles per man in the 1870s was generally low.

At Khambula Wood noted that the Line battalions expended an average of 33 rounds per man in four hours' fighting, while at kwaGingindlovu Hutton noted his own men expended seven rounds per man, and the Marines next to him sixteen. At Ulundi the average was ten rounds per man in half an hour's fighting. By comparison, in other battles of the period in which British troops were armed with Martini-Henrys, at Charasia in the 2nd Afghan War 'the 72nd fired 30 rounds a man, being heavily engaged for some hours', while at El Teb and Tamai in the Sudan – both battles in which the enemy launched extremely determined charges – 'the troops most committed fired about 50 rounds a man'.[226] When assessing the debates about ammunition expenditure at iSandlwana it is worth noting that the 1/24th, in particular, was not an excitable draft fresh from home but, as Frere put it, 'old steady shots', while a survivor, Lieutenant Horace Smith-Dorrien, memorably described them as 'no boy recruits, but war-worn matured men, mostly with beards, and fresh from the long campaign in the old colony where they had carried everything before them'.[227]

Even such an apparently small expenditure per man of course directed a huge volume of shots at the target, often to surprisingly little effect. Wood's Line battalions at Khambula, the 13th and 90th, amounted to about 1,238 effectives, who, firing an average of 33 rounds per man, must have expended a grand total of 40,854 rounds. In addition there were several hundred Irregulars actively engaged in the battle, together with six 7-pdr field guns which, by all accounts, caused great devastation, particularly using case shot against the enemy when the charges drew to close range. All in all it is likely that over 60,000 rounds were fired at the Zulus, together with a significant quantity of artillery ammunition, much of it at ranges of less than 300 yards. Yet after the battle just 785 Zulu dead were found close to the British defences. Many more lay further off, of course, where they had crawled away to die or had been overtaken by the rigorous pursuit. In all some estimates put the Zulu dead as high as 2,000 men – although some hundreds of these were not killed in the fighting around the camp but were cut down in the pursuit. An unknown number were of course wounded, but the fact remains that in battle conditions the expenditure of a large number of rounds was necessary to incapacitate a single enemy. The point certainly struck one of those present, George Mossop of the Frontier Light Horse:

It is a strange fact, and very puzzling, that a very small percentage of the bullets fired into the mass are effective, either with game or humans ... The Zulus were thickly packed, trained, and disciplined men in regiments, who were under a hail of bullets at from two hundred yards to two feet, and, considering the expenditure of ammunition, a very, very small number took effect.

Probably double the number of Zulus would have fallen had a stiff breeze been blowing that day ...[228]

Of course what mattered in battle was not merely the number of casualties inflicted on the enemy but whether the volume of fire produced the required tactical result. Statistics from Rorke's Drift illustrate this. In some ten hours of sporadic fighting, roughly 150 men[229] fired off something close to a company reserve of ammunition – some 200,000 rounds. On average, each man fired rather less than 15 rounds per hour, inflicting by the end of the fighting some 650 dead and an unknown number of wounded on the Zulus (a kill ratio of something like 33 rounds per casualty, which is not incompatible with the experience of Khambula). Yet the bald averages do not reflect the varied intensity of the fighting. Some men found themselves in positions where they were required to fire off more rounds during the battle than others of their comrades, and the firing probably took place in any case in short bursts to counter each attack, with lulls in between. Moreover, the firing in the first two hours of the battle – during the last of the daylight – was undeniably more destructive because the enemy were at close range and could clearly be seen. After nightfall a great many volleys were fired into the dark in the direction where the Zulus were thought to be assembling in the bush. It is doubtful whether many of those rounds actually caused casualties – but they were sufficient sometimes to break up the Zulu concentrations and thereby discourage attacks. In tactical terms, therefore, they were very effective at securing their objectives.

All military firearms, of whatever age, become stressed by repeated use in action, and the Martini-Henry was no exception. The heavy charge of the Boxer cartridge meant that it fired with a loud crack – the sound enveloping the firer, clapping around his ears – and with a deep thump into the shoulder. After about ten rounds a greasy deposit began to form in the chamber, and the barrel – which would have been uncomfortable enough to touch anyway after hours in the hot African sun – began to warm noticeably. After prolonged firing the recoil causes an ache in the shoulder which it becomes difficult not to anticipate, affecting the aim.[230] Experienced veterans in the field stitched leather covers around the stock to protect the tips of their fingers. Once the breech became hot and increasingly fouled there was an increased risk of the thin brass cartridges sticking in the chamber or, worse, of the retractor tearing off the iron base leaving the body of the cartridge still in place. Most of these blockages could be cleared by using the cleaning rod, but sometimes it was necessary for a soldier to resort to his pocket-knife. In actions like Ulundi, where the expenditure was low, it is unlikely that the troops suffered any significant number of malfunctions; they certainly occurred at Rorke's Drift, but there the defenders were able to duck behind the barricades long enough to repair the damage. Certainly malfunctions did not affect the outcome of any of the battles, although it is possible that for some unlucky individuals in the closing stages of iSandlwana an unlucky jam rendered the odd rifle useless with fatal consequences when the fighting was hand-to-hand.

The Martini-Henry was equipped with a bayonet – an 18-inch triangular socket bayonet nicknamed 'the lunger' for the rankers and a broader sword bayonet for sergeants. Firing with the bayonet fixed had a detrimental effect on accuracy, not merely because the weight pulled the barrel to one side but also because it upset the pattern of reverberations in the barrel on discharge, potentially imparting an irregular spin to the bullet. While the bayonet was a fearsome enough weapon – it gave a reach of over 6 feet – it is worth noting that, although trained to bayonet drill, most British soldiers went into Zululand with little practical experience of close-quarter fighting. Their Zulu enemy, on the other hand, had been used to handling shields, spears and sticks on a daily basis.

Although the Martini-Henry rifle was largely confined to the British regular infantry, most mounted units in Zululand were equipped with the Swinburne-Henry carbine. This was a shorter, lighter version which employed the same basic mechanism and was particularly appropriate for use by mounted troops. The carbine also fired a .459/.577 Boxer cartridge, although the charge for carbine ammunition was lighter. In extreme circumstances, however, rifle ammunition could be fired from the carbine, although this had a marked effect on the recoil.

Because of a shortage of Swinburne-Henry carbines some Irregular and auxiliary units, particularly those raised later in the war, were issued with the obsolete Snider rifle. This was a percussion breech-loader and fired a .577 bullet to a maximum range of 2,000 yards. It was 49.25 inches long and weighed 8lb 9oz. Although considered effective a decade before, the Snider was generally less accurate than the Martini-Henry, and slower and more cumbersome to use.

The British Army had gone to war in Zululand with great faith in its weapons. 'I am inclined to think', wrote Lord Chelmsford on 28 November 1878, 'that the first experience of the Martini-Henrys will be such a surprise to the Zulus that they will not be formidable after the first effort.'[231] He was wrong in that judgement, of course, but the fault did not lie with the Martini-Henry, which performed consistently well throughout the campaign. As Captain Hutton observed, 'we all had the utmost confidence in our rifles, which at that time were the most perfect weapons in the world'.[232]

Small Arms (Zulu)

After the battle of Nyezane on 22 January the British collected up a number of firearms lying among the Zulu dead, and were curious to note their origins:

> There were all sorts of guns. From Potsdam, from Danzig, Murzig, and Tulle, from 'Manchester, N.H., United States', etc. The majority, however, were Tower muskets. The foreign weapons are very ancient indeed; some of them manufactured in 1835. As far as I could make out by the inscriptions, the continental weapons were condemned army ones. The sights were the most extraordinary contrivances.[233]

The Zulu army in 1879 was undeniably equipped with large numbers of firearms; sadly the reality of the international arms trade, through which obsolete weapons were sold off by the major powers to unsophisticated markets around the world when more efficient ones replaced them, meant that the quality of those firearms was usually poor.

The gun trade had been an element in the interaction between the Zulus and British interlopers from the earliest days. King Shaka had demanded demonstrations of the firearms carried by the first white traders to visit his court; seeing that their smooth-bore muskets were largely ineffective at individual targets beyond 50 yards' range, and that they took a long time to reload, he pondered whether, in a battle against them, it would be feasible for his men to absorb the casualties inflicted by the first discharge and then charge home before the riflemen had time to reload. It was a shrewd assessment of the relative merits of the two fighting systems, and one which would be put to the test in almost exactly those terms in 1879 – although the consequences of the technological changes of the intervening fifty years could not then be foreseen.

None the less, Shaka had persuaded his tame white men to supply musketry contingents to his military expeditions and after his death his successor, King Dingane, went a step further and pressured the whites to sell him guns directly. With the annexation of Natal as a British colony came an increase in European economic activity in Zululand and from the 1850s parties of white hunters and traders regularly operated in Zulu territory, and King Mpande often demanded a payment in firearms as the price of their admission. But whereas Shaka, Dingane and Mpande had striven to maintain a royal monopoly of the firearms trade, the very increase in the numbers of passing whites facilitated contact between them and ordinary Zulu, allowing regional *amakhosi*, and later ordinary homesteadheads, access to the sources of supply. Traders originating from Natal were prohibited from supplying guns to Zululand without a licence, and many were in any case uncomfortable at doing so – but others were not. One of the functions which the white *inkosi* John Dunn fulfilled for his patron, Cetshwayo, was procuring firearms for his supporters – a practice at least connived at by the Natal authorities from the late 1850s in the belief that by strengthening Cetshwayo's parties in the succession disputes they reduced the risk of the instability in Zululand spilling over into Natal.

Between 1872 and 1877 some 60,000 firearms were legally imported into Natal – there is, obviously, no record of those imported illegally – of which some 40,000 were re-exported to Portuguese Mozambique, intended for the African trade. The majority of these probably ended up in Zululand. Between 1875 and 1877 some 20,000 guns, including 500 breech-loaders, were admitted by Portuguese officials to have entered Delagoa Bay. One report of August 1878 suggested that there were as many as 20,000 stands of arms in Zululand, of which 500 were modern, good-quality breech-loaders, 2,500 were recent percussion muskets, 5,000 were older percussion muskets and the rest obsolete muskets, mostly flint-lock smooth-bores. As the Nyezane report suggests, the guns had come from all over the world – and it is interesting to note that many bore the Tower proof-mark of weapons tested by the British Government. Certainly the increasing availability of firearms of all sorts had been reflected in falling prices; a good-quality double-barrelled muzzle-loader, when introduced into the country by John Dunn in the 1860s, had commanded the impressive price of four cows, but by 1878 the same type of gun fetched only one. By the same time an Enfield percussion rifle – standard British military issue in the 1850s – could be purchased for as little as one sheep.

Nevertheless, the distribution of firearms within the country reflected patterns of wealth and status rather than military exigencies. Many of the *amakhosi* had come to possess fine sporting guns, and most ordinary family heads owned a firearm of some sort – and yet it was the young, unmarried men, who still lived at their father's homesteads and had little wealth in their own right, who had the least opportunity to buy guns, and these were the very men upon whom the greatest burden of the fighting would depend. In 1878, during the tense months running up to the break-down between the Zulus and the British, King Cetshwayo had recognised this. Summoning the young men of the uVe *ibutho* before him he instructed them to lift up their guns; seeing how few they were, he ordered them to go home and return with a beast to buy a firearm from Cetshwayo's supplier, John Dunn.

By the beginning of 1879 the Zulus possessed firearms in such quantities that they allowed themselves to think they might match British firepower. To ensure they functioned to the best of their capabilities, guns were the subject of a special feature in the doctoring ceremonies which took place before the assembled army marched to the front; an *inyanga* burned special medicines over a pot-sherd and the men filed past, holding their rifles barrel-down, so that the smoke drifted into them. The ceremony was designed to make the guns fire straight and true – but the early battles of the war soon dispelled this illusion. Not only were the guns themselves inferior to the modern weapons carried by the British, but the Zulus had to make do with inferior quality powder. Black powder was in short supply from traders, and Cetshwayo had recruited the services of a Sotho man to make powder for him; while this addressed something of the need for quantity, the quality was not ideal.

Many traders often supplied only a handful of shot, too, and the Zulu were forced to improvise bullets from roughly hammered pieces of metal, or even stones dipped in lead. As a result they were erratic in flight, although many observers on the receiving end acknowledged the intimidating whirr they made as they passed overhead; they could inflict unpleasant wounds on the rare occasions when they struck home, too, for lacking penetrative power they tended to tear through muscle and soft tissue, taking erratic courses as they bounced off bone. The colonials knew them as 'pot-legs' in the belief that they had been cut from the legs of three-legged iron pots which were a staple of the Zulu trade; perhaps some were.

Most Zulus were also poor shots. They had not, of course, been trained in the use of their weapons by the traders who supplied them, and few understood the basic principles of sights, believing that by raising the back-sight to maximum elevation they imparted extra power to the bullet. As a result most Zulu fire during the battles of 1879 either failed to reach the target, owing to the inadequacies of the weapons, or passed overhead. This contrasted starkly with the devastation wrought by British weapons in return, and helped to reinforce a natural conservatism among many Zulus who preferred to rely on the tried and tested advantages of the stabbing spear instead. Indeed, many Zulus came to regard firearms as little more than a variety of throwing spear; knowing that their guns were slow to reload, they advanced as close as they could to the enemy, fired one shot, then dropped their guns and charged with their spears.

That this was an opportunity tragically squandered is highlighted by those rare opportunities when the Zulus were able to exploit firearms effectively. A few in the Zulu ranks did understand the potential of the weapons they possessed; not only had some of the *amakhosi* persuaded sympathetic whites to teach them to shoot – Prince Dabulamanzi, for example, had been taught by John Dunn, and was a noted marksman – but the professional European hunting parties who had passed through Zululand for more than two decades had trained up some Zulus to assist them. Even in the early stages of the war there were incidents enough to suggest that a handful of Zulu riflemen were capable of inflicting damage on the British. At Rorke's Drift, for example, in the firefight which developed between Zulu riflemen on the terraces of the Shiyane hill and the men of B Company 2/24th posted on the rear wall facing them, several soldiers were shot in their shoulders or arms in quick succession despite presenting a very small target – only their helmets and arms were visible above the barricades – at ranges of 300 yards. Such impressive marksmanship may have been due to Prince Dabulamanzi himself, or his retinue, who had apparently taken up a position on the hill.

The capabilities of these men were undoubtedly enhanced by the capture of hundreds of modern British weapons at iSandlwana. The Zulus captured the best part of 1,000 Martini-Henry rifles and Swinburne-Henry carbines at iSandlwana, together with 500,000 rounds of ammunition – those men who looted rounds but not a rifle tore the bullets out and used the powder in their muzzle-loaders – and perhaps a further 200 weapons at Ntombe and Hlobane. In theory, these guns were the property of the king, to be presented to him on return from battle and redistributed according to his favours, but Cetshwayo wisely recognised the attachment of his men to guns they had captured at iSandlwana and allowed those who had taken them to keep them. Most of these guns, therefore, remained concentrated among the *amabutho* which constituted the king's main striking arm; rather fewer found their way into those forces contesting the British advance on a local basis. After the battle of kwaGingindlovu – where the Zulu force included a high proportion of men living locally – some 435 firearms were recovered by the British, of which just five were Martini-Henrys. One was a revolver (presumably another piece of iSandlwana loot), while the rest were old muskets.

In contrast, at Khambula just a few days before – a battle largely fought by men who had been present at iSandlwana – the improvements afforded by access to British weapons was immediately apparent. Zulu riflemen, firing captured Martini-Henrys, enfiladed British positions from the overgrown rubbish heap outside the British lines, not only forcing the British to abandon their positions in the cattle-laager, but inflicting considerable damage on British forays. As Wood himself put it:

> on five separate occasions, a plank of the hoarding on which I leant was struck. This jarred my head, and reminded me that the Zulus firing from the refuse heap in the right rear of the Laager were fair shots. A few had been employed as hunters, and understood the use of the Martini-Henry rifles taken at Isandlwhana.[234]

Yet the success of such incidents merely serves to undermine the failure of Zulu firepower throughout the war as a whole. Discouraged by the inadequacies of their weapons early in the war, they consistently failed to grasp the tactical potential of firearms and did not alter in the slightest their dependence on close-quarter combat. As a result they were condemned to learn a grim truth: that in the half-century since Shaka's death the balance of military technology had tilted overwhelmingly in favour of the invaders, and the price to be paid in casualties for attacking in the open men armed with firearms was ultimately no longer to be borne.

Snakes

The human conflict which took place in Zululand in 1879 did not take place in an empty landscape. The area had once teemed with a rich variety of African wildlife, and although this had been greatly affected by European hunting methods over the previous half-century, game still survived in those areas that were thinly populated by humans. Since most of the war was fought out in areas of comparatively heavy human settlement, and since troop movements were sufficient to scare most animals away, encounters between the combatants and larger animals, while they did occur, were rare throughout the war. Nevertheless, the major Zulu river-systems still supported large populations of both crocodiles and hippos, while snakes were common in the countryside at large. Although most snake species, too, generally prefer to avoid human contact, the movements of troops across country, through long grass or patches of bush, inevitably brought the combatants into contact with snake habitats. The timing of the war is also significant, in that it began in the summer months, when snakes are more active, in what was in any case an unusually warm and wet year.

There are, in southern Africa as a whole, over 140 different species of snake, of which about 30 are dangerous to humans. Of these, some 14 species have been known to cause fatalities. Some 74 species are to be found in Zululand, of which the most dangerous to humans are the predominantly grass-dwelling black mamba, the tree-dwelling green mamba and *boomslang*, the *mfezi* (Mozambique spitting cobra), the cobra-like rinkhals and the puff-adder. The country also supports a viable population of the African rock python which kills its prey by constriction. Of these, arguably the most potentially dangerous to troops on campaign in 1879 was the black mamba, which still enjoys an awesome reputation today. Individuals can grow above 2.5 metres in length and are known to be particularly aggressive when cornered; when irritated, they can raise a third of their body length off the ground. They deliver a bite with a potentially fatal dose of neurotoxin venom with devastating speed and accuracy. Victims of mamba bites suffer paralysis and can die within as little as seven hours. The *mfezi* is also extremely dangerous, and similarly rears up when irritated, spitting its venom towards its target's eyes, causing pain, irritation and, if untreated, permanent blindness. The chief risk from the puff-adder arises from its habit of lying still rather than fleeing when cornered; well camouflaged by its markings, it often goes unseen until trodden on when it reacts with a deep bite. Its venom, too, is extremely poisonous, being cytotoxic with haematoxic and cardiotoxic effects. A victim of a puff-adder bite experiences severe pain, swelling and nausea; death is caused by secondary effects due to swellings or by necrosis around the wound.

The Zulus, of course, were familiar with the snakes which shared their environment on a daily basis; they knew which were venomous and which were not, and they recognised tell-tale signs of snake habitat or activity. Indeed, some larger species – particularly mambas – were believed, when encountered living in the fences of cattle-kraals in homesteads, to be the incarnation of powerful family ancestors, and were left undisturbed as a result. Lieutenant Henry Charles Harford (99th Regiment, serving as staff officer to the 3rd NNC) encountered one such snake during a patrol after the battle of Ulundi:

on reaching a kraal where we intended to sleep the night, Stewart and I were lying on the ground just at the edge of the zereba [i.e. fence or palisade] outside, cooking our meal, when only a few feet from us, stretched almost full length in the dried scrub, was a snake that I had often heard of and much wanted to see, and that very few white men have ever come across. It was the *idhlozi*[235] of the [Zulu], a beautiful creature, vivid green with jet-black marking, between two and three feet long, and thick like a puff-adder. I would have given anything to be able to bottle it, and the opportunity was such as could scarcely ever occur again, no [Zulu], either men or women, being about. Being held sacred, and looked upon as the incarnation of some ancestor of the kraal, to kill one, if it became known, would certainly mean an assegai put through you, so having no collecting material we left our friend alone.[236]

An association with the ancestral spirits was also made when British troops discovered a powder store attached to the royal homestead of Mayizikanze (oLalandlovu), in the confluence of the Black and White Mfolozi rivers – although by the sound of it, on this occasion it was a rather more aggressive species: 'Just as our men were about to enter the cave they were startled by the sudden appearance of a huge snake, which raised itself in threatening attitude, and which the natives declared to be the spirit of the late King Panda keeping guard over his son's hidden treasure.'[237]

Captain Molyneux of Chelmsford's staff had an even closer encounter one morning:

Next morning Crealock rose at dawn to stir the servants up; just as he got outside the tent he asked me to give him his watch which he had left under his pillow. My blankets were on the ground alongside his, and I was pulling on my boots, so I jerked the pillow over, and there coiled around his watch was a big puff-adder! As it began to crawl away I flattened its wide head still more with a tent-mallet; but it was a near thing for both of us, for they are most deadly brutes. Had he not forgotten his watch, but felt for it as usual; or had I slipped my hand under the pillow instead of jerking it off! It seemed like a reminder that Providence watched over us to the last day in Zululand. The tent had been pitched in the dark over a foot-path. This should never be done; in wet weather it is a little river, and on cold nights snakes travel along it for warmth, as the dew does not condense there as on the grass. Our snake had been travelling along it from his spoor, and had been induced to lie up by the warmth of the blankets.[238]

Harford was one who witnessed an incident that might have served as a warning to the unwary:

One afternoon Major Duncan, RA, and I took a turn out to look for buck, and on beating down a ravine where he was on one side and I on the other, I saw his spaniel working very excitedly in a thick bit of scrub a little way behind him, and called out to him to look out as I thought that there was something there. In a few minutes the dog jumped out, uttering a little whine as if he had pricked himself in the thorns, and we went on. Then, as we got further down the dog lagged behind considerably, and I said to Duncan, 'Your dog is a long way

behind. I think he's got a prickle in his foot, as I heard him whine as he got out of that bush. We'd better go back and see.' So we went back, and found his head all swollen and a trickle of blood running from the tip of his nose. Seeing at once that he had been bitten by a snake, Duncan took him in his arms and I carried the guns and we made for the camp as hard as we could go.

By the time we got in, the animal's head was quite the size of a football, his eyes were closed up and his tongue an enormous size. Duncan at once got his medicine-chest and produced a bottle of Sal volatile, rubbing some on his nose, and with the greatest difficulty getting some down his throat. We continued this treatment every now and then till the last thing at night, adding an occasional drop of milk. For three or four days the dog remained in a state of stupor, but eventually pulled through alright ...[239]

For the most part snakes were in greater danger from the troops than the other way around. While a few officers, like Harford, had a genuine interest in naturalism, and appreciated the grace, beauty and complexity of snakes, they nevertheless still killed them when they found them, if only to preserve them as objects for study. Most soldiers had little knowledge of snakes, however, and regarded them all as potentially dangerous and therefore to be exterminated. Even before the war began, Lieutenant Thomas Main of the Royal Engineers, who was working on Fort Pearson on the Lower Thukela and the pont across the river nearby, noted that:

Moving about in the bush here was dangerous, on account of the number of big snakes (mambas) which would attack you, a rare action with snakes. John Dunn told me that one had risen up while he was riding and struck at his horse and it was dead in ten minutes. I only saw one mamba. It came out of the bush on the river bank and proceeded to advance on a body of blue-jackets who were making up my barrel raft on a dry sandbank, but it was foolish as, on the dry sand, it could neither advance nor retire, and so they easily killed it and bore it up in triumph to the camp, 9 feet long.[240]

Captain W.E. Montague of the 94th also recalled seeing a snake killed by troops, this time a rock python: 'On the banks of the river, over which a party of sappers was constructing a foot-bridge, a conductor had just killed a boa-constrictor which measured 14 feet, and was hideous in proportion.'[241]

Such was the general ignorance and concern about snakes that the men of the 1st Division were greatly unsettled by the advent of a plague of 'snakes' in their camp, some over a metre in length, following a severe storm in the coastal districts on 6 July 1879. In fact the snakes turned out to be a species of worm (*Catecilian*) disturbed by the unusual weather conditions.

Surprisingly, no fatalities were officially attributed to snakebite during the war. However, in 1883 an incident occurred which showed just how dangerous snakes could be to troops living out in the open. By that time King Cetshwayo had been restored and Zululand partitioned; a corridor of land north of the Thukela and Mzinyathi rivers had been annexed by the British as the Reserve Territory. Following the outbreak of the Zulu civil war and the attack on Cetshwayo's oNdini by *inkosi* Zibhebhu's Mandlakazi section in July, the country was greatly disturbed, and British troops were moved across the Thukela and concentrated at Eshowe. Among those troops were five companies of the 1st Bn The Welsh Regiment, commanded by Lieutenant-Colonel W.G. Montgomery.

On 25 September, while based at Fort Pearson, Lieutenant-Colonel Montgomery crossed the river, accompanied by his adjutant, to shoot birds on the Zulu bank, near the remains of the old Fort Tenedos. Montgomery was walking through waist-high grass when he suddenly complained of a sharp pain on the inside of his thigh. Within minutes he began to feel ill, and his adjutant helped him to his horse. By that time Montgomery was exhibiting signs of paralysis, could hardly speak, and was in danger of falling

unconscious. The adjutant managed to get him to the pont and he was ferried to the Natal bank where he fell from his horse. He was carried to the hospital tent and attended by a doctor; the wound inside his leg was identified as a snake-bite, probably from a black mamba. Montgomery became delirious and was unable to move his limbs before finally becoming unconscious. Despite the doctor's best efforts he died some hours later.

He is, curiously, remembered in two monuments nearby, both of which have been regarded as his grave. A stone memorial erected by his regiment stands near the site of Fort Tenedos on the Zulu bank; his name also appears on a cross in one of the cemeteries near Fort Pearson. The most likely explanation is that the regimental memorial was erected in remembrance near the spot where he was bitten; since he died in camp on the Natal bank, he was presumably actually buried in one of the existing 1879 graveyards closer to hand.

Spears

Seldom in history has a weapon been so identified with a particular people as the stabbing spear has with the Zulu. Much of what is said about it is fable, and even the name by which it is popularly known is inappropriate. Although the stabbing spear continues to be referred to as an *assegai*, the word is not of Zulu origin; although its etymological origins remain obscure, *assegai* seems to be a corruption of a Portuguese word for a spear which passed into general usage among whites following the early establishment of Portuguese trading enclaves on the eastern seaboard. The Zulu word for a spear is *umkhonto* (pl. *imikhonto*); each type of spear moreover has its own particular name. R.C. Samuelson, whose father was a missionary, and who grew up in Zululand before the war and later worked as Cetshwayo's translator during the king's captivity at the Cape, lists ten names for different contemporary spears, and there may well have been more. Use of these weapons was not confined to the adherents of the Zulu king but was widespread throughout Natal.

Although the heavy-bladed, short-handled stabbing spear is popularly associated with King Shaka, the story that he invented it was a product of the imagination of author Ernest Ritter.[242] In fact most oral traditions suggest that Shaka's innovation lay rather in exploiting a pre-existing weapon, which had been largely regarded as the preserve of a few eccentric individuals, and developing around it an entirely new system of fighting – training his men to move rapidly in concert to bring them to the point of contact, where the weapon's advantages were best demonstrated, as quickly and efficiently as possible. The classic stabbing spear of the Shakan age was called *iklwa*; pronounced *i-chwa*, where 'ch' is as in the Scottish *'loch'*, it is said to represent the sound the weapon made on being thrust into and pulled out of a victim. The size varied but blades were sometimes up to 18 inches in length, between 1 and 2 inches wide, and mounted on a haft about 30 inches long.

The blades were of iron and produced indigenously by skilled smiths. The working of metal in Zulu society, as with many African cultures, was considered a mystic art, and smiths not only maintained a degree of secrecy about their art but tended to keep aloof from ordinary society. Some groups – such as the amaChube in the Nkandla forest – were reputed to produce the best smiths, perhaps because of the ready availability of appropriate natural resources in their areas. Iron ore was collected from surface deposits and smelted over charcoal fires in clay furnaces heated with goat-skin bellows. The liquid metal was then poured into roughly shaped ingots using moulds cut into the hard earth and hammered into the finished article using stones. The presence of charcoal in the process meant that Zulu blades assumed some of the qualities of a poor-grade steel. Since the Zulus lacked the technology to wrap iron, blades were cast with a long shank which would serve to be set into the spear's wooden handle. Blades themselves were often finely wrought, and some examples have a degree of fluting around the central spine of the blade. The best blades were tempered with fats and secret magical ingredients, and it was widely rumoured that human fats produced the best results. Blades would be sharpened by rubbing them against rocks and could retain a sharp edge.

Once the blades were manufactured they were passed over to a different specialist, the *inyanga yokupisela*, who was responsible for hafting them. Sticks were cut commensurate with the balance of the blade, usually with a swollen 'stop' at the butt end, which served as a grip to stop the weapon slipping when it was wet with blood during heavy combat. A hole was drilled at the opposite end, and a thin wet tube cut from a cow's tail slipped over the end. The hole was then filled with a natural resin to serve as a glue, and the shank of the blade set into it. This was then bound round with a fresh animal sinew which shrank as it dried, further holding the blade in place, and finally the cow-hide tube was rolled over the join. Sometimes a split tree-root was bound over the join in place of the cow-hide tube. In either case the blade was firmly fixed in place as befitted a weapon designed to withstand the stresses of close combat. Nevertheless, damage did sometimes occur in battle and it was common for men to re-haft their weapons after a particularly hard fight.

The stabbing spear was designed to be used under-arm in combination with the war-shield. A man would run down on his enemy and batter him with his shield, blocking his opponent's own attacks; the hope was that this move would expose the opponent's stomach or rib-cage to a thrust with the spear. The fatal blow was delivered by skilled exponents with a slight upward cut for maximum effect. Often in the heat of battle a man would stab his enemy several times, not merely to ensure a kill but as a result of the emotional release produced by combat after lengthy pre-battle rituals.

By 1879 some smiths used iron imported by white traders. This was not held to be as strong as indigenously produced iron, and blades sometimes bent in combat. After iSandlwana it was noted that stabs aimed at the chest area were often less effective than those aimed at the stomach because they were sometimes deflected by a combination of the soldier's equipment straps, tunic and ribs.

Unlike the war-shields carried by the *amabutho*, spears were the personal property of the men who carried them. Men bought spears for the price of a beast from smiths; sometimes the king commissioned spears *en masse* and distributed them to his favourites or exchanged them for cattle or goats with his men. There was, therefore, some scope for favoured, wealthy or dedicated individuals to carry particularly large or fine weapons; young men – whose spears were paid for by their fathers – often carried less highly worked items. Sometimes weapons were passed down from father to son, but in the case of men who enjoyed a fierce reputation as warriors it was more common for the hafts to be broken on the death of the owner and the remains to be thrown into some inaccessible spot, to prevent the man's spirit wreaking havoc should he be angered in the after-life.

Tradition has it that before King Shaka's time wars were prosecuted by means of lighter throwing spears. Shaka is said to have outlawed these but they were permitted again by his successor King Dingane, perhaps as a counter of sorts to European muskets. The flintlock muskets carried by early white travellers had a very limited accuracy – 40 or 50 yards – while a Zulu spear could be thrown up to 30 yards. It was possible for a Zulu man to wait until his white opponent had discharged his musket then to run in and throw a spear at him before he had time to reload. Although most Zulu men were able to throw spears with considerable accuracy over distances of 10 or 20 yards, at longer range the shaft of the weapon produced a greater drag, causing it to fluctuate in the air with a corresponding loss of accuracy. Most throwing spears – which were equally used in the hunt – had smaller blades than their throwing counterparts (between 5 and 9 inches long) but at short ranges had considerable penetrative power.

In 1879 most men carried one or two throwing spears and a stabbing spear (and many carried firearms). The usual practice was to throw spears shortly before contact during a charge so that they caused damage and panic among the enemy seconds before the attack struck home. As a result throwing spears were often lost on the battlefield; since Shaka's time, however, it had been the custom for men never to leave their stabbing spears on the field, for to return home without one was held to be indicative of cowardice.

Stimulants (British)

Throughout the nineteenth century the British Army's drugs of choice were alcohol and tobacco. The Duke of Wellington, indeed, thought most of the rank and file in his day had enlisted for drink, and throughout the Victorian era the attitude of the Establishment remained decidedly ambivalent. On the one hand drink was recognised as a serious cause of indiscipline; to be drunk on duty was a military crime in itself, and it facilitated other crimes such as desertion and sleeping on sentry duty. Excessive drinking led to friction within and between regiments and encouraged fighting. On the other hand, so dependant was the ordinary soldier believed to be that it was considered dangerous to deprive him of the relief that alcohol provided, particularly to the aching boredom of barrack-room life in a peace-time garrison. Canteens were a feature of barrack life where beer could be bought in numbing quantities at a cheap rate; one reason why Army pay was calculated at a daily rate was to prevent men drinking themselves into a stupor when they received accumulated pay. In Wellington's day officers were by definition gentlemen – the Iron Duke himself believed that only those born to a state of authority in civilian life could be expected to exercise it over men in the Army – and while officers were expected not to transgress the codes of gentlemanly conduct by allowing drunkenness to interfere with their duty the consumption of large amounts of champagne, brandy, claret and whiskey were an essential part of the social life of the mess.

Obviously the practicalities of campaign life prevented the consumption of peace-time quantities of alcohol in the field. Nevertheless, the men were entitled to an issue of a dram of rum a day and bottled beer was carried with the invading columns. The column commanders took advantage of the remoteness of the theatres of operation to try to keep their men as 'dry' as possible, and civilian traders were usually prevented from entering the camps. Evelyn Wood was particularly strict on this point, partly because his column – operating out of Utrecht on the Transvaal border and in sparsely populated country – was easier for civilian traders to reach. Indeed, the profits to be made from selling gin – known as 'Squareface' from the shape of the bottles or, more romantically to the Africans, 'The Queen's Tears' – or brandy, 'Cape smoke', to thirsty soldiers was more than enough to tempt some to take the risk:

In February, when the Column was encamped at Kambula, a trader, who had a brother-in-law in the Volksraad in Pretoria, came into camp with waggons, asking to be allowed to sell groceries to the troops. I saw the man, and he assured me that he had no alcohol of any description; but I would not allow him to unpack his waggons until he had given me a certificate in writing that his verbal statement was accurate.... [One of Wood's officers later] came on the trader, who was selling trade gin at 1s a glass to the soldiers, some of whom were already drunk. Campbell had the man seized and sent for me. There was a full moon, and I exercised summary justice by its light; ordering the man to be tied up to the wheel of his own waggon, I sent for two buglers, and gave him two dozen lashes on the spot, upset the whole of his liquor (which must have been a considerable loss, for he had a large quantity under his groceries) and informed him that unless he trekked at daylight, I would impound his waggons and oxen for the rest of the campaign.[243]

The presence of the rum ration (stored in wooden kegs), intended to satisfy the men's needs, was also a source of perennial frustration since it was permanently watched, either by men of recognised good conduct or by tee-totallers – of whom there were some, a reflection of the evangelical success of religious and other Army reform societies. Nevertheless, the temptation provided by those barrels was sometimes too much, even at the risk of a flogging. Shortly after the war

had begun a fatigue party of men of the 99th Regiment were unloading stores on the Zulu bank of the Thukela when the sergeant in charge became suspicious because several of his men came to him in turn and requested to be excused. Following them he found they had secreted a rum barrel from the supplies and had broached it. The sergeant immediately reported to an officer, and the 99th's commander, Colonel Welman, collected a group of officers and trustworthy other ranks. They set out to arrest the drunkards but found that these had by then crossed the river and retired to the civilian hostelry, Smith's Hotel, on the other side. Welman pursued them and surrounded the place; several men were arrested as they tried to run away, and the rest were already found to be insensible. They were taken back to the camp and, when they had sobered up, court-martialled and sentenced to remain on guard duty on the lines of communication for the rest of the war.

Some months later a group of the 88th Regiment committed a similar offence and compounded it by going on a drunken brawl. They were punished with two dozen lashes each. In the closing stages of the war a group of 27 men found a rum barrel at Landman's Drift, hidden by another regiment; they opened it, drank themselves unconscious and awoke to the prospect of a stomach pump and a court martial. Even at Rorke's Drift Lieutenant Chard was concerned at the temptation afforded by a supply of rum in the storehouse and placed it under guard, threatening to have any man who interfered with it shot. The ban on strong liquor was felt even by the officers, who could neither acquire alcohol themselves nor risk openly drinking it when their men were deprived; the war correspondent Melton Prior managed to smuggle a few bottles to the front in his cart loaded with 'sketching materials'.

Tobacco was a luxury greatly prized by all ranks. The men in the ranks smoked pipes, while most of the officers preferred more sophisticated – and expensive – cigarettes. For the most part tobacco remained in moderate supply throughout the war but for Colonel Pearson's men, cooped up for three months at Eshowe, being deprived of a good smoke became more of a daily torment than the shortage of rations. At first the garrison ransacked the supplies at the fort to turn up every available ounce of tobacco. Some mouldy cakes of it were discovered, and distributed among the good to eke out the supply. When this began to diminish those who had husbanded theirs found a burgeoning market developing, and prices rose from 3 or 4s an ounce at the beginning of the siege to 22s an ounce. For those who would not or could not afford to pay, the ingenious offered alternatives ranging from dried tea to coffee grounds or likely-looking herbs gathered around the fort. One of the first things the garrison asked of their relievers was a supply of tobacco, and on the night after the relief a contented fug of tobacco smoke hung over the fort.

Stimulants (Zulu)

The Zulu army in the nineteenth century never had access to even the restricted levels of alcohol enjoyed by their British counterparts; indigenous Zulu beer was only mildly alcoholic, and it could not in any case be transported in any quantity on campaign. The Zulu man, therefore, went to war stone cold sober, but on the occasion of battle he did have recourse to other forms of stimulants.

Perhaps the most powerful of these was simply adrenalin. Zulu men embarking on a campaign were prepared by complex rituals which bound them together, cut them off from civilian society for the duration of the expedition, and focused their minds upon the prospect of combat. They existed in a common mental universe shaped by a collective aggression towards the enemy, a feeling veterans described as one of great anger and indignation. This condition was further channelled by the application of last-minute pre-battle rituals and stoked by chants and war-songs so that the experience of combat itself produced a rush of release, often expressed in the ferocity of the fighting itself. This state of mind the Zulus characterised as 'seeing red', and its passing after a battle left the men more than usually drained, physically and spiritually. For some the strain produced an almost hallucinogenic state of mind in which the confusion of battle pro-

duced distorted and surreal memories – of apes manning the British positions at Khambula, for example, or of flocks of birds attacking out of the sky.

This state was probably further enhanced artificially by the ingestion of small quantities of *cannabis sativa*. Cannabis grew wild in Zululand in types which modern chemical analysis suggests contained high levels of stimulants. Smoking it was widely held to induce courage and aggression, and indeed in traditional society its use was confined only to mature men, who were considered responsible enough to handle the consequences. Cannabis was smoked by means of a horn, known as an *igudu*, in which the leaf was burned in a small carved stone receptacle and the smoke drawn through water in the horn.

The Swazi army certainly relied heavily on cannabis to enhance aggression and stave off fatigue in the night marches and dawn attacks which characterised their favourite tactics. Certainly there is some evidence of the use of smoking-horns by the Zulu on battlefields in 1879; at least one stone part from an *igudu* has been found on the battlefield of Khambula, while Trooper Harry Lugg of the Natal Mounted Police shot a man at the height of the battle at Rorke's Drift as he was in the act of lighting his smoking-horn from the embers still smouldering in the cookhouse outside the British perimeter.

Perhaps more significant, however, is the suggestion that the special war-medicines which many men procured privately for use in battle prior to the start of a campaign, and which they carried in horns or small skin pouches attached to charm necklaces, contained powdered cannabis among the ingredients. This medicine was separate from that applied to the group as a whole by the specialist *izinyanga* on the immediate eve of an attack; instead, men would be instructed to take any medicines they had about them as they hurried towards the enemy. These might have a supernatural effect, such as 'when going to battle, the induna giving the word "Lumani umabope!"[244] – "bite *umabope*"[245] – or a physiological and psychological one induced by taking 'snuff'. There are many accounts of *amabutho* taking 'snuff' before entering a battle – the uThulwana were seen to do so after crossing the Mzinyathi on their way to attack Rorke's Drift – or in lulls between the fighting, and it is highly likely that this 'snuff' included cannabis.

Some modern Zulu diviners have suggested that the *abaqawe*, the 'heroes' – noted warriors who enjoyed a particularly high reputation for courage in battle – may have further stimulated their aggression by taking a particular herb known to induce a temporarily heightened state of focused rage and physical energy; this claim has, however, remained controversial.

Suicide

On 21 February, just under a month after Colonel Pearson's column had occupied the old Norwegian mission station at Eshowe, Private W. Knee of the 99th Regiment slipped out of his bed in the hospital quarters, set up in the mission church, and made his way through the perimeter lines. Pearson's column was, at that time, cut off from the outside world, the mission heavily fortified and the surrounding countryside full of parties of Zulus who had cut the lines of communication to Natal. Private Knee, however, had been ill for some time, and the doctors had come increasingly to think him unstable – and certainly on this occasion he did not behave like a rational man. After dark he managed to slip past the sentries guarding the outer lines, and disappeared unnoticed into the night; his comrades were astonished to find his body lying face-down in a nearby stream the following morning. His death was officially listed as suicide, as it almost certainly was; there was nothing to suggest that the Zulus had killed him.

Quite why Private Knee behaved as he did remains a mystery, as is the case with many of the suicides which took place in Zululand in 1879. Suicide was not a common occurrence – on either side – but when it happened to the men in the ranks the causes which drove them to such despair were seldom recorded. Mostly, like Knee's, they were probably the result of depression or temporary instability brought on by the effects of fever; sometimes they were rather more rational, the result of a letter from home with bad news – a 'dear John' or a report of some family disaster or financial catastrophe – but if so the reasons usually went unrecorded.

Quite why Sergeant Stratton of the 2/24th had killed himself during a skirmish on the Cape Frontier, six months before the battalion marched to Zululand, is, for example, unknown; Stratton had appeared cheerful to his men, but in the midst of a desultory fire-fight with the Xhosa – in which he was at little obvious risk – he had suddenly called out a brief farewell, then blown out his brains with his own rifle. The strangeness of his death had been underlined the following morning when he was found sitting bolt-upright in his grave, as if he had changed his mind; on closer examination, it turned out that someone had disturbed the body while trying to deprive Stratton of his boots.

Strange, too, was the death of a private of the 99th regiment during the Zulu campaign. He was in the hospital tents at Fort Pearson, suffering from fever, when on 13 March he suddenly dragged himself out of his sick-bed, ran down the hill-top towards a steep cliff which dropped down into the Thukela river – and threw himself off.

Less bizarre, but no less mysterious, was the death of Lieutenant Robert D'Ombrain of the 1/1st NNC on 8 April 1879 near Fort Cherry at Kranskop, above the Middle Drift. D'Ombrain had arrived in Natal from Kent in July 1877, and had accepted the hospitality of a family friend, a former regular officer who had become one of the settler gentry, Alexander Montgomery. Later, when the Natal Native Contingent was raised in late 1878, Montgomery offered his services and was given command of the 1st Battalion of Durnford's own 1st Regiment. D'Ombrain himself volunteered and was accepted as a lieutenant in the same unit. Montgomery's role in what followed is not clear; he was a strong-willed officer and rather restless, and his personal life was to be the subject, later, of a scandal. Although he was married – his wife bore him nine children – Montgomery was alleged to have had an affair with a young house-guest who bore him a child. The child later died and Montgomery was implicated in an investigation of infanticide. What this had to do with D'Ombrain, if anything, is not clear, except that a woman played on D'Ombrain's mind somewhere along the line.

Montgomery's men were stationed at Fort Cherry, on the escarpment above the Thukela at Middle Drift. This was an important strategic position – there was considerable Zulu activity at the drift throughout the war – but it was a dull duty, and many of Montgomery's officers apparently alleviated their boredom in drink. At the beginning of April life was enlivened by the visit to the post of Montgomery's 16-year-old daughter, who was apparently accompanied by a local admirer. Miss Montgomery was still in the area when, on the afternoon of 6 April, Lieutenant D'Ombrain apparently reported to the fort's medical officer suffering from a hang-over. He was duly prescribed an appropriate remedy and retired to his tent. Over the following two days, however, he complained of feeling ill, and friends who visited him said that he spent most of his time on his bed, smoking. He could not stomach solid foods, and under the doctor's guidance D'Ombrain's servant fed him on beef tea. He seemed restless and fretful, and told a fellow officer that he was concerned lest the nature of his illness became common knowledge. He seemed to be verging on paranoia, becoming convinced that the men of the regiment were talking about him in isiZulu, a language he could not understand. He warned one visitor that 'they are coming', and to another confided that 'there was only one woman who had threatened him'; both comments were regarded as being the product of an incipient fever. Early that after-noon D'Ombrain was in his tent when a shot rang out; Montgomery and his officers rushed over to find that D'Ombrain had shot himself with a Martini-Henry rifle. He had placed the barrel in his mouth, wedged a riding crop across the trigger, then pulled it with his foot. He had died instantly from massive head injuries, and the bullet had afterwards torn a great split in the canvas of the tent.

D'Ombrain was buried nearby, and his is un-doubtedly one of the most remote and poignant of the lonely graves relating to the war of 1879. Montgomery held an inquiry into the cause of his death, but no evidence emerged of what had been troubling D'Ombrain, and his suicide was put down to the effects of his fever. Years later, the local story had it that D'Ombrain had received a note shortly before his death from a woman breaking off her relationship with him; whether that was connected with the visit of Miss Montgomery is not at all clear.

Rather more common was an attitude among many serving soldiers that suicide offered a means of escape from the threat of worse horrors should a battle go badly wrong. The war correspondent Melton Prior was riding one day with the Revd George Smith, of Rorke's Drift fame,

> when he asked me, 'Why do you carry a revolver, Prior?'
>
> 'Well,' said I, 'for a very good reason. If I unfortunately get into a tight corner I intend five shots for the enemy and the last one for myself, for I am never going to be taken alive by a Zulu.'
>
> 'Oh, do you think that very brave?' he smilingly asked in reply. 'Do you really mean that? Would you really wantonly and with premeditation take a life that had been given you? Would it not be better to suffer a little agony, that you might have to bear if you fell into the hands of the enemy, than to take the life which God gave you?'
>
> I had never looked at it in that light before, but so much was I impressed with his seriousness and the nice way in which he put the matter, that I in turn looked at him and said, 'Smith, you are right, and I promise you that I will never take my own life.'[246]

Yet the idea of 'saving the last bullet for yourself' was quite a common one. It had little basis in rational fears – there is no evidence that the Zulus ever tortured anyone to death during the battles of 1879 – but it was perhaps the inevitable result of a mind-set in which British and colonial troops saw themselves engaged in a war of civilisation against savagery. Suicide in the last moment of defeat, when death is anyway inevitable, offers a last desperate trace of comfort, a sense of retaining control even *in extremis*, and of a last gesture of defiance, depriving the enemy of the satisfaction of your death. It is something which has often occurred in battles across the ages, and it happened in Zululand in 1879. Psychologically, it is a product of isolation, despair and terror, and it tends to occur more among troops whose *esprit de corps* has either been badly shaken during an action, or was never highly developed to start with. Suicide in battle, in other words, is a symptom of men and their units falling apart, and it is no coincidence that at the battle of the Little Big Horn in America in 1876, when George Custer's command was famously overwhelmed – an action which had much in common with some of the Zulu War engagements – American Indian eye-witnesses commented on a high number of suicides among the men of the 7th cavalry, a unit which had a high proportion of new and foreign recruits.

There are remarkably few references from Zulu sources of British troops at iSandlwana killing themselves under similar circumstances. There are two possible reasons for this. First, the infantry of both battalions of the 24th Regiment were experienced men who had served together, under officers they knew intimately, for a long time beforehand, and they had developed a strong sense of the regimental family. Such a feeling, even under such drastic conditions, tends to draw men together for psychological comfort and the hope of survival rather than causing them to break down into panic-stricken individuals. The second reason is rather more pragmatic; as Lieutenant D'Ombrain would discover, it is a difficult thing to kill yourself with a long Martini-Henry rifle.

Of course, it may well be that a number of men did commit suicide at iSandlwana, and their stories are simply not recorded. By contrast, however, there were a significant number of self-inflicted deaths among the Irregular corps during the battle of Hlobane. The Irregulars were by their nature largely anonymous; they were raised for temporary service in the campaign, had no long history of traditions to sustain a sense of

belonging and identity, and were recruited from men who were often rootless in their civilian lives. And, of course, the carbines they were armed with were a much handier weapon.

The Irregulars had performed well enough during the battle, but once the British attempted to retire off the mountain, under pressure from the abaQulusi on the summit and threatened by a large army coming from oNdini in the valley below, a sense of panic set in. A detachment of the Frontier Light Horse under Captain Barton and the Border Horse under Colonel Weatherley descended at the eastern end of the mountain but ran into the vanguard of the uKhandempemvu *ibutho* coming in the opposite direction. There was a brief fight and several of the Irregulars were killed before they were forced to turn about; at this point Trumpeter Reilly of the Border Horse, an Irishman, dismounted from his exhausted horse, fired several shots at the enemy at close range, then killed himself. Later, when the survivors of the same party had crossed the precipitous Ityenka Nek, still under pursuit, the Zulu *induna* Sitshitshili kaMnqandi, saw one man 'as he approached, turning his carbine and shooting himself'. Perhaps the most graphic account of a suicide at the battle, however, was given by George Mossop:

Many glancing sights had I seen that day of the Zulus with some of our men, who had fallen into their hands – whether dead or alive, I do not know! It is not good to write about such sights; all I can say is that it was a horror! Perhaps the man at my side had seen that which induced him to act the way he did.

I knew him well, but will not mention his name.

'Do you think there is any chance of pushing through?' I asked him. I was obliged to shout to make myself heard. The din was terrific.

'Not a hope!' he replied, and placing the muzzle of his carbine in his mouth he pulled the trigger. A lot of his brain or other soft stuff splashed on my neck.

> It was the last straw! I gave one yell,
> let go the bridle of my pony, and bounded
> down into the pass.

There were strong psychological reasons, of course, why the British invaders were more likely to suffer self-inflicted deaths than the Zulu. The latter were fighting in defence of their way of life in their own country – their sense of belonging and purpose could not have been greater. Nevertheless, as individuals they were subject to the same stresses in battle as the invaders, and there are suggestions that numbers of their men, too, killed themselves rather than face capture by the British. At least one man was seen clearly to stab himself with his own spear rather than fall to a British sortie in the closing stages of the battle of Khambula, and Mossop certainly noticed a degree of resignation – even defiance – in the face of inevitable death:

> When we overtook small bodies they made no attempt to resist; they were beaten, and that was the end. Many a man just turned, exposing his broad chest, saying 'Dubula M'lungu' ('Shoot, white man') – and the white man shot. The Zulu gave no quarter, and expected none.[247]

Of course, the damaging effects of exposure to the horror and violence of the war continued to afflict the participants for decades afterwards. Post-traumatic stress disorder was certainly not recognised in 1879, but its effects were real enough, and many of those who played a prominent part in the war were troubled for years with flashbacks, nightmares and feelings of guilt. That was, perhaps, why Cecil D'Arcy of the Frontier Light Horse – who survived Hlobane and earned the Victoria Cross for the skirmish on 3 July before oNdini – acted as he did. D'Arcy had continued to serve with colonial forces after the Zulu campaign, and had seen action in the BaSotho 'Gun War', but by early 1881, although he was still a young man, his health was suffering from the rigours of his active life. He was a lifelong asthma sufferer and had contracted both malaria and bilharzia. In August 1881 he went to stay with friends on the Eastern Cape, hoping the bracing winter air would help him. His friends found him tense and depressed, however, and on the morning of 7 August his room was found to be empty and his bed not slept in. Despite a search over the following days, no trace of him was found until 28 December, when the skeleton of a man was found in the hills nearby. The remains were identified as those of Cecil D'Arcy; he had apparently wandered off alone, quite deliberately, and died of exposure.[248]

There is very little evidence, of course, to determine whether Zulu veterans of the war suffered similar long-term psychological damage. In some respects the attitudes and beliefs of traditional society as a whole may have mitigated against the sense of isolation and taint which characterises post-traumatic stress. In their belief that the shedding of blood causes supernatural damage, and in their willingness to acknowledge the role of veterans within the community, Zulu life offered a framework of understanding which may have explained and eased the sense of recurring horror brought about by the visceral nature of Zulu combat. Nevertheless, here and there the odd snippet has surfaced to suggest that the events of 1879 left their mark, too, upon the souls of the Zulus who took part. A noted warrior named Muthi Ntshangase, who killed at least one white man at iSandlwana, is said to have been troubled by the spirits afterwards, and 'went mad soon after. Cetewayo was told of this incident. Muti was taken down to Ulundi from Isandlwana under control, and Cetewayo, who thought a lot of him, sent for some Shangane doctors, to try to make him right again, and they succeeded.'[249]

Swazi
In the run-up to the invasion of January 1879, Lord Chelmsford had pondered a number of strategic options. Conscious that his own troops were greatly outnumbered by the forces at King Cetshwayo's disposal, he attempted to split the Zulu response by attacking on a number of fronts. He initially hoped to invade with five separate columns from points along the Natal and Transvaal borders, although in the event

circumstances forced him to reduce the number of offensive columns to three. Nevertheless, even as he began to assemble his forces in November 1878, he still hoped that other – essentially diversionary – attacks might be made. One possibility was an attack by sea, either conducted through Portuguese territory in Mozambique or by direct amphibious landing on the Zulu coast. Lack of political support from Portugal ruled out the first option while the difficult nature of the coast – and in particular the lack of a viable natural harbour – mitigated against the second. Nevertheless, British warships continued to patrol the coast, and indeed towards the end of the war supplies were landed by sea on to the open beach at Port Durnford.

Another strategic possibility was an invasion via the Swazi kingdom, which bordered Zululand to the north-west. The British understanding of the relationship between the two African kingdoms was hazy, but for the most part they identified it as hostile, and therefore considered the Swazi to be potential allies. In November 1878 Captain Norman MacLeod, a retired officer of the 74th Regiment, was attached as political officer to Evelyn Wood's column, then at Utrecht, with the specific role of persuading the Swazi to enter the war. It was hoped that a Swazi *impi* might be attached to the nearest British column – Sir Hugh Rowlands', which was based at Derby on the Transvaal/Swazi border – or that at the very least the Swazi might mount their own foray south across the Phongolo river, and therefore force the Zulu army to deploy on another front to oppose them.

MacLeod visited the Swazi king, Mbandzeni waMswati, at his Nkanini royal residence. He found Mbandzeni full of professions of support, but curiously reluctant to commit himself. As two of the king's *izindvuna* explained to MacLeod privately,

> they had never seen the English fight. They were always saying that they would, but never did. They thought they never would. If we did we should be beaten. They had seen the Zulu fight. Until they saw the English fight the Zulus and beat them they could not

believe it possible. They would not fight the Zulus until they saw them running away to their caves, then they would come and help the English burn them out. When the English were ready to go into Zululand they might tell the Swazis so that the Swazis might be ready in case the English proved stronger, which would make them very glad.[250]

Although this was hardly the response MacLeod had hoped for, it was at least refreshingly honest – and as the British would discover as the war progressed, it was a very precise statement of Swazi royal policy.

The Swazi position owed much to their own complex relationship, not merely with the Zulu Royal House but with the neighbouring Transvaal Republic. The Swazi kingdom had emerged under the leadership of the Dlamini chiefdom early in the nineteenth century, at much the same time as the Zulus. For much of their history the Swazi had been squeezed uneasily between two powerful neighbours, the Zulus to the south and, from the 1830s, the Boer republic of the Transvaal to the west. Both parties had tried on occasion to assert their control over the Swazi but the Swazi, by an astute mixture of diplomacy and military force, had successfully resisted. During the 1840s and 1850s, when the Zulu kingdom was preoccupied with rebuilding its fortunes in the aftermath of its own catastrophic war against the Boers, the Swazi further consolidated their strength under King Mswati. None the less the Zulu kings – in their eyes, at least – had still retained a right to interfere in Swazi affairs, and three times during his reign – in 1847, 1848 and 1852 – King Mpande had dispatched his *amabutho* on raids into Swaziland. Although the Swazi maintained their own army of *amabutho* they were no match for the Zulus in open confrontation and had countered the raids by withdrawing to natural strongholds from which the Zulus could not dislodge them.

Moreover, from his accession in 1873 King Cetshwayo had maintained a keen interest in the Zulu/Swazi border area along the Phongolo river, seeing it as a natural route along which to expand the growing Zulu population. Since this area was also contested by Boer farmers expanding from the Transvaal in the opposite direction, the Phongolo basin had, even before the outbreak of the Anglo-Zulu War, become a potential point of conflict. It was partly to allow himself some influence over Swazi affairs that Cetshwayo, when still a prince, had extended his protection over the renegade Swazi prince, Mbilini. A son of the late King Mswati, Mbilini had lost out in a succession tussle to his brother Mbandzeni; Mbilini's hunger to rebuild his fortunes and his ambition to return to Swaziland had made him a useful ally to Cetshwayo.

It was these factors combined which had, of course, shaped Mbandzeni's reaction to the British invasion of Zululand. His enthusiasm for the British cause was genuine enough, but the Swazi knew enough to fear Zulu retribution, and with Mbilini waiting in the wings the risk of backing the losing side was prohibitive.

Nevertheless, when the war finally broke out many Swazi living on either side of the Phongolo border found themselves drawn into the conflict. Since Evelyn Wood's column, operating from the Transvaal, was not allocated any Natal African auxiliary units, he raised one himself – Wood's Irregulars – from Africans living on Transvaal border farms. Most of these men, 400 strong, were Swazis by origin, and, like the royal Swazi *amabutvo*, they mustered for service wearing their full regalia. Wood's Irregulars played a significant part in the early raids which characterised the war on the northern sector, and they were heavily involved in the battle of Hlobane on 28 March where they suffered heavy losses during the British rout. In the aftermath of Hlobane many of Wood's Irregulars dispersed to their homes for fear of a Zulu attack and the unit was disbanded in April.

On the other hand, many Swazis living in the border region had ties with the Zulu community and opted to support King Cetshwayo. When the king assembled his *amabutho* in January 1879, numbers of men from the Phongolo chiefdoms responded, and a handful of men of Swazi origin were subsequently present at iSandlwana.[251] Many more from the same area formed part of the irregular forces mustered by Prince Mbilini

and Manyanyoba Khubeka and took part in numerous raids, including the attack on the convoy of the 80th Regiment at Ntombe on 12 March. Mbilini himself was killed in a skirmish on 4 April, an outcome which must have caused considerable relief not only to the British but also to King Mbandzeni.

Although Mbandzeni was undoubtedly pleased at the growing British ascendancy, he still refused to commit himself, despite the pressure Mac-Leod put on him. He did offer to assemble his *amabutvo* if Chelmsford was prepared to dispatch British troops to support them in the field – an offer which Chelmsford was in no position to accept. Even after the British victory at Ulundi on 4 July, Mbandzeni prevaricated. The news that Cetshwayo had apparently retreated to northern Zululand to escape capture encouraged Chelmsford's successor, Sir Garnet Wolseley, to try to persuade Mbandzeni to cross the Phongolo with the specific intent to capture Cetshwayo. It seems, however, that Cetshwayo's capture was a basic requirement before the Swazi would commit themselves, since they remained concerned lest the British for some reason should fail in their resolve at the last minute. The most Mbandzeni was prepared to do was allow his *amabutvo* to raid the homesteads of Zulu loyalists in the Phongolo valley.

The capture of Cetshwayo in the Ngome forest by British dragoons finally brought an end to British demands upon the Swazi. It seemed briefly that they might be called to account for their failure to adopt a more proactive policy, but in fact Wolseley still had a use for them. In the aftermath of the Zulu defeat he was keen to resolve the long-standing Transvaal dispute with the baPedi king, Sekhukhune woaSekwati. Sekhukhune had defied not only the Transvaal republic in the 1870s but also a British expedition, led by Rowlands, at the end of 1878. With British fortunes running high, Wolseley was determined to reduce Pedi independence. He marched directly from Zululand to the Transvaal to confront them, and called upon Mbandzeni to support him. As astute as ever, Mbandzeni realised that sitting on the fence was no longer an option, and he mustered 8,000 of his warriors and sent them to Wolseley's assistance. By this time the Swazi had learned a little more about British determination and their capacity for a fight – and they preferred to be on the winning side. When Wolseley finally overran the Pedi capital at Tsate in November, the Swazis took a prominent part in the assault.

Mbandzeni's decision to support Wolseley's expedition effectively retrieved the goodwill among the British that he had nearly forfeited in Zululand, and the Swazi kingdom emerged as a clear winner in the shifts in the balance of power which resulted from the war. They had won the respect of the British while their old enemy, the Zulus, had been greatly reduced. As MacLeod himself put it, 'to the British mind in general, Russians and Zulus are fiends, Turks and Swazis are angels'.[252] None the less the war heralded a difficult time for the Swazi kingdom for the Zulu victory at iSandlwana had effectively destroyed the Confederation policy and following the Boer revolt in the Transvaal in 1880–81 the British abandoned their claims to the old republic. Over the following decades the Swazis would find themselves hard-pressed by renewed Boer interest in their country.

Tactics (British)

In 1879 the British Army was on the cusp of great changes with regard to the tactics it employed to physically win battles in the field. When Queen Victoria had come to the throne in 1837, tactical theory had remained dominated by the lessons of the Napoleonic Wars. At a time when the limitations of smooth-bore firearms – their inaccuracy and the huge quantities of smoke they produced – meant that it was necessary to manoeuvre troops in sufficient numbers to within 50 or 60 yards of the enemy in order for their fire to be effective, the emphasis remained on discipline and training and all independent thought was strictly discouraged as potentially damaging to the overwhelming importance of cohesion. Tactically, the Napoleonic Wars had been something of a struggle between two different theories, based on the column and the line. Napoleon had been a master of the column, a

dense, narrow mass of men which advanced on an enemy's weak-spot, punching a hole through his positions. As a formation the column was acutely vulnerable to artillery fire – a single cannon-ball could bowl down the length of it, knocking over entire rows of men – but it was very hard to stop with musketry because it was difficult to produce enough volume of fire to break up a column over the short distances at which muskets were effective. Wellington, however, was an advocate of the line, which while it could not stand up to an attack by column when it came to the crucial mêlée stage did at least maximise a unit's firepower, allowing the potential to bring fire to the head and flanks of a column as it closed in, and thereby break its impetus. Wellington's success with the line at Waterloo and elsewhere meant that his ideas continued to affect British military thinking long after advances in weapon technology had made them largely redundant. Moreover, although the British Army was involved in a number of military campaigns in the 1840s and 1850s in India and the Crimea, all fought out along conventional lines – the Sikh army had been trained by French veterans of Napoleon's Wars while the rebel sepoy armies during the Mutiny had been trained according to the British system – it was the incessant succession of small colonial wars which actually offered an insight into the shape of things to come. In warfare against the Afghans, Maoris, Boers[253] and Xhosa conventional tactics were not only inappropriate but often impractical, as a lack of troops on the ground forced British commanders to be flexible. As a result, by the 1860s there was a recognition that battles often turned upon the successful resolution of an important tactical contradiction: the need to balance the advantages of dispersal against the decisive application of concentrated firepower. In Zululand and elsewhere, any failure of judgement in this regard could prove disastrous.

By 1879 British tactics were beginning to move noticeably away from the Napoleonic mode. Infantry tactics still adhered to fundamental principles learned in the age of the smooth-bore, but sought to weld the advantages of both systems;

infantry battalions would manoeuvre into position in column, then attack in line. The attack itself, however, was generally well dispersed, the men advancing in a loose, open order, and accomplished in depth. Troops were trained to carry out ordinary movements at a rate known as 'quick time' – 120 paces per minute – and to attack in 'double time' – 165 paces per minute. Whereas rifle and light infantry regiments had originally been raised to carry out rapid and dispersed attacks, the Army as a whole was increasingly trained to perform their roles. An attack by an infantry battalion was supposed to be carried out with two companies extended as skirmishers, and two companies behind in support. The remaining four companies were to be positioned in the rear. The attack was carried out by firing and advancing in rushes with the supports closing up towards the skirmishers as the objective was reached; once fire superiority was achieved, the entire battalion closed with the bayonet. This was a concept that hinted at profound changes in attitudes towards the capabilities of ordinary soldiers, for inherent in any situation in which soldiers were widely dispersed was the assumption that greater responsibility would devolve not only upon junior officers but upon NCOs and the men themselves.

Such tactics, while they minimised the damage from enemies armed with firearms, were not always appropriate against those who were more flexible in battle, enjoyed numerical superiority, or who fought with close-quarter weapons. During the war on the Eastern Cape in 1877–78 it was found that the Xhosa lacked the discipline to withstand the heavy casualties incurred in mounting an attack to close quarters against even quite small bodies of British troops armed with effective breech-loading firearms. As a result, the old line formation was found to be the simplest method of inflicting a defeat upon the Xhosa, and to counter the Xhosa's use of the ground the troops were often widely dispersed with intervals of as much as 3 yards between individuals – a formation which both allowed small numbers of troops to dominate the terrain, and minimised the effectiveness of Xhosa return fire.

His successes in the closing stages of the Frontier War shaped Lord Chelmsford's tactical approach to the prospect of conflict in Zululand. In particular, Colonel Glyn of the 1/24th had won a decisive victory over the Xhosa at the battle of Nyamaga in 1878 by extending his infantry in an open line and placing his artillery support in the middle and his auxiliaries to protect either flank. Exactly this formation was specified by Lord Chelmsford in his Standing Orders prior to the invasion of Zululand, and it was employed at both Nyezane and iSandlwana on 22 January. While Pearson's position at Nyezane mitigated against too extended a position, however, and the numerical superiority enjoyed by the Zulus was uncharacteristically low, at iSandlwana the situation was reversed, with fatal consequences. The British firing line was far too extended to withstand the attack over a very wide front by a much larger Zulu force and collapsed under the pressure.

A tactical solution was handed to the British almost immediately, however, by the victory at Rorke's Drift later that same day. Here a Zulu force, again enjoying numerical superiority, had proved itself quite incapable of penetrating even the flimsiest of improvised barricades and, kept therefore at arms' length, beyond the range of its most effective weapons, had been acutely vulnerable to the concentrated firepower of the garrison. The British position at Rorke's Drift had, in effect, constituted a return to the 'square' – a formation which was by then anachronistic in conventional warfare, but which in Napoleonic times had provided a robust response to an attack by cavalry. As well as providing a position that could not be outflanked or surrounded, the square also offered a means of laying down a heavy fire in all directions and, *in extremis*, a hedge of bayonets to discourage close-quarter fighting. By forming up in square with the men in ranks two deep – one kneeling and one standing (or four deep, with two of each) – an almost continuous rate of fire could be kept up as men fired and reloaded alternately by ranks and by sections.

The lesson of Rorke's Drift was not lost on Chelmsford who thereafter abandoned his earlier preference for dispersal and fought instead in squares. Not that the square did not have weaknesses; because the field of rifle fire extended straight out from the sides, there was something of a blind-spot in the angles of the corners, but this was traditionally resolved by placing artillery pieces or Gatling guns there. Indeed, although tactical theorists had begun to consider the possibilities afforded by massed artillery batteries in preparing the enemy for an infantry assault, in reality there were too few guns in most colonial campaigns for them to offer anything other than close infantry support. None the less, it is worth noting that the Zulus were quick to appreciate these weaknesses, and at both kwaGingindlovu and Ulundi determined charges were mounted against the corners of squares; both these charges were halted just a few paces away only when Chelmsford ordered the corners to be reinforced by reserves inside the square.

The debate over the relative merits of dispersal and concentration were reflected within the role of mounted troops too. For the most part cavalry were expected to fulfil 'light' roles – scouting and skirmishing – or 'heavy' roles, the shock attack *en masse*. Many cavalry theoreticians remained attached to the romantic concept of the *arme blanche*, the attack with sword or lance, and considered the more practical day-to-day duties of scouting as at best drudgery or at worst beneath them. In fact, as Balaclava had demonstrated, the cavalry charge was increasingly redundant in a world of effective long-range weapons, and there was a growing need instead for an arm which combined the advantages of mobility with the ability to fight on foot with firearms. Although conservative cavalry ideologists consistently refused to embrace the possibilities afforded by 'mounted infantrymen', Chelmsford's experiences in Zululand would prove the worth of both approaches. Initially lacking regular cavalry, he benefited greatly in the early stages of the war from the services of locally raised Irregulars, Natal's Volunteer Corps and Mounted Infantry raised from his own troops, all of whom proved adept at light duties – scouting, raiding and skirmishing on foot. The victories at Khambula and kwaGingindlovu both highlighted

the need for shock troops, however, for the British pursuit of the retreating Zulus – although ruthless enough in its way – would have been far more destructive had there been available large numbers of regulars trained in the charge.

At Ulundi, of course, such troops were available and the 17th Lancers – whose initial performance in the war had proved disappointing when their shortcomings as scouts and skirmishers had become obvious – came into their own. In the closing stages of the battle they delivered a textbook charge which completely broke up the retreating *amabutho*.

It is one of the many ironies of the Anglo-Zulu War that Lord Chelmsford entered it employing tactics that were considered progressive by the standards of the day, but ultimately won it by abandoning them and falling back on tried and tested means which were already regarded as outmoded in conventional warfare, but which were to retain their relevance in a colonial context for a decade to come.

Tactics (Zulu)

In 1879 Zulu battlefield tactics were largely dictated by the constraints imposed by the nature of their military system. Because the Zulu army was not a standing organisation but a citizen militia, it was difficult to maintain large numbers of men in the field for a long period; historically therefore the Zulu army had adopted an aggressive outlook which was designed to resolve conflict as quickly as possible by initiating and deciding a confrontation as soon as possible. The Zulus remained committed to a battlefield formation known as *izimpondo zankomo*, 'the beasts' horns',[254] which emerged early in the kingdom's history and may have been developed by King Shaka himself to answer issues resulting from his adoption of the stabbing spear as his army's principal weapon.

The *izimpondo zankomo* consisted of four tactical bodies: the chest (*isifuba*), two horns (*izimpondo*), and the loins (*umuva*). Traditionally the youngest *amabutho* present with an *impi* were placed in the horns because their role required fitness and enthusiasm while more experienced *amabutho* were placed in the chest. During an attack the horns were thrown out to surround the enemy on either side and pin him in place while the chest launched a direct frontal assault to destroy him. The loins were kept away from the fighting – although some elements might be deployed in pursuit or to secure a specific tactical objective – and usually consisted of senior *amabutho* who could be relied upon to maintain discipline and not break ranks. Sometimes a cadet *ibutho*, not yet properly enrolled, was added to the loins to give the young men some experience in watching a battle unfold. Often, one horn was thrown out in advance of the other, and deliberately masked its advance through a good use of ground, concealing itself from the enemy until it had surrounded its objective. The other horn advanced in plain sight so as to confuse the enemy.

There are suggestions that the position of individual *amabutho* within the formation were decided long before a battle began, perhaps by the king and his councillors at the time of the preparatory rituals that took place before an army was launched on campaign. These positions were reflected in the order of march to the front – where the right to be appointed to the vanguard, for example, was jealously guarded – and in the overnight bivouacs before battle. Prior to an attack the Zulus usually effectively scouted the enemy's positions and the senior commander held a meeting with his regimental officers to ensure that each knew the role their *amabutho* was to play. This was essential because once an attack began it was difficult to make radical alterations to the plan because of the difficulties of command and control. In a battle Zulu commanders usually took up a position to the rear, out of immediate danger, and on a promontory which gave them a commanding view.

The Zulus did not advance into battle in a dense mass. They advanced to the periphery of the field in columns and then each *ibutho* threw out a screen of skirmishers – men who normally served as scouts, and who were renowned for their courage and initiative – who masked the deployment of the main body. Usually the main body attacked in loose, open lines, sometimes as

many as three or four rows behind one another, the intervals between each man more than enough to allow for the easy handling of shields and spears over rough terrain. In 1879 British observers were amazed to note the way the Zulus kept good order, even under fire, and made excellent use of the terrain, the men running, as they drew close to their objective, from cover to cover. At kwaGingindlovu Captain Hutton of the 3/60th took a professional delight in the sight of the Zulu deployment:

> The dark masses of men, in open order and under admirable discipline, followed each other in quick succession, running at a steady pace through the long grass. Having moved steadily round so as to exactly face our front, the larger portion of the Zulus broke into three lines, in knots and groups of from five to ten men, and advanced towards us ... In spite of the excitement of the moment we could not but admire the perfect manner in which these Zulus skirmished. A small knot of five or six would rise and dart through the long grass, dodging from side to side with heads down, rifles and shields kept low and out of sight. They would then suddenly sink into the long grass, and nothing but puffs of curling smoke would show their whereabouts. Then they advanced again ...[255]

Only as the Zulus drew near their objective, and their front constricted, did their formations become denser, in readiness for a final charge. The traveller Bertram Mitford, keen to form an impression of how this rush was accomplished, persuaded a few veterans of the war to show him

> how they made their charges which proved so fatal to our troops. They would rush forward about fifty yards, and imitating the sound of a volley, drop flat amid the grass; then when the firing was supposed to have slackened, up they sprung, and assegai and shield in hand charged like lightning upon the imaginary foe, shouting 'Usutu'.[256]

In many ways the victory at iSandlwana was a textbook battle, in which all the classic elements of a successful Zulu attack fell into place. Although the *impi* had only arrived in the vicinity of the British camp late on the evening of 21 January, the Zulus had thoroughly scouted their objectives on the morning of the 22nd and a command meeting was in progress when British detachments stumbled across the Zulu bivouac. This made it easier to overcome the initial confusion, when the *amabutho* were sucked into a spontaneous attack, and the advance continued with the chest screened by skirmishers[257] and the horns properly deployed. While the advance of the left horn was conspicuous, that of the right horn was accomplished with more stealth so that the British seem not to have recognised that it had occupied the Manzimnyama valley, behind iSandlwana, until it was too late. The final rush of the chest was sufficiently determined to drive back the British outlying positions and to prevent them reforming while the horns pinned them in place; only heavy firing by some British units prevented the horns from meeting, leaving a corridor through which the British survivors escaped. The loins were used to cut the road to Rorke's Drift and to harry fugitives at the Mzinyathi.

Nevertheless, it was clear, even at iSandlwana, that the *izimpondo zankomo* was acutely vulnerable to British firepower. In later battles the British learned to counter the surprise attacks of the horns by adopting formations that were protected on all sides, while at Khambula Evelyn Wood took advantage of the Zulu difficulties in deploying over a wide swathe of broken country to provoke the right horn into launching an unsupported attack, with the result that all subsequent Zulu assaults lacked the coordination they had achieved at iSandlwana.

In their reliance on the *izimpondo zankomo* – which was designed initially to facilitate a rush with stabbing spears – the Zulus effectively squandered any advantage their own firepower might have given them. Initial disappointment in those early battles at the performance of their largely obsolete firearms, compared to the much more effective British weapons, reinforced a general sense of conservatism within the Zulu ranks, encouraging them to rely instead on tried and tested methods. As a result many Zulus regarded the rifle as little more than a marginally improved throwing spear, to be fired and discarded before the final rush. This, together with a general failure to use the more efficient firearms captured at iSandlwana, Ntombe and Hlobane effectively, meant that firepower never achieved the results among the Zulus that it might. Nevertheless it is interesting to note that at Khambula Zulu marksmen occupying the camp rubbish heap were able to successfully enfilade the British cattle-laager, and force the troops stationed there to withdraw, thus offering a tantalising glimpse into what might have been achieved elsewhere.

For the most part the Zulus stuck to their conventional tactics even in minor skirmishes, although the lack of a comfortable numerical superiority often led to a greater emphasis on dispersal and the use of cover. In the skirmishing around Eshowe, for example, British patrols often found themselves attacked by small bodies of Zulus who had hidden in the long grass before rising up to try to surround them. In the skirmish before oNdini on 3 July the uMxapho *ibutho* had taken up a position in long grass in a semi-circle, and decoys were used to draw British mounted troops under Redvers Buller into it; the grass had been plaited to trip the horses. On that occasion the trap failed because of Buller's wariness, although during the subsequent retreat to the White Mfolozi the Zulu horns almost succeeded in cutting the British line of retreat.

The Zulu army was not ideologically suited to defensive tactics, partly because of its innately aggressive outlook, and partly because of the impossibility of sustaining large numbers of men in fixed positions over an extended period. None the less, it was usual for Zulu non-combatants – old men, women and children – to take refuge in natural strongholds when threatened by an enemy, hidden away among boulders or in caves, and their menfolk would naturally defend them there. Under such circumstances the natural advantages of a position would be reinforced by dry-stone walls, built between boulders to provide rifle-pits.

At both the actions at Sihayo's homestead and Hlobane, and again later in the Ntombe valley, the British came under fire from Zulus well placed among the rocks, who proved particularly difficult to drive out.

Ultimately, however, despite its occasional spectacular successes, the *izimpondo zankomo* formation was already anachronistic by 1879 in the face of the superior weapon technology of the invaders. Ironically, the success at iSandlwana obscured that fact, encouraging the Zulu high command to persist in its use beyond the point at which it could reasonably be expected to be effective. Tragically, it took the utter defeat of the *amabutho* in the field to emphasise the point.

Travellers and Tourists

'I cannot say what influenced me to select "The Cape" as the intended scene of a few weeks' wandering,' wrote R.W. Leyland, Fellow of the Royal Geographical Society and author of *Round the World in 124 Days*, 'probably the prominence into which it had been brought by the late Zulu War.'[258] The same sentiment has brought a steady trickle of visitors to the killing fields of Zululand over the years, and has given rise in recent times to a distinct tourism industry of its own.

At a time when travel was fashionable among the British upper classes, particularly among those with a military background, a taste for adventure, an interest in exotic foreigners or a penchant for slaughtering magnificent forms of wildlife, the press coverage of the war in Zululand gave the country an immediate allure which was rare among the scenes of recent British colonial conflicts. Almost as soon as the shooting stopped, travellers were keen to make their way to the battlefields to see for themselves the sites where so much drama had unfolded. In particular, the pleasing symmetry implicit in the story of iSandlwana and Rorke's Drift – of defeat vindicated by courage and expiated in victory, the mystery and horror of the former, the stalwart British heroism of the latter – has an appeal which has remained largely unchallenged over nearly 130 years.

For early travellers, however, tourism to Zululand was not easily accomplished. The physical constraints which had so challenged the British Army in 1879 – the lack of roads, impassable rivers, rocky hillsides – meant that visiting the battlefields remained an uncomfortable and potentially dangerous experience. Although a fragile network of wayside inns and hotels extended throughout Natal as far as the borders, there was no equivalent in Zululand beyond the occasional hospitality of white missionaries or traders. Travellers to Zululand faced the prospect of living out of wagons or tents, and of carrying all their equipment, clothes, guns and food with them.

There was, moreover, no guarantee that they would be well received. In fact the Zulu people seem to have reacted to early post-war travellers with good-natured curiosity but, for those about to embark upon the journey, there must have seemed a good chance it would be otherwise; the Zulus had only recently been defeated, after all, and the wounds were still raw. Thousands of men bore fresh scars of battle, thousands of others had been killed, homes had been burned and the country enthusiastically looted. The country was, moreover, in an unsettled state, the result of the gradual collapse of Wolseley's settlement into anarchy and civil war. A little resentment directed at representatives of the cause of so much woe might perhaps have seemed forgivable.

The fact that they might be vulnerable seldom seems to have occurred to the earliest travellers. Indeed, Captain Walter Ludlow, formerly of the Royal Warwickshire Regiment, did not seem to think it necessary to explain his motivation either, merely remarking that 'in the early spring of 1880, I found myself on board the SS *Melrose*, a few miles from Durban' before, with nary a second thought, clearing his guns through customs, buying a couple of horses and saddles – 'military stores were the only things that were cheap in Durban at this time' – and setting off alone for the Zulu border. He crossed the Thukela at the Lower Drift – where he found traders were required to pay a £25 licence fee to operate in *inkosi* John Dunn's territory – before visiting the battlefields of Nyezane and kwaGingindlovu and travelling up the coast to Lake St Lucia to marvel at the hunting opportunities. Along the way he saw plenty of evidence of the recent fighting:

> The saddest sight in Zululand is the number of these graveyards. Wherever there had been a halt, you saw one of these melancholy records of the war, some containing only three or four, others as many as twenty graves. Fever, caused by the defective water supply, was the chief cause of death. Fort Pearson is very strongly constructed, with gabions made of strips of galvanised iron, and filled with earth, with an inner citadel, and telegraph offices. The slopes in front were strewn with old biscuit and preserved meat cans, here an old ammunition wagon thrown on its side, and there a dilapidated gun-carriage.[259]

Although Ludlow was a keen observer of Zulu habits and customs, he showed little interest in securing a Zulu perspective of recent events. Instead, his opinions were coloured by conversations with John Dunn, with whom he was much impressed. Ludlow returned home convinced that the majority of the Zulus did not want King Cetshwayo returned.

R.W. Leyland, on the other hand, formed his opinions from conversations with Bishop Colenso, and reached exactly the opposite conclusion. Ludlow, whose object in his travels was clearly to see as much as possible in the shortest time, followed an itinerary which would have done credit to a modern tour operator:

> I busied myself today in trying to make arrangements for an excursion to Rorke's Drift and Isandhlwana, the former of which lies about 65 miles by road from Newcastle in a south-easterly direction ... My time, however, was very limited and it was imperatively necessary that I should be back in Newcastle not later than the following Wednesday, to be ready for Thursday's mail-cart going south.[260]

When Leyland reached Rorke's Drift, he found Otto Witt busily repairing his house. Leyland managed to cross the Mzinyathi with the help of another missionary, Charles Johnson, and finally achieved his aim of a day-trip to iSandlwana before returning to Rorke's Drift overnight, and then heading back to Newcastle. At iSandlwana he found plenty of evidence of the fight still on the ground, including the bones of fallen soldiers washed recently from their graves. Leyland did not trouble to meet anyone on the excursion beyond the missionaries and the Sotho *inkosi* Hlubi.

Perhaps the most remarkable of these early pilgrimages was accomplished by the Empress Eugenie and her escort in 1880. From the moment she had heard the dreadful news of the death of her son, Louis the Prince Imperial, on 1 June 1879, Eugenie had conceived a fierce desire to visit the spot where he was killed. Since that spot lay in as remote a corner of Zululand as any recently fought over her objective was not easily to be reached but Queen Victoria herself agreed to defray the expenses of the expedition and Evelyn Wood was instructed to organise it. The Empress arrived in Natal on 23 April 1880, accompanied by just one aide, the Marquis de Bassano, one lady in waiting, Katherine Campbell (whose husband Ronald was killed at Hlobane), and two maids. Wood himself brought his wife and two ADCs, Frederick Slade and Arthur Bigge, both young officers who had served with him in Zululand. Nevertheless, Wood felt that such an exalted personage as the Empress could not possibly travel in Zululand with any threat to her dignity, and by the time it left Pietermaritzburg the expedition included a 22-man escort of the Natal Mounted Police, 15 mule wagons, 78 servants and drivers and a French cook named Theodore.[261]

The Empress had left Wood to finalise the itinerary, and he planned the route with his own agenda in mind. Although he was one of the few to emerge from the recent fighting with his reputation enhanced, he was none the less troubled by the débâcle at Hlobane mountain, for which he had largely been responsible. Katherine Campbell wanted to visit her husband's grave – indeed, the expedition collected a large stone cross from a mason in Pietermaritzburg to place upon the site – and Wood wanted to lay his own ghosts to rest. As a result, although it was by no means the most direct route to the Tshotshosi river, where the Prince had been killed, Wood chose to travel by way of Helpmekaar, Dundee, Khambula and Hlobane. The Empress accepted his suggestions without comment, and so this curious little pilgrimage of the bereft trundled its way slowly through some of the most dramatic scenery in Zululand. At Khambula Wood, Bigge and Slade delighted in walking Katherine Campbell over the battlefield, and on 18 May the party reached Hlobane mountain. Katherine Campbell was pleased to find that her husband had been killed in such an intensely romantic location; the following day 40 or 50 Zulus who had probably fought in the battle manhandled the gravestone up the side of the mountain and placed it on his grave. Wood was concerned to find the body of a friend, Captain Barton, which had lain undiscovered on the field for a year; after inquiring among the Zulus Wood sent for an *induna*, Sitshitshili kaMnqandi, who had killed him. By the time Sitshitshili arrived the approaching anniversary of Louis's death had forced the party to move on, but Wood left an orderly to greet the Zulu, and together they found and covered over Barton's remains.

The party reached the Tshotshosi on 25 May, and for Eugenie it was a crushing disappointment. For a year she had imagined the spot where her son had died to be a wild, romantic ravine, a landscape in keeping with the dramatic events played out there; in fact it proved to be a muddy donga in an open and largely featureless landscape.

There was, however, one last distraction before Eugenie could commune with her son on the anniversary of his death. As the wagon train trundled slowly across the veldt, Wood received news that an interloper was apparently trying to intercept them. Since leaving Pietermaritzburg he had been at pains to deflect press curiosity, but now a woman calling herself Lady Avonmore had apparently ridden across Zululand, accompanied only by two troopers of the Mounted Police, to meet Eugenie on the spot where Louis had died. Lady Avonmore had a decidedly colourful past, not the least of which was that she was not entitled to her title. Born Theresa Longworth, she had been seduced into a secret marriage by a dissolute son of Lord Avonmore who had then regretted the marriage, had it declared illegal, and cast her out. Spirited and resourceful, Theresa Longworth had turned to making her own living by the highly unconventional means, for the time, of writing adventurous travelogues. She had already talked her way into the court of the Rajah of Sarawak and into the home of Mormon leader Brigham Young. Quite why she had decided to intercept Eugenie remains obscure, but Wood in any case would have none of it. He rode out with Bigge to her camp to politely warn her off, and then posted guards around the Tshotshosi donga. Defeated, Theresa Longworth could do little but resign herself to another adventurous ride back to Natal.

The party remained camped beside the donga until 1 June. Wood interviewed a number of the Zulus living in the vicinity who had taken part in the attack, carefully teasing out the details of Louis's death to reassure his mother that her boy had indeed died bravely. On the night of his death Eugenie kept a candle-lit vigil on the spot, during which she felt her son's presence close by; then, when it was over, they packed up and trekked back again, returning by way of iSandlwana.

Empress Eugenie, Theresa Longworth; the difficulties of life lived rough in 1880s Zululand did not seem to stop intrepid Victorian women travelling there. In 1881 the eccentric Lady Florence Dixie hurried to southern Africa with her husband and a commission to report on the Transvaal uprising for a London newspaper. To her chagrin she arrived too late, but instead she persuaded Wood – again – to take her to Zululand. She visited Khambula and iSandlwana, and Redvers Buller took her all the way to the battlefield of Ulundi, where Zulu bones still lay strewn across the ground. Lady Florence was present at Wood's meeting with the Zulu *amakhosi* at Nhlazatshe mountain on 31 August 1881 and she confessed herself disturbed by the obvious attempts to silence the appeals of royalist supporters for the king's return. The meeting converted her into an ardent supporter of Cetshwayo; it was partly due to her enthusiastic lobbying that Cetshwayo was allowed to visit London to argue his case in 1882.

Undoubtedly the sharpest observer among these early travellers was Bertram Mitford. Born in 1855, the third son of minor English gentry, he had gone in 1874 to the Cape to make his fortune in ostrich farming. He had not succeeded and in 1878 had joined the Cape civil service instead. In 1882, lured by the extraordinary stories which had recently come out of Zululand, he resolved to make a tour of the battlefields to see what evidence of the fight remained upon them, and to ask the Zulus what they thought about it.

This, and his remarkably complete itinerary, made his travelogue, *Through the Zulu Country. Its Battlefields and its People*, published in 1883 and reprinted several times since, unique as a historical source. Unlike most of his predecessors, who had little interest in the Zulu perspective, Mitford sought out and interviewed many of those who had been prominent in the war. He interviewed *inkosi* Sihayo and his son Mehlokazulu, Vumandaba kaNthathi, who had commanded the uKhandempemvu at iSandlwana, and Sobhuza, the headman of the homestead where the Prince Imperial had been killed. He talked to John Dunn and Hlubi Molife, those representatives of the new ascendant order, and Prince Dabulamanzi (although he is frustratingly vague about what Dabulamanzi told him of Rorke's Drift). He interviewed, too, a score of ordinary Zulus, providing vivid insights into their understanding of battles including iSandlwana and Ulundi. He visited each of the battlefields in turn and his impressions of the landscape and its moods will still strike echoes with modern travellers today. Like many Victorian travellers, Mitford struggled to reconcile his own essentially imperialist views with the political realities of the post-war Zululand he saw unfolding around him, yet he remained sympathetic towards the Zulu people. After his return from his travels he carved a new career as a writer of adventure novels, many of

them drawing on the people and places he had visited.

Bertram Mitford, of course, had accomplished his travels slowly, by ox-wagon. In April 1914 the novelist Sir Henry Rider Haggard accomplished his tour of Zululand in an American Overland motor-car.[262] Although Haggard had become famous as a result of his novels such as *King Solomon's Mines*, many of which had drawn heavily on mythic stories of the Zulu kingdom, he had never before visited the sites. He travelled some 400 miles in a week, accompanied by two of the great colonial experts on Zulu history, James Stuart and James Gibson. Although there were many Zulu veterans of the war still on hand to show Haggard round the battlefields, Zululand had changed immeasurably in the thirty years since Mitford's visit; parts of the country had been opened to white farmers, roads – of a sort – had been built, and there were hotels in many of the country villages which had sprung up with the arrival of colonial administration and law. Haggard left Zululand uneasy at the contrast between the Zulus of his youth – when he had supported British intervention in the 1870s – and those he found oppressed and dissatisfied by decades of white rule.

For many years Zululand remained a difficult place to visit. Under the Nationalist Government in South Africa and the artificial division of the country into black and white areas casual visits to rural areas were discouraged. In 1979 tourists hoping to visit the battlefields for the centenary found few places to stay closer than Dundee or Vryheid. Only in the late 1980s were the first tourist lodges opened near the sites – an act of determined optimism, since it was by no means clear then whether anyone would come to visit them. Not until the collapse of apartheid and the emergence of a majority government in the 1990s did large-scale tourism to South Africa take off, and with it came a steady flow of visitors to the historic sites. The area around Rorke's Drift and iSandlwana – still the main focus for those who, like Leyland, have only limited time – has spawned a small tourist industry of its own, and indeed apart from farming the area has few other means of generating income. Ironically this opening up of Zululand to international tourists has come almost too late for those who want to taste something of Mitford's experience, for the country itself has changed irrevocably, and many of the sites – largely untouched for more than a century – have steadily succumbed to the spread of commercial farming and the increase in local population; a motorway flyover now crosses the Lower Thukela where once Captain Ludlow was ferried across. Nevertheless, there are still many places where, in the shade on a hot, quiet day – under the steep banks of the Ntombe river, or among the boulders on the steep flanks of Hlobane, and always at the foot of iSandlwana – the past seems tangible enough to touch.

Travelling Shows

In April 1879 Astley's amphitheatre on the south bank of the Thames in London offered the public a theatrical extravaganza entitled *The Kaffir War*, which purported to re-enact incidents from the recent fighting in Zululand. The appearance of a number of fearsome 'Zulu warriors' provoked a good deal of interest among the audience, although Astley's made no pretence that the 'Zulus' were anything other than white men in black make-up.

This was, however, the first demonstration of a popular interest by the British public in the appearance and customs of the enemy who were even then giving their troops a run for their money in southern Africa. Comment and satire on the news of the day was a mainstay of popular theatre, particularly the music hall, and the news of the Zulu victory at iSandlwana had caused a sensation when it reached England in February. This had been reflected in the extensive coverage in the illustrated press – the depiction of the Zulu people becoming increasingly lurid in proportion to the publication's popular appeal – and the music hall had already, by April, produced a stream of artistically challenged patriotic songs celebrating the courage of British troops and the villainy of their enemy.

The success of Astley's production stimulated enterprising showmen to capitalise on the public desire to see real live Zulus on the London stage.

Over the following months several shows in both London and the provinces purported to offer demonstrations of Zulu life and warfare by real Zulus; the public were not, on the whole, convinced, and indeed one critic damned them as 'miserable specimens of humanity ... who are supposed to have been picked up at an East End hospital'.[263] It was left to a remarkable American showman, William Leonard Hunt (who called himself The Great Farini, and had cut his show-stopping teeth as a tight-rope walker across Niagara Falls in 1860), to bring the first genuine Zulus to the London stage.

Farini had sent an agent to Durban, who returned not only with a Zulu group but with a letter of endorsement from the Sergeant of Licensed Labourers there and confirmation from none other than Sir Theophilus Shepstone that one of the group was a son of *inkosi* Somkhele kaMalanda, whose Mpukonyoni people lived in Zululand's northern coastal plains. Farini billed his troupe 'The Friendly Zulus' – presumably lest anyone in the audience fear a repetition of iSandlwana – but their appearance none the less alarmed the government's Secretary of State for the Home Department, who refused Farini's chosen theatre permission to stage them. Undaunted, Farini found another venue and his Zulus were displayed in June, much to the public's delight; the performance apparently consisted of various traditional Zulu songs and representations of the hunt and of methods of warfare. In between performances Farini prevented the troupe from leaving their lodgings except in carriages and under escort, for fear of satisfying for free the public curiosity upon which his profits were based. The idea of displaying human beings as side-show curiosities may be unpalatable to modern sensibilities but it was undeniably popular at the time, and for the most part Farini's management of his troupe seems to have been sympathetic. What the Zulus thought of the experience is not recorded, although at one point they were wise enough to seek legal intervention when challenging some of the more restrictive clauses in Farini's contracts.

So successful were 'The Friendly Zulus' in London that Farini took them on a tour of Europe, and they may well have been the Zulu group involved in an altercation that winter in Bohemia, where young boys pelted them with snowballs in the street. In 1880 Farini tried to top his act by bringing three Zulu girls, described as King Cetshwayo's daughters, to London.

Music hall interest in the war continued for months after the final British victory at Ulundi, but any further attempt to produce live Zulu groups was upstaged by a spectacular turn of events which brought the real thing to London. In August 1882 King Cetshwayo himself arrived in England to argue his case before the Colonial Office for his restoration to Zululand. The public interest in the victor of iSandlwana, fed over the years by men like Farini, was intense. Crowds gathered every day outside his lodgings in Melbury Road, Holland Park, and the king was obliged every few hours to take a turn on the balcony, where he was received with rapturous applause. When he visited the fashionable London photographers Bassano's to sit for his portrait, the crowd which gathered outside was so great that the police had to intervene to clear a way for the king to leave. Souvenir photographs – mostly taken in Cape Town before his departure – for a few weeks outsold those of popular actresses.

The king's visit effectively eclipsed the music hall's more contrived representations of Zulu life and the interest in Zulu troupes faded. Politically, the visit had an ambiguous legacy: Cetshwayo was indeed restored to part of his old territory in Zululand, although civil war and defeat by fellow Zulus followed, but, together with Farini's shows, it had helped to reshape the Zulu image in the popular imagination of the British people, and had aroused a widespread appreciation of the injustices of the British policies that had led to the invasion.

Trophies

In the closing stages of the battle of Khambula young Trooper George Mossop was just riding out of the British laager to join in the pursuit of the treating Zulu when,

> A short distance outside the laager I saw a
> dead Zulu. He was on his back, and a good

portion of his head was blown away. He was a big powerful fellow, and from his neck was hanging a large, beautifully carved, horn snuff-box, attached to a thin rope of sinew. Dismounting, I went to him, and as I was putting out my hand to secure the snuff-box, he suddenly drew up one leg, and with the sole of his foot kicked me in the pit of my stomach, bowling me over and knocking the breath from my body – but that was not as bad as the fright I got from being kicked by a dead man! However, I was not going to be kicked and frightened to death for nothing, and setting to work more cautiously, I secured the snuff-box.[264]

The practice of combatants removing trophies from a fallen enemy is as old as humanity, an almost instinctive and primeval expression of the exultation of survival and triumph, and both sides indulged it freely in Zululand in 1879, even sometimes, as Mossop's account demonstrates, while the fighting was going on. For the most part, however, it took place in the immediate aftermath of a battle, when the victors, left in possession of the field, were able to walk over the field, to recover their own dead and take what they wanted from the fallen enemy.

For the British collecting was, in the Victorian era, very much part of the way they reacted to the expanding world around them. As British explorers, traders, soldiers and administrators expanded the Empire, so they encountered a world which seemed to them fresh and exotic, and with knowledge came a sense of possession. The alien and the unusual was examined in the field, collected and sent back to London to be categorised and placed within a natural order which seemed to revolve around Britain and its interests. With a sense of the vastness of a world just opening up, of its newness and richness, the British – and indeed Europeans and Americans – generally lacked that awareness of the fragility of cultures and eco-systems which characterises modern interaction with the environment. At a time when the Victorian upper classes, who largely directed the Empire's efforts, were accustomed to field sports and country pursuits –

when individual acts of destruction were part of their relationship with the natural world – there was little perception of the contradiction inherent in the destruction of exotic wildlife in the cause of understanding it. The world seemed then so limitless, the lesson of the Dodo only vaguely understood, and the rarer the species the greater the scientific honour in discovering, killing, pickling and collecting it, or the greater the satisfaction in shooting it for sport. And just as the triumph over the natural world could be charted by the growth in collections at the British Museum and by the trophies mounted on the walls of country estates, so could political and military triumphs be recognised by the carrying away of exotic enemy weapons of war.

For the British in Zululand certain items among the functional artefacts carried by Zulu men in battle quickly achieved an iconic status. While officers of the 24th were informed enough to recognise the significance of the wooden prestige staffs owned by *inkosi* Sihayo kaXongo, and to carry them away from his kwaSokhege homestead before they burned it on 12 January, the most favoured types of loot soon became shields and spears. Firearms were often collected after battles but, while they were carefully counted and the types noted, they had little appeal as souvenirs of the exotic and were generally destroyed. Shields and spears were so representative of Zulu military culture, however, and the shields so conspicuous and visually appealing, that they were obvious material for trophies and during the course of the war hundreds were picked up and taken back to England, usually to be mounted as wall-displays. After the battle of kwaGingindlovu the war correspondent Charles Norris-Newman and his friend Palmer sought out the spot where they had fired at a group of Zulus sheltering in a clump of grass; they found three bodies there 'close together, and Palmer and I took and divided the trophies of war, including their native dress, arms, and accoutrements; and we keep them yet, as most prized and hardly-won spoils'.[265]

Officers – and civilians like Norris-Newman – were generally better able to secure bulkier trophies than the men in the ranks since they enjoyed greater baggage allowances. At the beginning of the war it was clear that months of campaigning in all likelihood still lay ahead, and any souvenirs would have to be carried across Zululand before they could be taken home. Many items taken in the early battles were no doubt later discarded when the new owner found them cumbersome or became bored with them; none the less a good deal was squirrelled away, ordinary soldiers often making their trophies more portable by cutting down the length of spears, or by discarding shield-sticks and rolling up the hide. A photograph of a trophy collected by the 91st Highlanders, probably through the war as a whole, and displayed in some grand but unknown hall, reveals the range of items collected: a large war-shield, spears, firearms (unusually), head-dresses, axes, sticks, a prestigious kilt of animal-skins and beadwork.

It was immediately clear to most of the troops involved that the victory at Ulundi was a decisive one, and thus an appropriate moment to secure tokens of triumph and have some hope of getting them safely and quickly home. Looting after the battle was therefore particularly widespread, and there were hopes that King Cetshwayo's royal homestead at oNdini might contain tangible riches in the manner of the wealthy Indian houses looted during the Mutiny or the gold objects found in King Kofi Karikari's palace in Asante in West Africa. In fact dreams of caches of diamonds collected by African workers in the Kimberley diamond-fields or stacks of elephant tusks proved as illusory as the fabled riches of King Solomon's Mines, and the British had to be content with the ordinary Zulu artefacts that littered the homesteads after their hasty abandonment. There were shields in plenty – mostly white ones with small brown spots belonging to the uThulwana *ibutho* who were quartered at oNdini, or grey flecked ones from the uMxapho at kwaNodwengo – together with carved wooden headrests, meat-platters and milking-pails. Major Anstruther of the 94th Regiment wrote home to his wife that:

We walked about burning the whole place and picked up shields and assegais. I got 5 shields and 2 assegais – could not carry more ...

There was a nice little spruit just 28 yards off our rear faces where we were and there were 6 lying behind it. They had died very pluckily and I took one of their shields but it is a dirty piece of goods and nothing at all to compare with the 4 that I got from the kraal.[266]

One officer was seen to be collecting souvenirs so enthusiastically that he lost his grip and fell off his horse.

With the British victory came pacification and the Zulu surrender, and for the first time in the war the two sides were able to meet in comparatively relaxed circumstances. It offered the British a last chance to secure souvenirs, and written accounts of conversations between British officers and Zulu *amakhosi* are littered with references to last-ditch attempts to procure personal items ranging from sticks to snuff-boxes. Anything connected with King Cetshwayo himself was particularly prized and after his capture by dragoons in the Ngome forest on 28 August he was politely but enthusiastically relieved of everything from his sticks to the last milk-pail – carried by his female attendants – he had drunk from.

The Zulus, too, were undeniably enthusiastic looters. It was in any case part of their post-combat rituals that a man who had killed an enemy should remove part of the victim's clothing and wear it until he had undergone various cleansing ceremonies. This was of course only possible when the Zulus were victorious and were left in possession of the field, and on those occasions – notably at iSandlwana and Ntombe, and to a lesser extent at Hlobane – a rich cornucopia of European artefacts also fell into their hands. Although many ordinary Zulus had some experience of itinerant white traders before the war, for the majority the practical experience most had enjoyed of white material culture was extremely limited. At iSandlwana the Zulus captured all of the comforts that British troops had brought into the field with them, and for many of them this was no less exotic than the Zulu artefacts were to the British.

Some items were of course primarily of military interest, notably firearms and other weapons. The best part of a thousand modern Martini-Henry rifles and Swinburne-Henry carbines fell into Zulu hands, along with the entire column's reserve supplies of ammunition. It was usual for such prestige items to be taken to the king and then apportioned by him as rewards for those who had distinguished themselves in battle, but so sought-after were rifles, in particular, that Cetshwayo wisely allowed those men who had secured one to keep it. Even those who did not acquire a gun eagerly sought out British ammunition, pulling out the bullets with their teeth from the cartridges and pouring the powder into their powder-horns to service their old muskets. Revolvers and swords too had an appeal but largely of the exotic; in untrained hands they were less effective as a weapon than the stabbing spear, and the Zulus prized them more as curiosities.

There was a huge amount of other paraphernalia in the camp, however, almost enough to service an army of looters. There were uniforms and clothes – hats and helmets, tunics, shirts, trousers, boots – and not merely those removed from the dead but the officers' spares left in tents. Greatcoats were particularly prized because they were warm and comfortable and could easily be worn over traditional loin-coverings. There was food in sacks, tins and boxes – British burial parties commented on the number of meat tins scattered about the field which had been roughly punctured with spear-thrusts – and drink, both alcoholic and otherwise.[267] There were blankets, and if there were not enough to go round the tents could be pulled down and the canvas cut into strips as a substitute. There were saddles and harnesses from the mounted troops – the horses too, if they weren't killed in the fighting – and officers' folding beds and trunks, collapsible tables, utensils and cutlery, candle-sticks and ink-wells. When Lord Chelmsford's troops returned from Mangeni that evening, the last of the Zulus were still carrying away their captured treasures.[268]

Many of these items were carried miles away by hand. British rifles were recovered from Zulu dead after the battles of Khambula and kwa-Gingindlovu – which took place at opposite ends of the country – while a boot looted from Lieutenant Harford's tent at iSandlwana was found on the battlefield of Ulundi. Throughout the war the British routinely searched Zulu homesteads for captured British items before they destroyed them, and they recovered significant quantities of material, as Captain Montague of the 94th recalled during the destruction of *inkosi* Sihayo's settlements on the Ntinini river in June:

Everywhere were caves and holes cunningly hidden in the sides of dongas, and amongst them our native allies were busy. Isandlwana relics were abundant. Martini cartridges ripped open to get at the powder; a new saddle and saddle-bags complete; rifles of the 24th and 80th Regiments; soldiers' valises; a gunner's oil-bottle; a pair of ammunition boots; a pearl-handled knife; a cake of soap and a sponge, the last two very puzzling to the possessors.[269]

Occasionally these items were taken back into service, but for the most part they became trophies of another kind to be treasured by their original owners, redolent now of incidental defeat and ultimate victory, and invested with the poignancy and pathos of loss and regret.

Ulundi

Three different versions of the royal homestead known variously as Ulundi or oNdini existed, and all three were violently destroyed as a result – directly or indirectly – of the British invasion of 1879.

The names oNdini and Ulundi are different forms of the same root, *undi*, meaning a high place, like the rim of a bowl, or a mountain range like the Khahlamba (Drakensberg). The names were intended to convey a sense of impenetrability. In official correspondence before the war the British used both versions before generally settling on Ulundi, partly because

another homestead known as oNdini was also in existence. For the most part the Zulus used the version oNdini;[270] today oNdini is used to refer to the homestead destroyed by the British on 4 July 1879, while Ulundi is the modern town near which it stands.

The first oNdini was built by order of King Mpande in the early 1850s. At that time his sons, the Princes Cetshwayo and Mbuyazi, were first beginning to dispute the right of succession, and Mpande thought it wise to house each in a separate royal homestead. This oNdini was built on the lower reaches of the Mhlatuze river, in Zululand's sub-tropical coastal belt, and it remained Prince Cetshwayo's favourite homestead even after his defeat of Mbuyazi at the battle of 'Ndondakusuka in 1856.

When Cetshwayo finally became king in 1873, he decided to build a new, much bigger homestead in keeping with his new position. He chose a spot just north of the White Mfolozi river, on an undulating plain surrounded by hills. This area had been a favourite with his father Mpande, whose old kwaNodwengu homestead had stood there, together with a number of other *amakhanda*. Indeed, Mpande had been buried at the head of the central enclosure of the old kwaNodwengu complex, which had then been abandoned and allowed to fall into disrepair; Cetshwayo ordered a new, smaller version of kwaNodwengo to be built nearby, and at the time of the British invasion there were a total of thirteen major royal homesteads in the area.

From the first Cetshwayo intended the new complex to be memorably impressive. His predecessor and uncle, King Dingane, had been renowned for the magnificence of his royal homestead, eMgungundlovu, and Cetshwayo was determined that his should be better still. In 1838 eMgungundlovu had been destroyed during the war against the Voortrekkers, but in 1873 the clay floors were still clearly visible (many survive today) to provide inspiration.

Cetshwayo picked a spot on a broad slope overlooking the Mbiline stream which afforded good drainage and allowed for a clear view over the plain. Young men of the iNgobamakhosi and uKhandempevu *amabutho* were assembled and set to work clearing the slope of brush and grass, and then dispatched to the Nkandla forest to procure the huge quantities of saplings needed to make the frames for the huts. Hundreds of women were also assembled and set about preparing clay for the hut floors and cutting grass for the thatch. Each hut was dome-shaped, the framework supported by two or three central poles. The floors were made of clay with a hearth for a fire in the centre; the clay was then smeared with cow-dung and polished with stones to give the floor a deep bottle shine. There was no chimney; the smoke simply filtered out through the thatch. Since the smoke tended to hang in a fug a few feet off the ground, visiting such a hut when it was occupied could be unpleasant for those not used to it, although one side-effect was that the smoke tended to reduce the number of insects living in the thatch.

The homestead was broadly oval in shape with huts arranged in three or four rows around a large central enclosure. This enclosure served as a pen for the herds of royal cattle housed there at night, and during the day as a parade-ground for the *amabutho*. The huts were surrounded both inside and out by a stout fence of tree-trunks, each arranged in two rows, a few inches apart, so as to overlap at the top and provide a jagged barrier against attack.

At the top of the homestead were the king's quarters, known as the *isigodlo*. The most private of these, fenced off by screens, was known as the black *isigodlo*, which contained the king's personal hut, the huts of his wives, and those of the most elite of his female attendants (who were also known as *isigodlo*) who served the king's wives, and whom he also used as concubines. It was forbidden for a commoner to enter the *isigodlo* on pain of death. Flanking the black *isigodlo* on either side were less private royal quarters, known as the white *isigodlo*. Here lived some of Cetshwayo's 'mothers' – the widows of the late King Mpande – together with the rest of the *isigodlo* girls and the king's children. The king's personal hut was simply a bigger version of an ordinary Zulu hut; later, at the suggestion of a visiting missionary, Cetshwayo had an oblong European-style hut of mud-brick and thatch built

in the *isigodlo* area, but he was not generally impressed by its qualities and tended to use it only when receiving white guests.

The new complex was given the name oNdini, after the homestead where Cetshwayo had lived as a prince. In all it contained over 1,000 huts, and perhaps even as many as 1,400. A large number of royal functionaries – personal attendants, *izinduna*, messengers, praise-singers, herbalists and diviners – were always in attendance upon the king, while the great men of the kingdom often visited to discuss affairs of state. The great circle of huts around the perimeter of the complex was occupied by *amabutho*, in particular the uThulwana, iNdlondlo and iNdluyengwe. These were married middle-aged men.[271] It was unusual for married men to spend much time assembled in their *amabutho* – marriage generally marked the point at which men passed off the 'active service' list, mustering only for important occasions – but Mpande had established a precedent of maintaining 'white assemblies', and Cetshwayo followed his example. These were married men, carrying white shields, who none the less spent a good deal of time at the main royal homestead. They were generally free of the harsher constraints of such service; they were allowed to come and go as they pleased, and their wives came to visit them. The system ensured that the king always had a significant number of men available to him at his principal homestead without the need to assemble the more volatile younger *amabutho* for any length of time.

For much of the year oNdini was probably occupied by between 2,000 and 2,500 people, the overwhelming majority of them male. When fully occupied during the national ceremonies, however, when four or even five men were quartered in each hut, it might house between 6,000 and 7,000 people.

Between 1873 – when the complex was built – and 1877 oNdini also served as the barracks for the young iNgobamakhosi whenever that *ibutho* was assembled. The iNgobamakhosi was the first *ibutho* formed directly under Cetshwayo's supervision and he was particularly fond of it. However, there was considerable friction whenever they were assembled between the iNgobamakhosi and the older *amabutho* quartered at oNdini, and at the harvest ceremonies in December 1877 this led to a violent clash between them which started as the *amabutho* jostled each other one morning as they left by the main gate and spilled out across the neighbouring plain. The iNgobamakhosi were armed only with dancing sticks but the uThulwana had spears in their huts and armed themselves for war; over 70 men were killed, mostly iNgobamakhosi. Cetshwayo was appalled and directed that the iNgobamakhosi should thereafter be housed elsewhere. They were attached instead to the old oNdini, which still existed near the coast. Once Cetshwayo had built the new complex, the Zulus took to referring to the old one as kwaHlalangubo. It was still in existence in 1879, when the British called it 'old oNdini'.

In 1879 the British regarded the main oNdini as the Zulu capital, and made it the strategic target for their invasion. In fact, each of the many large royal homesteads across the country was regarded as a potential home for the king, and he often moved between them, taking up residence in one or another for a few months at a time. None the less, oNdini was undoubtedly his favourite – his *komkhulu*, or 'great place' – and, together with the other *amakhanda* nearby, it served as the administrative hub of the kingdom. To that extent the British objective was accurately chosen.

In their intelligence documents concerning the Zulu army, the British tended to lump together *amabutho* attached to particular homesteads as 'corps'. The *amabutho* attached to oNdini they called the 'Undi Corps' – these *amabutho* formed the Zulu reserve at the battle of iSandlwana, and went on to attack the British post at Rorke's Drift.

Both versions of oNdini were destroyed during the war. On 4 July Lord Chelmsford's forces crossed the White Mfolozi river and formed up for battle on the opposite plain. The Zulu army had gathered previously at the royal homesteads there – including oNdini itself – and then advanced to their defence but were defeated in the subsequent battle. Once the *amabutho* had retreated to a safe distance, Lord Chelmsford gave permission for his staff to race to oNdini – a race won by Captain Sir William Beresford, who apparently jumped his horse clean over the outer palisade. Although the king and his household had left the complex before the battle, there were a number of warriors, fleeing from the battle, still sheltering in the huts, and this made them unsafe for those British who became isolated while exploring them; the war correspondent Melton Prior, intent on sketching, only narrowly escaped when several warriors tried to ambush him. The British looted the complex, taking away large numbers of shields from the *amabutho*'s shield-stores, together with artefacts found in the *isigodlo* (all of which they fondly imagined belonged to the king himself), then set fire to the huts. Melton Prior drew a sketch of the square European-style house in flames. British cavalrymen were also dispatched to set fire to the other *amakhanda* nearby before Chelmsford withdrew his troops back across the White Mfolozi.

Over the next few days, as they retreated to the Mthonjaneni heights, the British could see oNdini burning in the distance, a great circle of flame, until a pall of ashes and smoke settled over what had once been the heart of the Zulu kingdom. In fact, here and there a few huts survived the conflagration, and when Sir Garnet Wolseley reoccupied the site in August 1879, during the pacification operations, several were still standing, together with some lengths of the palisade. These eventually succumbed to ruin, however, and for decades afterwards the site was marked by a great circle of different-coloured vegetation. It was easily recognisable to Bertram Mitford, who visited the spot in 1882:

Some idea of the dimensions of the kraal may be gleaned when I say that it takes full five minutes of tolerably quick walking to cross it. The floors of the huts still remain, with their fireplaces in the centre, but are thickly overgrown with coarse herbage. At the upper end . . . was Cetshwayo's [European house], a square tenement with glazed windows and a door; the other huts for his wives and attendants being of the ordinary shape. I was keenly on the lookout for relics, but could find none; a few bits of broken glass, remnants of ancient gin bottles, lay about, and fragments of native pottery, which is made of clay baked in the sun and very brittle and crumbly. On the site of the king's huts I picked up some pieces of a clay bowl, a fragment of an iron three-legged pot, and a smooth round stone such as would be used for polishing floors – a duty it had probably often performed on that of the royal dwelling. Other relics more curious or valuable there were none.[272]

Curiously, the violent destruction of oNdini was responsible for the survival of its foundations; the clay hut floors, so vividly described by Mitford, were baked to brick by the burning thatch above them. Until well into the twentieth century the site of the royal homestead was regarded with respect by those living locally; ordinary homesteads were not built upon it, and only in the 1930s was a small part of the outlying complex ploughed over. Much of it still survived below a layer of topsoil so that in the 1980s an archaeological survey was made of the site, and it was decided to clear the surface debris and reveal the hut floors in the *isigodlo* area. These included the remains of Cetshwayo's personal hut and his European-style building. A section of the outer palisade was then reconstructed, and huts rebuilt over the original floors to give some idea of what the *isigodlo* looked like in its heyday. Today there is also a museum on the site.

KwaHlalangubo – the old oNdini – survived oNdini proper by just two days. On 6 July 1879 a patrol of mounted men attached to the British 1st Division and led by Major Percy Barrow found the homestead deserted and set fire to it. It was said to have consisted of some 640 huts, in keeping with the fact that provincial *amakhanda* were notably smaller than those in the Zulu heartland.

Following the Anglo-Zulu War King Cetshwayo was of course captured by the British and sent into exile. The British attempted to control post-war Zululand through appointed nominees but the invasion had unleashed deep-

seated tensions within Zulu society and the country became increasingly unstable. In 1882 the British Government opted to partition the country for a second time and restore Cetshwayo to some of his former territory. He was granted a swathe of central Zululand, including the oNdini area, and returned to the country in February 1883.

Cetshwayo hoped to restore something of his old authority, at least over those areas he now controlled. The British banned him from reviving the *amabutho* system and of course the old *amakhanda* had not survived the war; nevertheless, many Zulu men still recognised their allegiance to their old *amabutho* and large numbers answered the king's call to serve him. Cetshwayo decided to rebuild oNdini as his *komkhulu*. The original site was no longer practicable – and indeed the bones of many of those killed in the battle were still lying across the plain – so Cetshwayo selected a fresh site a mile or two away. The new complex was slightly smaller than the old one, being only about 300 yards across, but it still consisted of nearly 1,000 huts. Once again saplings were collected by men who remained loyal to the king and the thatching was completed by women. In fact, however, this last version of oNdini was not quite completed when tragedy befell it. The king's restoration had provoked a confrontation with prominent Zulus who had enjoyed power during his absence, and the resulting violence escalated. On 30 March an army of royalist supporters – possibly without the king's knowledge – launched an attack on *inkosi* Zibhebhu kaMaphitha, the most prominent opponent of Cetshwayo's return. Zibhebhu first defeated the royalists, then prepared for a counter-attack. He made a daring night-march across country from his own territory in the north of the country and arrived at oNdini at dawn on 21 July. A large number of royalists had gathered at the new *komkhulu* in response to the crisis but they were taken by surprise by the speed of Zibhebhu's attack. The king's men attempted to make a stand outside oNdini but broke in the face of a determined attack. Fighting spilled into the complex itself and a number of huts were set on fire. Cetshwayo managed to escape but not before being wounded in the thigh by thrown spears. More than 50 prominent royalist supporters – former generals, councillors and *amakhosi* – were killed. For the third and final time the oNdini homestead was utterly destroyed.

The battle of oNdini on 21 July 1883 marks the true end of the old Zulu order. Although badly damaged by the British invasion in 1879, many of the individuals, structures and loyalties which had supported the kingdom survived and rallied briefly in 1883. The destruction of the last oNdini, the defeat of the king by one of his own erstwhile commanders and the death of so many prominent royalists shattered any further attempts to reunify the kingdom. Cetshwayo himself died in early 1884; oNdini was never rebuilt.

In the 1970s, however, during the height of the apartheid era, when the country was divided into areas of white land ownership and black 'home-lands', Ulundi was designated by the Nationalist Party Government in Pretoria as an appropriate capital for the KwaZulu 'homeland'. At that time the area was not heavily settled and had partly been owned by white farmers, and there was little economic activity in the region to support such development. Nevertheless a Legislative Assembly was built as the seat of government for KwaZulu and the modern town of Ulundi – including an airstrip and a hotel – was built around it from scratch. Following the collapse of apartheid the old black KwaZulu and white Natal areas were unified in a single province, KwaZulu-Natal. Since there was no longer a need for two capitals, Pietermaritzburg and Ulundi vied to be the new seat of provincial government – a contest in which Sir Bartle Frere, had he still been around, might have seen a certain irony. Because of its greater existing infrastructure and its proximity to the international port at Durban, Pietermaritzburg eventually won.

Uniforms (British)

In 1879 the age of the red-coat – which had so long been a characteristic of the British Army, and which dated to the formation of the New Model Army in 1645 – was drawing to a close. To modern sensibilities, accustomed to the widespread and imaginative use of camouflage fatigues, the idea of wearing so conspicuous a colour as red in combat seems fatally absurd, yet the red-coat was in fact a practical response to the realities that prevailed on the battlefield for some 300 years. The major imperial wars of the eighteenth and nineteenth centuries, including the protracted struggles against Napoleon, were waged with smooth-bore weapons which were accurate at ranges of only 50 yards or less, and which – using black powder as a propellant – produced huge quantities of smoke from the first volley. Under such circumstances, when troops only stood any chance of hitting an enemy when they blazed away within clear sight of each other, the imperative lay not on concealment but in the ability to differentiate friend from foe. All the major European powers adopted distinctive uniforms which made it marginally easier to identify friend from foe on the battlefield amidst the fog of war. Although campaigns such as the Revolutionary War in America hinted at the limitations of conventional and conspicuous military practice in the face of guerrilla tactics, the lesson was largely irrelevant in European warfare, and it was not until the widespread introduction of rifled weapons in the 1850s – which were accurate to a greater range – that the advantages of dispersal and concealment gradually came to outweigh the need for battle-field recognition. In South Africa, in the 8th Frontier War of 1851–53, British troops first began to strip their uniforms of unnecessary refinements to make them more comfortable and practical in warfare in the bush, while during the Indian Mutiny of 1857 some units began to wear drab dust-coloured clothing of a colour known locally as *khaki*. By 1879, however, khaki had been officially authorised for use in the Indian theatre only, and while British troops fighting in the 2nd Afghan War were dressed in it, the troops fighting in Zululand at the same time still wore the old red-coat. The situation was to change rapidly thereafter, however; indeed, when troops were rushed from Afghanistan in 1881 to assist in the suppression of the Transvaal Rebellion, they landed still wearing their khaki India dress, and fought alongside troops from the Natal garrison – most of whom were veterans of the Zulu campaign – who remained dressed in scarlet. In the Egyptian campaign of 1882 troops sent from England wore red, and those from India khaki; the last war fought entirely by British troops in scarlet was the Dinuzulu Rebellion in Zululand in 1888.

The uniforms worn by British troops in Zululand were essentially those designed for home service, with just a few concessions to the practicalities of campaign life. For the other ranks of infantry regiments, this meant either a smart seven-button scarlet tunic – usually preferred for parades – or a looser, more comfortable equivalent which had five buttons and was known as the 'undress frock'. Regimental distinctions were marked by a distinctive colour worn as a patch on the cuff and a tab either side of the collar-opening, known as 'facings'. On the tunic, the bottom edge of the collar, the shoulder straps, the leading edge of the front opening and the vents on the skirts at the back were all trimmed with flat white braid. The cuff patch was also edged in white braid which ended in a trefoil knot. On the plainer frock there was no edging to the front opening and the skirts, and indeed some battalions seem not to have worn the facing colour on the cuffs of the frock. Regimental badges were worn on the collar patches and a regimental numeral on the shoulder straps. NCO rank distinctions were worn for Line regiments on the right sleeve only – white chevrons to the rank of lance sergeant, gold for sergeant and above – but on both sleeves for Light Infantry. Trousers were a very dark blue/grey colour known as 'Oxford mixture' – which was almost black, with a slight blue cast – and had a scarlet welt down the outer seam. Black leather boots were worn with short black lace-up gaiters. For home service infantry battalions wore a dark blue helmet with brass badge, spike and fittings but this was clearly impractical for field use and it was replaced instead with a cork 'foreign service helmet' covered in white canvas. Although regimental badges were authorised for wear on the front, most battalions in the field soon realised that not only the badge but the white helmet itself offered a dangerously conspicuous target in the bright African sun, and it became commonplace

to remove all metal fittings and dull the helmet to a khaki colour with dyes made from tea, coffee or boiled bark.

Equipment was the integrated 1871 Valise Pattern which provided for the soldier to carry a black leather knapsack or valise – and a rolled great-coat as well as ammunition, all supported by white leather straps. In Zululand, however, it was more common for the valise to be carried on regimental transports, leaving the rolled grey greatcoat carried high on the back. Ammunition was carried in pouches on the waist-belt – 20 rounds in packets in each pouch on either side of the clasp, and a further 30 rounds carried loose in a black leather 'expense pouch', usually worn on the right hip. A white canvas haversack – often called a 'bread bag' as it carried the soldier's rations and other necessities – was worn over the right shoulder (on the left hip), and a wooden barrel-shaped water bottle on a leather strap was slung over the left. Like the helmet, all straps were usually dyed buff or khaki on campaign.

In the field officers' uniforms were largely devoid of the ornate rank distinctions which characterised home-service dress. Instead of the full dress-tunic, with its ornate gold braid on the cuffs, most officers preferred to wear their equivalent of the 'undress frock'. This was scarlet, with scarlet cuffs, but with the entire collar of the facing colour. Thin gold braid, according to rank, decorated the cuffs, and rank badges were worn on the collar. The frock was piped white down the front and around the edges, and the scarlet shoulder straps were white and bore an embroidered gold regimental number. As an alternative many officers preferred to wear a more comfortable jacket of very dark blue, known as a 'blue patrol'; this was edged around the collar, front and bottom with flat black mohair-braid which also decorated the back seams and cuffs. The front was fastened with hooks and eyes, and decorated with black toggles, and with ropes of braid ending in loops. In 1879 infantry patrol jackets bore no shoulder-straps. Trousers were dark blue with a red welt, and most officers carried their swords – with the belt worn either outside or under the jacket – and carried revolvers.

The fame of the Sam Browne belt had not generally spread beyond India at this time, and most officers in Zululand carried their revolvers on leather shoulder-straps.

Both officers and men of the Royal Engineers also wore scarlet jackets. For ORs the undress frock was red with a blue collar and cuffs, and yellow braid around the collar, shoulder straps and cuffs, where it ended in the usual trefoil knot. Trousers were dark blue with a broad red stripe. Officers wore a similar undress frock, trimmed with thin gold cord rather than yellow braid, and with a loop of braid instead of shoulder straps. Some Engineer officers preferred to wear their equivalent of the infantry patrol jacket which had blue velvet on the collar and cuffs and a different pattern of braiding. Officers on mounted duties usually wore yellow corduroy riding breeches.

Royal Artillery uniforms were of the dark blue Oxford mixture. Most ORs in 1879 wore the undress jacket, which was plain blue, with a breast pocket on the left, and no piping. Trousers were also dark blue with a broad red stripe. Men riding the limbers wore black leather riding boots, the rest ordinary boots and gaiters. Photographs suggest that a few ORs did wear the tunic in the field which had a red collar and was piped with yellow, including a trefoil over the (blue) cuffs. Artillery officers generally wore the blue patrol, which was of a similar pattern to the Engineers' version, but without the blue velvet.

Lacking regular cavalry in the early stages of the invasion, Chelmsford relied instead upon improvised Mounted Infantry squadrons. These were raised from volunteers in the infantry battalions who could ride. The men retained their regimental frocks – which gave them a decidedly mixed appearance – but were issued with corduroy riding breeches, Swinburne-Henry rifles and bandoliers carrying 50 rounds of ammunition in leather loops. They wore the ubiquitous foreign service helmets.

Of the cavalry units dispatched as part of the reinforcements, the 17th Lancers wore a distinctive uniform of very dark blue. This consisted of a plastron-fronted tunic which, for ORs, had a white collar and white pointed cuffs and was piped white around the edges and up the back

seams, including the arms. The plastron was white on one side and blue on the other; on parade it was worn with the white face showing but in the field this was such a conspicuous target that it was worn reversed, blue side out. Trousers were blue with a double white stripe. The impressive refinements of home-service dress – a lancer-style *czapka* helmet with a large badge and white plume, a yellow waist girdle with red stripes, a leather shoulder-belt and heavy white leather gauntlets – were abandoned in the field in favour of a Valise ammunition pouch waist-belt, haversack and water-bottle and dyed white helmet. Officers wore either a blue cavalry-pattern patrol jacket or the tunic, which was similar to the OR pattern but sported gold braid around the collar and cuffs. The men were armed with a 9-ft lance of male bamboo with a steel point and a red-over-white pennon. They also carried swords and carbines. Officers were armed with swords and revolvers.

The 1st (King's) Dragoon Guards wore scarlet tunics with dark blue collars, cuffs and shoulder straps, all edged in yellow braid. There was an ornate 'Austrian knot' design in yellow above the cuff. Trousers were blue with a broad yellow stripe. Officers wore a similar tunic but with gold braid, the patterning on the cuff becoming thicker and more complex with rank. ORs wore ammunition pouch belts, haversacks and water bottles and were armed with carbines and swords.

Of the support corps the Army Service Corps wore dark blue frocks and trousers with white collar and cuffs, and with a white stripe in the trousers and either a white helmet or blue forage cap with a white band. Army Hospital Corps staff wore a dark blue uniform with a red stripe in the trousers and a conspicuous circular white badge on the right arm bearing the red cross.

The realities of campaigning in Zululand were such that the British troops had a very different appearance from that popularly imagined by the Victorian public at home. Although replacement uniforms were issued in April each year, it often took months for them to reach colonial garrisons, let alone troops fighting in remote areas. In the meantime boots were at the mercy of long hard marches over rough and rocky terrain, and thorns snagged at tunics, jackets and pieces of equipment. Exposure to the elements caused some colours in the uniform to fade, and gradually distorted the shape of helmets. To all this the individual soldier had no recourse but 'make do and mend', and by the time the Zulu campaign was over every battalion sported an ingenious array of patched trousers and jackets, of boots in a state of virtual collapse, sometimes merely tied together, and – where they had not given way altogether to civilian hats – helmets crumpled out of all recognition. Tunics were faded and dusty and all white equipment straps had been dulled to a grubby khaki using improvised vegetable dyes. On taking over the command in July, Sir Garnet Wolseley made a determined effort to insist that his men present a smart and soldierly appearance, but many had little choice but to continue to serve in rags until the war was over and they were able to secure replacements.

Uniforms (Zulu)

On ceremonial occasions – notably the national gathering which ushered in the new harvest each year – the Zulu *amabutho* wore lavish and distinctive costumes. Although these included a number of elements in common to all (such as dense bunches of cow-tails, worn suspended from a necklace so as to hang to the waist at the front and the knees at the back, streamers of cow-tails around the knees and elbows and ordinary loin-coverings), each *ibutho* boasted a number of unique elements which, in combination with the patterns on their shields, were sufficient to distinguish them, and which therefore constituted a regimental uniform.

The chief distinction in ceremonial dress lay between the young unmarried *amabutho* and their married counterparts. Young men carried predominantly dark shields – black or brown – and older men spotted or white shields. Young men wore a headband of cat-skin – usually civet or serval, although those of rank used leopard-skin – stitched into a tube and padded with bull-rushes, while older men wore headbands of brown otter skin. Both wore supple oblongs cut from *samango* monkey pelts hanging from the headbands over the cheeks and ears, and feathers

tied neatly to stand upright above the headbands, but particular feathers carried associations of either youth or maturity. Younger *amabutho* wore thick bunches of the long, glossy black tail feathers sported by the *isakabuli* finch during its mating season, sometimes on either side of the head, or in a dense plume on top. They wore, too, stiff flat 'horns' of cow-hide, known as *amapovela*, to the tips of which were tied cow-tails which fell back down over the side of the face. Black ostrich feathers were associated with youth, white ones with experience. Some *amabutho* wore bunches of feathers apportioned to them by the king as a particular mark of distinction, while senior *amabutho* wore the long tail-feathers of the Blue Crane, either singly over the forehead or in ones and twos over the temples. Great men – members of the leading houses of the *amakhosi*, wore bunches of scarlet and green wing feathers from the Purple-Crested Lourie, cut along the spine and twisted so as to give a pleasing crinkly appearance.

The quantity of feathers and pelts needed to dress even a moderately sized *ibutho* reflected a very considerable slaughter of wildlife, and indeed many of the rarer items were acquired by the Zulu kings as tribute from neighbouring subject chiefdoms, notably the Thonga from the areas around St Lucia Bay, which were particularly rich in bird life. Although it was the habit of successive kings to distribute pelts and feathers to the *amabutho*, there were seldom enough to go round, and it fell to ordinary members to provide the appointed costumes themselves. Each costume represented considerable effort and expense, and for this reason – together with the impracticality of wearing them for long periods – most Zulu men did not wear their costumes in battle. Instead, they assembled in a war-dress which was a greatly reduced version of their ceremonial uniforms. Brushes of cow-tails around the arms or, particularly, the legs remained popular, and some men retained their headbands, perhaps with a characteristic feather or two thrust in. Personal choice seems to have been a deciding factor here, and senior men were generally more conservative – and therefore less inclined to reflect regimental distinctions – than younger ones. It may also be that men wore more into action in the early campaigns of the war, or if they lived closer to the scene of operations. The heaviest items, such as the great mantles of cow-tails, were generally left at home (although a lighter variant, with just a few tails covering the chest, shoulders and back, may have been retained by some), and lighter versions retained. Most men also took the precaution of privately procuring before the shooting started necklaces containing charms and ritual medicines to ward off harm and evil.

It also seems that many men of rank wore distinctive items reflecting their status. *Amakhosi* might wear a mantle of leopard-skin, known as a *mabatha*, which was proscribed to all except those of chiefly blood, while junior members of their families confined themselves to leopard-skin *amabeshu* buttock-covers. Crane feathers and lourie feathers were also indicative of status. Many senior men wore loin-coverings consisting of finely worked monkey- and cat-skins arranged to encircle the waist like a kilt.

For those in the youngest *amabutho*, such as the iNgobamakhosi and uVe, young men who had as yet few assets of their own in civilian life and enjoyed little demonstrable status, it seems to have been common to go into battle wearing little more than their every-day loin coverings. Nevertheless, at least one British survivor of iSandlwana thought that the men of the young *ibutho* who pursued him through the Manzimnyama valley were all wearing a single small red feather in their hair, and it seems that among most *amabutho* enough items were retained that, together with the shield-pattern, it remained easy enough for fellow Zulus to recognise their allegiance.

Wagons and Laagers

In many respects the question of transport largely dictated Lord Chelmsford's strategies during the invasion of Zululand. Unlike its Zulu counterpart, which was accustomed to moving freely across difficult terrain, and carried only limited supplies with it, the British Army had to transport everything it needed to sustain and house itself. Tents, equipment, ammunition, food and even water all had to be dragged along with the invading armies on a daily basis, and the lines of advance were largely dictated by the existence of viable tracks. The physical requirement of wagons was enormous: an infantry battalion (800 men plus headquarters detachment and band) required seventeen wagons just to carry its equipment, without the added necessity of food. Chelmsford had originally intended to invade with five offensive columns, but the difficulties in obtaining enough wagons forced him to reduce it to three, with two in support. Even so, Pearson's column at the beginning of the war included 384 wagons and 24 carts and 3,128 oxen to pull them. Durnford's column was originally intended for defence but even so had 30 wagons, 480 oxen and 350 mules. Glyn's column had 220 wagons, 82 carts and 1,507 oxen, Wood's column 41 wagons, 5 carts and 260 oxen, and Rowlands' column 17 wagons, 2 carts and 150 oxen. Under normal circumstances each wagon required a span of 16 oxen, yoked in pairs, to pull it, but the spans were sometimes doubled along difficult stretches of road or at drifts. When he began his advance on the coast, Colonel Pearson split his column in two in order to manage it better – the first section alone, which included just 50 of his wagons, took up more than 5 miles of road. It took hours to manoeuvre wagons across even the narrowest of streams, and throughout the war the British advanced at the speed of the oxen, and considered a march of 5 or 6 miles a day a good rate. Supply convoys – taking up food and ammunition, bringing down empty wagons – trailed in the wake of each column, and escorting them was considered an onerous and dull duty, despite the fact that they remained vulnerable to attack (as happened to the 80th's supplies at Ntombe on 12 March). During the second invasion the 2nd Division and Flying Column halted their advance for several days in the first week of June to send back wagons *en masse* and refill them; at the same time the 1st Division on the coast had been starved of transport necessities largely to facilitate the advance of the other columns. For the 1st Division this meant a painfully slow crawl forward by way of supply depots which had to be established in advance.

Although the British Army was equipped with mule-drawn 'General Service' wagons, there were far too few of these in southern Africa when the war began and the military authorities were forced to hire civilian wagons, usually at inflated rates. The indigenous ox-wagon was an enormous beast, 18 feet long with a maximum rear axle span of 5 feet 10 inches. The rear wheel was over 5 feet in diameter and the front one just under 4, and the wagon weighed 3000lb. Fully loaded, it could carry an impressive 8,000lb on a good road – sadly Zululand had no good roads, and the average load during the campaign was 3,000lb. Most civilian wagons were painted in jaunty colours – green bodywork and red wheels – in lead paints which helped to preserve the wood. The load was either open to the elements on 'buck wagons', in which case the load was protected by a tarpaulin, or covered by a canvas tent or half-tent stretched over wooden hoops. Each wagon with its team took up a minimum of 32 yards of road, often more under an inexperienced driver. The oxen were managed by African *voorloopers*, who walked alongside cracking a long whip with remarkable dexterity, and in order to manage the unwieldy convoys the Army employed a 'conductor' for every ten wagons. In order to keep the oxen healthy they needed to graze for eight hours a day, and rest for eight more – which left just eight for working. Any attempt to interfere with the mathematics of this equation usually led to oxen dying in large quantities from over-work.

At the end of each day's march the wagons had to be parked in some manner which would make them easy to protect. On the Cape Frontier from the late eighteenth century the Boer farmers had drawn their wagons into a circle – known as a laager – for defensive purposes and during the Great Trek the laager had assumed a central role in their military operations. At Vechtkop in 1836 and again at Ncome (Blood River) in 1838 small numbers of Boers had been able to defeat much larger African armies by fighting from within the protective circle of the laager. At the beginning of the Zulu war many settlers advised Lord Chelmsford to adopt a similar strategy. Although his failure to do so has been held against him, the

British columns in 1879 posed genuine challenges which had not troubled the often smaller and more mobile Boer *commandos*. At the battle of Ncome, for example, Andries Pretorius's laager consisted of 64 wagons; at the battle of kwa-Gingindlovu on 2 April 1879 Chelmsford's laager was double that. Chelmsford's initial plan was to simply park the wagons in each camp, then deploy from there with his troops to fight. The lessons of iSandlwana and Rorke's Drift – where an open camp was carried by storm in one case but a secure position was not – changed this just days into the war. Nevertheless, the practical difficulties of manoeuvring hundreds of wagons into an effective line remained, and the British struggled to adapt the laager concept to their own military thinking. They found it much easier to construct and defend square laagers than the traditional Boer circular variety, since this required less precision in managing the wagons and still allowed straight lines for troops to defend with concentrated firepower. The wagons were usually parked *en echelon*, with the *disselboom* (pole) of each wagon trailed outwards at an angle. Sometimes the traces and yokes were simply laid out in front of the wagon to provide an obstacle to any attack; often the laager itself was entrenched. In his camp at Khambula Evelyn Wood entrenched his laagers by cutting the turf and topsoil in a great line around the perimeter, and piling it up beneath the wagon-beds. During the battle on 29 March his infantry actually knelt under the wagons, behind the shallow rampart, or in the wagon-beds themselves. Lord Chelmsford, however, preferred to throw up a deep straight trench, 4 or 5 feet deep, around the perimeter some 15 yards in front of the wagons on all sides. The earth from the ditch was thrown up to form a rampart inside. During battle the transport animals and reserve troops were secured inside the laager itself, while the infantry formed up in the space between the wagons and the ramparts.

Even this compromise could not be easily realised, as Captain Molyneux wrote of the end of the first day's march of the Eshowe relief column: 'that night the wagon drivers, who had no practice in laagering, got so out of hand that the laager was made anyhow, and it would only hold one third of our oxen. So much for our first laager on our first trek.'[273]

The remaining oxen had to be left outside the laager that night, while the interior remained a jumble of animals and carts parked in confusion. Yet the British soon became more adept at making their form of laager, and while they were still unwieldy their military effectiveness remained inviolate. Just days later these same troops defeated the Zulu at kwaGingindlovu, and no properly constructed laager was ever overrun throughout the war.[274]

Wales and the Anglo-Zulu War

In the popular imagination the principality of Wales will probably always be associated with the Anglo-Zulu War, but in fact the image of 'brave little Welshmen from the valleys singing *Men of Harlech*' as they manned the barricades is almost entirely anachronistic and has more to do with the efforts of Sir Stanley Baker and Ivor Emmanuel in the 1960s and the battlefield tourism industry of today than with the reality of 1879.

The impression is fuelled by the obvious regional origins of today's Royal Welsh regiment, the successor to the old 24th. Yet in 1879 the 24th had only recently taken the first steps of its long association with Wales, and the connection was certainly not reflected in the regional origin of the men in its ranks.

The 24th was first raised by Sir Edward Deering in Kent on 28 March 1689. In 1782 a royal warrant decreed that all British regiments not already having some county affiliation within England should be given one; those regiments which received a new regimental title as a result included the 6th Regiment, which received the subsidiary title of the 1st Warwickshires, and the 24th, which became the 2nd Warwickshires. The 24th was ordered to establish a recruiting detachment in the Warwickshire town of Tamworth, although from the 1790s regiments were authorised to raise recruits wherever they could across the country. The 24th was initially a single-battalion regiment but in 1756 it raised a second battalion which was redesignated as a separate regiment – the 6th Foot – in 1759. The second battalion was reformed in Warwick in 1804 for the exigencies of the campaigns against Napoleon, but was disbanded in 1814. It was reformed in Sheffield in 1858 after the demands of the Crimean War and the Indian Mutiny had come close to overstretching the existing military establishment.

The Regiment's association with Brecon began in 1873 when the government of the day reorganised the Army establishment, dividing Great Britain and Ireland into military districts and subdistricts, and insisting that a brigade depot be established in each district. The depot companies of two regular battalions of the line were to be based at each depot, and command of all local volunteer and militia units was to be given to the colonel of the brigade depot. The 24th Regiment, notwithstanding its historic Warwickshire associations, was attached to the twenty-fifth subdistrict, which encompassed the counties of Cardigan, Radnor, Brecon and Monmouth. (At the time Monmouth was a border county – it was not redesignated as Welsh until the local government reorganisation of 1976.)

The appointment of a depot served to give each battalion a fixed administrative base but it did not unduly reflect its patterns of recruitment, nor were the service battalions often posted there. The 1st Battalion, 24th Regiment, spent much of the 1870s in Mediterranean garrisons – Malta and Gibraltar – before being dispatched directly to South Africa in November 1874. The 2nd Battalion was based in Aldershot in 1874, Dover from August 1875 and Chatham from 1877 prior to its departure for the Cape in February 1878. Throughout that time both battalions continued to receive recruits through the efforts of recruiting sergeants across the country, although there had been a slight increase in recruits from the area covered by the district depot as a result of its association with the local militia, some members of which, like Alfred Henry Hook, opted to go on to join the regular Army.

By the beginning of the Anglo-Zulu campaign in January 1879 neither battalion had spent time in Brecon. The 1st Battalion, moreover, still contained a high proportion of older, experienced men who had joined under the 'long service' system that had prevailed before the establishment of the Brecon depot. The recent time spent at home by the 2nd Battalion was reflected in a higher proportion of young recruits who had joined under the more attractive 'short service' system. Since the 1st Battalion had been at the Cape, a number of men had left it on the expiry of their term of enlistment, and had been replaced by drafts from home; despite this, any marginal increase in the Welsh character of the Regiment had fallen rather to the 2nd Battalion.

In fact, however, where records are available – and they are not always complete or reliable – they suggest there were very few Welshmen in either battalion during the war. Of the men of the 2/24th who defended Rorke's Drift (B Company, together with a handful of patients in the hospital) whose regional origins are known with any certainty, 62 were from England (including 5 from Monmouthshire), 25 were from Ireland and 17 from Wales. Of the rest, one had been born in Canada and another in India, presumably to English parents. Even this figure probably reflects a marginally higher proportion of Welshmen than the average within the Army as a whole, however. Nor do the origins of men of the Company who received the Victoria Cross after the battle reflect any emphasis on Welsh origins: Lieutenant Gonville Bromhead was born in France to members of an old Lincolnshire family, Corporal William Allan was born in Northumbria to Scottish parents (and considered himself 'a Scotchman' by birth), while Private Fred Hitch was a Londoner, Private Alfred Henry Hook was born in Gloucestershire and Private William Jones was born in Evesham (although there is a family tradition he was in fact born in Bristol). Two other privates were born in Monmouthshire – Robert Jones in Penrose, Raglan, and John Williams (whose real name was Fielding) in Abergavenny, a town now considered decidedly Welsh. John Fielding's father was in fact Irish, however, having emigrated to Wales to escape the horrors of the potato famines. Nor can the preponderance of names commonly associated with Wales be taken at face value: Jones and Williams are of course equally common English names, while Private Thomas

Griffith – the 1st Battalion's VC holder, killed at iSandlwana – had been born in Ireland and enlisted in Tamworth.

As the figures suggest, both battalions of the 24th largely reflected the general pattern of regional origins within the British Army at the time; the majority of them were English, many of them were Irish, and some were Scottish and Welsh. A similar pattern prevailed in other battalions who fought in Zululand, who similarly recruited widely whatever their county affiliations, and there were a number of Welshmen among them, too, as letters from serving soldiers published in Welsh-language newspapers attest.

Following the destruction of the 1/24th at iSandlwana replacements were hurried out from drafts appointed from no fewer than eleven Line battalions of very mixed origins. The 24th's lasting associations with Wales truly date from a new wave of Army reorganisation instituted in April 1881 when the old Regimental numbers were discontinued and new local titles allocated. The 1st and 2nd Battalions, based in Colchester and Secunderbad, were now designated, in recognition of their permanent depot, the 1st and 2nd Battalions, South Wales Borderers. At the same time the old regimental march, *Warwickshire Lads*, was ordered to be replaced with *Men of Harlech*. Not until 1936 were the old Regimental Colours – carried at the battle of Chillianwallah in the Sikh Wars – transferred from St Mary's Church in Warwick, where they had been laid up, to Brecon Cathedral. Only in the twentieth century, too, did the regiment begin to assume the characteristically Welsh stamp its successor, the Royal Welsh, enjoys today.

War Correspondents

The beginning of the invasion of Zululand largely caught the mainstream British press by surprise. Even those journalists from the London papers who had been present in southern Africa to cover the end of the 9th Cape Frontier War, and who heard the widespread military gossip about a possible Zulu war long before Frere had actually delivered his ultimatum, were taken by surprise by the outbreak when it came. Most had already moved on to other imperial flashpoints around the globe, particularly to Afghanistan where the 2nd Afghan War had broken out in November 1878. Only one professional London journalist, the enigmatic Charles Norris-Newman,[275] was on hand to cover the beginning of the war, and by choosing to accompany the Centre Column he scooped his colleagues in spectacular style – he was present throughout the iSandlwana campaign and, having accompanied Dartnell's foray to the Mangeni gorge, he lived to tell the tale. He did not, of course, enjoy his exclusive rights for long, for when news of iSandlwana reached London on 11 February it burst like a bombshell in the offices of the Empire's most prestigious newspapers, sending editors scurrying to dispatch their best men to the front. By the time Norris-Newman made his way again to the Thukela to join the start of Lord Chelmsford's Eshowe relief expedition at the end of March, he found a veritable gaggle of Britain's best-known war correspondents already waiting for him:

I found that I had been preceded by Mr Francis of *The Times*, Melton Prior, *Illustrated London News*, Fripp, the *Graphic*, Dormer, *Cape Argus*, and Mr W. Pearce, who represented the *Daily Telegraph* until the arrival of Mr P. Robinson from Afghanistan. Other English, Colonial, and Provincial papers were also represented.[276]

Francis Francis of *The Times* and Prior of the *Illustrated London News* were two of the three best-known war-correspondents of the day; the third, Archibald Forbes of the *Daily News* was even then on the steamer from Burma, where he had cut short a fact-finding mission to hurry to Zululand. In addition, most newspapers at the time had an open editorial policy and happily printed contributions from amateur correspondents; most commanders were prepared to allow officers under their command to write for the press on the tacit understanding that they did not criticise the conduct of the campaign.[277]

Archibald Forbes, a Scot from Morayshire, was then at the height of his powers. As a young man he had run away to join the Army and had

served in the Royal Dragoons; he found the constraints of military life irksome but it had left him with a deep sympathy for the soldier's lot which had informed his later career. Once free of the Army he moved to London and secured his first freelance commission as a journalist, and when the Franco-Prussian War broke out in 1870 he managed to secure a post to cover it. The war made his reputation; he managed to write home reports from inside Paris and from alongside the advancing Prussian armies – at one point he watched from a distance as the young French Prince Imperial narrowly escaped the effects of a shelling – and he had covered the rise and fall of the Paris Commune. He had gone on to report the Carlist wars in Spain, the Indian famine of 1874, the Serbian War of 1877 and the Russo-Turkish War. He had just recently accompanied the advance of British troops through the Khyber Pass and the storming of the fortress of Ali Musjid; when the Afghan War appeared – erroneously, as it turned out – to be won, Forbes had gone to Burma, only to change course on hearing of iSandlwana.

Forbes, Prior and Francis were all on hand to cover the expedition to bury the dead at iSandlwana on 21 May. Ironically, Prior had not, after all, accompanied the Eshowe expedition. No less experienced than Forbes – he was a veteran of the Asante, Balkan and Cape Frontier campaigns – he had had a premonition of his death and at the last minute refused to cross the Thukela; he had, he said, given his position to a friend who was duly killed at the battle of kwaGingindlovu.[278] Prior was not a journalist but the leading war-artist of his day; in the 1870s it was not possible for the printing process to reproduce photographs in newspapers, and instead illustrated papers relied on complex woodblock engravings, worked up by engravers in England working directly from sketches produced in the field. Such work required not merely artistic flair but an eye for the newsworthy and the ability to work fast under difficult conditions; Prior's technique was to produce pencil drawings from life, then work up ink-and-wash copies that night to submit for publication – it was not unknown for him to produce half-a-dozen sketches of some important incidents in a single night, working by lamplight alone.

The sight of the devastated field at iSandlwana had a profoundly unsettling effect on those who witnessed it, and the impressions of Forbes and Prior largely shaped the public perception of the Zulu campaign. Forbes's haunting description of the months-old British dead was one of the finest pieces of journalism to emerge from the war, and it provoked in his readers not merely horror at the true face of colonial warfare but the desire for British honour to be avenged – and later a more subtle questioning of the policies that had resulted in the invasion in the first place:

In this ravine dead men lay thick, mere bones, with toughened discoloured skin, like leather covering them, and clinging tightly to them, the flesh all wasted away. Some were almost wholly dismembered, heaps of yellow clammy bones. I forbear to describe their faces, with their blackened features and beards bleached by rain and sun. Every man had been disembowelled. Some were scalped, and others subject to yet ghastlier mutilations. The clothes had lasted better than the poor bodies they covered, and helped to keep the skeletons together . . .[279]

Forbes's eloquence was matched by Prior's acute artist's eye – but the grinning skulls which stared so accusingly from the latter's sketches were adroitly removed by the engravers before publication.

While Victorian war correspondents were 'embedded' to a degree their modern counterparts might envy – most befriended officers in the units they encountered and Norris-Newman unceremoniously attached himself to the mess of the 3rd NNC – they made no pretence of that other great modern virtue, impartiality, at least not when writing about British campaigns. Many of them came from the same background and shared the same values as the soldiers they lived among, and they knew in any case that their white skins would mark them down as enemies by the people whose country was being invaded. As a result many of them had few qualms about taking an active part in the fighting. At the battle of kwaGingindlovu Norris-Newman and a colleague potted happily at a group of Zulus sheltering behind clumps of long grass, and after the battle went over to collect trophies from the dead men; F.R. MacKenzie of the *Standard* was generally considered to have gone too far, however, when he ran down a wounded Zulu and beat the man's brains out with his own knobkerry.

Correspondents knew, too, that personal incidents added flavour to dry accounts of political wrangles and military manoeuvres, and they did not hesitate to cultivate something of a cult of personality, weaving their own adventures in among their reports. And many of them had adventures in Zululand. On 3 July Charles Fripp, the war artist of the *Graphic* – chiefly remembered now for his iconic painting of iSandlwana – was busily sketching British mounted troops returning across the White Mfolozi river after a skirmish before oNdini when Redvers Buller, riding past, ordered him to the rear. Fripp was too engrossed in his drawing to notice who gave the order – and Buller habitually wore civilian clothes – and was indignant at being addressed like a common soldier. When Lord Beresford passed by a few minutes later, his back smothered in the blood of a man he had rescued, Fripp angrily demanded to know who had insulted him and Beresford – a notorious bruiser known as 'Battling Bill' – took offence. He dismounted and demanded an apology, Fripp refused and, even as Zulu marksmen came down to the far bank in the wake of the retreat and began shooting at them, the two squared up to each other. Fripp made up in enthusiasm what he lacked in height and skill and when he landed a kick on his opponent's shin Beresford collapsed into laughter just as Fripp's fellow correspondents, Forbes and Prior, arrived to drag Fripp away.

Both Prior and Forbes were destined to have adventures, too, at Ulundi. Prior had sketched the battle from inside the square – to his horror he had lost a sketch-book full of complete sketches, but one of Chelmsford's staff had loaned him another – and had then followed the rush of staff officers to the oNdini homestead itself. Here he had become separated from his colleagues and was busily sketching the huts as they went up in flames when he noticed a Zulu lurking among them. Realising that he was alone, and that he had left his horse by the gate, he hurried away, convinced that he was being stalked; when he got back safely to the British square, watching officers confirmed that a group of Zulus had chased him all the way. Prior promptly sketched the incident in suitably dramatic terms, with himself in the foreground, and it appeared in the down-market *Penny Illustrated*.

Forbes's turn came after the battle. Desperate to send his despatches home quickly, he asked if he might send them with Chelmsford's courier. To his surprise Chelmsford replied that he had no intention of sending a courier that afternoon, and Forbes snapped 'Then sir, I shall start at once!' It was, he recognised as soon as he had spoken, a foolhardy exercise; the nearest telegraph was at Landman's Drift on the Ncome river, it was late afternoon, and the country was alive with parties of Zulus retreating from the battle. It was dark even before Forbes had climbed the long escarpment from the White Mfolozi valley, and in the distance great circles of fire marked the positions of the burning royal homesteads. For a while he became lost but the great lines of tracks made by the advancing column were easy enough to see once the moon rose and he soon regained the way. At the first fort on the line of communication he begged another horse and rode through the night, exchanging horses six times. He finally arrived at Landman's Drift in the early afternoon of the following day (5 July) having covered 110 miles in 20 hours. He had the satisfaction of knowing his account of Ulundi was the first to reach London, and his ride became a story in itself. It was christened 'the Ride of Death' and was the subject of a spirited engraving, and one of Forbes's admirers rather over-enthusiastically urged that he be awarded the Victoria Cross.

With that final victory the London professionals began to drift away from Zululand, leaving the closing shots of the war to the locals. Victorian war correspondents were very much men of their time and class, and they wrote for the educated middle and upper classes at home who were, by and large, imperialist by outlook. Yet the journalists who covered the war in 1879 were by no means immune to the uncomfortable truths that underpinned it. Forbes left Natal in a flurry of settler outrage following some outspoken comments about colonial attitudes towards the African population; back in London, he would become one of Lord Chelmsford's most persistent and influential critics, picking over the details of the conduct of the campaign in general and iSandlwana in particular. Francis Francis of *The Times* declared the war 'unjust' – no insignificant judgement from the representative of a paper which had almost single-handedly exposed the mismanagement of the Crimean War a generation before. Charles Fripp set a tone which became increasingly widespread among the general public when, in a memoir written in 1900, he wrote, 'whatever the rights and wrongs which brought on the war, these same brave Zulus died resisting an invasion of their country and homes. Naked savages as they were, let us honour them.'[280]

War Cries

In an interview with the Natal press after the disaster, Lieutenant Erskine, who had fought at iSandlwana with the 1st NNC and survived, was asked if he had heard the Zulus shouting out war cries during the battle; ' ''Usutu'', he replied, 'and ''Qoka a Amatye''. I don't know what they meant by calling ''Usutu'', but every time a white man was stabbed to death the cry was ''Usutu''.'[281]

War cries have of course been important to men in battle since the dawn of humanity, not merely as a means of focusing anger and aggression in the excitement of battle, but as a means too of reinforcing common allegiances, and they were particularly so to the Zulus for whom a sense of common identity was an essential part of the psychology of warfare.

The cry recognised by Erskine – 'uSuthu!' – was in fact a word associated with King Cetshwayo from his youth. During the succession crisis of the 1850s both Cetshwayo and his rival, Prince Mbuyazi, gathered factions about themselves.

Taking their cue from a recent campaign by King Mpande across the Khahlamba mountains, which had returned home with a rich booty of Sotho cattle, Cetshwayo's followers called themselves uSuthu, a term which not only suggested that they were as plentiful as those cattle but also had connotations of military supremacy. Prince Mbuyazi's followers called themselves the iziGqoza, from a verb meaning to drip, a wry acknowledgement that while they were not so numerous there was a steady and ultimately overwhelming trickle of support in their favour. Sadly the iziGqoza's vanities proved largely unfounded, and Cetshwayo's uSuthu had spectacularly defeated and largely destroyed them at the battle of 'Ndondakusuka in December 1856; thereafter *uSuthu* became the cry of those who identified themselves with the new order in Zululand. During the civil wars which followed the British invasion, royalists again identified themselves by the term, and during the Poll Tax disturbances in 1906 *uSuthu* was used as a rallying cry by the protestors, many of whom had, historically, never been part of the old Zulu kingdom, but who none the less wished to associate themselves with its heroic traditions.

Every Zulu *ibutho* also had its own particular chants and cries, although traditionally these were used at the climax of the ceremonies in which the men were prepared for war rather than in battle itself. None the less, certain words and phrases were popular among many of the *amabutho*, recalling as they did heroic incidents or boasts peculiar to each one; the other cry Erskine heard that day was '*Ngqaka amatshe phezulu*', meaning 'catch the hailstones!', the boast of the uKhandempemvu *ibutho* that they would treat enemy bullets as if they were nothing more than hailstones, to be turned aside by their shields.

When many Zulus stabbed an enemy in battle they also cried out '*Inkomo ka baba!*', meaning 'my father's cow!', an allusion to the cattle stabbed to appease the ancestral spirits on ceremonial occasions. Others called out '*Ji!*', a universal exclamation of exultation. At the battle of Khambula wagon-drivers in the British camp heard the Zulus calling out ominously as they advanced, 'We are the boys from iSandlwana!'

Members of the British Army have never used a single national war cry, although some regiments have particular words and phrases, steeped in regimental tradition, which have been used as a rallying cry, such as the old Gaelic war cry of the 88th Regiment (Connaught Rangers) '*Faugh a Balloch!*', meaning 'Clear the way!'. More typically, the British soldier has been known to curse and swear in the heat of battle, and indeed there is a telling story (probably apocryphal) from the Maori Land Wars in New Zealand in which, after one engagement, the Maori are said to have grumbled at the ill-manners of the British red-coats, 'who ought not to have sworn at us so, as we bore them no ill – we were merely fighting them'.

There was swearing, too, in Zululand, as Sir Garnet Wolseley noted:

> The Revd Mr George Smith who was at the defence of Rorke's Drift is reported to have corrected the men for cursing whilst the fight was at its height. 'Don't swear, men, don't swear, but shoot them, boys, shoot them.'[282]

'What do you come here for?': Popular Zulu Defiance

On 12 January 1879, as British troops prepared to attack the followers of *inkosi* Sihayo in the first action of the war, an exchange took place which summed up the respective attitudes of the combatants. According to George Hamilton Browne, an officer in the 3rd NNC, 'A voice hailed us asking by whose orders we came. My interpreter and right-hand man (Capt. R. Duncombe) answered "by the orders of the Great White Queen", and the enemy, or those of them who had exposed themselves, at once ran back to cover'.[283] Hamilton Browne was a man who enjoyed a good story, and this incident might perhaps have grown in the telling, although the essence is confirmed by a staff officer, Captain Henry Parr:

> As the Zulus saw the mounted men ... they began to taunt us, making their voices sound through the still morning air in the

curious way natives can. 'What were we doing riding down there?' 'We had better try and come up.' 'Were we looking for a place to build our kraals?' etc, etc. This badinage, which was accompanied by a few shots by way of emphasis, did not last long ...[284]

These exchanges cut to the heart of the false assumptions held by the British with regard to Zulu popular support for the war. So successful was Frere's propaganda war before the campaign began – and so readily believed was it by British troops who were convinced that the war represented a struggle between civilisation and savagery – that the British entered Zululand under the illusion that King Cetshwayo's administration was an unpopular one. The king himself had been portrayed as a tyrant, his councillors and generals as villainous die-hards who manipulated the natural war-like spirit of the people for their own ends; implicit in this view was a conviction that the population of Zululand would readily see the righteousness of the British intervention and would readily submit to British authority. In return they would recognise and appreciate the advantages of Christianity, of European concepts of justice, and of the introduction to Zululand of a cash economy.

Much of the evidence about the Zulu public's real reaction to the invasion is obscured by the contemporary British insistence of portraying them as an anonymous, faceless mass – a sea of charging warriors rather than an accumulation of individuals with views and opinions of their own. Nevertheless enough evidence survives to make it clear that ordinary Zulus simply did not want to buy the package offered to them by the British at bayonet point. It is true that a ritual exchange of insults – as at Sihayo's stronghold – was a recognised element in the Zulu way of making war, but the voices which emerge, even under such circumstances, give expression to more than just ritual challenge. They reveal a very real sense of a popular indignation which pervaded Zulu society, at least in the early part of the war. Ordinary Zulu people were prepared to express their defiance and rejection of British

attitudes, even under circumstances of considerable danger to themselves. On 13 January, for example, a patrol of mounted men under the command of Major Percy Barrow was scouting ahead of the coastal column, which was just then crossing the Thukela river, when a party of Zulu scouts was spotted. A skirmish ensued and several men were captured, one of whom asked, after being disarmed, 'What do you red-jackets want in our country?'

It was not merely a rhetorical question, for the issue genuinely concerned many ordinary Zulus at the time of the invasion who could not understand what business the British had to cross into an independent sovereign state. Most of the Zulus were deeply conscious that, unlike the African population of Natal who had given away their independence to the whites, Zululand was ruled by laws and traditions which were embodied in the person of the king and greatly valued, and it acknowledged the superior authority of none. The British had no place to come there and dictate to the Zulu people; they were not wanted. Nor were the Zulus – as the British had fondly assumed they would be – in the slightest bit overawed by the sight of white faces, red-coats or modern weapons of war. Those early prisoners captured by Barrow were taken to Pearson's camp at Fort Tenedos, and during interrogation one self-assured individual was knocked down by his guard. Despite his helpless position – a prisoner in the middle of the British camp – he was so indignant at this treatment that he stood up, twirled his impressive moustache, pointed at the distant hills and said 'You have taken me, but there are plenty more waiting for you over there'.

On the morning of 2 June, when British troops recovered the body of the Prince Imperial of France from the muddy donga by the Tshotshosi river where he had been killed the day before, they found an ancient Zulu woman who had been abandoned in the nearby homestead of a local head-man, Sobhuza. This old woman, scarcely less vulnerable than Barrow's prisoner, also had little time for the invaders, according to Captain Montague: 'They killed your great Inkoss; they are gone now to the king's kraal to fight you white men. What do you come here for? We don't want you. This is Zululand. Keep to your own side!'[285]

A few days later, when Zulu envoys arrived at the camp at Nondweni to try to open negotiations to bring the war to a close, Montague noted the same refrain:

'What do you English want here?' they growled. 'We don't want you; go away! We want to be friends with such a great people. Tell us what you want, and go away!'[286]

Montague himself was both amused and confused by the general refusal of the Zulus to see the fact that seemed self-evident to him and almost everyone else among the British – that the British were clearly their superiors, both materially and morally. Even after the battle of Ulundi, Montague noted that the Zulu sense of self-belief remained largely undaunted. He was witness to the surrender of a member of the Zulu Royal House, Prince Mahanana kaMpande, and was clearly unsettled by Mahanana's undented composure:

An officer, wishing to possess something of his as a memento, asked him to give him the rough stick he carried. Mahanana raised his eyes for a second, and replied in a low, soft voice, 'That stick has touched my hand, and there may be some of my own royal sweat upon it. I am a king, and nothing of a king's can touch a stranger and not be defiled!' The officer, foiled about the stick, asked for the tiny snuff-box he carried in his ear. Without a word the Zulu raised his hand and took it out, with hardly a motion of his body; then he held it out, and let the little bit of horn drop in the Englishman's hand. The latter, in return, brought out some sticks of tobacco and a couple of boxes of matches, both worth their weight in gold in a Zulu's eyes, and offered them to Mahanana. He quietly held out one hand, and as the present fell into his palm, just passed it over to his follower sitting next to him, as if the things were utterly beneath

his notice. And yet the man was a prisoner, and beaten. It is amusing to talk to the Zulus; they are so magnificent in their ignorance, and so full of their own superiority.[287]

Perhaps the most entertaining exchange, and one which reveals best the gulf in the respective perceptions of the two sides, took place on 2 May on the slopes of the Hlobane mountain between an unknown Zulu and the Boer Piet Uys Jnr. Hlobane had, of course, been a stronghold of the abaQulusi section, and had been resolutely defended by them during the action of 28 March in which Uys's father had been killed. Following the British success at Khambula the following day, however, the abaQulusi had dispersed and the Hlobane complex had been largely abandoned apart from a few men hiding out in the caves there. According to a report in the *Natal Mercury*,

Volunteer Burgher Piet Uys, jun., had a parley with one of the enemy, whom he saw peeping out of a cave in the mountain. When the Zulu was asked why he did not come into the camp and surrender, he said he did not require our protection. When told that he would be killed if he continued fighting, he asked in return, if he (Mr Uys) did not run the same risk? When the Zulu was asked when the army was coming to attack the camp again he replied 'Not so long as you remain in your earthworks; but as soon as you come out we will come and fight you; at the Zlobane we killed lots of you, and two of your great men, and we can do it again' ... Some of the patrol fired a shot in the distance and the parley ended.[288]

It is perhaps fair to say that by that stage of the war there was an element of bravado in such defiance. The heavy losses in the battles of late January had come as a shock to the Zulu population at large, but the knowledge that they had won a great victory at iSandlwana buoyed up their resolve. The twin defeats at Khambula and kwaGingindlovu, at the end of March and beginning of April, had been deeply unsettling, however, since the Zulu army had again suffered heavily and on both occasions had been undeniably beaten. While many persisted in the view that they could still beat the British fairly, in the open, as they had at iSandlwana, there was a growing sense of war-weariness, exacerbated by the inexorable British advance into the heart of the country. The Zulu army still retained enough determination to defend oNdini itself, but after the battle of Ulundi on 4 July it was clear that the war was lost. British patrols moving through the country in July and August found few signs of resistance, and indeed often encountered an open curiosity about the conquerors. Nevertheless, as Montague noted, the reality of military defeat had in no way reconciled ordinary Zulus to the imposition of a colonial lifestyle:

Their independence was capital, and almost laughable. Not one would sell us anything except at the most exorbitant of prices. They said out, without the smallest hesitation, 'What more do you English want? You have beaten us fairly – we own that you are better at fighting than we are – so now go away!'

When I asked them if they wanted to go on with the war, they shook their heads and said, grinning broadly, 'No, no; you kill too many of us, it isn't fair.'

Another added, 'You put iron all round your laager, and our bullets struck and fell back. I saw them.'

'Well, do you want peace?' I went on.

'Yes; of course', burst out half a dozen in chorus. 'You have beaten us – that is quite right; now go away!'[289]

Sadly, the reality of defeat was to bring about the eventual destruction of the very independence – of a way of life, and of spirit – which the Zulu people as a whole had fought so hard to retain.

Wives

For both sides the Anglo-Zulu War was a predominantly male affair. Although the character of the British and Zulu armies was very different – the one a self-contained professional body largely isolated from civilian society, the other a temporary mobilisation of civilian manpower for a military purpose – neither regarded campaign life as appropriate for women.

The British Army was a predominantly male preserve. It preferred to enlist unmarried men because they brought with them few emotional entanglements and no administrative complications. A recruit who admitted to having a wife might be refused, while serving soldiers were required to ask their commanding officer's permission to marry. It was often refused for it was felt that the Army functioned best with little emotional baggage. A very few wives were allowed to live with their husbands in the barracks 'on the strength'; they received half pay and rations in return for washing, cleaning and repairing the men's clothes. Although many colonels felt they were an asset to the regiment, curbing the worst excesses in the men's behaviour, there were in the 1870s no married quarters, and married men simply lived at one end of the barracks, their beds screened by blankets. The situation for senior NCOs was better – permission to marry was one of the perks of being a sergeant – but, ironically, given the huge social gulf which separated them, not much better for the officers. Here the unofficial rule was that 'subalterns cannot marry, captains may marry, majors should marry, colonels must marry'. Life as the wife of an officer was infinitely more private and genteel than it was for their counterparts married into the ranks but it carried with it both obligations and long periods of separation. The wives of senior officers were required to watch over the welfare of the rankers' wives and display a maternalistic interest in the regiment generally. Although officers did enjoy long periods of furlough on home postings, overseas postings often left wives at home. Although it was common for wives to accompany officers to India the climate dictated that most of them spent much of their time in the cool hill-stations while their husbands soldiered in the hot plains.

When a regiment was sent overseas on active service the other ranks were allowed to take a maximum of six wives per hundred men with them. These were chosen by ballot. In the first half of the nineteenth century it was quite common for wives to accompany their men to the front itself, although with the growing prevalence of colonial wars – fought out in uncompromising locations against determined enemies – this began to die out. None the less many battalions who fought in Zululand had brought their wives to southern Africa; the 1/24th had left theirs at the Cape when they were shipped to Natal to take part in the invasion. A number of the 3rd Regiment's wives, including famously Colonel Pearson's, had been left in Natal when the battalion crossed the border.

Among the Zulus, in contrast, warfare was a temporary state which merely separated men from their womenfolk for the duration of a particular campaign. None the less, while it lasted men were proscribed from having contact with their wives and girlfriends, largely because the process of ritual preparation was considered to unleash powerful spiritual forces which had to be contained within the all-male preserve of the *amabutho*. Once a man was cleansed and prepared for war he could not interact with women for fear not only of weakening his own state of spiritual readiness but also of spreading a dangerous taint throughout civilian society. He could not return to civilian life until the counterpart ceremonies were completed at the end of the campaign. Most Zulu campaigns, however, only lasted a matter of weeks.

Despite this, there are occasional references to women joining in when fighting occurred near their homes – some abaQulusi girls reputedly killed a white man who had become trapped between boulders in the cliffs of Hlobane – and non-combatants were known to go on to nearby hills to watch battles taking place in their vicinity. There were, moreover, particular rituals which Zulu wives were required to observe when their men were on campaign:

We must not forget the women-folk who were left behind. Married women always wear a skirt made of ox-hide, the hair having been scraped off. In ordinary life the upper edge of this is rolled outward, around the hips, but during war they turn the roll inside.

The young girls throw ashes over their bodies, a sign of mourning ... The old women take their brooms and run along the roads sweeping with them, thus indicating that they would make a clean sweep of their enemies in all directions.[290]

World Events, 1879

The British invasion of Zululand in 1879 was by no means the only important international event that year, even to the British. Indeed, one of the main reasons why the Disraeli administration had been reluctant to sanction military intervention in Zululand was the fact that British troops were already committed to a campaign in Afghanistan which, with regard to the broader security of the Empire, was regarded as an infinitely more important affair.

Afghanistan bordered British India to the northwest, and was considered by imperial theorists to control the gateway to and from central Asia. It was the route by which foreign invaders had entered India from the West since the days of Alexander the Great, and the British were concerned that the expansion of Tsarist Russia into Asia might lead Russia to challenge British supremacy in India. This fear had led to the first of many disastrous British interventions in Afghanistan in 1839–42, had influenced the British decision to support Turkey in the Crimea, and had resulted in the so-called 'Great Game' – the prolonged campaign of intrigue intended to secure India's north-western frontiers against Russian influence. In 1878 the British had become seriously alarmed when the Amir of Afghanistan, Sher Ali Khan, received a Russian envoy at his court in Kabul. The British demanded equal representation but a British envoy was turned away at the Khyber Pass. The British then declared war and in November 1878 three columns of British troops crossed the Afghan border. The Afghan forts in the Khyber Pass were quickly captured and over the following months the British occupied the cities of Jellelabad and Kandahar. Sher Ali died, and on 26 May 1879 his successor signed the treaty of Gandamak which guaranteed British diplomatic representation in Kabul.

A British envoy, Sir Louis Cavagnari, arrived in Kabul on 24 July 1879 but found the city tense and volatile. In September he was killed during an insurrection led by mutinous Afghan troops supported by the local population, and in response British troops again invaded Afghanistan. Kabul was occupied by Lord Roberts on 13 October, but the British found themselves facing widespread opposition across the country. Fighting continued throughout 1880 but in September the British were able to establish a more sympathetic regime in Kabul, and by April 1881 the last British troops had been withdrawn.

The 2nd Afghan War had proved prolonged and costly and the success of the outcome is debatable for although the British had, temporarily at least, established a more sympathetic regime in Kabul, their influence remained limited while that of the Russians had by no means been eliminated. The security of India's northwestern borders would continue to enjoy a greater priority for British imperial strategists than affairs in southern Africa, even allowing for the outbreak of the Anglo-Boer War in 1899.

British suspicions regarding Russian intentions were not without foundation, of course, and Tsarist Russia at the time had extensive ambitions in Asia. The Russo-Turkish War (1877–78) – fought out in the Balkans over the issue of Serbian independence from the Ottoman Empire – had only just ended, and in 1879 Russian troops began an invasion of Turkmenistan, which borders Afghanistan, modern Iran and Uzbekistan. The campaign culminated in a series of battles fought around the fortress of Goek Tepe which was stormed with great loss and brutality in January 1881.

In America the United States Government in 1879 was still largely preoccupied with the great move west, and with the suppression of the indigenous peoples which accompanied it. The war against the Sioux and other Great Plains groups had only recently been won; the spectacular defeat of George Armstrong Custer and his 7th Cavalry had taken place at Little Big Horn as recently as June 1876, while his nemesis, Crazy Horse, had been killed in September 1877. Sitting Bull was in exile in Canada, where he had fled in

1877, and he was not to return to the US until 1881. In Texas in 1879 the Apache chief Victorio had just embarked on a guerrilla campaign that was to last for several years, largely as a result of the skilful way he exploited the US–Mexican border.

In February 1879 a major war broke out in South America. A dispute between Chile and Bolivia over valuable nitrate resources (used both for fertiliser and to manufacture explosives) in the Atacama desert led to a political crisis which also embroiled Peru, an ally of Bolivia. Although major campaigns were fought out on land, the proximity of the Pacific Ocean coast meant that naval struggles soon assumed a strategic priority. Although Chile enjoyed supremacy both at sea and on land, the Peruvian ironclad *Huascar* severely disrupted Chilean shipping in a gallant series of hit-and-run attacks on vessels and ports. She was eventually run down and captured in the battle of Angamos on 8 October 1879, however. The defeat of the *Huascar* left the Chileans with unchallenged naval supremacy which allowed them to mount a successful invasion of Peru. The Peruvian capital Lima fell in January 1881 but Chile's attempts to control the Peruvian provinces had still not entirely succeeded when, after a further three years of fighting, peace was imposed by the treaty of Ancon in October 1883. Both Peru and Bolivia were forced to cede territory in return for an end to the Chilean occupation of Peru.

Curiously, there is a direct link between the *Huascar* and the Anglo-Zulu War. The *Huascar*, a turreted warship similar to the monitor type pioneered in the American Civil War, was commissioned by the Peruvian Government from Laird Brothers' shipyard in Birkenhead. During the Peruvian Civil War (which took place from 1877 until just prior to the war with Chile) the *Huascar* was seized by rebel forces and used to disrupt government shipping. In the course of this it attacked two British merchantmen. The Commander of the British Pacific Station, Algernon Roos de Horsey, was ordered to intercept the *Huascar*, which he did with two warships, HMS *Amethyst* and HMS *Shah* in the Bay of Pacocha on 29 May 1877. An afternoon of sporadic fighting followed in which the Peruvians manoeuvred to good effect and British shells – even when they hit their target – had little effect on the *Huascar*'s armour-plating. Commander de Horsey then took the bold step of authorising the use of a new weapon with which his ships were equipped – automotive torpedoes. These weapons, the first designed along modern torpedo principles, had never been used in action before, and legend has it that the captain of the *Amethyst* was so concerned that they might be illegal and inhumane that he requested confirmation of the order in writing. In the event the torpedoes fired by both British ships failed to hit their target and the *Huascar* escaped under cover of darkness shortly afterwards. She was forced to surrender to the Peruvian Government just two days later.

HMS *Shah* was returning to England at the end of her tour in the Pacific Station when she landed men in Natal in 1878 at Lord Chelmsford's request.

In Australia at the time of the invasion of Zululand the outlaw Ned Kelly was successfully robbing banks. After years of conflict with the authorities, Kelly had taken to the bush with a gang of supporters, and in October 1878 a fierce shoot-out with a police patrol at Stringybark Creek had left three policemen dead. With little to lose, Kelly began a campaign of daring robberies, 'bailing up' the banks at Euroa on 10 December 1878 and Jerilderie on 8 February 1879. The gang remained at large until the famous confrontation at the Glenrowan Inn on 27/8 July 1880 where Kelly, despite wearing a suit of home-made armour, was wounded and captured. The rest of his gang were killed. Kelly himself was tried and executed in Melbourne gaol on 11 November 1880.

Zibhebhu kaMaphitha

Zibhebhu kaMaphitha was arguably one of the greatest Zulu military commanders of his generation; he fought valiantly for Cetshwayo during the 1879 campaign, but later became a bitter opponent of the Royal House and was responsible for the king's spectacular defeat in the civil war of the 1880s.

Zibhebhu was himself *inkosi* of a section of the Royal House known as the Mandlakazi. His exact connection with the ruling lineage is obscure because it concerns the relationship between Zibhebhu's grandfather Sojiyisa and King Shaka's grandfather, *inkosi* Jama. Jama apparently took Sojiyisa – whose origins are difficult to determine – into his household and raised him as a son. He was regarded genealogically as a junior brother to Jama's heir, Senzangakhona (Shaka's father). When Sojiyisa grew to manhood, he established his own homestead in northern Zululand, not far from the Mkhuze river, which he called kwaMandlakazi – the place of the 'mighty seed' or 'great power'. His followers took the name Mandlakazi and enjoyed a status within the kingdom which reflected their close association with the House of Senzangakhona. After Sojiyisa's death his heir, Maphitha, became a firm friend and ally of King Shaka, and the Mandlakazi were appointed rulers of the northern marches of the kingdom on Shaka's behalf. Maphitha survived the culling of Shaka's supporters in the wake of the king's assassination and went on to become a councillor to both Dingane and Mpande. His support for Mpande during the various crises of his reign ensured that Maphitha remained one of the most powerful of the regional *isikhulu*, the 'great ones' of the nation, given a decisive voice in the affairs of state. Zibhebhu was born in 1841, Maphitha's senior son in his 'great house'. He was enrolled in Mpande's uMxapho *ibutho*, formed in 1861, and from an early age displayed a shrewd, ruthless and aggressive personality. During the 'war of the princes' between Cetshwayo and Mbuyazi in 1856, the support of the Mandlakazi played a decisive role in Cetshwayo's victory at the battle of 'Ndondakusuka. Zibhebhu himself would have been too young to have played a significant part in the conflict but was probably present as a mat-carrier. Cetshwayo expressed his gratitude in his friendship for the Mandlakazi heir apparent, and it is said that, later, when the elderly Maphitha became suspicious of his son's ambitions, it was Cetshwayo who intervened on Zibhebhu's behalf.

Both Mpande and Maphitha died in 1872, and Cetshwayo and Zibhebhu succeeded to the leadership of their respective houses at about the same time. Free from his father's constraints, Zibhebhu began to develop extensive trading contacts across northern Zululand and extending into Portuguese Mozambique. He formed close business associations with whites from Natal and the Transvaal, and in due course became more than usually at ease in the white world. He acquired and rode horses, was a good shot, and enjoyed the material products of white society; as an adult, despite his quiet and controlled manner, he would prove to be both ruthless and acquisitive.

In the tense run-up to the war of 1879, Zibhebhu argued against a direct rift with the British. As a realist, he undoubtedly feared for the consequences of a war, and he was no doubt troubled by the potential disruption of his trading empire. None the less, when war broke out Zibhebhu loyally joined the army Cetshwayo assembled at oNdini in the second week of January. Since he already enjoyed a reputation for his skill in military affairs, he was given command of the scouts during the advance to iSandlwana. Scouts were selected from among the most capable and dynamic men in the army, since they were expected not merely to watch for enemy movements but also to harass them where they could. On 21 January, when the army moved from its bivouac near Siphezi mountain to the Ngwebeni valley close to iSandlwana, it was a protective screen of Zibhebhu's scouts who drove off a patrol of British mounted infantry, and prevented them from exposing the Zulu strategy.

When the battle occurred at iSandlwana the following day, Zibhebhu was given command of the *amabutho* which constituted the Zulu reserve – the uThulwana, iNdlondlo, uDloko and iNdluyengwe. These were directed to cut the line of British retreat from iSandlwana to Rorke's Drift, which they successfully accomplished. Elements of the iNdluyengwe were detached to mop up British survivors at Sothondose's ('Fugitives') Drift. When Zibhebhu himself reached the river, believing that he had accomplished his orders and realising that the Natal border was now exposed, he left his command and crossed the river in search of abandoned cattle on the Natal bank. He successfully rounded up a small herd but by the time he returned to the river it was dark, and he injured his hand in crossing back to Zululand. He also narrowly avoided discovery by Lord Chelmsford's force, which was then bivouacked at iSandlwana. Command of the reserve had, in the meantime, passed to Prince Dabulamanzi kaMpande who had led it upstream, crossed the Mzinyathi, and unsuccessfully attacked the British post at the mission station of Rorke's Drift.

Zibhebhu continued to serve with the main Zulu army throughout the rest of the war. He was present at the battle of Khambula on 29 March, and it was he who, ever pragmatic, pointed out at the end of the battle to *inkosi* Mnyamana Buthelezi the impossibility of rallying the *amabutho* once they had begun to retreat. At the beginning of July Zibhebhu was given command of the detachments guarding the crossings of the White Mfolozi river before oNdini. It was his men who harassed British watering parties with sniper fire. When, on 3 July, Lieutenant-Colonel Redvers Buller crossed the river with a mounted party to scout the terrain to search for an appropriate spot from which to attack oNdini, it was Zibhebhu who orchestrated the response. Such a foray had clearly been expected, for Zibhebhu had laid careful plans. When the British horsemen emerged on to the plain near oNdini they saw and gave chase to several mounted Zulu scouts, among them Zibhebhu himself. As the scouts retired towards the Mbilane stream Buller became suspicious and ordered his men to halt; as they did so a force of several thousand Zulus – predominantly Zibhebhu's own uMxapho *ibutho* – rose up in an arc from the long grass around them. Zibhebhu had led them into a carefully prepared trap – a few yards further on the grass had been carefully plaited to trip the horses. The Zulus opened fire, killing a handful of Buller's men, and the British turned and retreated towards the river. Buller's quick thinking had saved his men, but Zibhebhu's warriors chased them all the way back to the river.

On the following day, when Lord Chelmsford crossed the White Mfolozi and drew up his forces in a square within sight of oNdini, Zibhebhu is said to have commanded the left 'horn' of the Zulu army. Displaying Zibhebhu's consummate understanding of the ground, the left horn advanced close to the British position under cover of the kwaNodwengu homestead. They then mounted a determined charge on one of the rear corners of the British square which Zibhebhu had correctly identified as a weak spot. Although this charge was broken by a hail of fire poured into it at close range, the nearest Zulu bodies fell only a dozen metres from the British line.

Zibhebhu himself survived the battle and returned to his homestead at Bangonomo in the north of the country. Here he offered shelter to some of the fugitive Cetshwayo's family, cattle and attendants, and the king gratefully accepted. Even before Cetshwayo was captured at the end of August, however, the British had approached Zibhebhu and offered him a role in the post-war settlement of Zululand. It was their intention to divide the country up among thirteen independently minded *amakhosi* who thereby would largely be committed to follow British interests. Despite his impressive war record, Zibhebhu was selected because his readiness to embrace the white world had marked him out as 'progressive' in British eyes. He accepted on the assumption that Cetshwayo would never be returned to Zululand. This irrevocably soured his relationship with the king's family, however, and in particular upset Cetshwayo's brother, Prince Ndabuko; Ndabuko complained that Zibhebhu had refused to return Cetshwayo's cattle when asked, and that he had mistreated Cetshwayo's heir, Dinuzulu, while he was in Zibhebhu's care. This was the start of a bitter feud between Zibhebhu and Ndabuko which was to have desperate consequences for the country as a whole.

The post-war settlement was in any case inherently unstable, not least because many ordinary Zulus, who had fought loyally for their king, regarded the British appointees as traitors, and the country gradually polarised between pro- and anti-royalist factions. Zibhebhu became one of the most determined of the latter, harassing royalists in his districts and confiscating their cattle.

By 1882 the situation in Zululand had become so volatile that it was no longer considered in Britain's best interests to sustain the post-war settlement. It was decided in London to restore King Cetshwayo to part of his old territory; a swathe of southern Zululand was to be set aside as a reserve, administered by the British, while Zibhebhu and his neighbour, Prince Hamu kaNzibe (who was also opposed to Cetshwayo's return) retained their independence in the north. Such were the festering resentments, however, that no sooner had Cetshwayo returned at the beginning of 1883 than his followers began planning their revenge on Zibhebhu. The royalists – known as the *uSuthu* – assembled about 5,000 men, under the command of Prince Ndabuko, and invaded Zibhebhu's territory. Zibhebhu's response was typically decisive; on 30 March he lured the royalist army up the shallow valley of the Msebe stream, then ambushed them. The royalists fell apart and over a thousand of them were killed; Zibhebhu lost just ten men.

The battle of Msebe, rather than those of the war of 1879, marks the true emergence of Zibhebhu as an independent commander, and he was to display a flair which marked him down as the greatest Zulu field commander since King Shaka half a century before. It was Zululand's great tragedy that his skills were directed not against foreign invaders, but against fellow Zulus.

The battle galvanised Zululand. Despite British prohibitions of the revival of the *amabutho* system, Cetshwayo began assembling his warriors at the newly rebuilt oNdini in anticipation of further violence. Rather than wait to be attacked again, Zibhebhu collected his own forces and on the night of 20/21 July 1883 he made a dramatic night march from Bangonomo across country, appearing at oNdini at dawn. Although Cetshwayo had assembled several thousand men at oNdini – many of them veterans of 1879 – the royalists were so taken by surprise that they were unable to mount effective resistance. Their army broke and fled, and in the pursuit dozens of leading royalists, being old and portly, were overtaken and killed, and Cetshwayo himself was wounded. Among the dead were *inkosi* Sihayo Ngobese – whose sons' actions in 1878 had precipitated the British invasion – and Ntshingwayo kaMahole, the victor of iSandlwana.

Zibhebhu's victory at oNdini marked the true end of the old order that so many Zulus had fought to protect in 1879. Cetshwayo's influence was destroyed – he fled to the protection of the British at Eshowe, and died in February 1884 – and the fabric which held the old kingdom together was irrevocably shattered.

The king's death none the less led to a hardening of resolve among his followers. His heir was his young son Prince Dinuzulu, himself a determined and dynamic young man. Dinuzulu was particularly close to his uncle, Prince Ndabuko – the man who had first quarrelled with Zibhebhu. Together Dinuzulu and Ndabuko planned an effective response to Zibhebhu; they invited the Transvaal Boers to intervene on their behalf, offering them farms in Zululand in return. A Boer commando duly assembled near the Hlobane mountain and proclaimed Dinuzulu king under their protection on 21 May 1884. A combined royalist and Boer force then advanced against Zibhebhu at Bangonomo. As he had done successfully on the day before the battle of Ulundi five years earlier, and then at Msebe, Zibhebhu tried to lure them into a trap, retreating up the Mkhuze river. He placed his army in carefully concealed positions at the foot at the Tshaneni mountain, where the Mkhuze river flows through the Lebombo mountains. As the cautious royalists and Boers pursued him, however, a gun went off accidentally, warning them of the impending trap. Zibhebhu's men broke cover to charge and might have routed the uSuthu had not the Boers, firing over the heads of their allies, caused such heavy casualties that Zibhebhu's men broke. Zibhebhu's army was destroyed: hundreds of his men were killed, many of his non-combatants captured and over 60,000 head of cattle carried away.

Even in defeat, however, Zibhebhu remained determined. Gathering his surviving followers together, he marched rapidly across Zululand to throw himself on the mercy of the British. The British, who had come to regard him as one of the staunchest allies of the post-war settlement, were happy to offer him refuge.

The battle of Tshaneni forced a British intervention in other respects, too. After it was over the Boers presented their bill to King Dinuzulu, and claimed a staggering tract of land, extending from Hlobane mountain almost to the sea. The British – who were reluctant to allow the Boers direct access to the coast, for fear that they would establish contacts with rival European empires – objected, forcing the Boers to restrict their claims to the Hlobane area. The Boer territorial gains were formalised as the *Nieue Republiek* – the New Republic – and a new capital town, Vryheid – 'Freedom' – laid out midway between the old Hlobane and Khambula battlefields. The rest of Zululand fell to the British who finally acknowledged the responsibility they had assumed by their invasion in 1879 by annexing the country in May 1887.

The delayed advent of British rule meant the return of favours to old allies. One of the first acts of the new administration was to allow Zibhebhu and his followers to return from the Eshowe area to their old homes at Bangonomo. To the royalists, this was of course a highly provocative act – the more so because King Dinuzulu himself had settled at Nongoma, not far from Bangonomo. The British built a magistrate's post at Ivuna, on top of the Nongoma ridge, midway between the two but their presence was not sufficient to diffuse the tension. By the end of May 1887 both Dinuzulu and Zibhebhu had begun assembling armies. On 2 June the magistrate from Ivuna marched out to Dinuzulu's homestead to arrest him on charges relating to the disturbances; he found Dinuzulu's *impi* waiting for him, and made a hasty retreat. Zibhebhu promptly called out his own forces and moved to Ivuna to support the magistrate. At dawn on 23 June, however, Dinuzulu swept up the slopes of the ridge at the head of an army and attacked both the British post and Zibhebhu's camp. For once it was Zibhebhu who was taken by surprise and his men broke and scattered down the hill with the royalists in pursuit.

Zibhebhu went into hiding, and for the second time in less than a decade British red-coats were hurried into Zululand. Dinuzulu and his family, including Prince Ndabuko, orchestrated a valiant attempt at rebellion but the odds were stacked too highly against them and the country was disunited by years of civil strife. A series of minor actions ensued before Dinuzulu and his uncles fled to Natal. They were tried for sedition and exiled to St Helena.

To his surprise, Zibhebhu was not allowed to return to Bangonomo immediately. The British had at last begun to recognise the destructive effects of their policy of 'divide and rule' and Zibhebhu – to his disgust – was called to Eshowe to account for his actions. It was not until 1898 that he was allowed to return to Bangonomo. Dinuzulu, recently freed from St Helena, returned to Nongoma at about the same time. The bad feeling between them had not dissipated but the intervention of the Anglo-Boer War (1899–1902) largely kept their animosity in check. By 1904 it seemed that fresh trouble was brewing when, on 27 August, Zibhebhu died. He was not yet 70, and his health was probably undermined by the long years of hardship he endured during his campaigns.

The rift between the uSuthu and the Mandlakazi was not healed until well into the twentieth century, and even today Zibhebhu's outstanding qualities as a general, and his contribution to the war effort in 1879, are largely overshadowed by the memory of his bitter animosity, in later years, towards the Royal House.

Zulu Royal House

On 14 November 1887 the Governor of the newly established British colony of Zululand, Sir Arthur Havelock, attempted to persuade King Dinuzulu and prominent members of his family of an uncomfortable political truth. 'Dinuzulu must know,' he said,

and all the Zulus must know, that the rule of the House of Chaka is a thing of the past. It is dead. It is like water spilt on the ground. The Queen now rules in Zululand and no one else. The Queen who conquered Cetywayo has now taken the government of the country into her own hands.[291]

It was not a view that the Zulu Royal House shared at the time – Dinuzulu orchestrated an abortive rebellion just months later – nor since. For the first half of the twentieth century the Royal House struggled against a concerted effort by white authorities to deny the validity of their monarchy, but the Zulu kings have never accepted that the invasion of 1879 and the subsequent domination by colonial authorities interrupted the line of legitimate succession that stretches back to the days of *inkosi* Senzangakhona kaJama.

Senzangakhona was the last *inkosi* of the Zulus whose world was bounded by the basin of hills framing the Mkhumbane valley. Senzangakhona was born into a world which was already on the cusp of great change as chiefdoms across Zululand were drawn into conflict, breaking down centuries-old patterns of allegiance and initiating a new order. Although Senzangakhona himself made little impression on these events, his remarkable sons were to shape the region's destiny for half a century.

Inkosi Senzangakhona died in about 1816, and the powerful Mthethwa chiefdom interfered in the succession for its own purposes, raising up Senzangakhona's estranged son Shaka. Shaka quickly threw off his allegiance to the Mthethwa and during his reign the political boundaries of the Zulu kingdom were drastically redrawn, establishing a framework which – with a good deal of ebb and flow across the years – survived to confront the British in 1879. Shaka was wary of raising up heirs in his household to challenge his position and fathered no legitimate heir – although Zulu tradition tells numerous stories of babies smuggled away from his household and into obscurity to protect them – and when he was assassinated in a palace coup in 1828 he was succeeded by one of his murderers, his brother Dingane. It fell to Dingane's lot to consolidate the kingdom after the period of rapid growth, a task which he accomplished with some skill until challenged by a new group of European interlopers, the Boers, in 1837. The subsequent brutal war which raged throughout 1838 severely damaged the bonds that had held Shaka's kingdom together. In 1839 Dingane's brother Prince Mpande defected to the Boers, and the following year defeated Dingane with Boer help. Mpande then became the third of Senzangakhona's extraordinary sons to assume the throne.

Unlike both Shaka and Dingane, however, Mpande fathered many children – 29 sons and 23 daughters. Although Zulu custom provides clear guidelines for establishing the precedence of an heir, and Mpande himself named his son Prince Cetshwayo as his heir when questioned by the Boers in 1839, he later preferred to maintain his own security by playing off the aspirations of his sons against one another. This led to a disastrous succession dispute in 1856 between the rival princes Cetshwayo and Mbuyazi. Mpande's family was largely split between the two factions but at the battle of 'Ndondakusuka in December 1856 Cetshwayo spectacularly defeated and killed Mbuyazi. Several princes who had sided with Mbuyazi were killed with him, but a number including Mthonga, Mkhungo and Sikhotha – escaped to Natal where they formed a nucleus of anti-Cetshwayo agitation.

Nevertheless the last twenty years of Mpande's reign were marked by a continuing power-struggle between the king and his ascendant heir. Mpande finally died peacefully of natural causes in 1873 – one of the few of Senzangakhona's sons to do so – and in 1873 Cetshwayo succeeded him. For the most part Cetshwayo was regarded by the Zulu people as a vigorous and able ruler but it was his misfortune to rule at a time of increasing British imperial ambition in southern Africa. Cetshwayo was defeated during the British invasion in 1879 and sent into exile in the Cape. The British were determined to eradicate the authority of the Zulu Royal House – which they regarded as hostile to their interests – and the country was divided up among British appointees. Many of the new ruling elite were not popular with their subjects – many of whom not unnaturally regarded them as traitors – and friction between royalist and anti-royalist factions increased to such a degree that the British were forced to intervene. In 1883 Zululand was partitioned into three, with the British assuming control over the southern sector while the northern portion remained in the care of factions hostile to the monarchy. King Cetshwayo was restored to the central sector, although he was forbidden to reintroduce the apparatus of state authority upon which his power had formerly been based.

The partition was a disaster. Civil war broke out and Cetshwayo was defeated by his relative, *inkosi* Zibhebhu (whose Mandlakazi section traced their descent from Senzangakhona's father, Jama). Cetshwayo himself took refuge with the British Resident at Eshowe, and died on 8 February 1884. Before his death Cetshwayo is said to have nominated his son Dinuzulu as his heir. Although still a young man – he was born in 1868 – he was determined and resourceful and, together with Cetshwayo's brothers, the princes Ndabuko and Shingana, he enlisted the help of the Transvaal Boers in his quarrel with Zibhebhu. On 21 May 1884 the Boer leader Conraad Meyer recognised Dinuzulu as King of the Zulus in a ceremony staged near Hlobane mountain, and the following month a combined royalist and Boer force defeated Zibhebhu at Tshaneni mountain.

Dinuzulu's triumph was short-lived, however. The Boers demanded payment in land and their claim was so exorbitant that the British intervened again. Zululand was now carved up between the British and the Boers; the Boer claims were limited to the New Republic – with a new capital built at Vryheid, near Hlobane – and the rest of Zululand became a British colony in May 1887. When the British signalled their support for Zibhebhu by restoring him to the lands he had been driven from in 1884, Dinuzulu promptly attacked Zibhebhu. British troops were hurried into Zululand and for a few weeks the Zulu Royal House again defied the might of the British Empire. Weakened and divided by a decade of intermittent civil war, however, the Zulus lacked the capacity for determined resistance and the rebellion collapsed. Dinuzulu fled to Natal and surrendered to the British authorities. He was tried for treason together with his uncles Ndabuko and Shingana, and all three were found guilty and sentenced to exile on St Helena.

Dinuzulu took two of his female attendants with him, each of whom bore him a son during his exile. Dinuzulu learned to wear western clothes, to read and to write, and to play the piano. In 1898 all three sentences expired and Dinuzulu and his uncles were allowed to return to Zululand. He was not allowed to retain the title of king, however, and was acknowledged by the Natal authorities as merely the *inkosi* of his own followers. On his return to Zululand he built a new royal homestead, oSuthu, near Nongoma.

While the colonial authorities remained wary of Dinuzulu's aspirations, many Africans in both Natal and Zululand looked to him increasingly as the embodiment of a nostalgic age of African power and independence. The first years of the twentieth century fell heavily upon African communities largely dispossessed by the settler government and forced to compromise their traditional lifestyle and beliefs. A widespread resentment coalesced around the imposition by the Natal authorities of a poll-tax early in 1906. Many groups refused to pay and in April 1906 protests broke into open rebellion. The rebellion was rapidly and ruthlessly suppressed by the Natal militia, and after it was over and the important leaders killed, many whites came to question Dinuzulu's role. In fact it seems that Dinuzulu was wary of supporting armed resistance after his own experiences of defeat, but the authorities saw in the rebel appeals to the Royal House proof of the lasting threat to white supremacy the Zulu kings represented. Dinuzulu was again arrested and tried for complicity in the rebellion. Although skilfully defended and acquitted of the main charges, he was nevertheless sentenced to four years' imprisonment. When Natal and Zululand were incorporated into the Union of South Africa in 1910, the Prime Minister, Louis Botha – who had known Dinuzulu in 1884 – commuted his sentence to internal exile. Dinuzulu was moved to a farm, Rietfontein, in the Transvaal. Overweight, depressed and increasingly dependant on alcohol, Dinuzulu's health declined, however, and he died on 18 October 1913 at the age of 42. His body was taken back to Zululand and laid to rest alongside his ancestors in the emaKhosini valley.

Dinuzulu's heir was his son Solomon Nkayishana, who had been born on St Helena on 2 January 1893. Solomon was the first of the Zulu kings born after the collapse of the kingdom's independence; he had also been baptised as a child,

and was therefore the first Christian king. The South African authorities would not recognise his position, however, and Solomon's life was characterised by a struggle to claim his birthright and defend the beleaguered traditions of his people. Solomon revived the tradition of raising *amabutho* – purely for ceremonial purposes – and in 1916 the Union Government acknowledged him as head of the royalist faction in return for his help in raising African labour battalions during the First World War. In 1920 Solomon was instrumental in founding the Inkatha organisation which sought to ally Zulu traditional leaders with the emerging black middle class in Natal and therefore channel traditional means of authority into specific political contemporary disputes. The Union Government remained suspicious of the influence of the Royal House, however, and continued to refuse to recognise Solomon as King of the Zulu people. When, in 1925, the British Prince of Wales went to South Africa on a state visit Solomon used the occasion to assert his position. After a subtle battle of protocols, Solomon and Prince Edward met and exchanged gifts in front of more than 60,000 Zulus at Eshowe on 6 June 1925. The occasion was seen by most Zulus as the British recognition of Solomon's position.

Yet the official title of king was destined to elude Solomon. Always at ease in both the European and traditional Zulu worlds – a Christian himself, he became a polygamist, wore western-style uniforms, liked sports cars and employed a white chauffeur – he none the less became increasingly frustrated by his inability to assume his rightful place in Zulu society. The promise of his meeting with the Prince of Wales came to nothing, and Solomon turned increasingly to alcohol. On 6 March 1933 he collapsed suddenly and died, just a few weeks after his 40th birthday.

Solomon's heir, Prince Nyangayesizwe Cyprian Bhekuzulu, had been born in 1924 and was just 9 years old when his father died. He was placed in the care of Solomon's brother, Prince Arthur Mshiyeni, who acted as regent, and Cyprian was not formally installed as *inkosi* of the royalist faction until August 1948. That same year the

Nationalist Party won the whites-only election in South Africa and instituted a number of programmes designed to entrench Afrikaner rule and cement racial segregation – the political philosophy of *apartheid*, or 'separateness'. Land ownership across South Africa was divided unequally along racial lines with the African population denied rights outside small, cramped and often physically fractured 'homelands'. Ironically, Cyprian now found himself under pressure from the government to accept the title 'King' as a means of legitimising the homeland policies. Under the influence of his friend and adviser *inkosi* Mangosuthu Buthelezi, Cyprian prevaricated but, worried that a refusal might exclude him from any influence over Zulu affairs, he eventually agreed. From 1959 over a hundred separate administrative districts were formally established which between them constituted the KwaZulu Homeland. It was perhaps the lowest point in the post-1879 struggles of the Zulu leadership who found themselves confronted with the logical consequences of defeat; shorn of any real political power, their sense of national identity was cynically manipulated by an oppressive government. The frustration of his position undoubtedly told on King Cyprian who was by nature a quiet and retiring man; like his father and grandfather, he turned to alcohol for relief. Although still a young man he suffered from diabetes and cirrhosis of the liver, and he died on 20 September 1968.

King Cyprian's heir was his son Goodwill Zwelithini, who had been born in Nongoma in July 1948. After a short regency King Goodwill was crowned king on 4 December 1971 in a traditional ceremony. No less than those of his illustrious predecessors, King Goodwill's reign has been characterised by the need to find a relevant role for the Zulu monarchy against the background of a rapidly changing society and the bitter political rivalries which followed the collapse of apartheid and South Africa's first free elections in 1994.

Notes

1. A.W. Lee, *Once Dark Country; Recollections and Reflections of a South African Bishop* (London, 1949).
2. The box of 1871 was officially designated the Mark VI, and was fractionally larger than the earlier boxes carrying Snider rounds. The sliding centre panel had been a feature since 1863. The Mark VI differed from the Mark V only in the addition of a washer beneath the screw on the lid. When this was introduced for the Mark VI, it was also added retrospectively to the Mark V.
3. The .450 Boxer ammunition used by the Martini-Henry was also supplied in the same boxes for use with the Gatling gun.
4. I am indebted to Lieutenant-Colonel Mike McCabe of the Royal Engineers for this point.
5. Reproduced in David Rattray, *A Soldier Artist in Zululand* (Fugitives' Drift, 2007).
6. Some may of course have been found but not remarked upon.
7. *Field Force Regulations for Southern Africa* (Pietermaritzburg, November 1878).
8. Sir Evelyn Wood, *From Midshipman to Field Marshal* (London, 1907).
9. Sir Edward Hutton, letter reproduced in the *Army Quarterly* in 1928, reproduced in Frank Emery, *The Red Soldier* (London, 1977).
10. Colonel C.E. Callwell, *Small Wars and their Principles and Practice* (London, 1896).
11. *Ibid.*
12. Captain Edward Essex, letter published in *The Times*, 2 April 1879.
13. Brigadier General Horace Smith-Dorrien, *Memories of Forty-Eight Years' Service* (London, 1929).
14. Smith-Dorrien, letter published in the *Brecon County Times*, 15 March 1879, reproduced in Emery, *The Red Soldier*.
15. White NCOs of auxiliary units were usually issued with bandoliers containing 50 rounds of Martini-Henry ammunition. Not being professional soldiers, and having had only minimal training, they were likely to fire off these rounds at a far quicker rate than would the steadier regular soldiers.
16. *Letters of Major-General Hart-Synot* (London, 1912).
17. Malindi, 3rd Regiment NNC, Chelmsford Papers, National Army Museum, London.
18. Bertram Mitford, *Through the Zulu Country. Its Battlefields and Its People* (London, 1883).
19. Royal Artillery batteries were designated as either field batteries or garrison batteries, according to whether they were apportioned primarily for offensive operations or static defence; field batteries bore letters and garrison batteries numbers. Thus N/5 was officially a field battery and 11/7 a garrison battery.
20. The two-gun section of 11/7 which fought at Khambula certainly had horse-drawn limbers. It is unlikely that the detachment with Pearson's column would have been any different, although a contemporary sketch does show limbers being pulled by mules.
21. Report by J.F. Brickhill.
22. Adrian Greaves and Brian Best (eds), *The Curling Letters of the Anglo-Zulu War* (Barnsley, 2001).
23. Curling, evidence before the Court of Inquiry, quoted in Greaves and Best, *The Curling Letters*.
24. To render them inoperable to the enemy it was the practice to hammer small spikes into the vents if guns were likely to be captured.
25. Wood, *From Midshipman to Field Marshal*.
26. Sergeant Edward Jervis, letter published in the *Dover Express*, 5 September 1879, reproduced in Emery, *The Red Soldier*.

27. Captain Allen Gardiner, *Narrative of a Journey to the Zulu Country* (London, 1836).
28. Mitford, *Through the Zulu Country*.
29. *Whom The Gods Love:* A Memoir of Nevill Coghill, compiled by Patrick Coghill, *c.* 1966.
30. George Mossop, *Running the Gauntlet* (London, 1937).
31. Captain W.E. Montague, *Campaigning in South Africa* (London, 1880).
32. Letters of Major Philip Anstruther, National Army Museum, London, reproduced in Dr Paul Butterfield (ed.), *War and Peace in South Africa 1879–1881* (Johannesburg, 1987).
33. Report in the *Graphic*, 30 August 1879.
34. G.C. Dawnay, *Campaigns, Zulu 1879, Egypt 1882, Suakim 1885* (Privately printed, *c.* 1886; reprinted 1989).
35. Lieutenant A.C.B. Mynors, *Letters and Diary* (Privately published, 1879).
36. Major Ashe and Captain E.V. Wyatt-Edgell, *The Story of the Zulu Campaign* (London, 1880).
37. Wood, *From Midshipman to Field Marshal*.
38. *Ibid.*
39. Sam Jones' account appeared in the *Natal Mercury* on 22 January 1929.
40. Private William Meredith, letter published in the *South Wales Daily Telegram*, 24 March 1879, reproduced in Emery, *The Red Soldier*.
41. George H. Swinney, *A Zulu Boy's Recollections of the Zulu War* (London, 1883; reproduced with notes by C. de B. Webb in *Natalia* (no. 8, December 1978).
42. H. Rider Haggard, *Diary of an African Journey 1914*, ed. Stephen Coan (London, 2001).
43. John Maxwell, *Reminiscences of the Zulu War* (University of Cape Town, 1979).
44. Glennie, Paton and Penn Symons, *Historical Records of the 24th Regiment* (London, 1892).
45. Mitford, *Through the Zulu Country*.
46. Swinney, *A Zulu Boy's Recollections*.
47. Donald R. Morris, *The Washing of the Spears* (London, 1966).
48. Daphne Child (ed.), *Zulu War Journal; Col. Henry Harford C.B.* (Pietermaritzburg, 1978).
49. *Ibid.*
50. Maxwell, *Reminiscences of the Zulu War*.
51. *Ibid.*
52. Swinney, *A Zulu Boy's Recollections*.
53. Archibald Forbes, account in the *Illustrated London News*, 12 July 1879.
54. British Parliamentary Papers C.2676.
55. Montague, *Campaigning in South Africa*.
56. Wood, *From Midshipman to Field Marshal*.
57. Report from a correspondent 'with Colonel Wood's Column', *Natal Colonist*, 11 April 1879.
58. Mitford, *Through the Zulu Country*.
59. *Letters of Major-General FitzRoy Hart-Synot* (London, 1912).
60. Mitford, *Through the Zulu Country*.
61. R.W. Leyland, *A Holiday in South Africa* (London, 1882).
62. A.W. Lee, *Charles Johnson of Zululand* (London, 1930).
63. A small chapel stands on the spot which has since been reconsecrated as 'the tomb of the unknown Zulu warrior'.
64. *Memoirs of Field-Marshal Lord Grenfell* (London, 1925).
65. Quoted in Cornelius Vijn, *Cetshwayo's Dutchman*, translated and annotated by Bishop Colenso (London, 1880).
66. H.P. Braatvedt, *Roaming Zululand With a Native Commissioner* (Pietermaritzburg, 1949).
67. *Ibid.*
68. Haggard, *Diary of an African Journey 1914*.
69. *Ibid.*
70. Reported in the *Illustrated London News*, 4 October 1879.
71. Child (ed.), *The Zulu War Journal of Col. Henry Harford*.
72. Letter from Wood to the Military Secretary, Horse Guards, dated 25 July 1881, reproduced in Emery, *The Red Soldier*.
73. Correspondent of the *Natal Witness*, report dated Luneburg, 9 September 1879.
74. *Paulina Dlamini; Servant of Two Kings*, compiled by H. Filter and translated by S. Bourquin (Pietermaritzburg, 1986).
75. Report in the *Graphic*, 11 October 1879.
76. *Paulina Dlamini*.
77. The *Frederick Post*, Maryland, USA, 6 February 1914. I am deeply indebted to Ian Woodason for this reference.
78. Comment in the *Natal Witness*, 3 June 1918, reproduced in Mark Coghlan's useful article on the film in *Soldiers of the Queen*, no. 84.
79. Child (ed.), *The Zulu War Journal of Col. Henry Harford*.
80. Mrs Frances Colenso, *Colenso Letters from Natal*, ed. Wyn Rees (Pietermaritzburg, 1958).
81. Fleet Surgeon Henry Norbury, *The Naval Brigade in South Africa During the Years 1877–78–79* (London, 1880).
82. *Ibid.*

83. Charles Norris-Newman, *In Zululand With The British Throughout The War of 1879* (London, 1880).

84. Major Charles Tucker, letter to his father, dated Luneburg, 19 March 1879, reproduced in Emery, *The Red Soldier*.

85. *Ibid*, letter by Lieutenant William Weallans, 2/24th, 26 January 1879.

86. *Ibid*, letter by Sergeant W.E. Warren, N/5 Battery RA, first published 29 March 1879.

87. *Ibid*, letter by Private Cook, 2/24th, first published 29 March 1879.

88. Account of Mpatshana kaSodondo in C. de B. Webb and J. Wright (eds), *The James Stuart Archive of Oral Evidence*, vol. 3 (Pietermaritzburg, 1982).

89. Account of Mehlokazulu kaSihayo given 27 September 1879, reproduced in the Zulu War supplement to the *Natal Mercury*, 1879.

90. Account of Mpatshana, Webb and Wright (eds), *The James Stuart Archive of Oral Evidence*, vol. 3.

91. Letter by Richard Stevens, dated Helpmekaar, 27 January 1879, reproduced in Emery, *The Red Soldier*.

92. Account of Kumbekha Qwabe, supplement to the *Natal Mercury*, 22 January 1929.

93. John Sholto's son – and Florence's nephew – was Wilde's friend 'Bosie', Lord Alfred Douglas.

94. Lady Florence Dixie, *In The Land of Misfortune* (London, 1882).

95. Account by Private Buckley of B Co. 2/24th c. 1930, *Events Remembered*, Lugg Papers, Campbell Collections of the University of KwaZulu-Natal.

96. There is no doubt that the dog present in the battle at Rorke's Drift was Reynolds', although some confusion remains about his name which is given variously as Dick or Jack. Since he seems to have been a Jack Russell terrier – which may have confused the matter – I have preferred Dick.

97. Account by Private Buckley, *Events Remembered*.

98. The *Graphic*, 17 May 1879.

99. My thanks to Ian Woodason for drawing attention to this point.

100. Maxwell, *Reminiscences of the Zulu War*.

101. Major Charles Tucker, letter to his father, dated Luneburg, 19 March 1879, reproduced in Emery, *The Red Soldier*.

102. Account included in Mitford, *Through the Zulu Country*.

103. L.H. Samuelson, *Zululand, Its Traditions, Legends, Customs and Folklore* (Marianhill, 1917).

104. H.W. Struben, *Recollections of Adventure 1850–1911* (Cape Town, 1920).

105. Account in Mitford, *Through the Zulu Country*.

106. Account by the *Natal Colonist*'s correspondent, reproduced in the *Natal Mercury*'s Zulu War supplement, April 1879.

107. Statement by Grandier submitted by Evelyn Wood, 16 April 1879, British Parliamentary Papers C.2374.

108. *Ibid*.

109. *Natal Mercury*'s correspondent dated 'Kwamagwaza, Oct 28 1879', reproduced in Vijn, *Cetshwayo's Dutchman*.

110. Mitford, *Through the Zulu Country*.

111. *Ibid*.

112. Vijn, *Cetshwayo's Dutchman*.

113. For these accounts see Ian Knight (ed.), 'Kill Me In The Shadows; The Bowden Archive of Oral History', *Soldiers of the Queen* (Journal of the Victorian Military Society), no. 74.

114. Melton Prior, *Campaigns of a War Correspondent* (London, 1912).

115. Major General William Molyneux, *Campaigning in South Africa and Egypt* (London, 1896).

116. Curiously these proceedings were later quashed, apparently because of the controversy surrounding the case of Lieutenant J.B. Carey, who was court-martialled for abandoning the Prince Imperial during a Zulu attack on 1 June.

117. Molyneux, *Campaigning in South Africa and Egypt*.

118. Diary of Lieutenant Julius Backhouse, 3rd Regiment, National Army Museum, London.

119. Lieutenant C.E. Commeline RE, letter in the *Hereford Times*, 15 March 1879, reproduced in Emery, *The Red Soldier*.

120. Letter from Captain W.R.C. Wynne RE, reproduced in Howard Whitehouse (ed.), *A Widow-Making War; The Life and Death of a British Officer in Zululand, 1879* (Nuneaton, 1995).

121. Montague, *Campaigning in South Africa*.

122. Champagne.

123. Montague, *Campaigning in South Africa*.

124. 'One Who Was There', believed to be Captain Pelly Clarke, 103rd Regiment, in 'The Zulu War With Colonel Pearson at Ekowe', *Blackwood's Magazine*, July 1879.

125. Whitehouse (ed.), *A Widow-Making War*.

126. Mossop, *Running the Gauntlet*.

127. Private Alfred Davies, 90th L.I., letter published in the *Brecon County Times*, 29 March 1879, reproduced in Emery, *The Red Soldier*.

128. Lieutenant W.N. Lloyd RHA, *The Defence of Ekowe* (RA Institution, 1881).

129. 'One Who Was There', *Blackwood's Magazine*, July 1879.

130. Captain H.R. Knight, 3rd Regiment, 'Reminiscences of Etshowe', *United Services Magazine*, October 1893, April 1894.

131. Private diary, family possession.

132. Lloyd, *The Defence of Ekowe*.

133. Mossop, *Running the Gauntlet*.

134. Swinney, *A Zulu Boy's Recollections*.

135. Mitford, *Through the Zulu Country*.

136. The Distinguished Service Order was instituted in 1886 as an officers' equivalent of the DCM. Since 1993 the DCM has been discontinued, but has been replaced by the Conspicuous Gallantry Cross.

137. Due to an error in the date of the action given in the official announcement, the award given to Lieutenant Edward Browne of the 24th Regiment is often credited to the battle of Hlobane on 28 March 1879. In fact independent eyewitness accounts make it clear that Browne's act of gallantry – saving the life of an unhorsed man in the face of a Zulu attack – took place the following day at Khambula.

138. I have included the award to Trooper R. Brown of the Frontier Light Horse in the total awarded for Hlobane.

139. Prior to 1881 the award could be given for acts of heroism performed not in the presence of the enemy, however; hence five men of the 24th Regiment were awarded the VC for braving heavy surf in a small boat to rescue several of their comrades who had gone ashore on Little Andaman Island in the Bay of Bengal to search for sailors believed to have been attacked by the islanders on 7 May 1867. One of those awarded the VC on this occasion, Private William Griffith, was killed at iSandlwana.

140. In fact 24 VCs were awarded for the relief of Lucknow on 16 November 1857, during the Indian Mutiny. Because these were won during a series of interconnected actions on the same day, however, Rorke's Drift is usually recognised as earning the highest number of awards for a single action. The proportion of awards to men involved was also, of course, much higher at Rorke's Drift.

141. In 1888 Captain R.S. Baden-Powell of the 13th Hussars saw King Dinuzulu kaCetshwayo in captivity wearing an *iziqu* (which Dinuzulu had earned in a battle with the Mandlakazi during the Zulu civil war of the 1880s). Years later Baden-Powell was inspired by the *iziqu* to invent the 'wood badge' for Boy Scouts.

142. Molyneux, *Campaigning in South Africa and Egypt*.

143. N. Devitt (ed.), *Galloping Jack; Reminiscences of Brig. Gen. J.R. Royston* (London, 1937).

144. Molyneux, *Campaigning in South Africa and Egypt*.

145. Mitford, *Through the Zulu Country*.

146. Haggard, *Diary of an African Journey 1914*.

147. Haggard has apparently confused two separate actions, those in the Mome gorge (10 June 1906) and the Izinsimba gorge (9 July 1906). On both occasions 'rebel' forces were trapped in narrow valleys by government forces and ruthlessly destroyed.

148. Haggard, *Diary of an African Journey 1914*.

149. From Haggard's dedication to James Stuart in *Child of the Storm* (London, 1913).

150. Prior, *Campaigns of a War Correspondent*.

151. Mossop, *Running the Gauntlet*.

152. Captain W.R. Ludlow, *Zululand and Cetewayo* (London, 1882). It is not entirely clear that Prince Dabulamanzi was present at Ulundi, however.

153. From *Paulina Dlamini*.

154. Montague, *Campaigning in South Africa*.

155. Mossop, *Running the Gauntlet*.

156. *Ibid*.

157. Haggard, *Diary of an African Journey 1914*.

158. The base of Bromhead's cairn – a circle of stones – can still be seen immediately behind the 1913 memorial. Recently a small cairn was added to this base by the curators of the site.

159. Lee, *Once Dark Country*.

160. George Chadwick, article on the battles of iSandlwana and Rorke's Drift in the *South African Military History Journal* (January 1979).

161. The author, although never a member of the military, was lucky enough to be offered one of a limited number of spare places made available to civilians on this trip.

162. In 1999 the author and Gillian Scott-Berning of Durban organised a visit by the Die-Hard Company – a British re-enactment group specialising in the drill of the Victorian soldier – to iSandlwana. The Die-Hards took part in a re-enactment at iSandlwana with a traditional *ibutho* on the

120th anniversary. The Die-Hards' contacts with local history enthusiasts led to the creation of the Dundee Die-Hards, who have since taken up the tradition of commemorative re-enactments.

163. James Young Gibson (1857–1935) was a magistrate in Zululand and author of *The Story of the Zulus* (1903).

164. James Stuart (1868–1942) was a Natal civil servant and an avid collector of Zulu oral tradition (some of his voluminous notes have been published by the University of Natal under the title *The James Stuart Archive*) and author of the semi-official *History of The Natal Rebellion.*

165. Haggard, *Diary of an African Journey 1914.*

166. Henry F. Fynn, 'My Recollections of a Famous Campaign and a Great Disaster', *Natal Witness* (22 January 1913).

167. Mitford, *Through the Zulu Country.*

168. H.C. Lugg, *Historic Natal and Zululand* (Pietermaritzburg, 1949). The late 'SB' Bourquin, a fluent Zulu linguist and former head of the Bantu Affairs Department in Durban in the 1970s, was also of this opinion (in conversations with the author).

169. For Gibson and Stuart see notes 163 and 164 above.

170. Haggard, *Diary of an African Journey 1914.*

171. Letter published in the *Colchester Mercury and Essex Express*, 15 March 1879, reproduced in Emery, *The Red Soldier.*

172. A copy was discovered on Durnford's body during the burials of May 1879. Pulleine was not of course a column commander but the evidence is strongly suggestive that Colonel Glyn (who did command the Centre Column) had left his copy of the orders with Pulleine when Glyn left the camp with Lord Chelmsford on the morning of the 22nd. Copies of the orders, dated December 1878 and addressed to the 'OC Helpmekaar' (which was then Glyn) were also found on the battlefield by burial details. They were passed to an officer in Durban and have remained in the possession of his descendants. They have only recently been made public.

173. Major-General Sir Robert Baden-Powell, *The Matabele Campaign 1896* (London, 1901).

174. Probably a significant underestimate, since the returns were incomplete.

175. Molyneux, *Campaigning in South Africa and Egypt.*

176. Child (ed.), *The Zulu War Journal of Col. Henry Harford.*

177. Lieutenant General Sir Edward Hutton, Recollections of the Zulu War', *Army Quarterly* (April 1928).

178. Dawnay, *Campaigns: Zulu 1879, Egypt 1882, Suakim 1885.*

179. Mossop, *Running the Gauntlet.*

180. Mitford, *Through the Zulu Country.*

181. Cardwell's other reforms also attempted to make service more attractive by curbing the worst excesses of Army life – flogging was abolished as a peace-time punishment – and by improving access for ordinary soldiers to educational facilities.

182. Rudyard Kipling, '*Route Marchin*', from *Barrack Room Ballads* (1892).

183. Letters of Lieutenant W. des V. Hamilton, HMS *Active*, National Army Museum, London.

184. An earthwork, dubbed Fort Pearson, had been built on a knoll commanding the Natal bank; a fort was then built on the Zulu side to secure the crossing, and was named Fort Tenedos.

185. Lloyd, *The Defence of Ekowe.*

186. *Ibid.*

187. Knight, 'Reminiscences of Etshowe'.

188. I am indebted to Gavin Wiseman of Eshowe for a Zulu oral perspective on this anecdote.

189. Colonel G. Hamilton Browne, *A Lost Legionary in South Africa* (London, *c*. 1913).

190. A term used by the Romans to describe a trophy taken from a fallen rival.

191. Hamilton Browne, *A Lost Legionary in South Africa.*

192. Account by Lieutenant Edward Hutton, reproduced in Emery, *The Red Soldier.*

193. Sir Henry Bartle Frere, 23 August 1879, published in the *London Gazette*, 7 November 1879.

194. Robarts family papers; letter reproduced in Ian Castle and Ian Knight, *Fearful Hard Times; The Siege and Relief of Eshowe* (London, 1994).

195. Maxwell, *Reminiscences of the Zulu War.*

196. On this point see Bishop Colenso's notes in Vijn, *Cetshwayo's Dutchman.*

197. Hamilton Browne, *A Lost Legionary in South Africa.*

198. Dawnay, *Campaigns: Zulu 1879, Egypt 1882, Suakim 1885.*

199. Haggard, *Diary of an African Journey 1914.*

200. L.W. Reynolds, *The Diary of a Civil Surgeon Serving with the British Army in South Africa during the Zulu War* (Duntroon, 1996).

201. Cecil D'Arcy, letter in the Cape *Eastern Star*, reproduced in Emery, *The Red Soldier.*

202. Frederick Schermbrucker, 'Zlobanie and Kambula', *South African Catholic Magazine* (1893).
203. Private John Snook, letter in the *North Devon Herald*, 29 May 1879, reproduced in Emery, *The Red Soldier*.
204. Account of Mgelija Ngema, Bowden Papers, KwaZulu-Natal Museum, Pietermaritzburg. Reproduced in Ian Knight (ed), 'Kill Me in the Shadows', *Soldiers of the Queen*.
205. Pay Sergeant Edwin Powis, letter in *The Cambrian*, 11 July 1879, reproduced in Emery, *The Red Soldier*.
206. Devitt, *Galloping Jack*.
207. Account in the *Cape Journal,* reproduced in Emery, *The Red Soldier.*
208. Lloyd did not accompany the burial expedition of 21 May, and his photographs clearly show a very different state to the battlefield, many of the wagons having been removed on the earlier occasion.
209. In fact Colonel Wood's Left Flank Column had crossed into the disputed territory – i.e. territory claimed by the Zulus – some days before the British ultimatum expired on the 11th.
210. Captain Warren Wynne, letter to his wife, dated Eshowe, 7 February 1879, published in Whitehouse (ed.), *A Widow-Making War.*
211. Unknown staff officer quoted in *The Queen's Colours, and Other Sketches of a Soldier's Life* (Religious Tract Society, London, no date (*c.*1880)).
212. For a detailed description of these ceremonies see Ian Knight, *The Anatomy of the Zulu Army* (London, 1995).
213. Account of Mpatshana kaSodondo, Webb and Wright (eds), *The James Stuart Archive*, vol. 3.
214. Mpatshana kaSodondo, *ibid.*
215. Lloyd, *The Defence of Ekowe.*
216. Prior, *Campaigns of a War Correspondent.*
217. It is not entirely clear whether the rocket attached to Buller's party at Hlobane, and commanded by Major Tremlett RA, was lost on the mountain.
218. Captain W.R. Ludlow, *Zululand and Cetewayo* (London, 1882).
219. Account in the *Natal Mercury*, 22 January 1929.
220. Lee, *Once Dark Country.*
221. A photograph which has been reproduced as showing signallers of the 24th Regiment at Helpmekaar in 1879 in fact depicts men of the Welch Regiment there in 1884.
222. The money was pooled and distributed to relatives of those among the garrison who were killed.
223. Hutton, 'Recollections'.
224. Lt E.O.H. Wilkinson, letter dated 13 April 1879, published in the *Eton College Chronicle* and reproduced in Emery, *The Red Soldier.*
225. John Dunn, *John Dunn, Cetywayo and the Three Generals*, ed. D.C.F. Moodie (Pietermaritzburg, 1886)
226. Callwell, *Small Wars and their Principle and Practice.*
227. Gen. Sir Horace Smith-Dorrien, *Memoirs of Forty-Eight Years' Service* (London, 1925).
228. Mossop, *Running the Gauntlet.*
229. The exact number of British troops present at Rorke's Drift is the subject of some debate, and is unlikely to ever be fully resolved because of discrepancies and omissions in the various original rolls.
230. After Rorke's Drift most of the defenders had badly bruised shoulders as a result of the heavy and persistent firing they had been engaged in.
231. Chelmsford Papers, National Army Museum, London.
232. Hutton, 'Recollections'.
233. Report in the *Natal Mercury*, 12 February 1879.
234. Wood, *From Midshipman to Field Marshal.*
235. Actually the Zulu name for an ancestral spirit; the snake itself is known in isiZulu as *inyande-zulu*, and is a harmless grass-snake.
236. Child (ed.), *The Zulu War Journal of Col. Henry Harford.*
237. Report in the *Graphic*, 11 October 1879.
238. Molyneux, *Campaigning in South Africa and Egypt.*
239. Child (ed.), *The Zulu War Journal of Col. Henry Harford.*
240. Lieutenant Main Papers, Royal Engineers Museum.
241. Montague, *Campaigning in South Africa.*
242. Ernest Augustus Ritter originally wrote his famous *Shaka Zulu* (London, 1955) as a novel, but because he based it on a number of genuine oral traditions it has been regarded as a non-fiction biography. The idea that Shaka should be credited as inventor of the stabbing spear was introduced by Ritter's publisher as an Arthurian flourish.
243. Wood, *From Midshipman to Field Marshal.*
244. Samuelson, *Zululand; Its Traditions, Legends, Customs and Folklore.*
245. *umabope* was a root, treated with medicines and worn on a necklace, which was believed to hold the power to tie up the enemy.
246. Prior, *Campaigns of a War Correspondent.*

247. Mossop, *Running the Gauntlet.*
248. Or had he? Oddly, in 1925 a Mr V.G. Sparks was captaining a cricket match in Newcastle, Natal, when he claimed to recognise a dishevelled bystander as D'Arcy. Confronted, the man admitted his identity and claimed that he had stumbled across a body in the hills that night and had changed clothes with him and had lived anonymously ever since; he begged Sparks not to disclose his identity as 'he wished to remain dead to the world'. How Sparks was so confident of his identification after forty years is not certain; probably the bystander told Sparks what he wanted to hear. Nevertheless, some small element of doubt remains about Cecil D'Arcy's ultimate fate.
249. Account of Mangwanana Mchunu, Bowden Papers, KwaZulu-Natal Museum, Pietermaritzburg, reproduced in Knight (ed.), 'Kill Me In The Shadows', *Soldiers of the Queen.*
250. MacLeod Papers, quoted in Philip Bonner, *Kings, Commoners and Concessionaries* (Cambridge, 1983).
251. Personal information from Mr Isaac Dlamini, whose great-grandfather lived north of the Phongolo and considered himself a Swazi, but who fought with the Zulus in 1879 and was present at iSandlwana. Malumbule, the grandfather of Obed Dlamini, a recent Prime Minister of Swaziland, also fought at iSandlwana (information from Mr John Doble, British High Commissioner to Swaziland, 1996–99).
252. MacLeod Papers in Bonner, *Kings, Commoners and Concessionaries.*
253. The British fought a number of small actions against the Boers in the Orange Free State and Natal in the 1840s.
254. Literally 'cow's horns', from *zankomo,* cattle. Sometimes translated as 'bull's horns' or 'horns of the buffalo', although the word for a bull in Zulu is *inkunzi* and for a buffalo *inyathi.*
255. Hutton, 'Recollections'.
256. Mitford, *Through the Zulu Country.*
257. It was skirmishers from the iNgobamakhosi who overran the British rocket battery. A determined stand by a handful of the NNC escort caused the skirmishers to hang back to await the arrival of the main body – a respite which allowed some of the survivors of the rocket battery to escape.
258. Leyland, *A Holiday in South Africa.*
259. Ludlow, *Zululand and Cetewayo.*
260. Leyland, *A Holiday in South Africa.*
261. For a detailed account of Eugenie's pilgrimage see Ian Knight, *With His Face to the Foe; The Life and Death of Louis Napoleon, the Prince Imperial* (Staplehurst, 2001).
262. Haggard, *Diary of an African Journey 1914.*
263. *The Entr'acte,* 31 May 1879, quoted in Michael Diamond, 'Popular Entertainment in the Zulu War', *Journal of the Anglo-Zulu War Historical Society* (December 1998) – a useful review of music hall attitudes towards the war.
264. Mossop, *Running the Gauntlet.*
265. Norris-Newman, *In Zululand with the British 1879.*
266. Major Philip Anstruther, letters to his wife, published in Butterfield (ed.), *War and Peace in South Africa 1879–1881.*
267. Not all of it safe to consume. Possessed of the thirst which accompanies the adrenalin-rush of combat, some Zulus drank the medicines in the overrun field hospital, not knowing of course what they were. Several were poisoned and died.
268. In 2000 during a partial archaeological survey of the battlefield a crushed Victorian chamber-pot was found a few inches below the surface on the line of the Zulu retreat.
269. Montague, *Campaigning in South Africa.*
270. See for example Guy Dawnay, 'the Zulus always call it Ondine, as I used to know it', *Campaigns: Zulu 1879, Egypt 1882, Suakim 1885.*
271. The iNdluyengwe were incorporated into the uThulwana not long before the war of 1879; it is not entirely clear whether they were allowed to marry at that point. Probably they were.
272. Mitford, *Through the Zulu Country.*
273. Molyneux, *Campaigning in South Africa and Egypt.*
274. The 80th convoy at Ntombe on 12 March is the only possible exception, but here the wagons were poorly placed with such gaps between them that they did not constitute a viable defensive perimeter.
275. Norris-Newman often described himself as a captain; details of his military experience, whether regular or colonial, have yet to come to light. It is not clear either why he alone of his colleagues was in Natal at the start of the invasion.
276. Norris-Newman, *In Zululand With the British.*
277. It was also common practice for relatives to pass on for publication private letters from the front. Sometimes this had embarrassing consequences, as when Private John Snook of the 1/13th wrote to his family gloating over the slaughter of

wounded Zulu after Khambula; when it was published Wood himself was forced to issue a rebuttal.

278. Although this is not apparently confirmed by the casualty returns.

279. Archibald Forbes, the *Daily News*, reproduced in the *Illustrated London News*, 21 July 1879.

280. Charles E. Fripp, 'Reminiscences of the Zulu War', *Pall Mall Magazine* (Vol. XX, January–April 1900).

281. Erskine, account reproduced in the *Natal Mercury*, 22 February 1879.

282. Professor A. Preston (ed.), *Sir Garnet Wolseley's South African Journal 1879–1880* (Cape Town, 1973). Entry for Thursday, 21 August.

283. Hamilton Browne, *A Lost Legionary in South Africa*.

284. Captain Henry Hallam Parr, *A Sketch of the Kafir and Zulu Wars* (London, 1880).

285. Montague, *Campaigning in South Africa*.

286. *Ibid.*

287. *Ibid.*

288. Report in the *Natal Mercury*, 17 May 1879.

289. Montague, *Campaigning in South Africa*.

290. Samuelson, *Zululand, Its Traditions, Legends, Customs and Folklore*.

291. British Parliamentary Papers C. 5331, November 1887.

Further Reading

The literature of the Anglo-Zulu War is immense. Since I have footnoted all direct quotes within the book, I have opted not to attempt an exhaustive bibliography here; it would no doubt be soon out of date. I did, however, include a critical bibliography in my *Brave Men's Blood*, and indeed many of John Laband's works include extensive academic bibliographies. Instead I have opted here for a largely subjective selection; I have listed below a number of books which, within their particular fields, I consider worthwhile reading. Between them they shed important light on many different aspects of the war and its impact on popular consciousness. In some cases – most notably when dealing with iSandlwana – they provide opposing viewpoints within the framework of continuing debates. As such, they do not always offer consistent interpretations of the same events – and indeed some of them reflect views very different from my own. I have also included some of the more important contemporary eyewitness accounts, many of which are regularly reprinted.

Ballard, Charles, *John Dunn: The White Chief of Zululand* (Craighall, A.D. Donker, 1985)

Baynham Jones, Alan, and Stevenson, Lee, *Rorke's Drift By Those Who Were There* (Brighton, Stevenson Publishing, 2003)

Bennett, Lt-Col. I.H.W. *Eyewitness in Zululand; The Campaign Reminiscences of Colonel W.A. Dunne, South Africa 1877–81* (London, Greenhill Books, 1989)

Binns, C.T., *The Last Zulu King; The Life and Death of Cetshwayo* (London, Longmans, 1963)

Brown, R.A., *The Road to Ulundi; The Water-Colour Drawings of John North Crealock* (Pietermaritzburg, University of Natal Press, 1969)

Castle, Ian, *British Infantryman in South Africa* (Oxford, Osprey, 2003)

Castle, Ian, *Zulu War – Volunteers, Irregulars and Auxiliaries* (Oxford, Osprey Publishing, 2003)

Castle, Ian and Knight, Ian, *Fearful Hard Times; The Siege and Relief of Eshowe* (London, Greenhill Books, 1994)

Child, Daphne (ed.), *The Zulu War Journal of Col. Henry Harford* (Pietermaritzburg, Shooter & Shuter, 1978)

Clarke, Sonia (ed.), *Invasion of Zululand 1879* (Houghton, Brenthurst Press, 1979)

Clarke, Sonia (ed.), *Zululand at War* (Houghton, Brenthurst Press, 1989)

Colenso, F.E., assisted by Durnford, Lt-Col. E., *A History of the Zulu War and its Origin* (London, Chapman & Hall, 1880)

Cope, R., *The Ploughshare of War; The Origins of the Anglo-Zulu War* (Pietermaritzburg, University of Natal Press, 1999)

Coupland, Sir Reginald, *Zulu Battle Piece; Isandhlwana* (London, Collins, 1948)

Drooglever, R.W.F., *The Road to Isandlwana; Colonel Anthony Durnford in Natal and Zululand* (London, Greenhill Books, 1992)

Duminy, A. and Ballard, C. (eds), *The Anglo-Zulu War; New Perspectives* (Pietermaritzburg, University of Natal Press, 1981)

Duminy, A. and Guest, B. (eds), *Natal and Zululand from Earliest Times to 1910; A New History* (Pietermaritzburg, University of Natal Press, 1989)

Emery, Frank, *The Red Soldier; Letters from the Zulu War 1879* (London, Hodder & Stoughton, 1977)

Filter, H. (compiler) and Bourquin, S. (tr. and ed.), *Paulina Dlamini; Servant of Two Kings* (Pietermaritzburg, University of Natal Press, 1986)

French, Maj. The Hon. G., *Lord Chelmsford and the Zulu War* (London, Bodley Head, 1939)

Gibson, J.Y., *The Story of the Zulus* (London, Longmans, Green & Co., 1911)

Gon, Philip, *The Road to Isandlwana; The Years of an Imperial Battalion* (Johannesburg, Donker, 1970)

Greaves, Adrian, *Rorke's Drift* (London, Cassells, 2002)

Greaves, Adrian (ed.), *Redcoats and Zulus; Myths, Legends and Explanations of the Anglo-Zulu War 1879* (Barnsley, Pen & Sword Books, 2004)

Greaves, Adrian, and Best, Brian (eds), *The Curling Letters of the Anglo-Zulu War* (Barnsley, Pen & Sword Books, 2001)

Greaves, Adrian, and Knight, Ian, *Who's Who in the Anglo Zulu War; Vol. 1 The British* (Pen & Sword Books, Barnsley, 2007)

Greaves, Adrian, and Knight, Ian, *Who's Who in the Anglo Zulu War; Vol. 2 The Colonials and Zulus* (Barnsley, Pen & Sword Books, 2007)

Guy, J. *The Destruction of the Zulu Kingdom: The Civil War in Zululand 1879–1884* (London, Longmans, 1979)

Haggard, H. Rider, *Diary of an African Journey 1914*, ed. Stephen Coan (London, Hurst, 2002)

Hall, Sheldon, *Zulu; With Some Guts Behind It; The Making of an Epic Movie* (Sheffield, Tomahawk Press, 2005)

Hamilton Browne, Col. G., *A Lost Legionary in South Africa* (London, T. Werner Laurie, *c*. 1913)

Holme, Norman, *The Noble 24th* (London, Savannah Publications, 1999)

Jackson, F.W.D., 'Isandlwana, 1879; The Sources Re-examined', *Journal for the Society for Army Historical Research*, XLIX (1965), 173, 175, 176

Jackson, F.W.D., *Hill of the Sphinx* (London, Westerners Publication, 2003)

Knight, Ian, *British Forces in Zululand 1879* (London, Osprey, 1989)

Knight, Ian, *Brave Men's Blood* (London, Greenhill Books, 1990)

Knight, Ian, *Zulu; The Battles of Isandlwana and Rorke's Drift* (London, Windrow & Greene, 1992)

Knight, Ian, *Nothing Remains But to Fight; The Defence of Rorke's Drift* (London, Greenhill Books, 1993)

Knight, Ian, *The Anatomy of the Zulu Army* (London, Greenhill Books, 1995)

Knight, Ian, *Go to Your God Like a Soldier; The British Soldier Fighting for Empire 1837–1902* (London, Greenhill Books, 1996)

Knight, Ian, *Great Zulu Battles 1838–1906* (London, Arms & Armour Press, 1998)

Knight, Ian, *Great Zulu Commanders* (London, Arms & Armour Press, 1999)

Knight, Ian, *Isandlwana 1879* (Oxford, Osprey, 2002)

Knight, Ian, *Rorke's Drift; Pinned Like Rats in a Trap* (Oxford, Osprey, 2003)

Knight, Ian, *The National Army Museum Book of the Zulu War* (London, Sidgwick & Jackson, 2003)

Knight, Ian, *With His Face to the Foe; The Life and Death of the Prince Imperial* (Staplehurst, Spellmount, 2003)

Knight, Ian, *British Fortification in Zululand 1879* (Oxford, Osprey, 2005)

Knight, Ian, and Castle, Ian, *The Zulu War; Then and Now* (London, After the Battle, 1993)

Laband, John, *The Battle of Ulundi* (Ulundi, KwaZulu Monuments Council, 1988)

Laband, John (ed.), *Lord Chelmsford's Zululand Campaign 1878–1879* (Manchester, Army Records Society, 1994)

Laband, John, *Rope of Sand; The Rise and Fall of the Zulu Kingdom in the Nineteenth Century* (Johannesburg, Jonathon Ball, 1995)

Laband, John, *The Atlas of the Later Zulu Wars 1883–1888* (Pietermaritzburg, University of Natal Press, 2001)

Laband, John, and Knight, Ian, *The War Correspondents; The Anglo-Zulu War* (Suffolk, Sutton, 1996)

Laband, John, and Thompson, Paul, with Henderson, Sheila, *The Buffalo Border 1879; The Anglo-Zulu War in Northern Natal* (Durban, University of Natal, 1983)

Laband, John, and Thompson, Paul, *Kingdom and Colony at War* (Pietermaritzburg and Constantia, N & S Press, 1990)

Laband, John, and Thompson, Paul, *The Illustrated Guide to the Anglo-Zulu War* (Pietermaritzburg, University of Natal Press, 2000)

Laband, John, and Wright, John, *King Cetshwayo kaMpande* (Ulundi, KwaZulu Monuments Council, 1983)

Lock, Ron, and Quantrill, Peter, *Zulu Victory; The Epic of Isandlwana and the Cover-Up* (London, Greenhill, 2002)

Mitford, Bertram, *Through the Zulu Country. Its Battlefields and Its People* (London, Kegan, Paul, Trench & Co., 1883)

Molyneux, Maj. Gen. W.C.F. *Campaigning in South Africa and Egypt* (London, 1896)

Montague, Captain W.E., *Campaigning in South Africa* (London, William Blackwood, 1880)

Mossop, George, *Running the Gauntlet; Memoirs of Adventure* (London, Nelson, 1937)

Norris-Newman, *In Zululand With the British Throughout the War of 1879* (London, W.H. Allen & Co., 1880)

Parr, Capt. H. Hallam, *A Sketch of the Kafir and Zulu Wars* (London, C. Kegan Paul, 1880)

Paton, Col. G., Glennie, Col. F. and Penn Symons, W. (eds), *Historical Records of the 24th Regiment* (London, Simpkin, Marshall, Hamilton, Kent, 1892)

Rattray, David, *A Soldier Artist in Zululand* (Kwa-Zulu-Natal, Rattray Publications, 2007)

Smail, J.L., *From the Land of the Zulu Kings* (Durban, A.J. Pope, 1979)

Snook, Lt-Col. Mike, *How Can Man Die Better; The Secrets of Isandlwana Revealed* (London, Greenhill, 2005)

Stevenson, Lee, *The Rorke's Drift Doctor; James Henry Reynolds and the Defence of Rorke's Drift* (Brighton, Stevenson Publishing, 2001)

Thompson, P.S., *The Natal Native Contingent in the Anglo-Zulu War* (Pietermaritzburg, 1997)

Vijn, Cornelius, *Cetshwayo's Dutchman* (London, Longmans Green, 1880)

Whitehouse, Howard (ed.), *A Widow-Making War; The Life and Death of a British Officer in Zululand, 1879* (Nuneaton, Paddy Griffith Associates, 1995)

Wood, Sir Evelyn, *From Midshipman to Field Marshal* (London, Methuen, 1907)